Africa's Agenda

Recent Titles in
Contributions in Afro-American and African Studies

Folk Wisdom and Mother Wit: John Lee—An African American Herbal Healer
Arvilla Payne-Jackson and John Lee; Illustrations by Linda Kempton Armstrong

Alice Walker and Zora Neale Hurston: The Common Bond
Lillie P. Howard, editor

A Journey into the Philosophy of Alain Locke
Johnny Washington

Time in the Black Experience
Joseph K. Adjayé

Folk Poetics: A Sociosemiotic Study of Yoruba Trickster Tales
Ropo Sekoni

Public Policy and the Black Hospital: From Slavery to Segregation to Integration
Mitchell F. Rice and Woodrow Jones, Jr.

Aunt Jemima, Uncle Ben, and Rastus: Blacks in Advertising, Yesterday, Today, and Tommrrow
Marilyn Kern-Foxworth

A World of Difference: An Inter-Cultural Study of Toni Morrison's Novels
Wendy Harding and Jacky Martin

African Market Women and Economic Power: The Role of Women in African Economic Development
Bessie House-Midamba and Felix K. Ekechi, editors

African Labor Relations and Workers' Rights: Assessing the Role of the International Labor Organization
Kwamina Panford

The Gong and the Flute: African Literary Development and Celebration
Kalu Ogbaa, editor

Masters of the Drum
Black Lit/oratures Across the Continuum
Robert Elliot Fox

Africa's Agenda

The Legacy of Liberalism and Colonialism in the Crisis of African Values

Harvey J. Sindima

Contributions in Afro-American and African Studies,
Number 176

GP

Greenwood Press
Westport, Connecticut • London

Library of Congress Cataloging-in-Publication Data

Sindima, Harvey J.
Africa's agenda : the legacy of liberalism and colonialism in the crisis of African values / Harvey J. Sindima.
p. cm.—(Contributions in Afro-American and African Studies, ISSN 0069–9624 ; no. 176)
Includes bibliographical references and index.
ISBN 0–313–29479–8
1. National characteristics, African. 2. Africans—Race identity. 3. Decolonization—Africa. 4. Africa—Politics and government—1960– I. Title. II. Series.
DT14.S56 1995
305.8′0096—dc20 94–43042

British Library Cataloguing in Publication Data is available.

Library of Congress Catalog Card Number: 94–43042
ISBN: 0–313–29479–8
ISSN: 0069–9624

First published in 1995

Greenwood Press, 88 Post Road West, Westport, CT 06881
An imprint of Greenwood Publishing Group, Inc.

Printed in the United States of America

The paper used in this book complies with the Permanent Paper Standard issued by the National Information Standards Organization (Z39.48–1984).

10 9 8 7 6 5 4 3 2 1

Copyright acknowledgments

The editors and publisher gratefully acknowledge permission to reprint the following copyrighted material:

Excerpts from *A Humanist in Africa* by Kenneth Kaunda and Colin Morris. Nashville, TN: Abingdon Press, 1966. Reprinted by permission of the Longman Group.

Excerpts from *African Socialism*, edited by William Friedland and Carl G. Rosberg. Copyright © 1964 by the Board of Trustees of the Leland Stanford Junior University. Reprinted by permission of the publishers, Stanford University Press.

Excerpts from *The Heavenly City of the Eighteenth-Century Philosophers*, by Carl Becker. New Haven, CT: Yale University Press, 1966. Copyright © 1966 by Yale University Press. Reprinted by permission of Yale University Press.

Excerpts from *Theology in Africa*, by Kwesi A. Dickson. Maryknoll, NY: Orbis Books, 1984. Reprinted by permission of Darton, Longman and Todd.

Excerpts from *The Ideologies of Developing Nations,* edited by Paul E. Sigmund, Jr. New York: Praeger, 1963. Copyright © 1963 by Praeger. Reprinted by permission of the Greenwood Publishing Group.

Excerpts from *Bantu Philosophy*, by Placid Tempels. Paris: Présence Africaine, 1959. Reprinted by permission of Societé Nouvelle Présence Africaine.

Excerpts from *Christianity Without Fetishes: An African Critique and Recapture of Christianity*, by F. Eboussi Boulaga, translated by Robert R. Barr. Maryknoll, NY: Orbis Books, 1984. Reprinted by permission of Orbis Books.

Excerpts from *African Cry*, by Jean-Marc Ela, translated by Robert R. Barr. Maryknoll, NY: Orbis Books, 1986. Reprinted by permission of Orbis Books.

For my beloved parents
who struggled so hard
that I may grow to know
the meaning of *moyo*
and realize my *umunthu*.

Zikomo kwambiri bambo ndi mai pa zonse

Contents

Preface

Writers become so obsessed with their work that not only does time cease, but the people around them seem not to exist. This is the pain suffered by loved ones of writers and scholars. I spent hundreds of hours in a world of my own, writing this book, but my wife never complained of being ignored. Instead, she always wished me "a clear mind and good writing." I cannot thank her enough for the love, patience, understanding, and encouragement she gives me. I am truly grateful to her. *Ndaombera kuphazi Anaphiri. Zikomo kwambiri.*

This book is a personal attempt to address the crisis of values in Africa. Although personal, I owe my sense of direction to all my teachers at the various institutions of higher learning I attended. They were all great teachers. I thank them for teaching me to say what I wanted and meant. Without them I would not have said what I have in the way it has been said. Above all, I thank them for their dedication and inspiration. I single out the following teachers to express my profound gratitude for their help at different levels in my academic career: Stephen Kauta Siska, Saimon Faiti Phiri, Bruce Gannaway, and Harry Welshman at the Presbyterian Theological College in Malawi; Alastair Campbell, Jim Gill, and Andrew Ross at New College, Faculty of Divinity, University of Edinburgh, Scotland; Ndugu T'Ofori-Atta and the late Rommey Mossely at Interdenominational Theological Center in Atlanta, Georgia; Peter Paris, Charles West, and Gibson Winter at Princeton Theological Seminary. I am indebted to them all. The last three were particularly important in sharpening my critical skills and seeing me through my terminal degree. I appreciate their help and guidance.

I thank Professor Segun Gbadegesin, Chair, Philosophy Department at Howard University, for reading through the manuscript and providing helpful suggestions.

Introduction

Several decades have passed since most of Africa became independent after many years under the liberal heritage brought by the colonial powers: the British, French, Portuguese, and Spanish. Under the liberal heritage African thought and society experienced a crisis of the meaning of life, persons, and community, for the liberal heritage imposed on Africans its notion of the world, values and manner of living. According to the liberal heritage, social evolution constitutes the basic principle of the world. The main assumption of the liberal paradigm is that technical knowledge is the key to the development of peoples. This is the understanding behind the concepts of "modernity" and "progress." This progress, imposed on Africans, emptied the substance of life and the being of persons.

In independent Africa, "modernity" is the goal toward which nations are striving, and modernity is understood as "catching up" with the West: its technology, infrastructure, and even way of life. The economic hard times of the eighties have not diminished attempts to "modernize," that is, to pattern Africa after the West. The first decade of independence, the sixties to the mid-seventies, African countries experienced some economic growth; there was a moderate rise in the GNP. During these "boom" years, most African leaders paid little or no attention to the development of basic values and needs. The development process focused on building national physical infrastructure, generating foreign reserves, and prestige projects. This orientation toward social change did not foster attempts to deal with the ethical issues caused by development. The leaders did not recognize or chose to ignore the ethical problems posed by so-called development. Ethical issues inform and define symbolic and institutional requirements of common life. Instead of encouraging those symbolic values that promote community life, Africans cultivated values of the liberal heritage, which corrupted the African way of life.

Following the liberal materialist philosophy, development was understood in purely economic terms. This philosophy is responsible for destroying the African holistic concept of the world and pushing religion into the realm of the private. Because the religious and the ethical are the foundations of identity and the way of living common life, religion orders and informs all social life in Africa. The Western paradigm undermined these religious and ethical powers even into the life of the church.

This book examines the impact of liberalism on African thought and values which resulted in a serious identity crisis. The book argues that a recapture of traditional values would open possibilities for a deeper understanding of self and society. Based on some traditional concepts of ultimate reality and meaning, namely, life, persons, community, and divinity, the book proposes a paradigm for social, political, and theological transformation of self, religion, and society.

The first two chapters are a general introduction to the problems of the African people as seen through their history. These chapters tell the story of Africa's contact with the outside world and how that exposure led to its incorporation into the Western social, political, and economic system. Social and political ideas arise out of a specific understanding of the world. Certain fundamentals ideas or values inform a manner of living. Social, political, and economic systems as well as religious ideas are not chosen arbitrarily; they are based on some fundamental values on what is perceived as ultimate meaning and reality. Chapters 1 and 2 show that Africa's incorporation into the Western political and economic system affected African social, political, economic and religious understanding and led to a corruption of people's value system. The result was a rupture of African societal thought and an identity crisis at a foundational level.

The struggle for independence in Africa was basically the peoples' attempt to reconstruct their societies. In order to reorganize their society people have to become the subjects of history, and historization implies taking control of one's destiny by controlling one's life and inserting oneself in the world. The quest for subjecthood inspired the African struggle for national independence, and independence produced a pride in the people by giving them a sense of identity. However, years of independence have painfully revealed that the roots of colonialism run deep. One of the aims of colonialism is to make people permanently dependent. Africans are discovering that in many subtle ways they are still under Western subjugation. The more obvious forms of Western grip on Africa are seen in economic control. In the past, Western economic control of Africa was through colonialism. It should be remembered that colonialism is an economic system designed to maximize profit for the colonial power. In terms of geo-politics, colonialism serves to protect economic interest. Open colonialism has disappeared, but the West now has different economic institutions to control Africa, such as the International Monetary Fund (Julius Nyerere, the first President of Tanzania, once called this body the International Ministry of Finance), the World Bank, and the so-called aid or donor agencies (aid always has an ulterior motive). Through mechanisms of control such as these organizations, Africa has been made dependent on the West. An analysis of African economies through a theory called dependence reveals how difficult it is for the former colonized world to fully realize selfhood.[1] Dependence discusses the question of authenticity or subjecthood of a people.

The problem of dependence is very serious in Africa because policy makers, the bureaucratic elite in post-colonial Africa, enjoy Western values as the result of the colonial heritage. Years of colonialism produced Africans who assimilated Western values a process called "civilization." To be "civilized" was to order one's life in light of the Western values. The liberal paradigm seeks to promote civilization, and it surely succeeds as long as African policy makers look to the West as the model for development and values.

Three modes of control are used in situations of domination: coercion/reward, dependence, and thought control. In chapters 3 and 4 the focus is on the most subtle of all the forms of control—thought control. The goal of this control is to get people obsessed with the values imposed on them till they define their life in light of the imposed values. By corrupting peoples' thought, colonialism destroyed their values. The task of African intellectuals who are aware of the problems inherent in the Western paradigm of development has been to disengage the African mind from Western values. Their approach has been to retrieve the African values of person and community and integrate these fundamental values in an economic process. This is the basic thesis of African socialism. The works of some prominent early African nationalists, such as Léopold Senghor, Julius Nyerere, Kenneth Kaunda, and Kwame Nkrumah, have very well discussed the African struggle for identity. In Chapter 3 I examine Senghor's negritude, his attempt to retrieve identity and dignity. Chapter 4 critically evaluates the works of African political elites on the concept of African socialism.

Chapter 5 discusses the contribution of African philosophers to the struggle. They have addressed the crisis of values at an ontological (foundational) level. Here the task has been to investigate how Africans construe their world, therefore the foundation of their values. The African project at this level is epistemological; that is, it focuses on how people arrive at knowledge, meaning, and value. In other words, the focus is on how people understand the structure of their world. In Western thought, knowledge has to do with being. It is because of this relationship between epistemology and ontology that Alex Kagame opened the discussion on African philosophy of being. Kagame's work was written in defense of African values and thought. He sought to establish the foundation of African values; and he has been followed by many Africans in this task. Chapter 5 explores the validity of this exercise in light of the African struggle for identity.

A key institution in "civilizing" Africans was the Church. Christianity has much to answer for in the uprooting and disorienting of the African people. Through its ministries—preaching, teaching, and healing—Christianity forced

Africans to totally reject their values. (It is important to point out that most of the first schools and hospitals in Africa were run by churches.) True values were those embodied in Western Christianity. It should be kept in mind that missionaries considered Christianity a Western phenomenon, not Middle Eastern. Christianity and Western culture were one and the same. The Church and state had the same goal: to "civilize" (Europeanize) the primitive people of Africa. This common goal led to a status quo mentality within the Church. It is not surprising, then, that structures of resistance to Western values should emerge in the churches. Chapter 6 is a general survey of the African resistance to Western Christianity and values. Taking their cue from the different forms of African resistance to Western values, African theologians have attempted to deconstruct missionary Christianity and reorder communities of faith. These theologians seek to develop an indigenous Christianity by allowing African culture to interact with the core of the Gospel. The chapter discusses the process and limitations of indigenization toward a recapture of identity.

The first six chapters clear the ground for developing a paradigm for transformation of society based on a hermeneutic of life, personhood, and community. These values stand in stark contrast to the Western paradigm, which places emphasis on self-interest, or individualism and materialism. The hermeneutic is informed by a particular understanding of life and personhood as symbols of ultimate meaning and reality and a manner of living fit for people. The Malawian terms *moyo* and *umunthu* are used to express this particular understanding of the world. If these fundamental symbols were allowed to inform all thought and action they would empower people to reorder society into a community of life. This is a community in which the human condition and all that supports it take precedence over everything else. To seek fullness of human life is the center of the community of life. This attitude toward living is what the Church should be about. Chapters 7 and 8 show how the proposed paradigm would affect biblical interpretation and the theological task necessary for transformation of both Church and society. It is important to look at the role of religion in social change because religion represents what people consider fundamental values.

The implications of *moyo* and *umunthu* go beyond Church life. If these symbols were taken as the organizing power of all thought and activity, decision making process in all sectors of life would be transformed by emphasizing their primacy. Social policy informed by these fundamental symbols would lead to justice and fairness in society; that is, sharing the benefits of people's labor in a development process. In the African world, life and people come first; therefore, development policies should focus on enhancing life. Similarly, political parties should respect the dignity of persons and allow people to realize themselves as makers of history. Politicians should make a deliberate attempt to structure their parties to facilitate building a community of life.

NOTE

1. I have done such an analysis on Malawi in my *Malawi's First Republic: An Economic and Political Analysis* (forthcoming).

1

Africa's Biography

The investigation into the crisis of African society and thought systems beings by considering the total experience of African people from a historical perspective. The experience of Africans is the story of a people's struggle for authenticity or identity in life and thought seen from social, political, economic, and religious perspectives. This story is Africa's biography. Biography brings to the open hidden and painful memories, and these provocative memories sharpen sensibilities and influence responses to the current situation and beyond. Biography is a conscience-raising and empowering process.

The concept of biography presupposes the understanding that history is the result of the intermeshing of political, economic, social, and religious factors. History is seen as an ongoing process in which there is a continual interplay of these factors, and those dynamics are reflected and furthered through institutional innovation. This means that all institutions of society are influenced by politics, economics and religion. All factors are then taken together and viewed as a whole in a historical process. That is to say, the concept of biography demands an integrative approach, one which seeks to raise history to its highest level, and to investigate its various dimensions. In an integrative approach history is treated as a totality of different factors, therefore all disciplines are taken as forming one whole, not departmentalized as it so often happens with academic disciplines.

It is only after history has been approached as a totality that it can be fully appropriated; that is to say, only after finding out what really happened and what the contributing factors were can the present condition of a people be fully understood. Lukacs reminds us that "only in context which sees the isolated facts of social life as aspects of historical process and integrates them into a totality, can knowledge of facts hope to become knowledge of reality."[1] In looking at history as a process and as a whole, we can see the African struggle for self-respect and self-determination.

THE CRISIS

The crisis in African society is a result of Africa's contact with the outside world. The consequences of this contact included involvement in a world political economy, receiving Christianity and Western forms of education, all of which undermined and caused the rupture of society and thought. This chapter explores Africa's integration into the world political economic system and the results thereof.

African society is experiencing a crisis of values and meanings occasioned by the rupture of traditional society. With the rupture also came a loss of cultural values and their meaning. In their place were put a new set of values of Western origin. The result of this clash of cultural values is that Africans fail to find meaning in their activities. Things do not hold, for the center of their value system has been moved; the bottom has fallen off, things are scattered! A search for meaning in Western values proves futile. Chinua Achebe, the great African novelist, has captured the feelings of contemporary Africans in their identity crisis and search for meaning in two of his bestsellers: *Things Fall Apart* and *No Longer at Ease.*[2]

Things Fall Apart focuses on the fall of African traditional society. Men of the village of Umofia, once proud of their unity and traditional values, find that those cherished values and the power of traditional society have been lost since the coming of colonial power. A feeling of defeat and impotence to stop the course of history prevails in the village as Okonkwo, the protagonist, burns a missionary school, murders a messenger sent by British official, and finally commits suicide as a final gesture of rebellion against the new order brought by the British. Okonkwo would rather die than submit to the order that has destroyed traditional structures and values.

In *No Longer at Ease*, Chinua Achebe follows up on the decay of social structure and the loss of traditional values. The loss of traditional values breeds an alienated and disoriented people. Loss of traditional values is evident among the African elite. Obi Okonkwo, the protagonist of *No Longer at Ease*, is the grandson of Okonkwo of *Things Fall Apart.* Obi Okonkwo returns home from his studies in England only to discover that his values have changed so much so that traditional African values no longer appeal to him. He has been "detribalized." While he likes the past, he is horrified by the thought of returning to a world that has almost fallen apart. "Detribalization" takes many forms, but the most powerful is the educational system, which strips a person's identity by undermining one's sense of self-worth, self-determination, and cultural values through doubt and suspicion about the validity of these values and beliefs.

This disorientation is present in both secular and religious education. In a very dramatic way, John Mbiti has demonstrated how fatal detribalization can be for the exercise of ministry of the church. Mbiti tells a story of a young man who returns home after years of pursuing a doctorate in theology overseas. Not long after he is home, his sister suddenly falls to the ground; everyone says she is possessed with spirits. People ask the young man what to do, and he tells them to rush her to the hospital. He is told, "She is possessed, hospitals will not cure her." Besides, the nearest hospital is fifty miles away. Then the chief turns to him and says, "You have been studying theology overseas for 10 years. Now help your sister. She is troubled by the spirit of her great aunt." The young man does not know what to do; he consults a book by Bultmann, a German New Testament scholar, to check on what he says about spirit possession in the New Testament, only to find that Bultmann has demythologized spirit possession![3]

The rupture of African society and loss of cultural values cannot be fully understood if not seen through Africa's contact with the outside world, particularly Western influence, the development of Western political and economic institutions, and the evolution of religious and philosophical thought in the last four hundred years. It was the coming of Western power to Africa that weakened traditional society, destroyed the great African civilizations of western and central Africa and the city-states of the east.[4] In the pretext of civilizing and saving Africans, Western civilization and Christianity undermined African traditional institutions, value systems and thought. The destruction of African society and thought followed several phases: incorporation into a world capitalist economic system (which began with the trans-Atlantic slave trade), evangelization of sub-Sahara Africa, education, and colonization.

AFRICA AND THE WORLD: EARLY CONTACTS

Africa's contact with the outside world dates back to time immemorial. Then, as it is now, people came to exploit Africans and their natural resources. In fact, every foreign power that ever set foot in Africa came to exploit. However, the magnitude of exploitation and destruction of the fabric of African society by the West in the last four centuries has reached alarming and dangerous proportions. This is not to deny or overlook the fact that early contacts changed the social, economic, and even political face of Africa. Let us briefly review the nature of relations Africa had with those early contacts.

It is recorded that Phoenician sailors under the orders of Pharaoh Necho circumnavigated Africa over the course of three years arriving home in 596 B.C.E.[5] Phoenicians established colonies in northern Africa, and Carthage, a city-state established near modern Tunis in 814 B.C.E. was their most powerful and important colony.[6] From there, they traded down the western coast as far as Senegal, reaching the coasts of modern Ghana.[7] They established trading settlements, but they confined themselves to the lands immediately around the cities. However, in Tunisia and Algeria, their major settlements, they intermarried with the local inhabitants and introduced Punic as the official language of the region.[8]

The Phoenicians were challenged by the Greeks who planted their colonies in Egypt and Cyrenacia and were later repulsed by Carthaginians. Carthage later fell to the Romans in 146 B.C.E. The Romans established five provinces in North Africa, extending their power to every cultivatable land, thereby making North Africa a colonial breadbasket. Areas of special interest were two adjacent rich provinces which the Romans called "Africa," namely, Tunisia and nearby Tripolitania, and Numidia, eastern Algeria. In these provinces fifty cities were built and integrated into the surrounding farmlands, thoroughly Romanizing the inhabitants. The Romans called the indigenous inhabitants Barbari (barbarians), from which came the name "Berber."[9]

Others who had contacts with Africa included Arab and Asian traders. As late as the twelfth century, Indian textile, Chinese porcelain, and Indonesian and Malaysian beads, all found their way to the east African coast in exchange for African gold, ivory, iron and tortoise shell.[10] Arab traders started establishing trading settlements on the east coast as early as the eighth century B.C.E. According to Al Masudi, an ancient Arab writer, Arab traders acted as middlemen in trans-Indian Ocean trade. Ivory from Africa would

> go generally to Oman, and from there are sent on to China and India. . . . In China the kings and their military and civilian officers are carrying chairs of ivory; no official or person of rank would dare to visit the king in an iron chair, and ivory alone is used for this purpose. . . . Ivory is as much prized in India: there it is made into handles for daggers . . . as well as for the hills of curved swords. . . . But the biggest use of ivory is in the manufacture of chessmen and other gaming pieces.[11]

Arab traders made inroads in northern and eastern Africa in search of Africa's natural resources including people later. Long before the European slave trade, Arabs sold Africans into slavery in the Middle East and beyond. In the seventh century, there were enough African slaves in Mesopotamia to sustain revolts on and off for two hundred years.[12]

It was under their expansion program that started in the seventh century that Arabs settled in northern Africa. Compelled by religious zeal, Arabs fought and conquered many places in battles that they believed to be holy wars or *Jihad* in Arabic. Arab religious campaigns entered Egypt in 639 C.E. and by the turn of the century almost all of northern Africa had fallen to Moslems. Long before the coming of Islam, Arabs were a dominant trading power in eastern Africa engaging in the lucrative trade of gold and ivory. Their strongholds were the islands of Zanzibar, Pemba, and Kilwa. From these islands they easily reached the mainland and into the interior as far south as Sofala, a town south of the Zambezi river on the east coast of Mozambique.[13]

The presence of Arabs in East Africa continued until the sixteenth century when they clashed with Portuguese sailors and traders seeking to avail themselves of the wealth of Africa and to find a sea route to India. The

Portuguese plundered Kilwa, the great commercial port of East Africa, in 1502 and Zanzibar in 1503. Portuguese interference in the region between 1505 and 1512 led to the decline of Kilwa, and thus Moslem commercial influence except in the interior commercial towns of Sofala and Sena. The Portuguese attacked Sena in 1531 to interrupt the Sofala gold trade.

The nature of African trade before the Western invasion is sometimes described as "equal exchange," a term introduced by Ricardo. This term is misleading, especially when used in connection with early African trade with foreigners, because there was no equal exchange value in the goods traded. For example, Africans traded in gold, copper, ivory, gums, shells, coconut oil, and kola nut in exchange for beads, bracelets, and other Asian ornaments. At best, the African trader got cloth. Such was not equal exchange. Samir Amin has suggested the term luxury goods to define the goods African traders were interested in. Amin defines luxury in terms of consumption: "In the strict sense of the term, luxury goods are those for which the demand originates from part of profit which is consumed" as opposed to demand from wages.[14] This was possible because it was trade between externals, or long-distance trade. In modern economic terms it would be said that there was no division of labor that resulted from free trade since there was no integration into one economic system; neither did transfer of surplus result from this trade.[15] "Luxury" goods do not form or determine a system because they are passive; that is, they are not used in production of other goods.[16]

Up to the time of slave trade, long-distance trade changed very little the dynamics of critical traditional institutions of African society. Since traditional institutions remained intact to a large extent, traditional thought and cultural values were maintained. The Arabs in East Africa, posed no threat to African social institutions and thought, because they intermarried with the Africans and became Africanized.[17] The crisis in African society and thought came with Europeans drafting Africans to provide both resources and human power to build a dominant economic system in the West. Once incorporated into the Euro-American political economy, Africa lost its economic and political independence, and its values and thought system were seriously undermined.

AFRICA AND WORLD POLITICAL ECONOMY

First Integration

Before Africa's integration into a world economic system or before 1800s and even as late as the nineteenth century, Europeans had no settlements in Africa except for the Dutch, who had built a settlement at the Cape of Good Hope by 1650. The Portuguese were interest in the wealth of Africa and Africa as a stopping place on their journey to India and the Orient. Lack of settlements did not mean that they had no interest in Africa. No. They had economic interest, they dumped on Africa wines, brandy, outdated firearms, cloth, and trinkets, and things that Africa did not need, in exchange for items they really needed: ivory, gold, gum, camwood and other products. Africa soon became an extension of the European capitalist market, dependent on what Europeans were prepared to buy and sell.

The Portuguese gained naval superiority in the 1400s. Problems of overland trade from Asia led the Portuguese to find a sea route to India. By the early 1400s they were on the islands off the west coast of Africa and by 1487 they had rounded the Cape of Good Hope, led by Bartholomew Diaz. Under the navigation knowledge and experience of Vasco da Gama, the Portuguese reached the east coast of Africa, thus opening the way to Portuguese traders to the treasures of this part of Africa. Portuguese activities in Africa were unwelcome from the beginning because when they arrived in Africa, "they began seizing Africans to take to Europe as 'curiosity pieces' which confirmed that a 'new' land had been reached."[18] The first African slaves reached Portugal in 1444, and 35,000 followed between 1450 and 1500. These slaves were taken to other places, mainly Spain, Italy and Sicily.

Slavery existed in Africa before the Portuguese and Arab slave trade but it was of a different nature. In African slavery, the slave was usually a criminal or a war captive and the person became a member of a household with defined duties and privileges. Marriage and participation in the social institutions assimilated the individual into full membership of a family or ethnic group. The motive for profit, gain and power, ideas brought over by foreign slave traders, sunk Africa into deep slavery. This was made worse by guns that the European and Arab slave traders provided African slave raiders. Sir Richard Burton, the British traveler, calculated that a slave raid to capture fifty-five women caused destruction of "at least ten villages, each with a population between a hundred and two hundred souls."[19] Slave raids destroyed African society but also African values of life and personhood. With European and Arab slave trade, a slave ceased to be a person and became property that could be dispensed with at the master's whim. The breakdown of traditional social and political institutions in the wake of the slaughter and destruction accompanying the capture of slaves was enormous. "No possible estimate can be made on human suffering and agony caused by separation of as many as fifteen million people of Africa."[20] Neither can the real cost be measured in the mass depopulation of Africa, for about 10-15 percent of the slaves shipped from West Africa died before they reached the New World.[21] Talking about these estimates Davidson says: "So far as the Atlantic slave trade is concerned it appears reasonable to suggest that in one way or another, before or after embarkation, it cost Africa at least fifty million souls. This estimate may be about one-fourth of black Africa's population today, and certainly on the low side."[22] It is indeed impossible to estimate the number of Africans shipped to the New World for all accounts are based on surviving records, but it is known that some smuggled Africans and, obviously, these withheld data.

Areas most affected by the slave trade in Africa were: West, East and Central Africa. On the west coast slave trade was notorious from Senegal to Angola, a belt covering two hundred miles inland. East and Central Africa covered the region now including Tanzania, Mozambique, Malawi, northern Zambia and eastern Zaire. By mentioning these areas we do not seek to give the impression that slave trade did not exist in North and South Africa, rather to emphasize that by comparison, the social and political infrastructure of the areas mentioned were badly destroyed by slave raids and human exportation.

Massive repatriation of Africans overseas as slaves was a response to the external factors of capital and labor. Africans did not start overseas trade in humans or chattel slavery. It was the expansion of capitalist economy in Europe and the genocide of indigenous peoples in the Americas and the Caribbean that created a demand for importation of slave labor from Africa. There was a direct connection between levels of export from Africa and demand for slaves in the Americas or the Caribbean. For example, when the Dutch took over Pernambuco in Brazil in 1634, the director of Dutch West Indian Company immediately informed their agents on the Gold Coast that they were to take necessary steps to ensure the supply of slaves from the adjacent coast of the Volta; thus the name "Slave Coast."

Eric Williams has documented the connections between the slave trade and the development of capitalism in England. Some English entrepreneurs built large enterprises from profits reaped from slave trade, including David and Alexander Barclay who got rich by being involved in slave trade since 1756. They formed Barclays Bank. Then there was Lloyds, who through the slave trade transformed a humble coffee house in London, to one of the world's leading banking and insurance houses in the world.[23]

The slave trade did not produce similar wealth in Africa yet it was impossible for any single state or authority to stop it. In 1630 Queen Nzinga of Angola and her people, established the state of Matamba on the river Kwango to resist Portuguese trade in slaves, but her effort did not succeed. About a century later, Agaja Trudo, Benin's greatest king saw that European slave trade had a crippling effect on the development of his land. From 1724 to 1726, he burned and destroyed European forts and slave camps and blocked paths to catchment areas. This reduced the trade to a trickle for a time, but in 1730 Trudo allowed Europeans to resume slave trading in exchange for firearms and cowries from Europeans.

The Mercantalist Network

Slave trade was accelerated by mercantilism—the creation of the closed imperial trade networks among European metropolis, the Caribbean and North America. The resultant economic activity from this imperial trade networks was slavery and expansion. This is how most of coastal Africa came to be incorporated into a capitalist world economy. As periphery zones, they retained their local sovereign political institutions for the most part, since it was seldom required to maintain the flow of commerce between the periphery and the metropolis. By the end of the nineteenth century, however, only Liberia and Ethiopia which still maintained their sovereignty. The loss of sovereignty was the first stage of integration.

Slave trade lasted for more than two centuries. The gradual demise of slave trade was caused by many factors. The first and foremost reason for its decline was that by the end of the eighteenth century it was no longer profitable. With the new forms of production brought by the industrial revolution, and styles of consumption in Europe, economic interest shifted from trade in slaves to finding sources for raw materials as well as markets overseas. The second contributing factor was reports of European travelers who wrote of vast mineral wealth in the interior of Africa. The reports painted a picture of instant wealth for anyone ready to work in the interior: "It was believed that the mineral wealth of Africa grew increasingly as one moved northward; this aspiration for sudden and great riches brought Europeans across the Limpopo into Southern Rhodesia [Zimbabwe] and later into Northern Rhodesia [Zambia]."[24]

The reports also spoke of destruction of African communities, the horrors caused by the slave trade, and the need for better trade to replace slavery. Some of the travelers urged their people to go to Africa not only to establish legitimate trade to replace slavery but also to convert Africans to Christianity. It was with this intention in mind that David Livingstone, the Scottish medical doctor and traveler, delivering his *Cambridge Lectures*, said: "I go back to Africa to make an open path for commerce and Christianity." Travelers' reports together with an improvement in economic circumstances brought about by the industrial revolution helped to create the third condition, a moral revulsion against slave trade. The fourth factor was a growing sense of nationalism in Europe: "The Third Republic sought to restore French grandeur; the newly unified German and Italian states were in search of their place in the imperial sun. Imperialist, missionaries and merchants converged on a continent whose defenses had been breached by an earlier generation of explorers and merchants and whose interior had been rendered vulnerable by two centuries of strife and dislocation accompanying the slave trade."[25]

Christian movements in England realized that it would not be enough for travelers to alert Europeans of the continuing horrors of the slave trade: something had to be done to stop the slave trade. Organized abolitionist groups started campaigns to exert pressure on the government to abolish slavery in Britain. It was not until Lord Mansfield's judgment on a test case in 1772 that "radical" Christians and philanthropists in Britain had their first victory. Total victory came when the British Parliament was prevailed upon to pass a law in 1807 which made the slave trade illegal for British subjects. Four years later, the 1807 law was followed up with another Act imposing heavy penalties on anyone who continued in slave trade. By 1811 slave trade had ceased in Britain. Britain began to use its naval, political, and economic power, to assert its moral superiority to protect its general economic position. Wolff has noted that British policy in East Africa was dictated by commercial interests. Britain wanted to protect its interest against private European companies, European national powers, and the Arabs:

> Facing this situation, the British government operating through Consul Kirk resorted to a strategy that had succeeded well for the previous half century. Put bluntly, the strategy involved the activation of anti-slave trade campaigns as a means of establishing British economic hegemony in an area. In the second stage [of the British campaign], from the 1890s, the British finally subjected the slave trade to a systematic attack sufficient to stop it and to confront the traders with economic ruin. The coup de grace followed, as Britain replaced the sultan and Arab-Swahili aristocracy with the direct economy and political hegemony of the British administration.[26]

The other nations gradually abolished the slave trade. By the end of the nineteenth century slavery was illegal in Europe and the United States of America.

The end of slavery created an economic vacuum, but this vacuum was quickly filled by trade in Africa's natural resources. This idea had taken a back seat during the trans-Atlantic slave trade. Now attention was on ivory, gum (copal), beeswax, honey, cloves, coffee, cotton, groundnuts, palm oil, and rubber. Palm oil and rubber were leading products from Ghana. By the 1890s Ghana had become the leading producer of rubber in the British empire and the third in the world. In eastern, central, and equatorial Africa, ivory was the main item of export. By the 1860s "ivory moving down the Congo . . . amounted to a sixth of all the ivory that was marketed in London, and . . . by the early 1880s the annual value of trade at the mouth of the Congo was about 3 million pounds sterling."[27] The direct consequence of the evolution of trade in natural resources was a steady decrease in the slave trade; but the slave trade did not end immediately. "For decades after abolition there was much sentiment in Europe (and in Africa) that the slave trade should be revived, and smugglers from England, France, the United States and other countries continued to engage in it until the risks far outweighed profits."[28] The other result of trade in natural resources was an acceleration of commercial linkage and strengthening of existing links within Africa. Almost the whole of North Africa had been integrated commercially by caravan routes long before European trade.[29] The old trade roots in the Nile valley continued to be active and by 1850s, trade linked Cairo through the Red Sea to points as far south as Darkfur and Kordifan. Commercial integration in the rest of Africa started in the first decade of the nineteenth century when Angolan traders started crossing the continent. These were followed by the Arab, Swahili, and Nyamwezi traders, who pushed from Tanzania into the interior in the 1820s. By the 1860s caravans of a Nyamwezi trader named Msiri had reached far west as Katanga and Kazembe. He established his empire there, from which caravans reached Benguel on the Atlantic coast, thus establishing trade links coast to coast. From Mozambique and Tanzania, the Bisa, Yao, and Chikunda traders penetrated the Shire valley and Zimbabwe by the 1850s. From the Atlantic coast, the Chokwe, Ovimbundu, and Tio established their routes into the kingdoms of Kazembe and Lunda.

The development of this network of long-distance trade, "promoted spatial specialization and helped to give greater elasticity to commercial relations over vast stretches of territory."[30] The system also became a vehicle for spreading cultures (the Zande-Mangbetu culture of equatorial Africa, for example) and creating lingua francas. Swahili spread from the east coast to the eastern part of Zaire and the copperbelt in Zambia. The network, then, set in motion the cultural unification of Central Africa. The end of slavery and the establishment of the new economic order also allowed for a greater centralization of political authorities—states and dynasties—which had been destablized by wars waged to capture slaves. Greater cooperation also emerged among political authorities. All this progress was cut short by the imposition of colonialism.

Another area in which significant changes took place in the nineteenth century was religion. By the nineteenth century Islam had established itself in areas hereto unreached in West Africa. This was done through the crusades of Usaman dan Fodio in Hausaland (1804), Sheik Ahmadu in Masima (1881), and Sheik Umar (1852).[31] Through Arab and Swahili traders Islam went on the rise in East Africa, especially in Baganda areas. Mombasa and Zanzibar had already received Islam.

Christianity benefitted greatly from the demise of the slave trade. At the beginning of the nineteenth century Christianity was mainly along the coastal areas and it was proclaimed by missionary societies. In West Africa it was the following societies: the Society for the Propagation of the Gospel (SPG), the Wesleyan Missionary Society (WMS) and the Glasgow and Scottish Missionary Society (GSMS). South Africa was the field of the Moravian Mission and London Missionary Society (LMS); in East Africa it was only the Church Missionary Society (CMS). The numbers of these organizations rose by the middle of the century from three to fifteen in West Africa, from one to eleven in South Africa, and from one to five in East Africa. The missionary enterprise was critical to colonization. In some areas missionaries were the forerunners to colonialism and collaborated with colonial administrators during the "pacification" period. Exceptions were few; on the whole, Christianity was a tool to European conquest.

The end of the slave trade ushered in a new era in which Africa experienced great social, cultural, political, and economic changes. Most of these changes were initiated from Africa and by Africans. Contrary to many reports, Africa was not sleeping when colonialism was imposed. There was much dynamism in all spheres of life; here only a few have been touched upon. One can only imagine what Africa would have been had Europeans not decided to divide Africa and impose their cultural, social, economic and political systems.

THE SCRAMBLE FOR AFRICA

The slave trade having thus become illegal, Africa was drawn into another phase of world political economy. This phase was anticipated by the influx of Europeans into Africa. By the end of the first half of the nineteenth century, three European nations—Portugal, Great Britain and France—had claimed areas in the interior of Africa, their presence being made visible by merchants, missionaries, and in some places by imperialists. They first established their presence along the coastal regions, by the 1850s, they were in the interior and by 1879, they had established political control in their strongholds along the coast and made more claims further inland. The race for colonies in Africa was sparked off by three issues: (1) the dispatch of three French missions to explore routes for the trans-Sahara railway, (2) the appointment of Major Gustave Borgnis-Desbordes as the commander of the upper Senegal to push French interests inland, and (3) the move of the King Leopold II of Belgium to join the three European nations already claiming land in Africa. Leopold had been in search of a colony for a long time and the travel reports of Sir Henry Morton Stanley, who in 1877, had completed a coast-to-coast journey descending the Congo river, gave Leopold an opportunity to realize his dream. His chances grew when Stanley began serving him in 1879 and for several years Stanley established land and water transport routes from the head of the Congo to Kisangani, a thousand miles inland. Leopold quickly prepared way for international recognition of his rule over the whole area of the Congo basin, becoming the first to secure international recognition of such a large African empire.

It was Leopold's claim on the Congo and German activities in Africa that upset the pre-existing balance of European power in Africa that precipitated a state of international hysteria in which all the European powers rushed in to stake claims to political sovereignty and to bargain furiously with each other for recognition of this or that region. Britain became alarmed when France annexed Port Novo in 1883 and began its activities on the Niger. To check both France and Belgium, Britain backed Portugal on the Congo issue and safeguarded its interest on the bight of Benin and Biafra, now threatened by French moves. In June 1884 Britain sent Hewett to declare a protectorate over the Oil Rivers and the Cameroons, only to find that Germany had its flags flying in Togo and the Cameroons. After Leopold had made his claim, the Germans had acted swiftly claiming Cameroon, Togo, South West Africa, and Tanganyika in an eighteen-month period from 1883 to 1885.

A conference to settle territorial disputes on who had claimed what area in Africa met in Berlin from 15 November 1884 to 31 January 1885. The conference was attended by every western nation except Switzerland and the United States. Although the conference was on Africa, no African monarch or political authority was invited. Four resolutions, rules of colonization were passed: (1) any power claiming an area should inform the other signatory powers for any who may deem it necessary to make counterclaim; (2) proof of effective occupation was required before annexations; (3) treaties signed with African rulers were to be considered as legitimate titles to sovereignty; (4) there was to be freedom of navigation on the Congo and Niger rivers. The conference also agreed to stop the slave trade, which was still being carried by the Arabs as well as Western nations. The conference also passed a resolution on free trade. These rules were embodied in the Berlin Act, which was ratified on 26 February 1885. This act cleared the way for the Partition of Africa, for it removed the possibility of military conflict between occupying nations. The need for the second resolution, namely, proof of effective occupation, during the time the conference met, a period characterized by flimsy annexations, especially on the part of Germany. While the conference was actually sitting, Bismarck announced his government's protectorate over the parts of East Africa where Karl Peters and his associates had obtained dubious treaties from bemused chiefs in the course of a single expedition lasting a few weeks. It was now clear to all that a quick partition of the whole continent was inevitable, and to consider further claims for their own countries could most usefully be developed.[32]

The Berlin conference accelerated the scramble for Africa by European nations. For the next several decades, Europeans engaged in dividing the interior areas of Africa for themselves. By 1911, Morocco ceased to be one of the independent nations of Africa and was partitioned by France and Spain. Of all the old African civilizations and empires, only Ethiopia succeeded in resisting European influence by forcing the Italians to limit themselves to Eritrea and Somalia in 1889. Liberia too was left alone because it was protected by the United States. (Although independent, Liberia bowed to American political, economic, and military pressures, which undercut the country's identity as a sovereign state.) Thus the European conquest of Africa was complete.

THE COLONIAL LEGACY

The main reason for the scramble for colonies in Africa was economic. The increased competition between principal industrial states on the world's markets, which led to a crisis in industrial capitalism, led some to believe that the political future of a state lay in the securing control of markets and raw materials, which Africa had in abundance. It is not surprising, then, that European conquest of Africa was quickly followed by occupation. Ferkiss has said it is important to clearly understand European occupation of Africa for what it was.

> Once European powers had conquered Africa they had to find means of ruling and exploiting it. The system they created for this purpose is usually called colonialism; but it is a misnomer. What is ordinarily called colonial period should be called the Era of European Occupation. This distinction is not merely a matter of semantics. Failure to understand the differences between colonialism and political and economic occupation is the cause of much misunderstanding about the African past and about Africa's present role in the world.[33]

The progress made by most Africans before the 1880s did not prepare them for European take over of their lands. Most African rulers saw Europeans as trading partners or allies, but there was not the sense of inferiority that colonialism was to introduce. If anything, most African rulers, especially those with centralized political authority, were proud and ready to defend their sovereignty and way of life from any external power. Examples abound. In 1890, Machemba, king of the Yao (what is now Tanzania) wrote Hermann von Wissmann,

> I have listened to your words but can find no reason why I should obey you—I would rather die first. . . . If it should be friendship that you desire, then I am ready for it, today and always; but to be your subject that I cannot be. . . . If it should be war that you desire, then I am ready, but never to be your subject . . . I do not fall at your feet, for you are God's creature just as I am . . . I am Sultan here in my land. You are Sultan there in yours. Yet listen, I do not say that you should obey me; for I know that you are a free man. . . . As for me, I will not come to you, and if you are strong enough, then come and fetch me.[34]

Similar sentiments were echoed in a 1891 letter by Prempeh I of Asante in Ghana in his reply to a British offer of protection.

> The suggestion that Asante in its present state should come and enjoy the protection of Her Majesty the Queen and Empress of India I may say is a matter of very serious consideration, and which I am happy to say we have arrived at this conclusion, that my kingdom of Asante will never commit itself to any such policy. Asante must remain as of old, at the same time to remain friendly with all white men. I do not write this in a boastful spirit, but in the clear sense of its meaning.

> . . . The cause of Asante is progressing and there is no reason for any Asante man to feel alarm at the prospects or to believe for a single instant that our cause has been driven back by the events of the past hostilities.[35]

Other African rulers were able to read the signs of the times and perceive the coming onslaught on Africa. For example, Makombe of Mozambique told a white man in 1895: "I see how you white men advance more and more into Africa; on all sides of my country companies are at work. My country will also have to take up these reforms and I am quite prepared to open it up. I should like to have good roads and railways, but I will always remain the Makombe my fathers have been."[36] While Makombe was ready for reforms, Wobogo, king of the Mossi, wanted whites out of his land. In 1895 Wobogo told a French Captain Restenave: "I know the whites wish to kill me in order to take my country, and yet you claim that they will help me to organize my country. But I find my country good as it is. I have no need of them. I know what is necessary for me and what I want: I have my own merchants: also, consider yourself fortunate that I do not order your head cut off. Go away now, and above all never come back."[37]

Most Africans did not take colonialism sitting down. They were aware of its political and economic implications to their society and way of life. Indeed, they were some who sought protection from Europeans against other Europeans. Those signed treaties of protection and trade cooperation. On the other hand, other African rulers came under colonialism as a result of being mislead into signing treaties whose full meaning was not clear. This was the case of Kabaka Mwanga of Buganda, who signed treaty with the British East African Company. From his diary we read:

> No man if he understood would sign it, and to say that a savage chief has been told he cedes all rights to the Company in exchange for nothing is an obvious truth. If he had been told that the Company will protect him against his enemies, and share in his wars as an ally, he has been told a lie, for the Company have no idea of doing any such thing and no force to do it with if they wished.[38]

The same would have happened to Menelik II, the emperor of Ethiopia, had he not been swift and decisive in his dealings with the Italy with whom he signed what he believed to be a treaty of friendship; the treaty was signed at Wuchale. When he discovered that the Italians had given a different interpretation to article XVII of the treaty, Menelik wrote directly to the king of Italy:

> When I made the treaty of friendship with Italy, in order that our secrets be guarded and that our understanding should not be spoiled, I said that because of our friendship our affairs in Europe might be carried on with the aid of the sovereignty of Italy, but I have not made any treaty which obliges me to do so, and today, I am

> not the man to accept it. That one independent power does not seek the aid of another to carry on its affairs your Majesty understands very well.[39]

The Italians did not change their position arguing, "Italy cannot notify the other powers that she was mistaken in Article XVII, because she must maintain her dignity." Ethiopia could not take that either. "We also," retorted Empress Ttaitu on behalf of Menelik, "have made known to the Powers that the said article, as it is written in our language, has another meaning. As you know, we also ought to respect our dignity. You wish Ethiopia to be represented before the other powers as your Protectorate, but this shall never be."[40] This misunderstanding made Menelik repudiate the Treaty of Wuchale on 12 February 1893 and the European powers two weeks later, declaring: "Ethiopia has no need of no one; she stretches her hand to God." Italy retaliated by attacking and occupying Tigre in January 1895. Menelik mobilized his army and defeated the Italians at Amba Alagi and Makale in December. In January 1896, Ethiopia gained its decisive victory at Adowa, giving Africa its greatest victory over a European army since Hanibal.

The subject of African reaction to colonialism is outside the present work. However, here let it be said that there were three reactions: submission, alliance and confrontation. There were two forms of confrontation: diplomatic and armed resistance.

Colonialism marked Africa's further integration into the world capitalist economy. European nations did not have a definite future plan for the colonies they acquired during the scramble. Each colonizing nation developed its own policy toward its colonies but that did not include a conscious planning for the welfare of the colonized. The policies were guiding principles in interacting with the people of the colonies. Britain chose a policy of indirect rule while Germany had a centralized and highly hierarchical bureaucracy of colonial officers responsible to the Chancellor and the Kaiser. French policy, on the other hand, was influenced by Enlightenment thought and the French Revolution with its motto, "liberté, fraternité, egalité." In theory, this concept, applied to the colonies meant that all under French rule enjoyed the same privileges and rights and that they could be assimilated into French culture and life—a kind of citizenship. The French called such people *evolvués*. In reality French rule in Africa treated Africans as anything but citizens. Claude Ake has shown that it was brutal. The Portuguese also had a program of assimilation (*assimilados* or *naos indigenas*). The *assimilado* program was based on paternalism—a civilizing mission or tutelage. Belgian policy was based on the idea of bringing civilization to Africa. Colonialism according to the European nations was not exploitation but salvation. It was with this idea that the British referred to their colonies as protectorates and "preferred to think of colonialism as a 'mandate' to help backward peoples."[41]

Different as the policies were, the prevailing understanding was that colonies were destined to be politically integrated with the metropolitan country. While that was so, the responsibility to "develop" the colonies rested on the colonial governments. At the beginning of colonialism, governments consisted of just a handful of people; for example, Harry Johnston (later Sir) was sent to found a colonial government in Malawi with ten thousand pounds sterling, being increased to one hundred thousand by 1900. With that money he could only afford seventy-five soldiers under a British officer. Any increase in civil and military expenditure had to be met by raising local revenue. It did not concern the colonizers how the colonial administration raised its revenue, even if that meant forced labor. Personal taxes was soon established and a system of labor in commutation of tax was used. Of course the introduction of personal tax and other demands by the governments for labor were met with opposition from Africans, and the colonial administrators often had to ask for more aid, sometimes in the form of military supplies, from their home governments to put down local opposition and "establish law and order."

At the beginning of colonialism aid was given to colonial governments not to develop the colonies but for police the colonies to ensure a steady supply of agricultural products needed in the metropolitan country or on the world market. The period of the scramble for Africa, 1873-1897 coincided with a period of contraction in the world capitalist economy.[42] Expansion came in 1900 and it lasted until 1913. During the expansion, world trade terms favored agricultural exports.[43] The contributing factor in favor of agricultural exports was short of world raw materials. It was then profitable for the European nations to begin or expand agricultural export in the newly acquired colonies of Africa. Since the crop growing areas in Africa were under their political control, it meant large profits for the colonizing nation. For Britain, the alteration in world prices in favor of agricultural products meant securing world dominance in political economy:

> In terms of supplying food and raw materials imports, colonial administration meant for Britain ultimate control and hence a greater measure of security than would have obtained if France or Germany or another power had annexed the territories. Also, whatever the final destination of food and raw materials export from any colony, British political control almost always meant British predominance in the financing, insurance and freight for the colony's exports, and hence British balance of payments advantages. Foreign political control could and frequently did deny Britain such predominance, regardless of the relative prices of the services provided by Britain and other countries. Finally, . . . colonial control enabled British authorities to determine to a large extent the choice of foods and raw materials developed and exported from any colonial territory. Thus, it is reasonable to conclude that, in the absence of Britain's new empire, her security, her gains from invisible exports, and both the general mix and quantities of food and raw materials supplied to world markets have been less favorable to her.[44]

Less favorable as the agricultural products may have been for Britain, the system itself was certainly disastrous for the African colonies in two ways: subsistence crops and peripheralization of the colonies. Increased production for overseas markets had a negative effect on subsistence needs. Colonial governments neglected subsistence crops in favor of those in demand on world market. "One fact is clear. Whatever the hypothetical balance sheet of colonial economies might reveal, European domination brought Africa into the world economy. There was no motive for anyone to seek in Africa anything which was not marketable elsewhere; hence on the whole, increased production for domestic subsistence needs was neglected except for the efforts of few individual civil servants and missionaries."[45] Peripheralization of the colonies was gradual. Ferkiss tells how this marginalization developed:

> The European merchants came in search of slaves, gold and exotic tropical products such as ivory and spices. They stayed (or their successors came) to obtain two things not found as conveniently elsewhere in the necessary quantities: tropical agricultural products such as palm oil, rubber, tea, sisal, cacao, peanuts, certain kinds of cotton or minerals such as gold, diamonds and copper. They did not seek these in order to sell them to Africans, who did not need or could not pay for them, but in order to sell them to other Europeans. As a result the resources of Africa were developed in terms of what could be sold elsewhere. This was the real crime of colonialism economically.[46]

It cannot be overemphasized that Europeans badly needed these resources. Of course topping their list were gold and slaves. Walter Rodney points out that

> Europeans were anxious to acquire gold because there was a pressing need for gold coin within the growing capitalist money economy. Since gold was limited to very small areas of Africa, as far as Europeans were then aware, the principal export was human beings. . . . African gold was also the main source for the mintage of Dutch coin in the seventeenth century, helping Amsterdam to become the financial capital of Europe in that period; and further it was no coincidence that when the English struck a new gold coin in 1663, they called it the "guinea."[47]

The other reason for turning to the colonies for production of raw materials and agricultural exports was cheap or "surplus" labor. The coming of colonialism brought wage labor, but wages were extremely low in all types of employment: farm, mine, and urban jobs. In most cases the employees had to have a plot of land to grow food to survive. Employers justified these low wages by arguing that the standard and cost of living in Africa were low, and they were backed by legislation. Africans who qualified and got senior positions were also subject to low pay, even if they held the same rank as a white. Africans working on farms, in mines, in construction, and in domestic service often worked ten to fourteen hours a day, and sometimes without breaks for meals, to produce surplus that they would not enjoy. Those who preferred to work on their own land rather than seek employment in the white establishment were not better off, for their produce, often cash crops, was sold at giveaway prices set and controlled by colonial marketing boards. Theoretically, these boards were supposed to buy African produce at a reasonable price, sell the crops overseas, and keep the surplus to improve African agriculture. In addition, marketing boards were to pay African farmers a stable price when prices fell on the world market. In reality, the boards paid the smallholder a low fixed price even when prices were rising on the world market. Profits went not to Africans but to the home government. Yet the European imports manufactured from African raw materials were sold to Africans at an inflated prices. The exploitation of the African was total.

Thus, colonialism meant loss of political authority for Africans and repatriation of profit, the consistent expropriation of surplus produced by African labor out of African resources. This was natural for colonialism, for that is how it expresses itself, that is, as "a system of rule which assumes the right of one people to impose their will upon another. This situation inevitably leads to a situation of dominance and dependency which . . . systematically subordinates those governed by it to the imported culture in social, economic and political life."[48]

Europeans did only dispossessed Africans of their land, but they also forced them to work on the land. Land utilization through forced labor had two intentions: (1) to maintain a steady flow of economic needs of the metropolis through expanded cash crop export production; (2) to provide ideological reinforcement through export production. The ideology was capitalism which "was seen as a 'civilizing' process, as well as an alternative to slave trade."[49] Claude Ake says that the notion of *mission civilisatrice* was the basis of African suffering and exploitation under colonial political economy.

> The ideology of the colonizer complemented political economy of colonialism very well. It justified the system in terms of its benefits to the exploited without in any way compelling mitigation of the harshness and the brutality of the exploitation. Every assault on the colonized person could be defended as a necessary concession to the realities of his state of development. In the meantime, the assault on his life and on his dignity became the very tool for creating those "realities." In other words, the systematic brutalization of the colonized became the very instrument for reducing him to subhuman existence, the condition of existence he would have to be in order to deserve colonization. Thus, somehow, the more inhuman the practice of colonialism, the more plausible its ideology.[50]

There was also another factor involved—prudence. Barber points out that "The *Pax* in Africa, it was widely believed, depended on the provision of opportunities for Africans to earn money incomes. Otherwise, idleness among African men might well breed mischief and thereby expensive threats to the new order."[51]

Three modes of development were used to utilize land and surplus labor force for what was taken to be three different political situations in Africa. The modes were chosen to make sure the metropolitan economic interests would be met and allow for easy administration. These modes were African smallholder farming, European concession, and white settler farming. In light of these modes, Samir Amin divides colonial Africa into three macro-regions: Africa of colonial economy, Africa of concession companies, and Africa of labor reserves.[52] The first was for the West Africa, the second for Equatorial Africa and the last for East, South, and North Africa. In the concessionary mode of development the head of colonial administration, out of financial interest, invited companies to buy the "vacant" land. The concessionary companies that bought this land felt they had the right to exploit the Africans for their own profit, thereby reaping "unheard-of profits" and creating "veritable hells-on-earth," wherein "the lot of the Africans was tragic," says Stenger.[53]

The white settler development model in East Africa was chosen on the grounds that East Africans would not respond to cash-crop market opportunities, in contrast to West Africans, because the slave trade had weakened the political structural system and thus the cohesiveness of society. The argument was that cash-crop market required a well structured society with a centralized authority. To avoid a return to "primitive" modes of production—tribal subsistence economy—it became necessary to "implant non-African settlers in order to organize, invest in, and manage agricultural production of cash crops."[54] The crops to be grown in this area were coffee, tea, tobacco, sisal, and cotton wherever possible.

Africans were not drafted into the world political economy without any resistance. The development model was a source of constant conflict between the settlers and the indigenous people. The direct cause of the conflicts was land. Often settlers moved the natives from their traditional land to some distant and/or infertile land. These moves were not limited to farming areas alone; people were moved from their land in areas where mining companies existed and also in the whole of Equatorial Africa. Oliver and Fage write about African experience under settler and companies.

> Here there were many hundreds of thousands of Africans who in one way or another lost the lands they had previously cultivated. Many were forced to move to new and perhaps inferior land in "native reserves." Many others were left in possession of the lands they were cultivating at the time of occupation, but lost the surrounding uncultivated land which in a sense was their "fallow." Accordingly, when they moved, in the course of shifting cultivation, they found themselves rent-paying "squatters" on alienated land.[55]

When Africans were allowed to remain on the "settler's land" they did so on condition that they would work for the settler as rent-in-kind. In some places the colonial administration tried to discourage the practice (to lessen opposition to colonial power), of demanding the natives to pay rent-in-kind. Instead the colonial administrators proposed that the Africans pay rent (the idea did not make any difference for people owned the land). For example, in Malawi legislation was passed to this effect including the Land Ordinance (Native Location) of 1904. Settlers never followed the ordinance "for what the landlords wanted was not rent but work."[56] "Thus, if an African resident did not provide his quanta of labor as rent-in-kind (the *thangata* system), many Europeans felt that they ought to resort to their only means of disciplining their labor force: eviction from his land holding," comment Shepperson and Price.[57]

The practice of wage labor was widespread in colonial Africa. Settlers and Europeans owning plantations and mining companies all demanded wage labor. This practice had also been carried out by different governments upon their subjects in the colonial territories. The government demanded "labor for the construction and maintenance of roads and railways, labor for building and clearing government stations, and (above all in the early days) labor for porterage. Nominally such labor might be given in commutation of tax. In practice, however, it was compulsory labor."[58]

The problem of forced labor, "de-enspacement" through forced removal from traditional land holding, and other grievances was the seed bed of political struggle for independence. Space is very important to Africans. The village space, which includes cultivated and uncultivated land, embodies a certain historical consciousness that cannot be had elsewhere. A village is a particular space; its particularity arises from the understanding that it is a place where special events of historical significance for a people have taken place. This historical significance cannot be transferred to any other place. To force an African to leave traditional land, is to rob one of his or her of historical consciousness. Land to Africans is both a political and a sacred entity, not a trade commodity, as the government saw it or a vehicle of the feudal system that the white settler scheme brought. The *thangata* system itself was immoral: land was to be shared by all and owned by none, for it was the source of life and livelihood for all. Thus the struggle for independence was not only a political struggle but also a moral struggle.

Colonialism had other effects on Africans, which can be summed up as a crisis of identity due to loss of power. Africans lost power over their social, political and economic institutions to their colonizers. Africans lost their ability to control and defend their interests and the institutions that gave them cultural unity. This meant that Africans had lost control of their cultural goals and standards, thus how to determine their destiny. They could no longer train their young in their way of life. A society that cannot train its youth, has lost control of its future. Africans were no longer makers of their history.

With colonialism European domination of Africa had become complete. European influence and control left no area of African thought and society untouched. European determination to the change African way of life was based on *mission civilisatrice*, which was an attempt to bring the "backward" people of Africa into civilization. Although the metropolitan countries used different methods and policies, their basic goals were the same.

> No colonial power believed that Africans had a history; all of the powers gave evidence of regarding Africans as inferior. In this context, no colonial power was prepared to treat Africans as free people. Thus political and economic domination were principal goals for colonial rule, and the European commitment to racial superiority which was part and parcel of the European administrators' approach to Africans was always evident—in dress, language, housing, recreation, religion and sex.[59]

European domination brought a new concept of rule. Colonialism was not just a rule by foreigners but it was also a rule by the executive. In all colonies the style of government was the same: rule without checks and balances. The attitude of the colonial power toward its colony, be it direct control (as did the French, Belgians, and Portuguese) or indirect (like the British), did not give rise to a different system of rule; colonial rule was all the same: rule without the effective check of legislatures representative of local interest. This was contrary to African political systems, in which a chief ruled with a council of elders who represented their nuclear and extended families. Chiefs discussed matters with their council and ruled in the name of the common good. Politics was based on participation, an the exercise of power which gave a sense of worth to all in the community. The people had power to "stool" (enthrone) or "destool" the chief. Colonial politics, on the other hand, was politics of subjugation. Unfortunately, the politics of subjugation did not die with colonialism: the same rule by executive was common in post-colonial Africa, where the single political party was in many ways was a successor to colonial authority. "The very same 'emergency regulations' under which African political leaders were imprisoned by the imperialists are once again being used in many independent African states to silence and destroy political opposition."[60]

In places where the traditional office of chief is still recognized, the chief's role in government is minimal with few exceptions. The chief is not a traditional authority, the one who embodies the norms and values of the people; no longer a symbol of historical consciousness by which people find their identity. In some places chieftaincy has become a political office as in Kenya; in other places the chief has to be "a card-carrying party member." In places where the chief is still seen as the bearer of traditional values—in Malawi, for example—until the 1993 multiparty referendum, a chief had to work with the local party chairperson and other political figures or be deposed.

Seeing what colonial rule was like one wonders why the West blames Africans for not continuing the "democratic" tradition left by Europeans. What sort of democracy? Is rule by subjugation democratic? Europeans never brought democracy to Africa. The African condition in the post-independence era is in large measure the direct result of the undemocratic rule practiced by the colonialism administrators. African leaders are to be blamed for mistakes, but their colonials masters have no right to point a finger.

The crisis and rupture of African society and thought was thorough. The crisis came in all fields: economic, political, social, religious, and philosophical thought. The crisis deepened even further with every form of contact and involvement that Africans had with the Western world. With incorporation into the world economy Africa produced capital for the West, but it lost more than resources; it also suffered a crisis of values of sanctity of life and meaning of persons: people could be traded like commodity. The slave trade disrupted societies, displaced many people, and weakened social infrastructure. This was followed by exploitation of land and its resources, thereby displacing even more people. Most Africans lost their time-honored means of livelihood, with nothing taking its place. As the result of losing their land, they also lost political control, and a new notion of power, alien to them, was introduced.

This produced a situation of dependence on the master and a conviction of inferiority. Dependence took many and different forms, some of them had disappeared by the time of political independence. However, other forms are still going on, namely, social, economic and psychological or cultural. The presence of social and economic dependence has been a barrier to a full realization of authentic African life or "Africanicity." Central to this Africanicity is culture, that set of values, lifestyle, and vision that a people cherish and share. Culture is about self-understanding; it is therefore concerned with ethos and a manner of living informed by that ethos. In colonialism as in any situation of oppression, the dominated become disoriented in their values for they follow lifestyles that alienate them from their true selves. This is because the ethos or organizing logic of their life—culture—is eclipsed. Thus they ordered their life according to the values and vision of the dominant culture. Their own proper values fall into disuse and are not appreciated, so that they lose their national and cultural identity. Economic domination is closely related to cultural alienation for those who plan and run the economic system also impose their values on those they subjugate. Simply put: any economic system or development model is bound to cultural ideology. The loss of national or ethnic character in Africa is to be explained by this fact.

Culture serves as a vehicle for propagating the ideology of the dominant group and creating a market for its products. Cultural imperialism alienates the colonized from their aesthetics as the master's work of art and concept of beauty become norm. Through education, and other medium, the colonized are led to believe that their concept of the good and beautiful is inferior. Cultural domination is an element of political and economic alienation. Dependence produces cultural alienation.

Social and economic issues are always connected with politics; and politics as the art of living together as a community should reflect the values of the people. Socio-economics then raise ethical issues that define the symbolic and institutional requirements of a good life. Socio-economic dependence undermines the African ability to define those values that constitute their idea of a good life and a community. The realization of African values, or what Kwesi Dickson has termed selfhood, is tied to socio-economic and political issues facing Africans today.[61] A reconstruction of African life and thought will require an integrative approach to the foundational issues facing African society and thought systems.

NOTES

1. Georg Lukacs, *History and Class Consciousness* (London: Merlin, 1971), 8.

2. Chinua Achebe, *Things Fall Apart* (London: Heinemann, 1958); *No Longer at Ease* (London: Heinemann, 1960).

3. John Samuel Mbiti, "Theological Importance and the Universality of the Church" *Lutheran World*, no. 3 (1974). Also in Gerald H. Anderson and Thomas F. Stransky G. S. P. eds., *Mission Trends Number 3*, (New York: Paulist Press, 1979), 6-8.

4. Joseph Harris, *Africans and Their History* (New York: New American Library, 1972), 34-65.

5. Victor C. Ferkiss, *Africa's Search for Identity* (Cleveland, OH: World, 1966), 48.

6. John G. Jackson, *Introduction to African Civilization* (Secaucus, NJ: The Citadel Press, 1970), 148.

7. Basil Davidson, *The Lost Cities of Africa*, revised ed. (Boston: Little, Brown, 1987), 13.

8. E. Jefferson Murphy, *History of African Civilization* (New York: Dell, 1972), 67.

9. Jackson, *Introduction to African Civilization*, 160.

10. Davidson, *The Lost Cities*, 179.

11. Quoted by Basil Davidson, *The African Past: Chronicles from Antiquity to Modern Times* (New York: Grosset and Dunlap, 1967), 109.

12. Davidson, *The Lost Cities*, 180.

13. Harris, *Africans and Their History*, 62.

14. Samir Amin (an African dependency theorist) quoted by Immanuel Wallerstein, "Three Stages of Africa's Involvement in the World-Economy," *Political Economy of Contemporary Africa*, 2nd ed, Peter C. W. Gutkind and Immanuel Wallerstein, eds. (Beverly Hills, CA: Sage, Sage series on African Modernization and Development, 1985), 36.

15. For details on division of labor see A. V. K. Fitzgerald, "The New International Division of Labor and Relative Autonomy of the State: Notes for a Reappraisal of Classical Dependency," *Bulletin of Latin America Research*, 1, no. 1 (October 1981).

16. Piero Sraffa has given full treatment of the subject in *Production of Commodities by Means of Commodities* (London: Cambridge University Press, 1972), 6-7.

17. Harris, *Africans and Their History*, 62, 64.

18. *Ibid.*, 73.

19. L. H. Gann and P. Duigan, *White Settlers in Tropical Africa* (Baltimore, MD: Penguin, 1962), 26.

20. R. R. Kuczynski, *Population Movements* (1936); quoted in Basil Davidson, *Black Mother* (London: Victor Gollancz, 1961). Philip Curtin's estimates are lower. His view is that about 9.5 million slaves arrived in the New World. *African Slave Trade: A Census* (Madison: University of Wisconsin Press, 1969).

21. A detailed study of the trade has been made by Daniel P. Manix and Malcom Cowley, *Black Cargoes* (New York: Viking, 1962).

22. Davidson, *Black Mother*, 88.

23. Eric Williams, *Capitalism and Slavery* (Chapel Hill, NC: University of North Carolina Press, 1944).

24. Fred Burke, *Africa's Quest for Order* (Englewood Cliffs, NJ: Prentice-Hall, 1964), 83.

25. *Ibid.*, 84.

26. Richard Wolff, *The Economics of Colonialism: Britain and Kenya 1870-93* (New Haven, CT: Yale University Press, 1974), 33-35.

27. P. Curtin, S. Fierman, L. Thompson, and J. Vansina, *African History* (London: Longman, 1978), 418-43.

28. Murphy, *History of African Civilization*, 296.

29. A. A. Boahen, *Britain, the Sahara, and Western Sudan* (Oxford: Claredon Press, 1964), 103-4.

30. Curtin, et al., *African History*, 420.

31. J. F. A. Anjayi and M. Crowder, eds., *History of West Africa*, vol. 2 (London: Longman, 1974), 1-29.

32. Oliver Roland and J. D. Fage, *A Short History of Africa*, 5th. (New York: Penguin, 1978), 190.

33. Ferkiss, *Africa's Search for Identity*, 69.

34. Quoted Davidson, *The African Past*, 357-58.

35. Quoted by J. Fynn, "Ghana-Asante," in *West African Resistance*, M. Crowder, ed. (London: Hutchinson, 1971), 43-44.

36. Quoted by A. Isaacman, *Anti-Colonial Activity in the Zambesi Valley 1850-1921* (Berkeley: University of California Press, 1976), 128-29.

37. Quoted by I. G. Wilks, *Asante in the Nineteenth Century* (Cambridge: Cambridge University Press, 1975), 304.

38. Terrence O. Ranger, ed. *Aspects of Central African History* (London: Heinemann, 1968), 195.

39. Quoted by M. B. Akpan, "Ethiopia and Liberia," in *General History of Africa*, vol. 7, A. Adu Boahen, ed. (London: Heinemann, 1985), 270.

40. *Ibid.*

41. Claude Ake, "The Congruence of Political Economies and Ideologies in Africa," in *Political Economy of Contemporary Africa*, Peter C. W. Gutkind and Immanuel Wallerstein, eds. (Beverly Hills, CA: Sage, 1985), 230.

42. Joseph Schumpeter, *Business Cycles* (New York: McGraw-Hill, 1939), 321-325, 335-341, 356-366.

43. W. E. Lewis, "World Production, Prices and Trade, 1870-93," *Manchester School of Economics and Social Studies* (1952), i, 20.

44. Wolff, *The Economics of Colonialism*, 23.

45. Ferkiss, *Africa's Search for Identity*, 75.

46. *Ibid.*, 75.

47. Walter Rodney, *How Europe Underdeveloped Africa* (Washington, D.C.: Howard University Press, 1981), 77, 83.

48. E. A. Brett, *Colonialism and Underdevelopment in East Africa: The Politics of Economic Change 1919-39* (New York: Nok, 1973), vii.

49. Wallerstein, "Three Stages of African Involvement," 46.

50. Claude Ake, "The Congruence of Political Economies," 230.

51. W. J. Barber, "The Movement into World Economy," in *Economic Transition in Africa*, M. J. Herskovits and M. Harwitz, eds. (Evanston, IL: Northwestern University Press, 1964), 301.

52. Samir Amin, "Modes of Production and Social Formations," *UFAHAMU*, 4, no. 3, (1974), 57-85.

53. J. Stenger, "The Congo Free State and the Belgian Congo Before 1914," *Colonization in Africa 1870-1960*, vol. 1, L. H. Gann and P. Duigan, eds. (Cambridge: Cambridge University Press, 1969), 270-71.

54. Wolff, *The Economics of Colonialism*, 135.

55. Oliver and Fage, *A Short History of Africa*, 203.

56. Findings of the Land Commission Reports, on 19 July, 1920, a commission to inquire into certain Matters connected with the Occupation of Land in the Nyasaland Protectorate (Zomba, 1921: 10582), 13; in I. Abraham, *Land Commission Report 1946* (Zomba: Government Printer, 1947).

57. George Shepperson and Thom Price, *The Independent African* (Edinburgh: Edinburgh University Press, 1958), 198.

58. Oliver and Fage, *A Short History of Africa*, 204.

59. Harris, *Africans and Their History*, 182.

60. *Ibid.*, 72.

61. Kwesi A. Dickson, *Theology in Africa* (Maryknoll, NY: Orbis Books, 1985), 85.

2

Liberalism and African Culture

THE LIBERAL DISCOURSE

The current value crisis among Africans is the result of impact of liberal philosophy and discourse. This chapter examines this philosophy, explores the nature of the liberal discourse to ascertain how it affected the African mind and traditional social and religious institutions, and examines the means that were used to inculcate this philosophy and its attendant manner of life among Africans.

The term liberalism is often used to refer to the political and economic theories that have influenced the Western tradition in the last four centuries. The common factor among liberal theories is the value placed on individual freedom to pursue interests and goals. This is why classical liberals such as Locke and Mill emphasized freedom from social control. From this foundational value of freedom follows the welfare state, wealth, and power—manifestations of a mindset centered on individualism. Of course Locke and Mill were aversed to wealth and power, but for them as all liberal theorists, it is the individual that matters. Liberalism cherishes anything associated with the individual. African thought on the other hand, respects individuality but abhors individualism. African traditional thought holds that people are bonded to each other in a web of life, therefore, what affects one affects all and community takes priority over individuals. "We are many yet one," maintains African traditional thought. Liberalism concentrates on individual materialistic concerns while African society focuses on the material as well as the spiritual welfare of the community and individual. With the coming of liberalism, Africans started to lose their values and consequently, suffered an identity crisis.

The Metaphor of the Machine

The liberal paradigm undermined the hermeneutic power of Africans to interpret the world through their symbols. People live their symbols, for symbols represent ultimate reality and meaning. Let us examine the European world to note the forces that destroyed the ability of Africans to organize their society around their symbols. The concept of the world and manner of living which inform Westerners is best described by the term mechanistic. The metaphor of the machine holds that the world is like a machine with so many parts, each working according to the laws of nature. To understand the world then, one has only to know the laws of nature. Knowledge of the laws of nature enables one to "put" the world into its component parts, that is, the building blocks which make up the "machine," for the whole equals the sum of its parts.

The mechanistic metaphor conceives society as a megamachine.[1] In this megamachine, nature and people are objectified. People are seen as atomistic individuals. Interaction and communication are determined by function. People are seen in light of what they can do. The model of living in this megamachine is accordingly mechanical. The key concept in understanding relations in mechanistic society is utility; feelings and emotional needs are not important. Therefore, concern and care do not enter everyday living. Moral conduct in a mechanistic society is guided by self-interest, and there is no agreement on what is moral. Work and relations or the manner of life together, are reduced to a means-end process.

Mechanistic society undermines the ties that bind persons to their communities and the cosmos. The absence of the moral can be attributed in part to the eclipse of common cultural symbols on which all moral action can be based. In a mechanistic society, cultural symbols and ritual processes that orient life are suppressed. This is what sociologists call secularism.[2] This loss of cultural moral matrix has been described by Alasdair MacIntyre as emotivism.[3] We may conclude by saying that the mechanistic metaphor is another name for determinism.

The mechanistic concept of the world can be traced as far back as 400 B.C.E to Democritus, who declared: "There is nothing but atoms and space, all else is an impression of the senses." His world was nothing but atoms bumping into each other. This atomistic theory was later advanced by Epicurus (342-270 B.C.E.) and Lucretius (96-55 B.C.E). These views were to become part of modern science through the works of the forerunners of contemporary physics or mechanics such men as Copernicus, Bruno, Galileo, and Newton. The work of Newton opened the way for science to explain how the world works.

One of the best exemplars of the mechanistic notion of the world was René Descartes (1596-1650). Echoing Democritus, Descartes wrote, "Give me matter and motion and I will construct a universe." He believed that through scientific reductionism the totality of creation could be ascertained simply by measuring and quantifying all of its various components. It was not surprising then that Descartes, a mathematician and engineer turned philosopher, set out to explain the phenomenon of life by two forces, namely, matter and motion. Mechanics was the key to the workings of nature. Although Descartes considered people as machines, he saw them apart from nature. They were machines that had distinguished themselves from nature by thought or mind. Descartes argued that nature could be understood as a machine-like organism simply by following logical, objective, and disinterested thinking or rationality. Descartes, declared: "we can thus render ourselves the masters and possessors of nature."[4] This division of mind and matter is known as the Cartesian doctrine of bifurcation. Here we see Descartes dividing nature into mind and matter, thus clarifying western cosmology.

In the last paragraph, I have not claimed that Descartes was a materialist, rather a dualist. My point is simply this: Descartes's ontology, mind-matter bifurcation, set the stage for a materialist philosophy. As it is known, Descartes' mission was to confirm the method introduced by the New Science of the sixteenth and seventeenth centuries, which relied on mathematics to understand the universe. He thought that the human mind was capable of understanding and therefore mastering nature. It is this idea of mastering nature, or perceiving matter as an extension of mind, which, I am contending, made some successors of Descartes emphasize the material aspect of his philosophy. For sure, others put stress on the mental, but here we are examining the impact of the materialist emphasis.

Descartes was not the only one who advocated setting humankind apart from nature and arguing for its mastery and possession. As the result of the New Science of the sixteenth and seventeenth centuries, it was a general occupation among European thinkers of the time to look for scientific ways in which humankind would rise and control nature. One of the most influential in this era was Francis Bacon (1561-1626), the prophet of science and nature. Bacon argued that the purpose of science was to become "the enlarging of the bounds of human empire, to the effecting of all things possible."[5] He also wrote: "The command over all things natural—over bodies, medicine, mechanical powers and infinite others of this kind—is the one proper and ultimate end of true natural philosophy."[6] Bacon was aware that for the new world to come, the mind had to be "from the very outset not left to its own course, but be guided at every step and the business be done as if by machinery."[7] He knew the power a particular concept of the world can have over the mind, and that people live their vision of the world.

The works on philosophy and science by Descartes and Bacon along with Newton's discoveries in mechanics transformed the metaphysical understanding of the West. A new era had come. In this new age nature was no longer considered part of the human species and sacred, and it was reduced to mathematics or transformed to a quantitative physical phenomenon grasped by rationality. Nature was now the other, only material to be subjugated and manipulated. It had no value; its value was to the extent that people used it. With this way of construing the world, a stage was now set for a materialist philosophy and manner of living to emerge.

The Myth of Progress: The Question of Development

Materialist philosophy was helped by the works of social philosophers such as Thomas Hobbes (1588-1679), who understood reality as composed of entitative forces.[8] With this notion of the world, Hobbes attempted to bring political theory into close relation with systems of thought, scientific principles and facts of nature including human behavior. In so doing, Hobbes became one of the early advocates of scientific materialism. John Locke (1632-1704) did for political science what Bacon and Newton had done for physical science. As Bacon understood the purpose of science as to learn to control nature; Locke understood the purpose of government as to allow people freedom to use their power over nature to produce wealth.[9] In fact, Locke considered it a duty for people to generate wealth by mixing their labor with nature. Thus he wrote, "Land that is left wholly to nature . . . is called and it indeed it is, waste."[10] With this idea he introduced his trickle-down theory:

> He who appropriates land to himself by his labor, does not lessen but increases the common stock of humankind. For the provisions serving to the support of human life, produced by one acre of inclosed and cultivated land are . . . ten times more than those which are yielded by an acre of land, of an equal richness lying waste in common. And therefore he that incloses land and has a greater plenty of the conveniences of life from ten acres than he could have from a hundred left to nature, may truly be said to give ninety acres to humankind.[11]

Locke's treatise was against the feudal authority of his day and he sought to establish "natural" basis for society and government. Through rationalism he had come to the conclusion that it was wrong to make religion and tradition the foundation of social order. Since God was unknowable, how could the unknown be the basis of government? So he argued that religion be a matter of private concern and not the basis of government. Locke understood society as an aggregate of individuals, creating meaning in their lives and having one purpose and one purpose alone, namely, to protect and allow for the increase of property of its members. Self-interest then was the sole basis for creating the state and society was secular, materialistic, individualistic, and humanistic. This, according to Locke, is the natural order of things. It was within laws of nature that people, as individual social atoms, should amass personal worth.

With Hobbes and Locke joining Descartes, Bacon, and Newton, a new vision of the world that could be rationally explained had been created. These people established the new world on the foundations of science and philosophy whose way of life was to be basically materialist. This way of life has captivated Western civilization ever since and has been exported to all parts of the world where this civilization has gone in search for material resources and in fulfilling its expansionist philosophy. This manner of seeing the world has eroded the African concept of nature, persons, and the whole creation as belonging to one community.

The Western view of the world allowed for the notion of unlimited growth. Since through science humankind would have power over nature, there would be no limit to growth. The growth of science would lead to economic increases. In short, science held the key to "a line and race of inventions that may in some degree subdue and overcome the necessities and misery of humanity."[12] Here we find the roots of the notion of progress. Put in its simplest form, progress is the ordering of the natural world to create a better material environment for people. It is creating greater value from natural resources than is found in their original state. To achieve this goal is the task of science and technology. Science is perceived as the means by which people gain control over nature, that is, ordering principles and rules of nature to be consistent with human goals. Science viewed from this perspective, technology becomes the application of those rules (of nature established by science) to specific needs to reorder nature for human ends. Through science and technology, human mastery over nature is complete and progress assured.

The idea of progress has been very compelling in Western civilization. Many believe progress is the way by which misery can be eliminated in the world. However, as the centuries have shown, the alliance between progress, science and technology has not eliminated misery; on the contrary, destitute has emerged and the future of all creation hangs in balance. Progress through (industrial) technology creates exploitation of resources and people. The demand for more productivity through some scientific innovations damages the ecological balance and thus threatens the life of those whose livelihood depend on what nature provides. The livelihood of fishermen, for example, is destroyed by anything that affects or changes the composition of water or marine life.

Perhaps more serious, is the fact that the alliance of progress, science and technology leads to a social and spiritual bankruptcy. Having objectified nature and people, God too becomes impersonal. God is not seen as part of nature. Believing that the creator of the world was not part of nature the Enlightenment removed God from nature. The enlightened minds of the eighteenth century Europe argued that God, having created the world, let it to go on following its own laws—laws of nature. This was the argument advanced by deists or those who considered God a divine watch maker. In a world without Divinity, morality is dictated by self-interested ends, consequently, there is no sense of community since relations are based on utility.

Briefly, let us look at the sort of cosmology the West imported to Africa. First, the cosmos was no longer sacred and people were not part of nature. Second, nature was reduced to mathematical quantification and could be understood by way of rationality. Mechanics was the principle for understanding it. Third, nature simply existed; its value was in connection with human use. This is to say, nature was for manipulation and subjugation. This way of discerning the world was the foundation of a materialist philosophy which permeated Western civilization. Finally, there was no moral foundation for way of life together for God having been removed from nature, there was no ground for establishing moral principles.

This concept of the world and manner of living imposed on Africans ruined their traditional system of thought and values. Their ability to interpret the world as they understood it and live accordingly became weakened. Their sense of basic values affected and their vision of life was undermined. Greatly affected were all those who received Western education or became Christians. The more Western education one received, the more disoriented one became. The elite became so disoriented that their vision of the world was informed by the metaphor of the machine and the myth of progress. Soon a crisis of values emerged as the result of the clash between the African and Western concepts of the world.

In the last few decades the crisis has been compounded by the recommendations that Africa has received from the "experts" on development. The concept of development has its roots in the notion of progress, which is fundamentally a materialist philosophy bent on unlimited growth or exploitation and accumulation. The African bureaucrats and political elite operating within the Western paradigm continue the philosophy of accumulation and development. This explains why politicians and the bureaucratic elite are unable to draw on their concept of community or bondedness of life as they decided on national policies.

Christianity, though a Middle Eastern phenomenon, came to most of Africa in the last century as part of Western civilization, compounding the problem of the crisis of values for Africans. Through preaching and education churches changed traditional African value systems. As traditional values crumbled, the hermeneutic ability of Africans became deeply affected. Here I am contending that Christianity weakened or impaired their ability to interpret and reconstruct their systems of representations of values and norms that give meaning to their lives. When people lose their sense of values and norms, the symbolic function itself becomes blocked, because there is no possibility for the "theological" work required to analyze past traditions and gain a new understanding. People understand the present in light of their interpretation of past experiences. Since in the African world there is no dichotomy between the sacred and the secular, interpretation of the past is always a theological interpretation.

ON INDIVIDUALISM

Africans who received Western education soon learned that individualism controlled one's relationships and perspective on life not only inside class but also in society in general. The African learned that "to get help in writing your essay at school could be a case of cheating, certainly copying from your friend in an examination is a great violation of the code of honor. One is judged in an examination as an *individual*."[13] Western education claimed as its task awakening the critical mind, enabling one to discover one's identity and freeing one from one's social identity group. African students were taught to be rational and "independent," free themselves from the memory of their descendants since "one knows himself to be as singular and he [she] glories in not being like others. . . . Each private person considers himself as possessing the status of an historical personage."[14] The person who discovers personal identity seeks personal security through private property as opposed to communalism.[15] Furthermore, a critical person discovers personal values, for "the thought which seeks and finds the truth is a thought which reflects, and this means a thought which concentrates, which folds back over itself."[16] John Newman explained what liberal Western education does: "It is the education which gives one a *clear, conscious view* of one's own opinions and judgement, a *truth* in developing them, an *eloquence* in expressing them and a *force* in urging them."[17] By bombarding young African minds with the ideas of critical reason and freedom that come with discovery of personal identity, Western education undermined the traditional African value of community life.

One of the corner stones of traditional African society is the concept of community. In African thought, community includes the living, the dead, and the unborn. In some societies a child is considered an incarnation of the spirit of a departed member of a family (immediate or extended). The dead belong to the community through their dynamic presence:

> But while the departed person is remembered by name, he is not really dead: he is alive and such a person I would call the *living dead*. The living-dead is a person who is physically dead but alive in the memory of those who knew him in his life as well as being alive in the world of the spirits. So as long as the living-dead is thus remembered, he is in the state of *personal immortality*. This personal immortality is externalized in the physical continuation of the individual through procreation, so that the children bear the traits of their parents or progenitors.[18]

In connection with the African idea of community there are values associated with the living dead. Kwesi Dickson has summarized those values: (1) "They [the dead] give a sense of solidarity and security; (2) The ancestors integrate for the African his world view, seeing that they are believed to mediate between God and man; and (3) the ancestral cult serve to remind the living of those virtues which define the morally good life."[19]

According to Africans, people are not atomistic individuals who group themselves for a common goal, first and foremost because of their individual interest. In other words, society is not a means to satisfaction of ends which one could not achieve except through a particular community—"this is the principle of individualism" according to Unger.[20] In African thought, persons are part of an ongoing human community and constituted by their past. It is through this community and this past that persons come to self-awareness and a sense of responsibility. Ritual practice has two functions: (1) it is a means by which society creates an individual through incorporation and (2) it seeks to emphasize this basic concept of bondedness of people, that people are a fused collective "we." This "we" seals the fact that whatever happens to one in life and death, since we are, therefore I am."[21] The dictum underscores the idea of an organic relationship between individual members and their community.

In such a relationship one's duty comes first over one's interest. Consequently, African society is organized around the requirements of duty whereas the West puts individual rights first. Menkiti sees a profound difference between the West and Africa on the issue of rights, arguing that "whereas the African view [of society] asserts an ontological independence to society, and moves from society to individuals, the Western view moves from individuals to society."[22] This does not mean that Africans disregard rights. Rather, concern for the common good comes first and, most important, is that the individual owes her or his "existence to other people including those of past generations and his/her contemporaries. He/she is simply part of the whole."[23]

African concept of community encourages teamwork and communalism, while at the same time offering possibilities for self-awareness, sense of responsibility, and development of one's potential. All activity is oriented toward fostering community life. Children are inculcated with the concept of community through sayings such as, *Mutu umodzi susenza denga* (One head does not hold a roof), meaning, more than one beam is needed for a roof to be in place. Children are encouraged to play and eat with others. Initiation rites seek to emphasize the idea of one being bonded to one's age group and to others in the community. With such heavy emphasis on community, one would think that children would not develop self-awareness, the African concept of community allows development of human capacities and individuality without encouraging individualism, which promotes competition and self-interest. Cornel West, the African-American philosopher, argues that the concept of individuality "stands in stark contrast to those doctrinaire individualism which promote human selfishness, denigrate the idea of community, and distort holistic development of personality. The norm of individuality conceives persons as enjoyers and agents of their uniquely human capacities, whereas doctrinaire individualism views them as maximizers of pleasure and appropriators of unlimited resources."[24] This emphasis on community in African society does not imply that consciousness of self is lost. There is a very strong notion of self in African society. Zahan observes:

> African psychology attributes to the self a broader and richer content than our classic treatises on the study of the soul. To define the self, we separate it from the other, whereas in Africa the opposite is the rule; nowhere is the African psyche ever limited to "that which is not the other and does not come from him." On the contrary, the African carries within himself, physiologically and physically, his own genitors and respective ascendent. His self is thus more "social" than "individual"; he defines himself precisely by that which he receives from others at any moment.[25]

Individualism has been with Western society so long that it has become one of cultural values; people cannot imagine living a different life. Unger states the problem of individualism in Western society:

> Individualism is so deeply rooted in our thought that it is hard to understand. A great part of the difficulty lies in imagining a different principle that might help define it by contrast. Yet such a polar view has been a staple of social thought in the West since the Romantic movement and birth of sociology as a discipline. It is the principle of collectivism, exemplified by romantic organicist conceptions of the group. These conceptions view the group as an entity with independent existence irreducible to the lives of its members, with group values that stand apart from the individual and subjective ends of its membership, even with its own "personality." Collectivism is one of the most partial critiques of the liberal doctrine.[26]

It has been argued that not only individualism is a problem in formation of community life but also that the road to individualism leads to destruction of the true meaning of being human. Society must be built on categories which will enable building community life that will respect individuality without the idea of individualism. Dallmayr argues that "individualism can no longer (or can only with greatest difficulty) be justified or buttressed on 'individualist' premises, mainly because these premises—revolving around the practical and other cognitive ego—have become tenuous or implausible."[27] Dallmayr has introduced a dimension of individualism that runs through all the works and arguments of liberalism, namely, epistemological individualism. Epistemological individualism is the principle idea in the subject-object dichotomy, which is a key concept in the liberal theory of knowledge, that is, how people know or arrive at meaning. This form of individualism was a result of the Enlightenment's freeing of individual reason, or the "thinking subject," from unexamined beliefs. The idea continued to be shaped in the following centuries. The notion of *ego cogitans* (knowing subject) was originated by Descartes. Steven Lukes has explained epistemological individualism as Descartes saw it and how his ideas were later understood.

> Descartes' thought began from this position from the individual's certainty of his existence—*cogito ergo sum*—from which he derived knowledge of the external world and the past via the transcendental route assuming God's veracity; . . . Kant saw the categories as innate in the (abstract) *individual.* But the paradigm epistemological individualist is perhaps the empiricist, who holds that (individual) experience is the source of knowledge, that all knowledge arises within the circle of the individual mind and the sensations it receives.[28]

Dallmayr points out that even in Western society, people are beginning to realize that the prevailing crisis in society is due to the concept of *cogito ergo sum*: "The malaise of modern and contemporary life can be traced, either directly or indirectly, to its anthropocentric and subjectivist thrust or its focus on thinking subject; according to some, the malaise has already reached a crisis stage with the result that the 'end' or 'death of man' is imminent (if not an accomplished fact)."[29]

Liberal individualism is sometimes called possessive, utilitarian, radical, abstract individualism. These adjectives are indicative of the principle and nature of liberal individualism whose view of the world is one in which each person is confined purely to a subjective viewpoint. This is the world that arises out of Hobbes's state of nature, a world in which each person is considered singularly and has only private and self-centered thought. In this theory, people look at the world, and others, through the perspective of subjective self-interest, and in terms of the protection and enlargement of their property, which for Hobbes means the property they own in their persons and lives. In Hobbes's state of nature each person has a natural right to everything that is required for self-preservation. Since persons judge their needs entirely subjectively, it follows that there can be no limitation upon their natural right. According to Hobbes, individuals have natural "right to every thing; even to one another's body" since "there is nothing he can make use of, that may not be a help, in preserving his life against enemies."[30]

The natural right to everything leads people to acquire whatever they have the means and power acquire. Power, therefore, holds the key to "felicity" and "continual prospering." To be happy one has always to seek more power; thus Hobbes arrives at the conclusion that the "general inclination of humankind, [is] a perpetual and restless desire of Power after Power that ceaseth onely [sic] in Death."[31] One needs power because of the competition for felicity. In this competition for happiness individuals will attack each other, it is therefore necessary to have power in anticipation of another's actions: "There is no way for man to secure himself, so reasonable, as anticipation; that is, by force, or wiles, to master the persons of all men he can."[32] Hobbes's state of nature is a state of mutual war between individuals (*bellum omnium contra omnes*, as Hobbes called it); war will break out every time any individual judges it advantageous to attack the other. Hobbes was of the opinion that this generalized war a natural way of human society. The reasoning of liberal individualism is entirely self-interested, likewise its morality, since people act only if they judge something to be for the benefit of themselves and their property. The "natural morality" of abstract individualism is completely possessive, resting entirely on individuals' subjective judgment of personal advantage and profit. These are the characteristics of Hobbes's state of nature which inform the attitude of radical, possessive individualism.

Abstract possessive individualism was responsible for the development of the ideas of a society in which the main concern was personal interest. It might be remarked in passing that thought always informs structure of society or how people are to live. Western society that emerged from abstract individualism was capitalist in nature. Horkheimer stresses the role of abstract individualism in the formation of a capitalist society:

> Bourgeois thought is so constituted that, in reflecting on the cognitive subject, it discovers with logical consistency the supposedly autonomous "ego." Its approach is essentially abstract and its guiding principle is an individuality which is sealed off from concrete events and which bombastically considers itself the ground of the universe, if not the universe itself. . . . The thinking subject (*ego cogitans*) is not the locus where thought and object coincide and which could function as launching pad for acquisition of absolute knowledge. Such an illusion—nurtured by idealism since Descartes—is ideology in the strict sense; for the limited initiative of the bourgeois individual here takes on the illusory form of absolute freedom and autonomy. However, in a non-transparent and unconscious society, the ego—whether thinking or as practical subject—cannot have a secure footing. In the (traditional) conception of man, subject and object are surrendered; their identity lies not present but the future.[33]

Liberal individualism was given a theological interpretation by John Locke. In his second *Treatise on Government*, Locke begins to deal with the state of nature by stating that all individuals are "by nature" free and equal to each other. Like Hobbes, Locke speaks of individual morality, saying that individuals are free to "order their Actions, and dispose their Possessions, and Persons as they think fit."[34] Locke understands the state of nature as a condition of people "living together according to reason, without a common superior on Earth, with authority to judge between them."[35] This condition is possible because God has given each individual reason in order to know how to live peaceably with others. This reason, unlike that of Hobbes, is not purely subjective; it is reason of individuals who live socially and can consult one another and follow the rules embodied in the law of nature that God has provided to regulate their interaction with each other. The difference between Locke's position and Hobbes's on the state of nature is that Locke's argument is "grounded on the theological conviction that God cannot have issued rules for men to obey and then have created beings who, in their most natural state, are necessarily unable to follow those rules."[36] Locke attempted to move away from Hobbes's abstract individualism by putting reason, capacity to keep faith, and natural law as sign posts to the way people should live together. It should be noted that this faith is based on individuals' capacity for reason and choosing whether to follow the laws of nature.

This is the background of liberal individualism, taught and practiced in liberal education in Africa. This individualism was linked to a particular vision of the world, and by introducing individualism, educators were bringing into conflict two different, incompatible ways of interpreting the world in the African mind. It was, as it were, uprooting the African from her or his culture and asking her or him to make sense of the new condition without reference to the old. With the old traditional practices "unroofed and pulled down" Africans were left with no frame of reference and were made aliens in their own land.

Uprooting the African was understood as a necessary step toward converting and bringing the African into modernity.[37] The general understanding of African world was that it was mythical. The mythical world or consciousness, which bred superstition and fear in the African mind, had to be replaced with a rational view of the world. In other words, *mythos* had to be replaced with *logos* or truth that could be empirically demonstrated. African culture was considered unscientific; a culture in which the human was not separated from reality, in which no distinction was made between the knowing subject and the known (object or nature), mind and matter—the subject and object bifurcation rising from the Cartesian epistemology. In a word, the African world was inseparable reality of aesthetic qualities. It was argued then, that because of this lack of differentiation or individuation, Africans were unable to develop a scientific mind, hence a scientific truth, since that truth demands objectivity. In the absence of objective, rational truth, African religious life was unreasonable, meaningless and mere superstition. It was in light of these views that some Christian missionaries believed they brought religion to Africa.

FAITH AND REASON IN LIBERAL THOUGHT

In order to understand the baggage Christian liberalism brought over to Africa, it is necessary to go beyond the period of colonialism. In tracing the roots of Christian liberalism one is taken to the eighteenth century. The philosophical thought or the vision of the world of the eighteenth century shaped the moral and religious life of liberalism. Eighteenth century philosophical thought and discussion was informed by the notion of natural law, as Becker points out: "In the eighteenth-century climate of opinion, whatever question you seek to answer, nature is the test, the standard: the ideas, the customs of men, if they are to attain perfection, must obviously be in accord with those laws which 'nature reveals at all times.'"[38] Becker adds, "In the eighteenth-century the words without which no enlightened person could reach a restful conclusion were nature, natural law, first cause, reason, sentiment, humanity, perfectibility (these last three being necessary only for the more tender-minded, perhaps)."[39]

Natural law answered all questions of human life and concern, including religious and moral life. Volney's definition of natural law explains why nature was believed to be the foundation of religious and moral life, "*Qu'est-ce que la loi naturalle? C'est l'ordre regulier et constant des faits, par lequel Dieu regit l'univers*" (What is that natural law? It is the regular and constant order of facts by which God rules the universe).[40] Voleny further states that this order given by God in divine wisdom offers humankind "sense and reason" which are to serve as a common rule of conduct and guide to human beings toward perfection. The same mind is found in Locke's conclusion that society, its institutions and thought, should be patterned on the laws of nature. He argued that since the mind is created by nature which God created, then it is possible for human beings "barely by the use of their natural faculties," to order their ideas and their conduct and hence the institutions by which they live with the universal natural order.[41] This way of thinking and living produced a religious and moral life based on the laws of nature. This is made clear by Voltaire's definition of natural religion: "I understand by natural religion the principles of morality common to the human race."[42] Voltaire states that the function of religion for the enlightened people of the eighteenth century was basically to produce moral life: "*ce fonds de rectitude et de bonté morale, qui est de la vertu*" (the concern for uprightness, and moral goodness is the foundation of virtue), said Marmontel in his *Memoires*.[43] To be a virtuous person "was both sufficient and efficacious, and likely to give one, without any painful searchings of the heart, the assurance of being in a state of justification, or even, if the esteem were general enough, of complete sanctification."[44]

Natural law was the ontic category of eighteenth-century thought. It is to be remembered, though, that natural law was not the product of eighteenth century minds. The eighteenth century only appropriated and re-interpreted or highlighted the concept of nature, more so because it suited its idea of human mastery of the creation whose path had been prepared by Newton's ideas. The notion of natural law is traced to Aristotle, however, it was not, till the time of Thomas Aquinas that the notion received much attention. Aquinas appropriated the concept for a theological understanding of the relation between divine nature on one hand and created life (people and the total universe) on the other. Concerning natural law Aquinas said:

> Since all things subject to Divine providence are ruled and measured by natural law . . . it is evident that all things partake somewhat of the eternal law, in so far as, namely, from its being imprinted on them, they derive their respective inclinations to their proper acts and ends. Now among all other, the rational creature is subject to Divine providence in the most excellent way, in so far as it partakes of a share of providence, by being provident both for itself and for others. Wherefore it has a share of the Eternal Reason, whereby it has a natural inclination to its proper act and end: and this participation of the eternal law in the rational creature is called natural law.[45]

The meaning of natural law for the people of the eighteenth century was different from that of Aquinas. Whereas Aquinas appropriated the concept of natural law from a position of religious faith in a God who was the provider of humanity and sustainer of all creation, the eighteenth century minds approached the term from a position of doubt in God and used the term to deify human mind and its rationality. Aquinas used the concept of natural law in connection with participation of the divine or what he called "the eternal law in the rational creature." In the eighteenth century people pushed God out in their idea of natural law. The world had come of age: God was no longer needed to run the world. The "rational creature" was no longer "subject to Divine providence." This thinking was the foundation of the causal theology of the eighteenth century, which held that divine intelligence could be discerned or inferred by looking at nature just as one can interpret the mind of a painter by looking at the artist's work. God was the mind behind nature. Causal theology was based on cause and effect theory.

In this intellectual climate, a substitute had to be found for the idea of a provident God who controlled the world. In his place were substituted the "First Cause," "Prime Mover," Great Contriver," and "Author of the universe," to mention some of them. All these designations were intended to make clear the idea that God was an absentee landlord, "a *Deus absconditus*, hidden somewhere behind the silence of infinite space."[46] *Deus absconditus* had "ceased to be personal and inconvenient. No longer demanding propitiatory sacrifices." God "could be regarded as that Omniscience with respect untempered with fear or adoration."[47]

The idea that God was an absentee landlord developed from Newton's discoveries and philosophy of "General Laws of Nature, by which the Things themselves are form'd."[48] Newton's philosophy paved the way for a mechanical view of the world. Newton's philosophy argued that since nature behaved according to natural law, what people needed to do was to understand the rules of nature and they would be able to control nature. It is through Newton's philosophy or "natural philosophy" that the philosophy of human domination emerged. To Newton's philosophy must also be added the concept of individualism, particularly on its domineering attitude over nature. This attitude "found overt expression in Francis Bacon's *instauratio magna* of modern science as an instrument of human mastery. Through their implication in the mastery of nature, individual reason and thinking subject were part and parcel of *anthropocentricism*, construed as the quest for general-human supremacy or *species* liberation."[49] The philosophy of domination has been responsible for the exploitation of resources and people all over the world.

The theological implications of this thinking included the erosion of faith in society by undermining the claims of the magisterium that divine purpose for the world is made known through the Holy Scriptures and the Church. Eighteenth century philosophy advanced the idea that divine purpose was made manifest in creation; nature had recorded the laws of God. As far as the eighteenth century enlightened minds were concerned, one did not need the Scriptures or the Church to know divine laws. To know this double truth was to be enlightened:

> Renunciation of the traditional revelation was the very condition of being truly enlightened; for to be truly enlightened was to see the light in all its fullness, and the light in its fullness revealed two simple and obvious facts . . . the fact that the supposed revelation of God's purposes through the Holy Writ and Holy Church was a fraud, or at best an illusion born of ignorance, perpetuated, or at least maintained, by the priests in order to accentuate the fears of mankind, and so hold it in subjection. The other factor contained the sum of those affirmations . . . that God revealed his purpose to men in a far more simple and natural, a far less mysterious and recondite way, through works. To be enlightened was to understand this double truth, that it was not in Holy Writ, but in the great book of nature, open for all mankind to read, that the laws of God had been recorded.[50]

The views of eighteenth century world and religious life did not go unchallenged. At the middle of the century David Hume (1711-1776) set out to correct what he had seen as a wrong conclusion by thinkers of the early part of the eighteenth century. Hume's project was to reconstruct the earlier philosophical and theological thought of his century. His self-given task in *Dialogues Concerning Natural Religion* was to show that reason alone was not adequate to prove or disprove divine existence or nature. He argued that reason was insufficient to answer ultimate questions of human concern, that is, of human life, nature, and God.

> If the whole Natural Theology, as some people seem to maintain, revolves itself into one simple, though somewhat ambiguous, at least undefined proposition, *That the cause or causes of order in the universe probably bear some remote analogy to human intelligence*: if this proposition be not capable of extension, variation, or more particular explication: if it afford no reference that affects human life, or can be the source of any action or forbearance: and if the analogy, imperfect as it is, can be carried no farther than to the human intelligence; and cannot be transferred, with any appearance of probability, to the other qualities of the mind: if this really be the case, what can the most inquisitive, contemplative, and religious man do more than give a plain, philosophical assent to the proposition, as often as it occurs; and believe that the arguments, on which it is established, exceed the objections, which lie against it?[51]

Having argued that "natural reason" was imperfect to be the basis of constructing a "system of theology," Hume concluded: "To be a skeptic is, in a man of letters, the first and most essential step towards being a sound, believing Christian."[52] Hume dislodged the claims of the enlightened people, the claims of causal theology, that by the use of reason, one could move from cause to effect.

Hume not only shook the foundations of eighteenth century theology, but also pulled down the walls of the faith of the time, leading some to despair and others to a lose faith. Hume's analysis of the concept of cause and his ability to demonstrate that reason was not enough to know the future left an impression on Immanuel Kant (1724-1804). In the *Prolegomena* Kant admits the impact of Hume's analysis on his work: "I openly confess my recollection of David Hume was the very thing which many years ago first interrupted my dogmatic slumber and gave my investigations in the field of speculative philosophy a quite new direction."[53] Concerning the task before him Kant wrote: "Our age is, in a special degree, the age of criticism, and criticism to everything must submit. Religion through its sanctity, and law-giving through its majesty, may seek to exempt themselves from it. But they then awake just suspicion, and cannot claim the sincere respect which reason accords only to that which has been able to sustain the test of free and open examination."[54] Kant calls for criticism of authority (dogmatism) through knowledge or subjection of all authority to knowledge, criticism of the religious tradition of Christianity. Through criticism he hopes or attempts to rescue or introduce sure foundations of faith. Kant seeks to bring God back into Christianity through the theory of knowledge. He believes everyone can come to the knowledge of the truth not through the magisterium but through criticism or one's understanding. Taking this position, Kant was able to formulate the principle of liberalism: Have the courage to make use of your own understanding.[55] His burden in *Critique of Practical Reason* and to some extent in *Critique of Pure Reason*, is to challenge dogmatism through knowledge and build a religious system based on ethics. In book 11 of *Critique of Practical Reason*, Kant sets himself to give the moral proof of the existence of God.[56] In *Critique of Pure Reason*, Kant attempts to demonstrate that reason has failed to grapple with transcendental problems. Kant also rejects the notion of "religious experience" because it is personal, therefore impossible to be empirically verified by others—it is not knowledge accessible to all for criticism. He does not accept claims to "communion" with God for that cannot be practically demonstrated.

Kant's idea of God, like his views of freedom and immortality, comes from his understanding of moral law which demands that people live a moral life. Morality, then, is the only way by which faith in God can be empirically manifested. The place of moral life (ethics) in Kant's work is central for the reason that it "avoids misunderstanding to abstraction" since ethics "can present its principles together with practical consequences, one and all *in concreto*, in what are at least experiences."[57] Placing ethics as *a priori*, Kant claimed God was an ethical principle because, he claimed, "belief in God and in another world is so interwoven with my moral sentiment that there is little danger of my losing the latter, there is equally little danger that the former can never be taken from me."[58] With his eyes set on the theory and praxis (demonstrable empirical evidence of theory), Kant rejected earlier theological claims of causality, arguing that the concept could not be empirically derivable. Kant's intention to reconstruct eighteenth century thought, particularly the work of Hume, was limited by his attempt to make God merely a ground for moral principle. For Kant, God was an ethical idea and obedience to God consisted of following the moral principle. Such a God can only be an impersonal God. Note also that for Kant soul freedom consisted in absolute obedience to the categorical imperative which is the personal dictate of reason.

The work of Kant fell short of its noble ideal: to demonstrate that God was essential to humankind as creator and sustainer. To say God was the provider of humankind was to claim complete divine control over all creation and human history, which is the claim of the biblical faith. Although Kant had not succeeded in his attempt, he had nevertheless taken a step in the right direction, that is, toward the restoration of faith in God in a skeptic society.

The task of Georg Wilhelm Friedrich Hegel (1770-1831) then was to reconstruct or build on the work of Kant, to demonstrate that God was in total control in the world: that events of the world (history) are set in motion and directed by divine knowledge. Hegel did this in two ways: (1) by demonstrating that consciousness cannot be objectified, that is, that all consciousness is self-consciousness; and (2) by introducing the notion of spirit. Hegel first examined and appropriated Kant's theory of knowledge. Kant had concluded that there are three modes of knowledge: intuition, understanding, and apperception (self-consciousness). Hegel set to show how these various modes were actually internally related. Hegel treated self-consciousness, Kant's apperception, not as something previously given, but as something to be specifically demonstrated as truth in all consciousness. In other words, Hegel treated all consciousness as self-consciousness. "Hegel assumes from the start that in which knowing will fulfill itself, that in which alone the concurrence of certainty and truth can be given, cannot merely be consciousness of the objective world which becomes conscious of itself. Rather, it must transcend the ontological status of individual subjectivity. It must be a spirit," says Gadamer.[59]

It is within the concept of consciousness that he attempts to bring God to the center of Christianity. Hegel refers to God as the self-conscious Spirit who is the Absolute Truth: "For Spirit is the knowledge of oneself in the externalization of oneself; the being that is the movement of retaining its self-identity in its otherness."[60] "Spirit," according to Hegel, "is that which is not static, nor unstained self-identity; on the contrary, it is of its very essence that is dynamic, is development, is sublimated otherhood."[61] Hegel's God was the dynamic self-conscious spirit, informing teleology of nature and history, that is, guiding the development of world events. This was a God revealed in a historical process of peoples and the world. In this revelation God "is known as Spirit, as a Being that is essentially a *self-conscious Being*."[62] In other words, for Hegel, God was the spirit *(weltgeist)* of the world and spirit *(volksgeister)* of nations.

Within the concept of Spirit, Hegel joined Kant in discussing the place of morals in the world. Hegel dealt with morality under the rubric of spirituality. By morality, Hegel referred to the "dutiful subjectivity" which is closely connected to spirituality.[63] He did not treat morality as a personal cult of virtue as the case was with earlier thinkers. To him, like Kant, morality represented an individual's practical attitudes arising from a deep reflection on conduct. The moral world was, for Hegel, a world in which people were called to fulfill their duty, which was the purpose of nature, life itself, and consciousness beyond the limits of the present human state.

Hegel sought to bring God back into Christianity by centering his arguments on the doctrine of providence. His appropriation of the doctrine was not from a theological perspective but rather from a philosophical standpoint. In Hegel's thought, theology had failed to demonstrate the centrality of God in human history. He therefore appealed to philosophy to vindicate Christianity by demonstrating the execution of divine purpose in history, because for him the Christian idea of God as redemptive was essentially a philosophy "of self-alienation that returns to self in victory." Findlay comments: "If Hegel was nothing better, he was at least a great Christian theologian."[64] Hegel says:

> Our intellectual striving aims at realizing the conviction that what was intended by eternal wisdom is actually accomplished in the domain of existent, active Spirit, as well as in that of mere Nature. Our mode of treating the subject is, in this

> aspect, a theodicy, a justification of the ways of God . . . so that the ill that is found in the world may be comprehended, and the thinking with which the fact of the existence of evil. Indeed, nowhere is such a harmonizing view more pressingly demanded than in Universal History.[65]

Hegel saw his task as to bring the kingdom of God on earth by transposing Christian expectation of the *eschaton* (the end of the world) into a historical process, thereby seeing the world as consummating itself. According to Hegel, the historical process was the judge of the world (*Die Weltgeschichte ist das Weltgericht*). Here lies the weakness of Hegel's thinking: that Christianity could be realized by reason in history. Therefore, philosophy, not theology, could lead to a true knowledge of God and providence, realizing the divine in the present. The God that is known through philosophy is not a personal God of the biblical tradition, but the Absolute Being, Spirit. This is a God not clothed in religious myths of the Christian theologian. In his attempt to present true God and religion to a skeptical society, Hegel eliminated Christianity altogether, leaving the worship of philosophy in its place. With Hegel, the corruption of biblical Christianity in liberalism is made complete.

By way of closing, it is well to mention that Hegel's liberalism was different from that of Locke or Mill. For whereas Hegel absolutized the state, Mill relativized it by absolutizing the individual.

The history of liberal thought has been traced at some length in order to put into perspective the world and religious life of liberal Christianity as it was brought to Africa during the period of christianization of Africa. The history of liberal thought shows the primacy of reason, or philosophical interest concerning the nature of the world and development of faith. Liberalism marked the beginning of rational reason and belief in human power to dominate nature. God was pushed out of human affairs. Hume's skepticism about how reason is unable to discern the future or prove divine existence, did nothing to restore faith in God; neither did Kant's theory of knowledge and its categories, nor did Hegel's consciousness and its development to the Absolute.

The world and religious life shaped by liberalism was one in which rational thought and analysis were keys in any investigation of faith. In sum, faith itself was reduced to an intellectual assent to a philosophical proposition. While reason held a critical position in the question of faith, there was skepticism of its ability to prove the existence of God. The result of liberal thought was the crisis of both faith and reason itself. This crisis might be called a spiritual crisis of Western civilization. The result of the crisis was made manifest in several ways. In liberal thought sin became non-existent and grace was translated as virtue. The mysterious or the mythical had no place in it. It was a world in which reason was appealed to not only to clarify, edify or guide faith but to lead humankind to the idea of mastering the universe. Humankind itself was not conceived as part of the universe but separate from it. Similarly, the mind was separated from spirit. In all questions of faith, the focus was on the individual and not on people as members of the community of the faithful. The world of liberal Christianity was not the one of the biblical tradition in which myth and imagination, articulated in mythology and symbolism, freely interacted to produce faith. Instead it concerned itself with discrediting the bible (or biblical authority) by subjecting it to reason. Indeed, discrediting authority was the general goal of the Enlightenment. Gadamer notes:

> It is general tendency of the enlightenment not to accept authority and to decide everything before the judgment seat of reason. Thus the written tradition of scripture, like any other historical document, cannot claim any absolute validity, but the possible truth of the tradition depends on the credibility that is assigned to it by reason. It is not tradition, but reason that constitutes the ultimate source of authority.[66]

The biblical religion is one in which faith contends with elementary spirits and powers of the universe.[67] The Bible speaks of Jesus contending with evil spirits through people who were possessed with those spirits. Compare the healing of the Gerasene demoniac (Luke 5:1-13) or the charge that Jesus cast out demons through the power of the Prince of demons (Matt. 9:34) and the counter charge by Jesus (Matt. 12:27). Similarly, the New Testament also records angels appearing to the faithful.[68] When Christianity reached Africa in the second half of the nineteenth century it had developed a completely different vision of the world from its biblical heritage. Liberal Christianity and liberalism in general had no respect for African thought and religious life.

LIBERAL EDUCATION

The agents of liberalism in Africa were colonial administrators and their accomplices—mission educators and evangelists. In their self-appointed roles as agents of change, missionaries joined with merchants and colonial administrators to launch an onslaught on African society. The idea that missionaries were the bearers of civilization made mission schools and Christianity the most destructive forces to African traditional institutions and values. Joseph Harris has described missionary attitude and practices in this way:

> With an unquestioned belief in their own self-righteousness and depravity of Africans, missionaries were determined to change indigenous institutions and behavior and thus saw themselves as Christian agents of civilization. This conclusion meant that Africans had to be taught different values, goals, and modes of behavior. Consequently, missionary schools became the keystone of the missions' activities. The curricula of those schools either ignored or distorted African culture and emphasized European history and culture, thereby instilling the ideas that the important developments of the past, even for Africans, occurred in Europe. . . . It was only with greatest of perseverance, therefore, that mission-trained Africans retained a sense of pride and confidence in their heritage and people, and a commitment to African freedom.[69]

Mission schools were critical institutions of the colonial machinery. Colonialism with all its claims to civilization did not establish schools after declaring areas as territories. Commitment to schools came in the second phase of colonialism and in many ways it was accomplished by the help of missionaries. In the early days, missionary programs expanded greatly, but in the post-World War I period missionaries had difficulties running their institutions because of shortage in personnel and funds as a result of the war. The first schools in the colonies were founded by missionaries, and it was from these schools that colonial governments educated Africans needed to fill junior civil servant positions such as clerks, interpreters, and others.

Missionaries identified themselves with the colonial governments in other areas besides education and evangelism. In some countries this was because of a historical connection: they had been instrumental in establishing colonial rule. For example, the British declared Uganda a colony partly because of the influence of Bishop Turker had settled in Uganda. Likewise, Barotseland (Zambia) came under the British rule because of the work of François Coillard. The same was true in Malawi, where the Scottish missionaries asked for support from the home government

> first to reinforce the anti-slave trade campaign and reduce the difficulties involved in missionary participation in civil jurisdiction; and latterly to check the advance of the Arabs, whose attempt to establish political control at the north end of the lake from 1887 appeared to threaten their own position; and keep out the Portuguese who in the 1880's began to advance claims to the Malawi regions. Dr. James Stewart, founder of Livingstonia, produced a scheme as early as August 1877 for the appointment of a commissioner with a steamer on the lake and a small armed force; this was followed by frequent appeals to the British Foreign Office to prevent Portuguese and Arab encroachments, growing in desperation as the failure became increasingly plain of all attempts of the African Lakes Company to dislodge the Arabs from their stockades.[70]

Unlike other missionaries who remained somewhat in the background of colonial administrators and legislatures, the Scottish missionaries in Malawi had two of their numbers sit in the Legislative Council of the Protectorate "representing" native interests.

The general attitude of missionaries at the dawn of colonialism and beyond was endorsement of or at least acquiescence to colonial power acquiring and holding colonies. This manifested itself in missionaries in their contacts with Africans often seeking "to bridge the gulf between the administration and the people," says Baeta. In this task missionaries encouraged Africans, especially before World War I, "to welcome the benefits of European rule, to co-operate with it and give it full and glad obedience. The revelations attendant on the war and critical voices beginning to make themselves heard soon thereafter, seemed to be casting doubt not only on their idealism but even their good faith."[71]

Right from the beginning of Western education there was wide-spread fear among Africans about what this education might do to society and young minds in terms of African values. Africans felt their societies and culture were threatened by Western education. Mission education seemed to have little regard, to say the least, for African cultural and moral values and totally rejected African religious experience. African values of industry, sanctity of life, respect of persons, and community were all undermined. In place of industry and dignity of labor, young people were taught to look down on village industry and or manual labor and value more white-collar jobs. There was also a total disrespect of persons, especially if the old or uneducated. District Commissioners, writing their reports attested to the lament of Africans over their young people's lack of respect: "[Youths] have recent years evinced an inclination to emancipate themselves from the disciplinary responsibilities of village life and obedience to authority and to adopt habits of prejudicial native family life."[72] Traditional practices, likewise authority, were to be ignored since they were founded on ignorance and superstition. In 1904 Alfred Sharpe, governor of Nyasaland (Malawi), acknowledged that the lament of elders and chiefs concerning rejection of traditional values and lack of obedience by many people was becoming increasingly common. Colonialism had indeed undermined traditional institutions; traditional authority had been eclipsed, and chiefs were losing their hold on society. "At present day when chiefs are not allowed to use their old methods, the people formerly subject to them often refuse to obey or take notice of their direction," Sharpe observed.[73]

In a documentary novel translated as *Headman's Enterprise*, Simeon Nthara takes his readers to a village in central Malawi where they enter upon a chief's council in session; the subject being discussed is the school that the chief has allowed missionaries to build in the village. The councilors, elders of the village, express their fear in regard to the threat that Western education poses to traditional life and practices. The discussion goes as follows:

> *Msayamboza*: What I say is this: Here in our village there is school and school opposes many things. For this reason I do not wish you to have the drumming dances here in this village. . . . I do not wish drums and dancing of *Mzinda*. If a person dies, people will just follow the headshaving ceremonial . . . but will not beat the drums.
>
> *Senior men reply*: You have heard that drums should cease sounding at this village here; what about a wife brought here among us? Do you imagine that here people will consent to burial under these conditions? Or in case of a girl coming of age, is it just to be the shaving ceremony? Without drumming or dance? Do you do well in this, oh chief? Are you not about to unroof and pull down that which is of old, since the ceremonies are of our ancestors? We cannot give assent; you will see all this when there is a death or a coming of age![74]

The drums and dance mentioned here concern ritual practices on which traditional African life centers. To abolish ritual practice was to do away with critical transforming moments in personal and communal life. This is a moment of self-understanding brought about by physiological change and society's recognition of that change. Personal and community identity are realized through ritual pain and mortification of the flesh which sharpen one's sense of awareness and responsibility in a way that would otherwise not be realized. The elders wondered how a girl reaching puberty would realize her sense and responsibility of womanhood without going through the rite of passage to womanhood (*chinamwali*). How would a young woman know what to do, how to behave herself without ritual practice? The elders also raised a theological issue concerning the hereafter. The Achewa, like all Africans, believe in a continuation of life after death, but the proper rites have to be performed to guarantee the dead person's passage into spiritual community. For the Achewa the rite of passage into the spiritual community of the living dead could not be performed without the ritual dancing and drumming that Western influence suppressed.

Nthara has graphically depicted the struggle of the people against Western education in order to keep their identity. They were ready not to receive Western education because their sense of who they were as a people was threatened by that education. Traditions in all cultures have survived because of the people who held fast to what their ancestors taught them. Missionaries and their education were determined to do away with all fundamental cultural and religious practices. At a meeting between educators and local Achewa leaders, missionaries and teachers were told the Achewa would hold on to the institution of their ancestors: "We the Achewa cannot allow our customs to disappear. They are the precious legacy of our ancestors. We hold them as sacred things."[75]

All cultures and nations take pride in them but this was not just dance, but it was a ceremonial dance without which a rite was incomplete. These rites guaranteed a dead person's passage into the ancestral community of the living dead, which one enters after being transformed into *Mzimu* (spirit). Kings Phiri comments that "the Western school system threatened the existence of indigenous indoctrination societies of *Chinamwali* and *Nyau* initiation schools."[76] Cullen Young says that colonial administrators and missionaries formed an alliance to uproot Africans: "both Mission and Government in the early days saw only 'obscenity' or 'lawlessness' and so put *Mzinda* under ban as far as they could, not realizing that much of community value might be involved."[77]

After World War I missionaries began to assess their work in Africa. They noted that their presence in Africa had had a negative impact, especially in the field of education, specifically in two areas: the cultural arrogance of missionary educators and the failure of liberal education to prepare Africans for the life that most of them would have to face. In various mission circles discussions were held with the hope of finding a suitable education system for Africans that would not destroy African culture, and they consulted on how to work out common educational policies and curricula for African schools.

European mission boards and their agencies did not know of an effective way to bring about change in African schools. So they turned to American educators, who seemed to have developed a pattern of education that was more appropriate to African needs and traditions. The new pattern of education in America had started after the American Civil War, in the time of General Armstrong and the foundation of Hampton and Tuskegee Colleges. By the turn of the century the main advocate of the "new education" was Dr. Jesse Jones, who had written a book on these new methods in which he stated that "consciousness of community" was to govern all education.[78] By "consciousness of community" Jones was referring to "a comprehensive understating of community conditions on the basis of which the educator plans the whole educational process."[79] For Jones the purpose of education was to prepare students for life, and toward this goal he developed a curriculum that emphasized four areas, which he called these areas the "simples" of community: "[1] health and sanitation, [2] appreciation and use of the environment, [3] house-hold and the home, [4] recreation" by which he meant a mental, spiritual, and moral development.[80] Particular attention was also to be given to the development of village industries.[81]

It was not surprising then that when the foreign mission boards of the American and British churches met for a consultation in 1920, they elected Jones a chairperson of a commission that was appointed to "make a survey of educational conditions and opportunities in Africa." The trustees of the Phelps-Stokes Fund gave the commission funds to investigate education in Africa, hence the commission was known as the Phelps-Stokes Commission. During the period 1920-1921 the commission travelled to West and South Africa and another commission continued the work in East and South Africa in 1924. The findings of the two commissions were published in 1921 and 1925.[82]

The fact that liberal education had done harm to African society was also realized by the British Government. In 1923 the British Government set up Advisory Committee on Native Education in Tropical Africa to study African education and report its findings to the Colonial Office, which was to be responsible for education in British Africa. Up to this time education in British Africa had been largely in the hands of missionaries but World War I missionaries had come to realize they lacked the resources necessary to support an adequate educational system. The Advisory Committee created by the Duke of Devonshire published its recommendations in 1925. The report of the Advisory Committee agreed with the findings of the two Phelps-Stokes commissions that liberal education had weakened African communities by undermining cultural values. Further, all the studies agreed that since the break-up of traditional institutions and the coming of liberal education in Africa, character training, loyalty to traditional authority, honor of labor (or "habit of industry," in the words of Advisory Committee) had disappeared from African society. The Advisory Committee described the crisis of African culture and values brought about by liberal education in Africa as follows:

> The central problem lies in finding ways to improve what is sound in indigenous tradition. Education should strengthen the feeling of responsibility to tribal community, and at the same time, should strengthen will power; should make the conscience sensitive both to moral and intellectual truth; and should impart some

> power of discriminating good and evil, between reality and superstition. Since contact with civilization—and even education itself-must necessarily tend to weaken tribal authority and the sanctions of existing beliefs, and in view of the prevailing belief in the supernatural which affects the whole life of the African it is essential what is good in old beliefs and sanctions should be strengthened and what is defective should be replaced. The greatest importance must therefore be attached to religious teaching and moral instruction. Both in schools and training colleges they should be accorded an equal standing with secular subjects. Such teaching must be related to the conditions of life and to the daily experience of the pupils. It should find expression in the habits of self-discipline and loyalty to the community. With such safe-guards, contact with civilization need not be injurious, to the introduction of new religious ideas have a disruptive influence antagonistic to constituted secular authority.[83]

AFRICAN THOUGHT AND SENSE OF THE SACRED

The many fundamental differences between liberal Christian practices and African thought made the two incompatible. To begin with, traditional African thought does not assume that reality can be subordinated to human reason alone. "Imagination, intuitive experience and feelings are also modes of knowing. This is why the deepest expression of African cultural reality has been through art, music, folksongs and myths rather than logical analysis. Through these procedures, the African culture constructed an edifice of truth that enabled the people to achieve a relative balance with their environment."[84] The African world is a unitary religious universe in which experience and art (symbolism) play an important role. Art is the solution to the duality of experience the visible world and the divine and spiritual world of mystery. This artistic or symbolic solution to mystical experience enables Africans to create a world of aesthetic qualities in one inseparable continuum of hierarchical order, a world in which nature, the living, and the dead are all one under God.

In this vision of the world, the secular and the sacred form a totality, as Delafose observed: "There exists no institution in Africa, whether in the social, political and economic fields, which would not be based on a religious conception. The African people are among the most religious in the world."[85] Mbiti expresses the same idea.

> Africans are notoriously religious, and each people has its own religious system with a set of beliefs and practices. Religion permeates into all the departments of life so full that it is not easy or possible always to isolate it. . . . Wherever the African is, there is religion: he carries it to the fields where he is sowing seeds or harvesting a new crop or to attend a funeral ceremony; and if he is educated, he takes religion with him to the examination room at school or university; if he is a politician he takes it to the house of parliament. Although many African languages do not have a word for religion as such, it nevertheless accompanies the individual from long before his birth to long after his physical death.[86]

It is based on this understanding of African spirituality that John Malula rejected the idea that religion was introduced in Africa by Christian missionaries: "The Bantu peoples preserve in their heart the innate feeling of God and of their dependence on such a Supreme Being. Such a religious feeling is one of the African values of which we are proud and jealous. . . . Religion was not imported into our continent."[87]

Mbiti says the idea of a religious universe in African thought is not "an academic proposition: it is an empirical experience, which reaches its height in acts of worship."[88] Mbiti adds that the pervasiveness of religion allows Africans to see God in creation: "For African peoples this is a religious universe. Nature in the broadest sense of the word is not an empty impersonal object or phenomenon: it is filled with religious significance. Man gives life even where natural objects and phenomena have no biological life. God is seen in and behind these objects and phenomena: they are His creation, they manifest Him, they symbolize His being and presence."[89] Divinity is not realized through abstract knowledge or empirical analysis; neither do Africans consider what is felt through sense perception as a "shadow" of the sacred transcendental world, as Platonism would claim. The African world holds these two worlds together in an intuitive unity. Kwame Nkrumah explains how Africans solve the duality of beings or worlds:

> the dialectical contradiction between "inside" and "outside" was reduced by making the invisible world continuous with the invisible world. For them heaven was not outside the world but inside it. These African societies did not accept transcendentalism, and may indeed be regarded as having synthesized the dialectical opposites "outside" and "inside" by making them continuous, that is, by abolishing them.[90]

Nkrumah here shows that reality in the African world is discerned in a different way: there is no separation between the knowing subject and the known; the knower is part of the known. This is because of bondedness of all creation. In other words, the experience of truth is not objectified, merely thought of; it is lived experience. The term *experience* is important in understanding the theory of knowledge present in African world.

> What is experience? It is a procedure by which human beings become immediately and directly acquainted with the object of knowledge. That which is experienced is given to the individual who experiences it. We must bear in mind that this process of knowing involves certain assumptions and interpretations. Immediate and direct experience is a personal experience. An impersonal and mediate or direct experience also exists, namely, scientific experience. This is impersonal because it does not mean the knowledge of personal values, institutions, relations, meaning, relevance and significance . . . the greatest aspect of human knowledge does not come from science but from personal experience. The knowledge of truth about human experience does not call for self-detachment which scientific knowledge used to demand. To know the truth about personal experience, a person

> must put himself in the context of that experience to feel, live with and grasp its relations.[91]

Experience as described here is total experience, born by all human faculties. Total experience is lived experience which interacts with reason, and is intuitive, felt, and imagined.[92] This makes it personal experience. Since all experience in the African world is personal, reference to all reality is also personal. (The term *personal* here does not imply private but rather intimate or close.)

The notion of personal experience is grounded in the understanding that the human and the universe form a continuum and that activities in the world become meaningful only through their interaction with the human. This is so because only the human is the meaning-making or the discerning creature in the whole universe. The meaning referred to here is not self-interested, but purposeful meaning in divine providence. This idea arises from the concept of person. In the African world, the human has a special place in the created universe. The human is considered a microcosm of creation. This implies that the human is a caretaker of creation and that the future of the environment depends on the activities of humankind. Hence the Malawian saying "*Dziko ndi anthu, nthengo ndi mabala*!" (The world is human; nature an illusion! Without humans the world is without meaning and purpose.) In the hierarchy of creation the human is found at the top. After the human there is the realm of the ancestors, spirits, divinities, and, the Divinity itself. The task of the human is to seek harmony with nature, the spiritual world, and God.

> The need for harmony is primordial. Whether it be the other: parent, neighbor, chief or servant, foreigner or enemy; whether it be the world of things or the cycle of seasons, rain or drought; whether it be the Invisible Ones; whether it be evil, or God who governs all, the African seeks with them all the most peaceful and advantageous coexistence possible. . . . These harmonies emanate from the heart of man and converge on him. But the heart of man introduces us into the heart of his people; and beyond that, into the very heart of his creator.[93]

The African theory of knowledge which states that people know through personal experience of everyday life gives rise to the concept of God as personal. The term *personal* here refers to the nearness and availability of divine presence to humankind. The idea of a personal God emphasizes that the divine is not an abstraction grasped by reason but is known through lived experience. This is to argue that thinking about God only follows an encounter with the divine in things and events of everyday life and reality. Divinity is revealed and mediated by common human experience, not by reason which is a second-level knowledge of the divine. To declare that Divinity is made known in things of everyday life is not to claim that the Divinity dwells in everything in creation. There is no pantheism in African religious thought. Indeed, things in creation—trees for instance—may be used as aids or shrines; cows, snakes, or some reptiles may be called divinities but are not considered the Supreme Spirit itself.[94] The assertion that the divine is known through experience aims at emphasizing the double nature of divinity, that the Divinity is near to people and nature, and yet too far away to be captured by human thought. This nearness makes the universe a religious universe, for there is nothing in creation that does not reveal or mediate the presence of the divine. Since the universe is a religious universe, humankind can employ anything in creation to communicate with the divine. Things and beings are not an obstacle to the knowledge of Divinity; rather they constitute signifiers and indices which reveal the divine. This leads to the idea of sacrifice.

The idea that the world is a religious universe also recognizes the fact that it is a hostile universe. It is a universe of invisible powers of the spiritual world that manifest themselves in good and bad things that happen in the human world. Sometimes people may be possessed by these powers or "elemental spirits," leading them to cause harm to others, to do good, or to work wonders. In short, African spirituality realizes that it has to contend with powers beyond human control.

The Divinity who is near is also a Divinity who is beyond reach. Human beings draw nearer to the Divinity only through sacrifice and death. Death in the African world graduates the dead into the world of the spirits of the ancestors standing between the human world and the personal, yet distant Divinity. In a mystical yet dynamic way, these intermediaries inform the living about community life, and how the Divinity would have people live.

We have seen the difference between the way reality is construed in liberalism and African society. By way of reminder, the term liberalism is used in this book to refer to the mind or mentality that focuses on subjective view of the world or individual freedom, which leads to or feeds individualism. This is the mind we have said arises out of the Cartesian epistemology and Hobbesian state of nature. We have further argued that rationality also plays a part in the formation of the liberal mind. Myth is rejected in liberalism. Mythical consciousness and experience give Africans their vision of the world. Berdyaev's explanation of myth helps to illustrate the African notion of mythical consciousness.

> Myth is a reality immeasurably greater than concept. It is high time that we stopped identifying myth with invention, with the illusions of primitive mentality, and with anything, in fact, which is essentially opposed to reality. . . . The creation of myths among peoples denoted a real spiritual life, more real indeed than that of abstract concepts and rational thought. Myth is always concrete and expresses life better than abstract thought can do; its nature is bound up with that of symbol. Myth is the concrete recital of events and original phenomena of the spiritual life symbolized in the natural world, which has engraved itself on the language, memory, and creative energy of the people . . . it brings two worlds together symbolically.[95]

Liberal Christianity would have nothing to with this mythical life of the African world that gives provision to the existence of spirits and the practice of sacrifices, because it could not be rationally and empirically demonstrated, it was mere superstition: the very concepts that rationalism had struggled from in the sixteenth century. The result of the clash of two visions of the world was shown in what missionaries succeeded in doing: "preaching to and . . . teaching Africans about a Strange God whom they have somehow come to identify as the God of the white man . . . with two Gods on their hands and thus made of them people of ambivalent spiritual lives."[96] Idowu then asks the fundamental question: "What has happened to the God . . . who is the foundation of traditional belief?"[97]

An assault was launched on African thought and its foundational concepts of person and community. The power of eradication of African thought consisted in disorienting the African; making the African believe that anything African was inferior, including the very framework of traditional expression, living, and understanding the world—culture. The African system of thought was disregarded as illogical. The rupture of African society was systematic, and number of psychological and philosophical mechanisms were employed to make it impossible for Africans to break out of social, economic, and political bondage. Psychological mechanisms were also used to make the Africans internalize their condition and the cultural myths that served to perpetuate the status of the West. Paul Freire tells us that every situation of bondage is built on continuous "invasion" of the oppressed by the oppressor until

> the vanquished are dispossessed of their word, their expressiveness, their culture. In order to present for the consideration of the oppressed and subjugated a world of deceit designed to increase their alienation and passivity, the oppressors develop a series of methods precluding any presentation of the world as a problem and showing it rather as a fixed entity, as something given to which men as mere spectators must adapt.[98]

This is no different from the way liberalism was imposed on Africans. The following chapters demonstrate the various ways in which liberalism penetrated African thought systems and ways of life.

NOTES

1. This is a term Lewis Mumford has designated in describing the differences of the vision of the world and way of life between Western and other societies. Lewis Mumford, *The Myth of the Machine, Part Two: The Pentagon of Power* (New York: Harcourt Brace Jovanovich, 1970), Chapter 3.

2. See Gregory Baum, *Religion and Alienation: A Theological Reading of Sociology* (New York: Paulist Press, 1975), Chapter 7. I believe those who advocate the theory secularization do so to avoid critical assessment of the issues that have undermined and eclipsed the presence of the sacred in society. It is an act of faithlessness itself to claim that people can "become of age" to have no need of the Divinity.

3. Alasdair MacIntyre, *After Virtue: A Study in Moral Theory* (Notre Dame, Indiana: University of Notre Dame Press, 1981), Chapters 1 and 2.

4. René Descartes, *Discourse on Method and Meditations* (New York: Liberal Arts Press, 1960), part 6.

5. Francis Bacon, *Novum Organum*, trans. R. Ellis and James Spedding (London: Routledge and Sons, n.d.), Book 1, Aphorism 2.

6. Jean Houston, "Prometheus Rebound: An Inquiry into Technological Growth and Psychological Change," in *Alternatives to Growth*, vol. 1, Dennis Meadows, ed. (Cambridge, MA: Ballinger, 1977), 274.

7. Bacon, *Novum Organum*.

8. Elizabeth Sewall, *The Human Metaphor* (Notre Dame, Indiana: University of Notre Dame Press, 1964), 68 ff.

9. Leo Strauss, *Natural Right and History* (Chicago: University of Chicago Press, 1953), 250, 251.

10. *Ibid.*, 315.

11. *Ibid.*, 312.

12. Jean Houston, "Prometheus Rebound."

13. Ali A. Mazrui, *The African Condition* (London: Cambridge University Press, 1980), 67. His emphasis.

14. Georges Gusdoff, *Mythe et metaphysique* (Paris: Presses Universitaries de France, 1949), 114.

15. *Ibid.*, 116.

16. Quoted by E. A. Ruch in E. A. Ruch and K. C. Anyanwu, *African Philosophy: An Introduction to the Main Philosophical Trends in Contemporary Africa* (Rome: Officium Libri Catholici, 1984), 30. Also see D. Essertier, *Les Formes Inferieures de l'explication* (Paris: F. Alcan, 1927), 268.

17. John Henry Newman, *The Scope and Nature of University Education* (London: Oxford University Press, 1915), 171.

18. John S. Mbiti, *African Religions and Philosophy* (London: Heinemann, 1990), 25.

19. Dickson, *Theology in Africa*, 177.

20. Robert Mangabeira Unger, *Knowledge and Politics* (New York: The Free Press, 1975), 81. Also see Jeremy Bentham, *An Introduction to the Principles of Morals and Legislation,* J. H. Burns and H. L. A. Hart, eds. (London: Athlone, 1970), 12; K. Arrow, *Social Choice and Individual Values* (New York: Wiley, 1963), 61-62.

21. Mbiti, *African Religions and Philosophy*, 106.

22. Ifeanyi A. Menkiti, "Person and Community in African Traditional Thought" in *African Philosophy: An Introduction*, 3rd. ed. Richard A. Wright, ed. (Lanham, MD: University Press of America, 1984), 180.

23. Mbiti, *African Religions and Philosophy*, 106.

24. Cornel West, *Prophesy Deliverance: An Afro-american Revolutionary Christianity* (Philadelphia: Westminster Press, 1982), 16-17.

25. Dominique Zahan, *The Religion, Spirituality, and Thought of Traditional Africa*, trans. Kate Ezra and Lawrence M. Martin (Chicago: University of Chicago Press, 1979), 9.

26. Unger, *Knowledge and Politics*, 82.

27. Fred R. Dallmayr, *Twilight of Subjectivity: Contributions to a Post-Individualist Theory of Politics* (Amherst: University of Massachusetts Press, 1981), 3.

28. Steven Lukes, *Individualism* (New York: Harper and Row, 1973), 107.

29. Dallmayr, *Twilight of Subjectivity*, 11.

30. Thomas Hobbes, *Leviathan: Or the Matter, Forme and Power of a Commonwealth Ecclesiastical and Civil.* Selected and introduction by Richard S. Peters; Michael Oakeshott, ed. (London: Collier Macmillan, 1962), 103-4.

31. *Ibid.*, 80.

32. *Ibid*, 99.

33. Max Horkheimer, "Traditional and Critical Theory," *Critical Theory: Selected Essays,* Matthew J. O'Connell et. al., eds., trans. (New York: Herder and Herder, 1972), 210-211.

34. John Locke, *Two Treatises on Government*, P. Laslett, ed., 2nd ed., (London: Cambridge University Press, 1967), Section 4.

35. *Ibid.*, S. 19.

36. Ashcraft, "Locke's State of Nature: Historical Fact or Moral Fiction?" *American Political Science Review*, 42, 902-3.

37. Fabian Eboussi Boulaga, *Christianity Without Fetishes: An African Critique and Recapture of Christianity*, trans. Robert R. Barr (Maryknoll, NY: Orbis Books, 1984).

38. Carl Becker, *The Heavenly City of the Eighteenth-Century Philosophers* (New Haven, CT: Yale University Press, 1932), 53.

39. *Ibid.*, 47.

40. C. F. Volney, *Oeuvres*. 2nd ed. (Paris: s.n., 1836), 1. 249.

41. John Locke, *An Essay Concerning Human Understanding* (Oxford: Claredon Press, 1894), Book 1, Chapter 2, Section 1.

42. André Voltaire. *Oeuvres XX11* (Paris: Presses Universitaires de France, 1948), 419.

43. Cited in Becker, *The Heavenly City*, 49.

44. *Ibid.*, 49.

45. See Anton C. Pegis, ed., *Introduction to Saint Thomas Aquinas: The Summa Theologica* (New York: Random House, 1948), 618.

46. John Miller, *The Disappearance of God* (London: Cambridge University Press, 1963), 6.

47. Becker, *Heavenly City*, 50.

48. Sir Isaac Newton quoted by Cecil William Dampier-Whetham in *A History of Science and Its Relation with Philosophy and Religion* (New York: Cambridge University Press, 1929), 183.

49. Dallmayr, *Twilight of Subjectivity*, 9.

50. Becker, *The Heavenly City*, 50-51.

51. David Hume, "Dialogues Concerning Natural Religion," in *The Empiricists* (New York: Anchor Books, 1974), 516. His emphasis.

52. *Ibid.*, 516.

53. Immanuel Kant, *Prolegomena to Any Future Metaphysics Which Will Be Able To Come Forth as Science (1783)*, trans. Mahaffy-Carus (New York: Library of Arts, H. W. Sams, 1950), 8.

54. *Ibid.*, Preface to first edition (1781), 9.

55. Immanuel Kant states this at the beginning of his essay *Beantwortung der Frage: Was ist Aufklarung? (1784)* (Frankfurt: Neuer Frankfurter Verlag, 1905).

56. Immanuel Kant, Critique of Pure Reason, Chapter 2, sections 4-5.

57. Quoted by A. C. Ewing, *A Short Commentary on Kant's Critique of Pure Reason* (Chicago: University of Chicago Press, 1938), 251.

58. Immanuel Kant, *Critique of Pure Reason*, trans. Norman Kemp Smith (New York: St. Martin's Press, 1965), 650.

59. Hans-Georg Gadamer, *Hegel's Dialectic: Five Hermeneutical Studies*, trans. P. Christopher Smith (New Haven, CT.: Yale University Press, 1976), 36.

60. Georg Friedrich W. Hegel, *Phenomenology of Spirit*, trans. A. V. Miller (London: Oxford University Press, 1977), 459.

61. Walter Kaufmann, trans. *Hegel: Texts and Commentary* (New York: Doubleday, 1966), 57.

62. Hegel, *Phenomenology of Spirit*, 459.

63. Hegel understands spirituality as "Spirit Sure of Itself" or "Morality." See *Ibid.*, 424-72.

64. J. N. Findlay in Foreword, Hegel's *Phenomenology of Spirit*, xxvii.

65. Georg Friedrich W. Hegel, *Lectures on the Philosophy of History*, trans. E. S. Haldane and Frances H. Simon (London: Routledge and Kegan Paul, 1955), 16, 477.

66. Hans-Georg Gadamer, *Truth and Method* (New York: Crossroads, 1982), 241.

67. Compare Paul's letter to the Romans 8:39 or letter to the Ephesians 6:13.

68. The appearance of angels is recorded in many places in the New Testament: An Angel appears to Zechariah in the temple (Luke 1:11, 12); an angel tells Mary that she will conceive (Luke 1:28); Joseph is told not to put Mary away secretly (Matthew 1:20); Mary and Joseph are told to flee into Egypt (Matthew 2:13); Mary Magdalene and the mother of the Lord talk to an angel at the sepulchre; Peter and Andrew are released from prison by an angel.

69. Harris, *Africans and Their History*, 180.

70. John McCraken, "The Nineteenth Century in Malawi," *Aspects of Central African History*, ed. Terence O. Ranger (Evanston, Il: Northwestern University Press, 1968), 107.

71. C. G. Baeta, "Missionary and Humanitarian Interests, 1940 to 1960," in *White Settlers in Tropical Africa*, ed. L. H. Gann and Peter Duigan (Baltimore, MD: Penguin, 1962), 425.

72. *Annual Reports, British Central Africa Protectorate 1912-13*, Cmd. 7050 (London: His Majesty's Stationery Office [hereafter designated by H.M.S.O.]).

73. *Colonial Reports, British Central Africa Protectorate 1904-5* Cmd. 2684 (London: H.M.S.O.), quoted in Barnekov, *An Enquiry*, 45-46.

74. S. Y. Nthara, *Headman's Enterprise*, trans. Cullen Young (London: Lutterworth Press, 1949), 140. *Mzinda* is a place where central Achewa ceremonies are held.

75. Report of the Conference sent by Fr. Roy to Fr. Ernest Paradis, September 27, 1929. Quoted by Ian Linden, *Catholic, Peasants and Chewa Resistance in Malawi* (London: Heinemann, 1974), 128.

76. Kings Phiri, "Chewa History in Central Malawi and Use of Oral Tradition 1600-1920" (Ph.D. dissertation, Michigan University, 1975), 183.

77. Footnote in Nthara, *Headman's Enterprise*, 140.

78. Jesse Jones, *Four Essentials of Education* (New York: C. Scribner's Sons, 1926).

79. Edwin W. Smith, *The Christian Mission in Africa* (London: The International Missionary Council, Edinburgh House, 1926), 56.

80. Jesse Jones quoted by Smith, *Ibid.*

81. An interesting discussion on what education in Africa should be about has also been given by J. H. Oldham, "Aims of African Education," *International Review of Mission*, 14 (1924), 514-22.

82. Thomas Jesse Jones, ed. *Education in Africa: A Study of West, South and Equatorial Africa By Africa Education Commission under the Auspices of the Phelps-Stokes Fund and Foreign Mission Societies of North America and Europe* (London:

Phelps-Stokes, 1921). Also see Thomas Jesse Jones, ed. *Education in Africa: A Study of East, Central and South Africa by the Second African Education Commission under the Auspices of the Phelps-Stokes Fund, in cooperation with the International Education Board* (London: Phelps-Stokes, 1925).

83. For a detailed discussion on the Advisory Committee see "Education Policy in British Central Africa," in *Traditions of African Education*, D. G. Scanlon, ed, (New York: Columbia University Press, 1964), 92-95, 97-98. Also see Bruce Fetter, ed. *Colonial Rule in Africa: Readings from Primary Sources* (Madison, Ws: The University of Wisconsin Press, 1979), 131.

84. K. C. Anyanwu, "The African World-view and Theory of Knowledge," in *African Philosophy*, Ruch and Anyanwu, 89.

85. Maurice Delafose, *Les Civilisations Negro-Africaines*; quoted in A. Pavian, *Da Postioma, Filosofia Africana* (Milano: Estere Capucini, 1967), 5.

86. Mbiti, *African Religions and Philosophy*, 1, 2.

87. John Malula, "Speech to the Congolese Elite and to Missionaries," *Revue du Clegé Africain*, no. 5, 1960. 499-500.

88. Mbiti, *African Religions and Philosophy*, 57.

89. *Ibid.*, 56-57.

90. Kwame Nkrumah, *Consciencism: Philosophy and Ideology of Decolonization and Development with particular reference to the African Revolution*, rev. ed. (London: Heinemann, 1964), 12.

91. Anyanwu, "The African World-view," *African Philosophy*, 84.

92. The term *lived experience* comes from the work of Alfred Schultz, *On Phenomenology and Social Relations*, ed. Helmut R. Wagner (Chicago: University of Chicago Press, 1970). Here the term has been used as developed by Gibson Winter in *Elements For a Social Ethic: The Role of Social Science in Public Policy* (New York: Macmillan, 1971), 54, 55, 58.

93. Dominique Nothomb, *Un Humanisme Africain: Valeurs et Pierres d'attent* (Bruxelles: Editions Lumen Vitae, 1965), 14.

94. Godfrey Lienhardt, *Divinity and Experience: Religion of the Dinka* (New York: Oxford University Press, 1987).

95. N. Berdyaev, quoted in John V. Taylor, *The Primal Vision: Christian Presence Amid African Religion* (London: SCM Press, 1963), 30.

96. Bolaji Idowu, *Biblical Revelation and African Beliefs*, ed. Kwesi Dickson and Paul Ellingworth (Maryknoll, NY: Orbis, 1969), 13.

97. *Ibid.*

98. Paulo Freire, *Pedagogy of the Oppressed* (New York: Herder and Herder), 134.

3

The Struggle for Authenticity

It is not by raising Africa to the level of the West that we Africans can answer the world's invitation.
It is not by endowing Africa with every material good that we shall grow.
It is not by integrating Africa into world commerce that we shall hand over to the world what Destiny asks of us.
Certainly Africa must be modernized and, as quickly as possible, Africa must be enriched. We must work for that with all our strength, not with any ambition to equal or compete with the West, but so that these goods may be a cloak to cover us as we go forward to build up a renewed humanism.
This cloak must cover our own hearts.
Our conception of *ubuntu* (human qualities).
Our love of *ubuvyeyi* (parental dignity)
Our practice of *ubutungane* (nobility of origin)
Our sense of *ubutungane* (integrity).
The respect of *Imana* (God)—our father's legacy to us.
Let us throw ourselves into such a commitment.
There is not time to lose.

—Michael Kayoya, "A Struggle That Is Human."[1]

Michael Kayoya, was a young Burundi priest whose life was cut short in 1972 when he was executed by a firing squad during the ethnic conflict that raged in Burundi in that year. Kayoya held that Africans will not be able to achieve true humanity without reaching deep into their cultural systems. In many poems he contended that neither capitalism nor communism, nor Western thought in general, can provide the proper requisite for transformation of social structures toward a vision of a dignified human life.

The idea of modernization mentioned in this prose-poem is problematic because it is based on the notion of progress, the flaws of which have argued in the previous chapter: modernization means patterning Africa after the Western values, culture, and technology. This liberal ideology of development is so powerful that even some of Africa's best minds have bought into it. The ideology has the power of a drug; the elite has become so intoxicated by it that they accept the principles of liberal economics and political theory as the only way forward for Africa. Is this not the ideology which brought cultural imperialism and alienation that Africans are experiencing? This chapter and the next, examine African reaction to cultural imperialism, liberal economics, and political theory. Through education, liberalism easily took control of the African mind. This chapter will demonstrate how liberal education corrupted African minds, thereby destroying African values system and uprooting and alienating the African elite.

The African struggle is a struggle for authenticity and identity; a fight against different modes of domination. A situation of domination uses specific modes of control to preserve power. Beker has identified three modes of control employed to preserve power: coercive/reward, dependence, and thought control.[2] The first mode uses military or coercive force to establish control. The second form uses psychological and material means to lock the dominated into a relationship in which their well-being and future depends on those who dominate them, including economic and political ways.

Thought control is the third and most subtle of all the modes of control. This form of control is established and encouraged by cultural dependence. Thought control uproots and disorients people by imposing on them a different value system until they become obsessed with the values imposed upon them. This disorientation begins by corrupting thought and language, for people interpret and understand their experience reality through these media; consequently their emotions and relationships are conditioned by this "reality." Corruption of a people's thought destroys their value system, the "world" or reality that informs their way of life. Without self-conscious realization of their own identity, a people cannot reject the disorienting language; the process of alienation becomes total.

Mohiddin argues that total disorientation and alienation were the aim of colonial politics: the colonizers sought to corrupt the African mind for good: "Western colonization of Africa, language and culture proved to be the most effective and least costly means not only of establishing and maintaining colonial rule but also of extending and perpetuating Western cultural domination of Africa beyond the period of formal independence."[3] Ezechiel Mphahlele expresses the same idea when he laments that Western values "have become part of your [African] personality equipment" and that psychologically "we [Africans] are hooked on something that is never going to let go."[4] Similarly, Albert Tévoédjré laments:

> It is twenty years since the majority of independent countries of Africa have appeared on the international scene. Dare I say it? The problem of their cultural identity remains unsolved without practically any change having taken place. From

time to time one dips one's hat to "authenticity" and "desalienation," but the mentalities remain lastingly colonized.[5]

The African struggle has been to undo what colonialism did to the African mind and society. The challenge has been to create a new mentality and a new social order in which the African values mentioned by Michael Kayoya can exist. African initiatives to recover traditional values have taken several forms: negritude (also African Personality), African socialism, humanism and a theological-philosophical approach. The next two chapters will examine the concepts of negritude, African socialism, and humanism.

NEGRITUDE: THE PHILOSOPHY OF AFRICAN PERSONALITY

Senghor: The Making of a Mind

One of the historical intellectual forces of recovery of traditional values was the negritude movement, an attempt to undo the distortion, disorientation, and alienation brought about by colonialism. Frantz Fanon, the Martiniquean psychiatrist of African descent, has described how colonialism works:

> colonialism is not content to impose its rule upon the present and the future of a dominated people. Colonialism is not satisfied merely with holding a people in its grip and emptying the native's brain of all form and content. By a kind of perverted logic, it turns to the past of the oppressed people, and distorts, disfigures, and destroys it.[6]

Negritude was a movement of the elite whose alienation was deep and painful. An attempt to recover lost selves, negritude is identified with Léopold Senghor, the first president of Senegal, but its architects included Léon Damas and Aimé Césaire. This chapter examines Senghorian negritude. Senghor's life presents a good illustration of African alienation and the struggle for authenticity.

Léopold Sédar Senghor was born in 1906 in Joal, Senegal. His journey to being a statesman, philosopher, poet, and scholar of international prestige began at about age seven when he was entrusted to a local parish priest, Father Léon Dubois, who introduced Senghor to Christianity, French, then France itself. From the custody of Fr. Dubois at Joal, Senghor passed through several institutions of learning, the first being Ngazobil, an outpost of the Fathers of the Holy Spirit. Ngazobil, was only six miles away from Joal, but this was very far for a boy of about seven in 1914. Here Senghor was introduced to literature, the arts, and Wolof, a language spoken by most people in Senegal, he was himself a Serer. Looking back at his years at Ngazobil, Senghor attributed to the priests three important lessons: "reasonableness, self-mastery, and a tendency not to be satisfied with mere talk."[7]

In 1923 Senghor entered the newly opened Libermann Seminary as one of its first seventeen students. At Libermann, Senghor studied for the French baccalaureate examination with emphasis on Catholic philosophers. For three years he studied hard, but shortly before graduation, Father Lalouse, the director of the seminary, with whom Senghor had several clashes, told him that he was not suitable for the priesthood. Senghor judged him a racist who treated white and black students different.[8] In the fall of the same year, Senghor enrolled at the new Cours Secondaire de Dakar, a French school, where, for the baccalaureate, examiners came from Bordeaux to administer the orals to ensure uniform standard between metropolitan France and the colonies. There students learned nothing about Africa, but French heritage. Senghor recalled learning the history of "our ancestors the Gauls, men tall, robust, with skin white as milk, blue eyes, and long blonde or red hair which they let hang on their shoulders."[9] The effect of such intense indoctrination into French culture and civilization and the complete negation of African values was devastating to young minds: one life in two separate worlds. Cheikh Hamidou Kane, the Senegalese writer, later described the experience as "strange nature in distress in not being two."[10] Senghor was moved up a class in two months in the year he arrived, and in same year, on July 7, 1928, he earned his second baccalaureate in philosophy with *assez bien*. Senghor received scholarship from the Federation of West Africa, to study literature in France.[11] He was the first African to receive such a scholarship.

Senghor left for France in October 1928. There he registered at the Sorbonne, only to withdraw in December to enroll at Lycée Louis-le-grand, a Jesuit secondary school founded in 1853, considered the best in France, whose graduates included writers such as Victor Hugo, Alphonse Daudet, Charles Baudelaire and such thinkers as George Sorel and Emile Durkheim. Most graduates of Louis-le-grand went into high government and public positions; the class of Senghor included George Pompidou, future president of France. At Louis-le-grand Senghor enrolled in a special class called *khâgne*, a boarding section for top students from all over France and the colonies. These students prepared for the most rigorous of all French academic competitions, the examination for the Ecole Normale Supérieure, the institution that provided professors to all French universities and best secondary schools. Senghor attempted the examination in 1931, but he did not get the required grade to enter Ecole Normale Supérieure; he had however done so well that on the day of graduation in July his name was on honor roll. He was awarded *Licence en Lettres*.

He then studied literature at the Sorbonne where he was awarded the *Diplôma Supérieure* in the spring of 1932 after completion of study on "Exoticism in the Works of Baudelaire." He received an *agrégé* of the University of Paris in Grammar in August 1935, thus distinguishing himself as the first African to earn that academic honor. For this academic excellence, he was received with full military honor upon his short visit to Senegal in 1937. The *agrégé* gave him the privilege to teach classics and grammar at Lycée Descartes in Tours; he also gave lessons to workers at Maison de la Culture, thus began his commitment to the Socialist Party. In 1938 he was assigned to Lycée Marcelin-Berhelot at Saint-Maur-des-Foss near Paris. He commuted to Paris to take courses in ethnography at the Institut d'Ethnologie with a view toward earning the Doctorar d'Etat in the field of linguistics and ethnography. For his research he chose to focus on African languages and oral Serer poetry.

He was naturalized as a French citizen in June 1933, and as a citizen was required to do military service. At the outbreak of World War II his unit was called and surrendered to Germans within four days. Senghor was taken to various POW camps. While in captivity he wrote poems, which were published in 1948 in a volume entitled *Hosties noires*. He also wrote an article in which he argued that Africans must learn more about the customs and languages of traditional Africa. This would have to be done quickly, he wrote, for Africa was being transformed rapidly by its contact with the West. He further asserted that Africans must assimilate, but that this assimilation would only be possible when Africans knew their own background. The key point then, was for Africans "to assimilate, not to be assimilated." Senghor was released in February 1942 on the pretext of ill health.[12]

In 1944 Senghor was appointed professor of African languages at the Ecole National de la France d'Outre-Mer. In the same year he published articles on African languages. In 1948 he published *Chants d'ombre Hosties noires*, and *Anthologie de la nouvelle poésie nègre et malgache*.

In 1946 Senghor entered political life and was elected deputy from Senegal to the French National Assembly, through the Socialist Party (SFIO). In 1951 he was reelected to the Assembly, this time through the Bloc Démocratique Sénégalais (BDS), a party he had founded in 1948. He gained more political responsibilities in 1955 when Prime Minister Edgar Faure named him Secretary of State for Scientific Research. In 1958, Charles de Gaulle called Senghor to serve in the Constitutional Assembly. In 1960 Senghor became President of Senegal, a position he held till his voluntary retirement on December 31, 1980. In 1984 he was elected to the most esteemed of all French institutions, the Académie Française (French Academy), thus becoming one of the "immortals." In the following year, Senghor was recognized by the distinguished Bibliothéque Nationale in Paris, in an exhibition of his literary work, a very unusual honor for a living writer.

THE AFRICAN RENAISSANCE

In the fall of 1931 Senghor moved to the Cité Universitaire. In September, he met Aimé Césaire, the man who would be his greatest friend in the struggle for Africa's identity. Césaire had come from Martinique to prepare at Lycée Louis-le-grand for entrance to the Ecole Normale Superiéure. When Senghor visited Martinique in 1976 as President of Senegal, Césaire, then mayor of Fort-de-France, the capital city, recalled their life long friendship:

> For forty years, we have lived in parallel . . . leaving each other, as life went, but nonetheless never truly separating. Was this surprising? After all, our adolescence was entirely blended. We read the same books, and often the same copy, shared the same dreams, loved the same poets. We were torn by the same anguish and, above all, were weighted down by the same problems. . . . Our youth was not banal. . . . It was marked by the tormenting question, who am I? For us, it was not a question of metaphysics, but of a life to live, an ethic to create, and communities to save. We tried to answer that question. In the end, our answer was Negritude.[13]

"Who am I?" The beginning of the quest for identity for the founders of negritude must be seen as part of a larger picture of a struggle of a race. In the twentieth century the quest was initiated by the emergence of renaissance of culture in America among the descendants Africa. This new spirit was spearheaded by African American artists, musicians, dancers and writers, most of whom lived in Harlem, on the east side of New York city. This rebirth known as the Harlem Renaissance, created a new sense of self-understanding and humanism expressed by the term *New Negro*, coined by Alain Locke, the African American philosopher. Writing in *Fire*, a Harlem Renaissance magazine, Langston Hughes expressed the sense of pride and optimism, that the new spirit had brought to young people. "We younger Negro artists who create," he wrote, "now intend to express our individual darkskined selves without fear or shame. If white people are pleased, we are glad. If they are not, it doesn't matter. . . . If colored people are pleased, we are glad. If they are not, their displeasure doesn't matter either."[14]

The new cultural expressions of African Americans, especially in Jazz, blues, and dance, had an enthusiastic welcome in Paris. Some African American artists had handsome rewards for their trades. Writings of African Americans as well as of those from the Caribbean were read in Paris. Langston Hughes poems and Claude Mackay's *Banjo*, for example, were read in the salons of Paulette Nardal (from Martinique) and René Maran. The Harlem Renaissance was inspired by the writings of two African American intellectuals—Alain Locke, a philosopher, and W. E. B. Du Bois, a sociologist—especially their writings on the sense of self of Africans in America, which were inspiring to students in Paris as they struggled with racism and assimilation. African Americans were also enriched by what they read in Paris. For instance, Mercer Cook put together an anthology of French-speaking descendant of Africa to be used in his seminar on French literature at Howard University.

The Harlem Renaissance was long in the making, for in spite of a dehumanization of untold magnitude suffered by the descendants of Africa through slavery, they never lost their sense of humanity and nobility of origin. The abolition of slavery allowed attempts to recover that sense of humanism, thus the beginning of African American churches and schools. These institutions enabled African Americans to assert and define themselves in light of their values. The founding of such African churches as African Methodist Episcopal (EME) Church, the African Methodist Episcopal Zion (EMEZ) Church, and of schools, colleges, and other institutions, was the beginning of the rebirth in America. Of importance for an international rebirth of African humanism was the founding of the American Negro Academy in 1897 by Alexander Crummel in Washington. The aim of the academy was to bring together intellectuals of African descendants for research in issues of their concerns. In 1909 Du Bois pushed forward the idea of seeking solutions to African American issues by establishing a magazine *The Crisis*, and in the following year, he organized the National Association for the Advancement of Colored People (NAACP), an organization which continues to champion African American issues. These years of change had been preceded by Booker T. Washington's philosophy of self-improvement of African peoples. Born a slave on a Virginia plantation, Washington founded of Tuskegee Normal and Industrial Institute in Alabama in 1881. Through personal achievements with the institute and his speeches and writings calling for African American self-improvement, he won national and international acclaim. He outlined his philosophy in his Atlanta Exposition Address of 1895, in which he warned African Americans, "It is at the bottom of life we must begin, and not at the top."[15]

In the Caribbean in 1900, the Trinidadian lawyer Sylvester Williams and Bishop Alexander Walter of the EMEZ Church organized the first Pan African Congress, a movement which inspired the spirit of nationalism among African intellectuals all over the world. It was around this period that Marcus Garvey, a Jamaican, started advancing the "Back to Africa" movement. In 1910 he sought to promote the interests of the working class in Jamaica through his first political organization, the National Club. He established the Universal Negro Improvement Association in Jamaica in 1914 and in Harlem in 1917. In 1919, he could claim a membership of one million in the United States, the Caribbean, Latin America, Europe, and Africa. The preamble of the constitution of the association defined the organization as "social, friendly, humanitarian, charitable, educational, constructive and expansive . . . founded by persons, desiring to the utmost to work for the general uplift of the Negro peoples of the World."[16] Garvey's journal, *The African World*, motivated intellectuals of African descent everywhere.

Elsewhere overseas, Africans were on the move toward forging a new identity. With the effort of Blaise Diagne, an African representative from Senegal to the French National Assembly; Gratien Candace, a deputy from Guadeloupe; and W. E. B. Du Bois, the third Pan African Conference was held in Paris. In

1924, Kodjo Tovalou Houénou, a follower of Garvey, created in Paris the Lingue Universelle de Défense de la Race Nègre (Universal League for the Defence of the Black Race), later to be changed to Comité de Défense de la Race. Lamine Senghor, Léopold Senghor's cousin, was the organization's first president; he was also a founding member of the Ligue Contre l'Impérialisme et l'Oppression Coloniale in 1927 in Brussels where he was subsequently arrested and imprisoned. He died not long after his release, and the presidency was filled by Malian Tiémoko Garan Kouyaé, who was a student at Ecole Normale in Aix-en-Provence, a founder of the journal *Africa*, and with Léo Sajous from Haiti, established the Comité Universel de l'Institut Nègre de Paris in 1930. There were also congresses of African issues and culture in Lisbon and London.

Such was the social and political climate of the African world at the time Senghor arrived in France in 1928. Paris itself was experiencing a rebirth of African culture through art, music and literature of the Harlem Renaissance and writers from the Caribbean. There was a general awareness of Africa and black culture in Paris from the twenties. The number of students, poets and novelists of African descent in Paris was significant between 1929 and 1940. Popular names included Léon Damas, Aimé Césaire, and Etienne Léro from the Caribbean; from the continent were Léopold Senghor, Alioune Diop and Paul Hazoumé. Their awareness of issues facing Africans everywhere was raised by the writings of African descendants in America and the Caribbean: Counte Cullen, Langston Hughes, Jean Toomer, Richard Wright, Zora Neal Hurston, Alain Locke, and the Jamaican-born writer Claude MacKay, among others. They also read René Maran's *Batouala*, the 1922 Prix Goncourt-winning novel. This politically conscious literature raised serious questions concerning race, nation, and colonialism. Take, for instance, Claude Mackay's *Banjo*, Alain Locke's *The Negro*, Langston Hugh's poem "I too sing America. I am the Darker Brother," or Maran's challenge of convectional belief in the "civilizing and colonizing mission of the West" in *Batouala*, or the impact of articles in *The Crisis*, *Opportunity* and Garvey's *The African World*. These works brought awareness of self, race and nation.

Senghor imbibed all these works of African literature. Janet Vaillant, the author of *Senghor: Black, French and African*, records that when Senghor returned home on a brief visit in 1937, his cousins heard him reciting the poems of Langston Hughes and African American writers as he walked along the beach. When developing his ideas on negritude, Senghor was informed by these works but also other political writings such as those of George Padmore, a Caribbean political analyst and Du Bois. Senghor was particularly impressed by *The Soul of Black Folk* by Du Bois. Senghor very much identified with the experience of Du Bois, expressed by the concept of double-consciousness or twoness in *The Souls of Black Folk*. "One feels," wrote Du Bois, "his twoness—an American, a Negro; two souls, two thoughts, two unreconciled strivings; two warring ideals in one dark body, whose dogged strength alone keeps it from being torn asunder."[17]

The new consciousness brought by the African renaissance raised serious questions concerning the French system of education and the policy of assimilation. In other words, French system of education and social policy were put on trial and found wanting; the result was the revival of, or at least an interest in African culture. Student activists and others turned to the power of the pen to express their anger at cultural imperialism. Put simply, French policies created poets and added more writers to the African renaissance. Their writings were accompanied by political ferment expressing rejection of French assimilation and exultation of their heritage and culture. These views started appearing in the fall of 1931 in the journal *La Revue du monde noir* (The Review of the Black World), founded by two Haitians, Dr. Sajos and Andrée Nardal. The editors of the journal said their purpose was

> to give to the intelligentsia of the black race and to their partisans an official organ in which to publish their artistic, literary and scientific works. To study and to popularize . . . all which concerns NEGRO CIVILIZATION and the natural riches of Africa . . . to create among the Negroes of the entire world, regardless of nationality, an intellectual and moral tie which will permit them to better know each other, to love one another, to defend more effectively their collective interests and to glorify their race. . . . By this means, the Negro race will contribute along with thinking minds of other races and with all those who have received the light of truth, beauty, and goodness to the material, moral and the intellectual improvement.[18]

In keeping with its aim of creating a worldwide African consciousness, *La Revue* published articles in both French and English. The idea that all people of African descent shared a common heritage was a new one in Paris. The journal therefore marked a departure from the view of many African peoples in Paris, most of whom identified themselves as French and had nothing to do with Africa, its culture, and values. In his book, *Black Skin, White Mask*, Fanon says Caribbeans never thought themselves black and it was a rude awakening for them to discover that in France, as in the whole of Europe, they were identified as *nègre* along with those from Africa and America. Subjectively and intellectually, the Caribbean was white, asserts Fanon.[19] Commenting on this attitude, Césaire wrote, "In Paris at the same time I discovered culture, I better understood the reasons for my own malaise. I became conscious of belonging to basic category of Negro."[20] Even some Africans from French colonies believed themselves to be French. When Senghor registered at Lycée he identified his nationality as French, not Senegalese.[21] The fact that the elite rejected or did not want to be identified as having an African connection was a testimony to the success of colonialism in distorting the image of Africa. In colonial media and literature Africa was backward in both technology and culture, so the elite assimilated French culture and believed themselves to be French people who happened to be black.

The editors of *La Revue* sought to raise consciousness of Africa's past and present greatness. It was for this reason that they published excerpts from leading ethnographers, Maurice Delafosse and Leo Frobenius. They also published articles about the work of African Americans at the Tuskegee Institute and in Liberia, and a sampling of the works of two contemporary African American poets, Claude Mackay and Langston Hughes. There were also contributions by young Caribbean writers and poets such as Loius Achille, Etienne Léro, René Maran, Andrée Nardal, Gilbert Gratiant, and René Menil. Felix Aboué, a Guyanese who had served in French colonial administration in Central Africa, retold folktales in the journal.

As can be seen from the list of literary contributions given above, *La Revue* devoted itself to cultural matters. In its short life of six issues, the journal avoided articles on politics. There were two exceptions: *La poésie ethnique* (Ethnic Poetry) and *Eviel de la conscience de race* (The Awakening of Race Consciousness).[22] The first article was a review a book in which a former colonial administrator warned that one day colonies would rise against France. The author was saying that already there was a counter-movement to colonialism, that the "penetration of Negro art and literature into the white world constitutes a far reaching offensive."[23] In the second article the author identified three stages race consciousness had evolved in the Caribbean: assimilation of European language and culture, slave revolts, and literature of moral protests and creation of independent culture at the turn of the twentieth century.

La Revue was followed by a student publication, *Légitime Défense*, in 1932. The aim of this journal was to make a connection between culture and politics. The students activists who organized the journal said they were tired of moderation and superficiality of *La Revue*. Speaking in a Marxist rhetoric, they called for a break with Western bourgeois because it was too materialistic and degenerate. *Légitime Défense* was against the Caribbean middle class and exposed its deep alienation, its search for an assumed personality, and treason towards its own race. Etienne Léro, the editor, denounced the misery of workers, and the racial prejudice and corruption of the elite. Léro urged experimentation with communism and surrealism but his friends considered these unacceptable since these had European origins, and as such, would be a hindrance in the search for authentic sources. They then agreed that the way forward for the workers was to discover the authentic self, abundant in dynamic reserves from which the black personality springs. The writers of *Légitime Défense* pledged themselves to the liberation of African peoples everywhere. The journal was short lived too for it was banned immediately.

Légitime Défense never took up the issues of unity and culture of African peoples which *La Revue* had sought to address. A replacement of *La Revue* appeared in 1934 under the title *L'Etudiant noir* (The Black Student). It is not clear whose idea it was to launch this new journal, but it could have been Césaire and Senghor, for they had been elected presidents of Martiniquean and West

African Student Associations respectively. It is also illuminating to note that Senghor, Césaire, and Damas, the would-be leaders of negritude, were involved in its organization and planning. It was in this journal that Senghor published his first article in 1935. It is here too that Césaire published his critical assessment of black people who sought to assimilate French culture. "If assimilation is not madness," he wrote, "it is most certainly a stupidity, for to wish to be assimilated is to forget that no being can change its biological type, its true nature."[24] Césaire went on to strongly condemn several generations of "progress" for the Caribbean.

Senghor's article, *L'humanisme et nous: Réne Maran*, was indicative of the direction his writings would take in the future. He opened the article by claiming that self-knowledge is the essence of humanism and asserted that for African peoples humanism is "a cultural movement that has the black person as its goal, and Western reason and the black soul as instruments of research. . . . It requires both reason and intuition. . . . To be black is to recover the human being crushed under the wheel of inhuman conventions."[25]

The development of the idea of negritude was gradual. After World War II, yet another journal, *Présence Africaine*, appeared in 1947. Alioune Diop, the guiding force behind the journal, said the journal was not exclusively for African peoples and that it did "not fall within the range of any political or philosophical ideology." The editorial of the journal attracted scholars with notable influence in France including: Emmanuel Monod, Paul Rivet, Georges Balandier, Emmanuel Mounier, and Jean-Paul Sartre. The first issue of *Présence Africaine* was dated October-November. Stating the *raison d'être* of the journal, Diop wrote: "It seeks collaboration of all people of good will (white, yellow or black) who are capable of helping us to define the nature of the African essence, and hastening its integration into the modern world."[26] The succeeding issues showed clearly that the journal would have a cultural orientation. *Présence Africaine* occasionally carried articles on political issues, for example, Maghemout Diop's devastating article on colonialism, "*L'Unique Issue: Independence totale*," which appeared in a special edition devoted to students of African descent, *Les Etudiants noirs parlent*.[27]

The literature of the descendants of Africa was a committed literature. There was a sense of responsibility, a vocation, and a mission. Rabemananjara, a Malagasy poet, said of it:

> The black writer will not only have to solve, as it is required of every poet, the discomfort of his own conscience in facing the essential mystery of life. He will also realize, as he strives toward liberation, that, under penalty of his complete failure, his personal deliverance imperatively demands the simultaneous deliverance of the brothers of his race. . . . Nobody will be saved if everybody is not saved. The solidarity of the poet with his people is not open to choice; it constitutes the very foundation of his poetry and insures its only chance for greatness and beauty. The *raison d'être* of his work is its existential originality.[28]

The same commitment was declared by Joseph Ki Zerbo, who wrote: "Since we have been sent to equip ourselves by contact with the West, our debt is very heavy with regard to our fellow countrymen [and women]. They expect us to testify for our people that we will help them find a place in a completely changing world and, eventually, to choose a way to adapt to that world."[29]

A NEW AFRICAN CONSCIOUSNESS

This brief survey of the journals shows that negritude emerged from a conflict and a resultant search for identity. Slavery and colonialism were more than economic exploitation, they also brought European cultural imperialism to which negritude emerged in reaction. Negritude was an attempt to prevent obliteration of the heritage and culture of African peoples, or as Césaire put it, negritude struggled to prevent absorption which the "grand-children of the Gauls" wished to impose.[30] What led intellectuals to negritude was their common experience of alienation and a discovery that in spite of their love of France, assimilation, and achievements, the French considered them unequal and downright inferior. It did not matter what their place of origin was be it the Caribbean, America, or Africa, they were all the same—nègre! They discovered that it was the color of their skin which made them unequal and inferior. This was very hard for people who had been led to believe in the ideology of assimilation. Harder still was to accept their blackness, the badge of their inferiority, but they did so with pride and set out to challenge traditional negative French attitudes concerning people of African descent. Senghor marked this turning point in his life by destroying the writings of his youth. "I accepted myself such as I was [black]. . . . I was born again."[31] Then borrowing from a term current in the Harlem Renaissance writings, he identified himself a "*Nègre nouveau*" (new Negro). (In a speech made in 1937 in Dakar, Senghor identified himself as "Afra-French" as well as "new Negro.") This was a major break with the past for one who had tried to "hide [his] ancestor" for fear that he might "burst the dam of scandal,"[32] as he wrote in poem at Lycée Louis-le-grand.

"Negritude is the cultural heritage, the values and particularly the spirit of the negro-African civilization," said the founders of negritude. While there were many influences on Senghor, he considers the African American philosophers Alain Locke and Claude Mackay the real originators of negritude. He also mentions René Maran as a forerunner. Born in Martinique of Guyanese parents, Maran lived in France from his early childhood, educated and joined the French colonial service, and was sent to West Africa as a colonial administer. While there, he wrote *Batouala*, a novel of an African village, based on notes he wrote during his service. Senghor argued that Maran's accurate portrayal of an African village was due to two essential arts, Western and African. The Western tradition was symbolized by the note-taking, while his African descent allowed him to intuitively understand the spirit of the village. His African origins were also illustrated by his writing style, which was poetic, alliterative, elegantly concise and repetitive—marks of the African oral tradition. Here Senghor advanced his assertion which he would elaborate later, that the difference between African and Western civilizations is appeal to reason for the latter and emotion for Africans. In the preface to the book, Maran strongly criticized French colonial policy in that it was failing in its civilizing mission and that French values of equity and justice did not prevail in the colonies. France, he charged, was interested only in financial and gain.

Senghor revealed that it was he and Aimé Césaire who coined the term negritude. They transformed the French adjective for a black person, *nègre,* into a noun by adding a suffix, *itude*, thereby creating an abstract noun, négritude. Senghor explained the circumstance in which négritude was coined.

> In what circumstances did Aimé Césaire and I launch the word negritude between 1933 and 1935? At that time, along with several other black students, we were plunged into a sort of panic-stricken despair. The horizon was blocked. No reform was in sight and the colonizers were justifying our political and economic dependence by the theory of *tabula rasa*. . . . In order to establish an effective revolution, our revolution, we first had to divest ourselves of our borrowed attire—that of assimilation—and assert our being, that is to say our negritude.[33]

Although the term *negritude* appeared in the early 1930s, Senghor said he had started thinking about the subject much earlier, while still in Senegal.

> I began to experience the reality of negritude when I was a student at the College Libermann in Dakar, before going to France, even before going to secular secondary school, in 1927. It was at the Lycée Louis-le-Grand, in the 1930s and then at the Sorbonne, that we began to elaborate, among black students, the concept of negritude in endless discussions, but especially between Aimé Césaire, Léon Damas and myself. . . . We developed our theory in opposition with that of the West Indians like Etienne Léro and René Menil. They wanted to subordinate cultural action to political action. Politically, they declared themselves "Marxists-Leninists."

While sharing the same goal, Senghor and Césaire had different emphasis on negritude. Césaire focused on color consciousness, race, psychology, and history. He understood negritude as "simply recognition of the fact of being black, and the acceptance of that fact, of our destiny of black, of our history and our culture."[34] For Césaire negritude was an attitude, but for Senghor it was an objective reality that meant "the manner of self-expression of the black character, the world, black civilization." Thus his approach was African-centered. He lamented Africa's past which colonialism had destroyed. For him, negritude became a way of self-asserting identity and dignity by centering on what he believed to be unique characteristics of African life. The starting point of this assertion was appreciation of African life and culture. Senghor explained why the project first focused on culture, which he defined as "a racial reaction of humankind to milieu tending towards an intellectual and moral balance between humankind and this milieu. As the milieu is never immutable then race, culture becomes a perpetual effort towards a perfect balance, a divine balance. Education is . . . the instrument of culture. It consists for the child in the acquisition of experience accumulated from previous generations in the form of concepts, ideas, methods and techniques."[35]

Negritude was a cultural revolution. Its basic aim was to give people of African descent a sense of worth, a sense of being somebody. The founders of negritude hoped to achieve this by (1) developing a philosophy of personality rooted in African culture and civilization and (2) rejecting European culture, which had failed to see the human as an emotional as well as rational creature. It was necessary to develop a philosophy of African personality because "We [of African descent] had been taught, by our French masters at Lycée, that we had no civilization, having been left off the list of guests at the banquet of the universal. We were '*tabula rasa*,' or, better still, a lump of soft wax which the fingers of the white demiurge could mould into shape. The only hope of salvation you could hold out to us was to let *ourselves be assimilated*."[36] Senghor was determined to prove that there was an African civilization. To this end he turned to French and German ethnographers and commuted to Tours from Paris to audit courses in ethnography. He read and discussed with Césaire the works of Frobenius, Delafose, and Delavignette, among others. Frobenius confirmed his feeling that there was a unified African culture and civilization.

With his knowledge of ethnography, Senghor started writing on the distinctive qualities of African life, contrasting them to Western society. Senghor used linguistic and literary forms of African languages to demonstrate their complexity and sophistication. The first three of his essays on African culture showed the movement of his thought. In 1939 he published "What the Black Man Brings," followed by "Views of Black Africa, or To Assimilate, Not to Be Assimilated" in 1943, and "Defense of Black Africa" in 1945. In all these essays Senghor never used the new term negritude, although he had mentioned it once in a poem in 1936. It was not until the late 1950s that Senghor started using negritude for certain African qualities, especially sensibility and culture. Senghor developed negritude as a theory of African personality or identity.

Proponents of negritude argue that it is necessary to reject Western civilization for its overemphasis on rationality makes it insensitive to deep human emotional needs. Negritude, they contend, envisages people first as emotional creatures and second as rational as a creature. According to Senghor, in no other race other than African is emotion a central concept in understanding of human life and relations. This theory was developed in a 1956 paper presented to the First Congress of Black Writers and Artists. Senghor elaborated his views on the essential content of Negritude in a paper presented to the Second Congress in 1959. In the 1956 paper "*L'esprit de la civilisation ou les lois de la culture négro-africaine*," Senghor discusses the "physiopsychology of the Negro-African," a theory that there is a connection between physical and psychological predisposition and the way people construe the world.[37] In other words, physiopsychology determines the distinctive characteristics of a people's culture. African physiopsychology produces emotion and empathy, which create societies and understand the world. This is to contend that emotion integrates consciousness. "Emotion is Negro and Reason is Greek," Senghor quotes Joseph de Gobineau to show the difference between Africans and Europeans. Drawing from Placid Tempels's Bantu ontology, Senghor further argues that African physiopsychology furnishes a metaphysic in which a single life force binds all creation and divinity. In this metaphysic, interdependence establishes harmony between all creation and divinity. That is to say, the African lives in harmony with all being and feels the essence of all. African physiopsychology informs art, music, and poetry and rhythm orders them all.

In his 1959 paper "*Eléments constitutifs d'une civilisation d'inspiration négro-africaine*," Senghor rejects the term *physiopsychology* in favor of *psychology* arguing that the former term connoted biological factors. He had come to the conclusion that cultural orientation had nothing to do with biological factors. He regards geographic reason as important in shaping culture. The black soul, he argues, is influenced by a tropical climate, agricultural, and pastoral conditions. Senghor had updated his theory of identity to include cultural and economic forces. In line with cultural-economic factors, he discusses the place of the family or the importance of the group in African society. In both the 1956 and 1959 versions of the theory, Senghor contrasted African with European views of the world. European sensibility was characterized as depending on reason, materialistic and bent on mastery of the world. Community is avoided since it limits individual freedom necessary for personal fulfillment. Individualism, then, is considered as a way of self-asserting and actualization. This manner of viewing the world, breeds conflicts as well as limit emotional, spiritual and artistic capacities.

Both versions of Senghor's theory of African personality create two societies with different orientations: one African, the other European. Africans experience the world with all their senses and are therefore intuitive, empathetic, emotional, spiritual, artistic, and community-oriented. Europeans, on the other hand, seek mastery of the world through technology and are materialistic, individualistic, and emotionally and spiritually impoverished. Their advances in technology make them arrogant to a harmonious living with nature. Like Max Weber, Senghor views rationality as the guiding principle of European society. Of course Weber was describing *Gesellschaft*, a society in which people are bound and ordered by group interest based on rational calculation. Weber contrasted *Gesellschaft* with *Gemeinschaft*, a society in which emotional ties keep people together, and described the process of social change from "traditional" to "industrial." For Senghor, however, those characteristics were unique to different cultures, African and European.

Senghor's criticisms of European civilization were in agreement with what some French thinkers were saying. Existentialists such as Mounier, Maritain, Sartre, de Chardin and those thinkers who formed the review *Esprit* all encouraged and supported Senghor in his criticism of European materialism, which they saw as getting out of hand. Sartre even wrote the introduction to Senghor's 1948 publication *Anthologie de la nouvelle poésie nègre et malgache de langue francaise*.[38] In the introduction, "Orphée nègre" (Black Orpheus), Sartre is alleged to have misinterpreted negritude, but by writing the introduction he gave Senghor and the other writers in the book, visibility and acceptability in French public and academic communities. In French colonies, especially in Africa, Sartre's introduction gave an ideological force to negritude and colonialism.

> A Jew, white among white men, can deny that he is a Jew, can declare himself a man among men. The negro cannot deny that he is negro nor claim for himself this abstract uncolored humanity. . . . The negro who vindicates his négritude in a revolutionary movement places himself, then and there, upon the terrain of reflection, whether he wishes to rediscover in himself certain objective traits growing out of African civilization, or hopes to find the black essence in the wells of this soul.[39]

Of colonialism and racism Sartre said: "The Negro creates an anti-racist racism. He does not at all wish to dominate the world; he wishes the abolition of racial privileges wherever they are found; he affirms his solidarity with the oppressed of all colors. At a blow the subjective, existential, ethnic notion of *négritude* passes, as Hegel would say, into the objective, positive, exact notion of the *proletariat*."[40]

The support Senghor received from Sartre, Delafosse, and other leading intellectuals reveal that Senghor took advantage of European self-criticism to make his point about the values and unique characteristics of African society. Of those values it was on emotion which Senghor placed emphasis. For him, emotion is human and totality of African culture: "I don't know how else to account for our specific quality, that *negritude* which is the sum total of the cultural values of the Black world," he declared.[41] In a presentation at Oxford University in 1961 Senghor defined negritude.

> Negritude is the whole of the values of civilization—cultural, economic, social, political—which characterize the Black peoples, more exactly the Negro-African world. It is essentially instinctive reason, which pervades all these values, because it is reason of the impressions, reason that is "seized." It is expressed in the emotions, through abandonment of self in an identification with the object; through

myth, I mean by images—archetypes of collective soul, especially by the primordial accorded to those of the cosmos. In other terms, the sense of communion, the gift of imagination, the gift of rhythm—these are all the trails of Negritude, that we find like an indelible seal on all the works and activities of the Black people.[42]

Senghor's arguments for negritude might be summarized as follows: (1) the unique characteristic of African peoples is emotion; (2) emotion is expressed through poetry and not discursive reason; (3) this characteristic manifests itself in African's love of nature and not logic; (4) emotion leads to spontaneity as opposed to ceremony. In other words, negritude is an ontology by which African peoples can be understood. Negritude is a humanism of the twentieth century which understands the inadequacy of discursive reason and therefore calls for intuition to complement it. Senghor said: "Negritude, by its ontology (that is, its philosophy of being), its moral law and its esthetics, is a response to the modern humanism that European philosophers and scientists have been preparing since the end of the nineteenth century."[43]

A charge has been made to the effect that the emphasis on emotion implies that African culture does not employ discursive reason. Senghor denies ever saying that Africans lack discursive reason but that every ethnic group has different aspects of reason and virtues, and that each stresses only one aspect of reason, and only certain virtues. He says it is not possible to build a civilization without discursive reason and techniques, and African civilization is no exception to the rule.[44] Senghor shows the different ways in which reason has been used or appropriated in Western and African cultures: the West uses analytical and discursive reasoning; Africa use intuitive reason through participation:[45] "to know an object, it no longer suffices to see it, dissect it, to weigh it, even if one has the most perfect precision instruments. One must also touch it, penetrate it from the inside . . . and finger it. . . . More specifically, knowledge coincides with *essence* of a thing in its innate and original reality, in its discontinuous and undetermined reality, in its life."[46] This is what Senghor calls African epistemology: confrontation and intuition or knowledge through sense experience.

Senghor argues that since African epistemology does not draw a distinction between the self and the object of knowledge, it leads people to abandon their personality. In participation, Senghor states, the self is subsumed in the other, individual identity (consciousness) into collective identity. It is this constitutive character of African thought and life that in some ways accounts for the identity crisis, contends Senghor: "The Negro-African sympathizes, abandons his personality to become identified with the Other. He dies to be reborn in the Other. He does not assimilate, he is assimilated. He lives a common life with the Other; he lives in symbiosis. . . . 'I think therefore I am,' Descartes writes. . . . The Negro-African could say: 'I feel, I dance the Other; I am.'"[47]

The philosophy of negritude manifested itself in African art, poetry (Senghor himself is a poet), literature, and drama. Commenting on African esthetics, art in particular, Senghor states: "For in black Africa art is not a separate activity, in itself or for itself: it is a social activity, a technique of living, a handcraft in fact."[48] In literature, the spirit of negritude set free descendants of Africa to appreciate and assert their past, and their traditional values and practices. They were ready to embrace it: "I am no longer ashamed to be the primitive you call me," Césaire was to declare later.[49] This positive attitude was evident in the works of Paul Hazoumé, the author from Benin, who wrote on the importance of traditional practice of pacts.[50] Jomo Kenyata, Kenya's first president, anticipated the spirit of negritude with his anthropological book, *Facing Mount Kenya*.[51] Novels with the negritude motif were many, and the most popular were Camara Laye's *L'enfant noir* (The African Child) and *L'aventure ambigue* (Ambiguous Adventure) by Sheik Hamidou Kane.

SENGHOR AND HIS CRITICS

Negritude was criticized by some as racist in its approach to assert identity and dignity for the African race: as emotion was not just for Africans, neither was reason only for whites. In opposing Senghor's claims S. Okechukwu Mezu argued: "In the final analysis, reason is as much black as it is Hellenic. Emotion, too, is present in both whites and blacks. Blacks may possess exceptional qualities in the area of dance, music, and the arts, but to term these the only and exclusive endowments of the negro is, at least, misleading. If there is any race that exclusively possesses dance, music and arts it is certainly not the black, yellow or brown race, but rather the *human race* in all its colors, in all its ramifications."[52] Ezekiel Mphahlele, while affirming the contribution of negritude, agrees with Mezu:

> Who is so stupid as to deny the historical fact of negritude as both a protest and a positive assertion of African cultural values? All is valid. What I do not accept is the way in which too much of the poetry inspired by it romanticizes Africa—as a symbol of innocence, purity and artless primitiveness. I feel insulted when some people imply that Africa is not also a violent continent. I am violent and proud of it.[53]

Senghor responded to these charges of racism by stating that negritude was a cultural concept and a racial one. He defined culture as "the psychic constitution which, in each people, explains its civilization. In other words, it is a certain way, proper to each people, of feeling and thinking, of expressing itself and acting. And this 'certain way,' or character as we would say today, is the symbiosis of the geography and history, or race and ethnic group."[54] In rejecting the charge that the traits of negritude can be found in other cultures, Senghor retorted: "I do not deny it. Each people's countenance reflects the diverse traits of the human condition. But I maintain these traits are found nowhere else in exactly the same balance, this same lighting, nowhere else has rhythm reigned so despotically."[55] Replying to the charge that negritude was mere romanticism of Africa's past, Nazi Boni says: "Africa would not be itself if it were ashamed of a past of which it has to be proud and from which it must draw the inspiration essential for revival."[56]

Others argued that negritude was an intellectual exercise lacking in real praxis by which Africa would be transformed and thereby be able to fully show its identity. The problem with negritude, according to Frantz Fanon, was that it did not take seriously into account socio-economic and political reality of African people, thereby being only theory and romanticism. Fanon emphasized that liberation seeks a concrete and total praxis, that is, a praxis which takes into consideration the socio-economic and political reality of a given context.

> It is around the people's struggle that African-negro culture takes on substance and not around songs, poems or folklore. . . . Adherence to African-Negro culture and to the cultural unity of Africa is arrived at in the first place by upholding unconditionally the peoples' struggle for freedom. No one wish for the spread of African culture if it does not give practical support to the creation of the conditions necessary to the existence of that culture; in other words, to the liberation of the whole continent.
>
> I say again that no speech-making and proclamation concerning culture will turn us from our fundamental task: the liberation of national territory; a continual struggle against colonialism in its new form; and an obstinate refusal to enter the charmed circle of mutual admiration at the summit.[57]

Many intellectuals in French-speaking Africa followed Fanon in dismissing negritude as lacking commitment to political and economic issues. Fanon went from a lukewarm enthusiasm to a complete rejection of negritude. Interestingly, he was introduced to negritude by his teacher, Aimé Césaire at Lycée Victor Schoelcher in Martinique. To some in the French-Speaking Africa, negritude seemed to have nothing to say about the problems of contemporary Africa. This feeling was expressed by the editorial of *Afrique Nouvelle*:

> The discovery of a like conception of life would never be able to solve our current problem. It would never help us live in the modern world. Our world is no longer that of the ancestors, nor will their conception of life ever be able to be ours.
>
> It is important for us to realize this, lest we waste time chattering about a long gone "blackness." . . . This is not a time for slogan-shouting about our "originality" and our "values." It is time to put that originality to work, for all to behold.[58]

In his in-depth analysis of Senghor's work, Towa rejected Senghor's view of a unique and unchanging characteristic of the African person: "The transformation of one's present condition signifies at the same time the transformation of one's essence, of what is particular to the self, of what is original and unique about it; it is to enter into a negative relationship with self."[59] Towa declared that "blackness" fosters servitude.

> Senghorian negritude, and enthnophilosophy which seeks to perpetuate it, encourage the illusion that Africa can offer Europe a heightening of its soul before the complete elimination of imperialism in Africa. In reality, no cultural development of any significance will be possible in Africa until [Africa] has built up a material strength capable of guaranteeing [its] sovereignty and power of decision not only in the political and economic field but also in the cultural. Our inferiority in material terms leaves our culture at the mercy of the great powers in our time.[60]

Adotevi agreed, saying, "This 'blackness' that we hate, but that we hear is the 'only way to go' for the nations of Africa, is purely and simply a way of 'putting the negro in his place.' 'His place,' of course, is moving along in low gear over field and furrow, in the cheap, tinny hour of neocolonization."[61] Adotevi's attack of Senghor's ideas declared negritude an ideology, a veil in the Marxist sense, serving the interests of the new African bourgeoisie.

Senghor was aware that a younger generation of scholars was critical of him and the negritude movement. He later commented:

> The generations following my own—those of Francophones Cheikh Anta Diop and Adotevi and of the Anglophones Mphahlele and Soyinka, to cite only those four names—wanted to be more radical than us, forgetting that Césaire and Damas, Rabemananjara and myself, had preceded them down the path of radical negation. . . . One must distinguish the quarrel of generations from the quarrel of culture. The quarrel of generations has always led me to say that the reaction of the generation which followed ours was legitimate. It was normal that this generation had the ambition to contribute something new and to deepen negritude. These writers wanted to go beyond the negritude of Senghor, Césaire and Damas.[62]

Those people who have closely followed Senghor's academic journey maintain that in negritude Senghor reproduced the eighteenth century and nineteenth century European image of the African: Rousseau's noble savage, Kant's negro, the African of Hegel, Gobineau, and Lévy-Bruhl's "primitive mentality." Actually, some of these critics argue that Senghor's negritude was a mixture of Lévy-Bruhl's primitivism, Bergson philosophy, which recognized inner life of things not grasped by the intellect, and Surrealism with its interest in investigating the depths of human consciousness lying beyond discursive reason. It is these and other philosophical nuances which move Hauser to indict negritude of clothing itself in mythical forms and its philosophy being an inversion and a reversal of Western theses.[63] Other critics maintain that in his search for an African past, Senghor uncritically appropriated the works of

Frobenius and other European ethnologists. His admiration and espousal of Frobenius and German scholarship and his emphasis on ethnicity and culture made him vulnerable to charges of being close to Nazism. Diop commented that it was alienation which led negritude poets such as Senghor to embrace German pseudo-science of "*caracterologie ethnique*" and its view that certain races "fluctuate," that is, they are dominated by the power of their emotion. Diop remarked:

> It is frequent that some blacks of a high intellectuality remain victims of this alienation to the point of searching in good faith to codify those Nazi ideas of an alleged duality between the sensitive and emotional Negro, the creator of art, and the White, especially made for rationality. It is this manner that a black African poet sincerely expresses himself in a verse of an admirable beauty: "*l'emotion est negre et la raison hellene*" (Léopold Sédar Senghor).[64]

Upon reflection years later, Senghor himself agreed, to a degree, with Diop's assessment of negritude. Senghor wrote:

> This return to the sources . . . this defiance in regard to European values turned quickly enough into scorn. Why hide it, to racism. We would think, and we would say, that we were, we Negroes, the salt of the earth, that we were the bearers of an extraordinary message that nobody else could prefer except us. Unconsciously through osmosis and reaction at the same time, we would speak like Hitler and colonialists, we would extol the blood. . . . After negation of white values the affirmation of negro values.[65]

Diop and Senghor were not friends, to put it mildly. Although they opposed each other intellectually and politically, their projects had the same aim, that is, to establish Africa's cultural identity. The affinity of their work has made some scholars, especially scholars in English-speaking Africa, to include Diop in the negritude movement. Although Diop's work is outside negritude, it is nonetheless important to outline it here.

The difference between Senghor and Diop was in their method: the former addressed Africa's identity crisis through poetry and metaphysics. Diop, on the other hand, considered historical and linguistic factors as key. He was also influenced by historical materialism of Marx—although he never became a Marxist—and he, too, read Gobineau. His aim was to establish a common historical and cultural unity of Africa, thereby to repudiate the West's claim that Africa had no civilization. This was the task Diop set for himself in *Nations nègres et culture*, a book that became a position of a classic among African intellectuals. In the book, Diop demonstrates that the origin of ancient Egypt was from the dark-skinned Africans in the south. He further contends that since European historians agreed that ancient Greece was influenced by Egypt, then Europe owes Africa a cultural debt. George James in *Stolen Legacy* and Henry

Olela in *From Ancient Africa to Ancient Greece* have made the same claim but at a philosophical level.[66] In his analysis of social and cultural institutions, linguistic kinship, and the cosmology of ancient Egypt, Diop found that they were similar to the people in the south. Here, he affirmed his hypothesis of cultural unity of precolonial Africa.

Diop concluded, "Egypt is to the rest of black Africa what Greece and Rome are to the West. The new disciplines in the African humanities must be built from the foundations of ancient Pharaonic culture."[67] Among his followers in scientific study of the African past is Theophile Obenga, who is considered his successor. Obenga continues to develop Diop's approach of establishing cultural unity between contemporary Africa and ancient Egypt. He argues against the Western historical approach, which fragments Africa:

> The European or American historian who is interested in Africa's past is irresistibly inclined to break the fundamental unity of African culture. He inevitably views things from the exterior, this on top of knowing the languages that support the reality described. The result, says Cheikh Anta Diop, is the pure and simple "atomization" of the African historical consciousness. The intellectual effort of the African researcher goes in the opposite sense: cultural unity and the continuity of the evolution of the blacks of Africa are the center of his reflection and his scientific reasoning.[68]

Diop, Senghor, and their followers demonstrate the depth and complexity of the identity problem colonialism created. These two schools of thought, in their own special ways, struggle with the issue and complement each other.

CONCLUSION

Negritude rose in part as a reaction to the alienation created by the French colonial policy of education and assimilation but the movement was also part of the greater African renaissance. Senghor was inspired by the writings from this greater movement, just as he drew some insight from European scholars in various disciplines and with different political orientations. Indeed, the similarities between him and some European scholars are startling, but the influence of the African revival and his own African experience should not be discounted. Senghor was as eclectic as the system he developed which had an inner cohesive force, a unity based on human intelligence, passion, spirituality and orientation to the world. Notwithstanding the influences upon him, Senghor forged a concept of African identity involving cultural and spiritual values as constitutive elements of an original mode of being for all Africans. Such a bold and general claim was bound to generate questions concerning authentic African life. Nonetheless, through negritude Senghor defined the limits of African personality. Negritude was a limiting concept, but one which should not be considered complete by all means, for it progressed in the 1930s from a gathering of young intellectuals and politicians in search of their personal identities, to a literature of decolonization, to an ideology of African development in the 1960s.

Given the broad strokes negritude made in the portrayal of the African, Senghor's negritude touched the lives of many elites. The movement spoke of the alienation they all experienced and knew all too well in their various disciplines. While negritude won the hearts of many Africans, it created enemies among whites. Senghor spoke about this fact, saying, "From the extreme right to the extreme left, almost all Europeans are the enemies of négritude, for négritude, as a theory and especially as a reality, is the one reality that provides the most effective form of resistance to their claims to hegemony and universality."[69]

In French-speaking Africa, the negritude movement marked a whole generation of artists, poets, writers, politicians, and theologians. Some of the scholars inspired by negritude focused on traditional thought systems to derive from them concepts that might form distinctive African philosophy and theology. Kagame's *La Philosophie bantoe-rwandaise de l'être* (Rwandese Ontology of Being) was one such attempt. A theological work that bears the marks of the time is *Des prêtres noirs s'interrogent* (African Priests Wonder).[70] This is a very important work for it marked the beginning of what was to become African theology and the project of inculturation.

Negritude did not have a strong impact in English-speaking Africa. The explanation, I think, lies in the fact, while cultural imperialism was experienced in all colonies, the impact and responses were different. This was first because of the French policy of assimilation and education of a small African elite, which was not the case with the British. Assimilation covered over the serious problems of economic and political colonization and racism. Negritude revealed that assimilation led to their cultural alienation. Therefore the elite in Francophone Africa contended mainly with the socio-cultural problems of colonialism. This is not to deny the fact that there, too, Africans had to struggle against political and economic problems, rather to emphasize that assimilation did not sharpen their awareness to the deep issues of colonial economics and racism. The British wanted people in their colonies to be "cultured" and "civilized," but they made it clear that no matter how much the people assimilated British culture, they would not be British. Of course there were some Africans who believed themselves "cultured," that is, the "Black Scots" or "Black Englishmen," but they too, found that the color of their skin would never make them equal in the eyes of whites. In British colonies people understood colonialism as economic and political. This point has also been made by Senghor: "The French policy of *assimilation*, in a certain fashion, I want to say, morally exiled and subjugated us: depersonalized us. Out of this came a traumatism that the African Anglophones did not experience and do not experience."[71]

This explains why negritude started as a cultural revolution and only later focused on political and economic issues. The French had succeeded in their assimilation and indoctrination. Senghor recalls a painful moment of truth when it became clear that he had been deceived by the French assimilation policy; that he would never become a French person:

> Very early on we had attested in ourselves the failure of assimilation: we had been able to assimilate the French language and mathematics, but we were not able to slough off either our black skin or our soul. Thus were led in search of a passionate quest for a Holy Grail: our collective soul. . . . We throw ourselves like unleashed swords into an assault on European values that we summed up by the trilogy: discursive reason, technique, market economy, i.e., capitalism. . . . We delighted in a radical opposition to Western civilization.[72]

It was this anger and quest that led to the development of negritude. The first stage of negritude was marked by radicalism, but although the origins of the movement were in disappointment and anger, negritude neither fed on anger nor produced hate, even at the height of its negative phase. Senghor remarks: "That here anger was never hate, nor grimace; that the racial sentiment was anti-racist. . . . Beyond the revolt of the colonized [there was] the appeal of person to person, to the great elementary need for justice, brother/sisterhood, love.[73]

Senghor defended negritude by arguing that in light of the background and experience of African peoples, the project was worthwhile to awaken pride and dignity in the African world.

> If it was . . . legitimate to cultivate the values of Negritude, to awaken in ourselves dormant energies, it should be for the purpose of bringing us into the current of cultural intermingling . . . into the current of panhumanistic convergence; to the edification of the Civilization of the Universal. Biological intermingling occurs by itself . . . encouraged by the very laws of life—against all the policies of apartheid. It is different in the cultural domain. Our freedom remains whole to accept or refuse cooperation, to provoke or not to provoke a synthesis.[74]

A strong affirmation of negritude has come from Bernard Dadie, who has put into perspective the facts that brought this intellectual movement into being.

> The desire to *be* gave birth to the theory of negritude: this negritude has caused so much ink to flow was stirred in us by frustration of being deprived in the course of history of the joy of creating and being regarded at our real value. Negritude is nothing but humble and tenacious ambition to rehabilitate the victims and demonstrate to the world what has been specifically denied up to this time: the dignity of the black race.[75]

Irele also says that the significance of the movement is

> in the fact that it is the culmination of the process of self-reflection implied in the

> intellectual reaction to colonial domination and, secondly, in the particular quality of its formulations of what I've called the African problematic, that is, of a long-standing question about the place and role of the African in a world dominated by the West.[76]

Negritude brought profound changes in the mind of a good number of French-speaking African intellectuals for it was an all-encompassing social and political theory advanced by descendants of Africa. Irele argued that negritude's influence arose

> from the fact that it formed so comprehensive a system of ideas, in one way or another, it responded to African interests in the colonial situation and this came to serve as a significant ideological reference—in both a positive and a negative sense—for the intellectual activity of French-speaking black intellectuals. We may even go further to observe that negritude was the most complete expression of the African state of mind in relation to the colonial experience.[77]

The term *negritude* has now drifted into the limbo of forgotten intellectual concepts, but the African project it started continues. Right from its beginning, negritude stressed going back to the sources; it called writers, artists, and politicians to stop wanting to be white. Negritude maintained that only art and literature rooted in the African world and expressing itself in African idiom could truly speak to the African condition. While negritude is no longer a force in literature, historians continue to use an African-centered approach. There are similar movements in other disciplines; even philosophy, after a long time of debating whether there is an African philosophy, has started becoming African-centered.[78] Gbadegesin is right when he says that the relation between philosophy and culture "is one of mutual influence. Culture influences philosophy by providing it with the basic materials for reflection, while philosophy influences culture by posing a critique, in various ways, of its foundation."[79] How else can philosophy in Africa proceed if it refuses to speak about African reality?

The current African-centered movement on the continent and diaspora is in some respects continuing the unfinished project of African identity—of negritude. It is true that some scholars of the African-centered approach distance themselves from negritude because of its biological emphasis, but they admit that negritude was a step toward the liberation of African peoples. However, leading persons in Afrocentricity such as Molefi Asante have a different view.[80] He and Kariamu Welsh Asante, for instance, defend Senghor, maintaining that "Senghor does not engage in extremes, only in tendencies, and although he has been mis-used to suggest a sharp dichotomy between reason and emotion, he never intended that misunderstanding."[81]

The same attitude would be expressed by Maulana Karenga and those in the Association for the Study of Classical Antiquity (ASCA), although these are more along the line of Diop than Senghor. (In *The Afrocentric Idea* Asante says he found Diop an inspiration.) Of course the focus of the association on "high culture" raises the question of how one determines what is "high culture." Often mentioned are those cultures associated with writing and large structures, the civilizations of the Nile Valley: Egyptian (Kemet), Nubia, and Ethiopia.[82] Songhai and Zimbabwe are also sometimes included. The high culture approach seems to suggest that writing and building determine the level of sophistication or civilization, like the European mind which considers writing and technology the essentials of civilization. The problem is that oftentimes focus is on only few scripts, those of the Nile Valley civilization: Egyptian, Meroitic, and Géez of Axum (Ethiopia). But studies are revealing other scripts, illustrations include the Arókò of the Yoruba, Mekutu alélé of Cameroons, ngombo of Angola.[83] It is also now known that every region of Africa had other forms of writing such as ideographs like the Nsibid of the Igbo, Edo and Efik, people of east-central Nigeria, or the Sona used the peoples of south western and eastern.[84] There were also phonological scripts the central and western parts.

The focus on "high culture" is certainly of importance but the emphasis on a few *might* give the impression that other cultures are not as important in human civilization. In that case, would that not be the same as European primitivism? The survival of culture does not depend on its physical structures, that is, buildings and constructions, but on its internal mechanisms, those social, political, and moral or religious factors which enable its people to survive. The fact that Africans have not been destroyed in spite of the hardships they have endured on the continent and elsewhere, is due to the religious and moral fiber that gives them dignity. Africans taken in slavery to the New World and elsewhere brought with them a nobility of birth that refused to be crushed. This was a dignity built on a deep understanding of being human, whose qualities we have in Michael Kayoya's poem at the beginning of the chapter, and on the African essence in them, the essence that Senghor struggled to identify and explicate.

Senghor's negritude was a serious attempt to recapture the essence of African personality, and in the process it started a discourse and inspired many people. It must be seen as part of a larger movement, the African renaissance. Senghor may not have succeeded in his own life and work to define the African essence, but the project of "going to the sources" must be seriously considered.

NOTES

1. Michael Kayoya, "A Struggle That is Human," in *My Father's Footprints*, trans. Aylward Shorter and Marie-Agnes Baldwin (Nairobi: East African Publishing House, 1973), 125-128.

2. Donald Beker, *Politics of Race: Comparative Studies* (Westmead and Lexington, MA: D.C. Heath, 1975).

3. A. Mohiddin, "Towards Relevant Culture and Politics in Africa," *Africa Development*, 2, no. 4 (October-December 1977): 59-60.

4. Ezechiel Mphahlele, *The African Image* (London: Faber and Faber, 1974), 30, 33.

5. Albert Tévoédjré, *La Pauvreté, richesse des peuples* (Paris: Editions Ouvriéres, 1978), 47 (English trans. *Poverty, Wealth of Mankind*, London: Oxford University Press, 1979).

6. Frantz Fanon, *The Wretched of the Earth*, preface by Jean-Paul Sartre, trans. Constance Farrington (New York: Grove Press, 1968), 210.

7. Ernest Milcent and Monique Sordet, *Léopold Sédar Senghor et la naissance de l'Afrique moderne* (Paris: Seghers, 1969), 27.

8. Janet G. Vaillant, *Black, French and African: A Life of Léopold Sédar Senghor* (Cambridge, MA: Harvard University Press, 1990), 31.

9. Léopold Sédar Senghor, "De la liberté de l'âme ou éloge du métissage," in *Liberté 1, Negritude et humanisme* (Paris: Seuil, 1964), 99.

10. Cheikh Hamidou Kane, *Ambiguous Adventure*, Katherine Woods, ed. (New York: Walker, 1963), 150-51.

11. The scholarship came through the help of Aristide Prat, teacher of Greek, director of the Lycée, and Inspector of Education for the French West Africa Federation. Prat so much wanted his brilliant student to go to France that he threatened to resign and publicize the case in France if scholarship was not offered.

12. Léopold Sédar Senghor, *La poésie de l'action*: *Conversations de l'action avec Mohamed Aziza* (Paris: Éditions Stock, 1980), 84.

13. Mbwill Ngal, *Aimé Césaire: Un homme à la recherche d'une partie* (Dakar and Abidjan: Les Nouvelles Editions Africaines, 1975), 45.

14. Langston Hughes, "The Twenties: Harlem and its Negritude," *Africa Forum*, 1, no. 4 (Spring 1966): 19.

15. Booker T. Washington, *Up From Slavery* (New York: Doubleday, 1963), 159.

16. Marcus Garvey, *Philosophy and Opinions of Marcus Garvey*, vol. 1, Amy Jacques-Garvey, ed. (New York: Atheneum, 1971), 102.

17. W. E. B. Du Bois, *The Souls of Black Folk* (Greenwich, CT: Fawcett, 1961), 17.

18. *La Revue du Monde Noir*, no. 1 (Nov. 1931): 1-2.

19. Frantz Fanon, *Black Skin, White Masks*, trans. Charles Lam Markmann (New York: Grove Press, 1967), 147-153

20. Aimé Césaire, "Paris," in Senghor, *Liberté 1: Negritude et humanisme* (Paris: Seuil, 1964), 313.

21. Senghor, "Lycée Louis-le-grand, haut lieu de culture francaise," in *Liberté 1*, 403-6.

22. Paulette Nardal, "Eveil de la conscience de race," *La Revue u Monde Noir*, no. 6 (April 1932), 25-31.

23. A. G. Perier, "La Poésie ethnique," *La Revue du Monde Noir*, no. 6 (April 1932), 46.

24. Aimé Césaire, "Négrerie-jeunesse noir et assimilation," *L'Etudiant Noir* (March 1935), 2.

25. Léopold Sedar Senghor, "L'humanisme et nous: Réne Maran," *L'Etudiant Noir* (1934).

26. Aloune Diop, "Editorial," *Présence Africaine* (October-November 1947).

27. Maghemout Diop, "L'independence totale," *Présence Africaine* (1959).

28. Jean-Jacques Rabemananjara, quoted in Lilyan Kesteloot, *Intellectual Origins of the African Revolution*, trans. Alexander Mborkov (Washington, D.C.: Black Orpheus, 1972), 23-24.

29. *Ibid.*, 25.
30. Aimé Césaire, "La Négritude en question," *Jeune Afrique*, no. 532 (March 16, 1971), 65.
31. Senghor cited in Michèle Dorsemaine, Alfred Fierro, and Josette Masson, eds. *Léopold Sédar Senghor* (Paris: Bibliothèque Nationale, 1978), 83-84.
32. Léopold Sédar Senghor, "Totem," in *Poésie*, 24.
33. Sylvia Bâ, *The Concept of Negritude in the Poetry of Léopold Senghor* (Princeton, NJ: Princeton University Press, 1973), 12.
34. Cited in Léopold Sédar Senghor, *Liberté 111: Négritude et civilisation de l'universal* (Paris: Seuil, 1977), 270.
35. Senghor, "Le Probleme Culturel en OAF," in *Liberté 1*, 12. In this quote and elsewhere in the chapter, the term *humankind* has been used in place of the term *man* in the original texts. Wherever the term *humankind* rendered an awkward reading, the term *person* was used instead.
36. Léopold Sédar Senghor, "Negritude and African Socialism," in *African Affairs*, ed. Kenneth Kirkwood. Number Two: St. Anthony's Papers, No. 15 (London: Chatto and Windus, 1963), 9.
37. Léopold Sédar Senghor, "*L'Esprit de la civilisation ou les lois de la culture négro-africaine*," *Présence Africaine*, nos. 8, 9, 10 (June-November 1956): 51-65.
38. Léopold Sédar Senghor, ed. *Anthologie de la poésie nègre et malgache de langue française*, preceded by *Orphée noir* by Jean-Paul Sartre (Paris: Presses Universitaires de France, 1948).
39. Jean Paul Sartre, *Black Orpheus* (Paris: Présence Africaine, 1967), 17.
40. *Ibid.*, 59.
41. Senghor, "Negritude and African Socialism," in *African Affairs*, 250.
42. Léopold Sédar Senghor, *Discours prononcé à l'Université d'Oxford*, Oct. 26, 1961. Hereafter called *Discours d'Oxford.*
43. Léopold Sédar Senghor, "Negritude: A Humanism of the Twentieth Century," in *The African Reader: Independent Africa*, ed. W. Cartey and M. Kilson (New York: Random House, 1970), 184.
44. Léopold Sédar Senghor, *On African Socialism*, trans. Mercer Cook (New York: American Society for African Culture, 1965), 72-73.
45. *Ibid.*, 74.
46. *Ibid.*, 71.
47. *Ibid.*, 72-73.
48. Senghor, "Negritude: A Humanism," 189.
49. Aimé Césaire, *Return to My Native Land = Cahier d'un retour au pays natal*, ed., trans. Emile Synder (Paris: Présence Africaine, 1971).
50. Paul Hazoumé, *Le Pact du sang au Dahomey* (Paris: Travaux et Mémoires de l'Institut d'Ethnologie, 1937); also see his article, "L'Âme du Dahoméen révélée par sa religion," *Présence Africaine*, nos. 14, 15 (1975), 5.
51. Jomo Kenyata, *Facing Mount Kenya: The Tribal Life of the Gikuyu* (London: Oxford University Press, 1938), 290-92, 305.
52. S. Okechukwu Mezu, *The Poetry of L. S. Senghor* (Rutherford, NJ: Fairleigh Dickinson University Press, 1973), 88.

53. Ezekiel Mphahlele, "The Fabric of African Culture," *Foreign Affairs* (July 1964), 624.

54. Léopold Sédar Senghor, *The Foundations of "Africanité" or "Négritude" and "Arabité"* (Paris: Présence Africaine, 1971), 37; Bâ, *The Concept of Negritude*, 161.

55. Senghor, "L'Esprit," 64; Bâ, *The concept of Negritude*, 165.

56. Nazi Boni, *Crépuscule des temps anciens* (Paris: Présence Africaine, 1962), 17.

57. Fanon, *The Wretched of the Earth*, 235.

58. Cited in *La Croix*, January 27, 1972.

69. Marcien Towa, *Léopold Sédar Senghor: Négritude ou servitude?* (Yaoundé: Editions CLE, 1971), 41.

60. *Ibid.*, 51-52.

61. Stanislas Spero K. Adotevi, *Négritude et négrologues*, collection 10/18 (Paris: Union Générale, 1972), 62.

62. Senghor, *La poésie*, 184, 90.

63. M. Hauser, *Essai sur la poétique de la négritude* (Lille: Université de Lille III, 1982).

64. Cheik Anta Diop, *Nations négres et culture* (Paris: Présence Africaine, 1954), 33.

65. Senghor quoted in Thomas Melone, "De la Négritude dans la littérature Negro-Africaine" (Paris, 1962).

66. James George, *Stolen Legacy* (San Francisco: Richardson, 1976); Henry Olela, *From Ancient Africa to Ancient Greece: An Introduction to the History of Philosophy* (Atlanta, Ga: Select, 1981).

67. Cheikh Anta Diop, *Parenté génétique de l'égyptien pharaonique et des langues nègro-Africaines* (Dakar: IFAN-Les Nouvelles Editions Africaines, 1977), xxv. Diop published a lot on historical and cultural unity of Africa. Some of Diop's work in English includes: *The African Origin of Civilization: Myth or Reality*, ed. and trans. Mercer Cook (Westport, CT: Lawrence Hill, 1974); *The Cultural Unity of Black Africa* (Chicago, Il: Third World Press, 1978); *Black Africa: The Economic and Cultural Basis for a Federated State* (Westport, CT: Lawrence Hill, 1978); *Precolonial Black Africa*, trans. Harold Salemson (Brooklyn, NY: Lawrence Hill, 1987). *The Cultural Unity of Black Africa: The Domains of Matriarchy and of Patriarchy in Classical Antiquity* (London: Karnak House, 1989).

68. Theophile Obenga, *L'afrique dans l'Antiquité* (Paris: Présence Africaine, 1973), 173. Obenga, like his mentor, has written more than fifty articles and about a dozen books in French on Egyptionology, historical method, poetry, and the customs, practices, and cosmologies of different peoples in Africa.

69. Daniel Garrot, *Léopold Sédar Senghor critique littéraire* (Dakar: Les Nouvelles Editions Africaines, 1978), 148.

70. A. Abble et al. *Des Prêtres noirs s'interrogent* (Paris: Cerf, 1957).

71. Léopold Sédar Senghor, "Problematique de la Negritude," in *Liberté 111: Négritude et civilisation de l'universel* (Paris: Seuil, 1977), 279.

72. Senghor, *Discours d'Oxford*. See also Irving L. Markovits, *Leopold Senghor and the Changing Social Function of Negritude as an Ideology: 1931-1966* (African Studies Association, n. d.).

73. Senghor, *Discours d'ouverture du colloque sur littérature africaine d'expression française*, March 26, 1963.

74. Senghor, *Discours d'Oxford*.

75. Bernad Dadie, "The Contribution of Religion to the Expression of the African Personality," quoted in K. A. Busia, *Africa in Search of Democracy* (London: Oxford University Press, 1957), 44-45.

76. Abiola Irele, "Contemporary Thought in French Speaking Africa," *Africans and the West: Legacies of Empire*, ed. Isaac James Mowoe and Richard Bjornson (Westport, CT: Greenwood, 1986), 125.

77. *Ibid.*, 129.

78. For the debate see Paulin J. Hountondji, "Historie d'un myth," *Présence Africaine* (1974); Hountondji, *African Philosophy: Myth and Reality*, trans. Henri Evans with Jonathan Rée (Bloomington, IN: Indiana University Press, 1983); Kwesi Wiredu, *Philosophy and African Culture* (New York: Cambridge University Press, 1980); E. A. Ruch and K. C. Anyanwu, *African Philosophy: An Introduction to the Main Philosophical Trends in Contemporary Africa*, rev. ed. (Rome: Catholic Book Agency, 1984), 11-24; Richard A. Wright, ed. *African Philosophy: An Introduction*, 3rd ed. (Lanham, MD: University Press of America, 1984), 1-92; Kwame Gyekye, *An Essay on African Philosophical Thought: The Akan Conceptual Scheme* (New York: Cambridge University Press, 1987), 3-57; Segun Gbadegesin, *African Philosophy: Traditional Yoruba Philosophy and Contemporary Realities* (New York: Peter Lang, 1991), 1-26.

79. Segun Gbadegesin, *African Philosophy*, Preface.

80. Molefi Kete Asante, *Afrocentricity*, rev. ed. (Trenton, NJ: Africa World Press, Inc., 1988); *The Afrocentric Idea* (Philadelphia, PA: Temple University Press, 1987).

81. Molefi Kete Asante and Kariamu Welsh Asante, eds. *African Culture: The Rhythms of Unity* (Westport, CT: Greenwood, 1985), 257.

82. See Karenga, Maulana, and Jacob H. Carrauthers, eds. *Kemet and the African Worldview: Research, Rescue and Restoration* (Los Angeles, CA: University of Sankore Press, 1986).

83. The following provide good information and illustrations on some African forms of writing: C. A. Gollmer, "On African Symbolic Messages," *Journal of the Anthropological Institute*, 14 (1985); M. Kibanda, "L'Écriture dans la civilisation Kongo: Problèmes théoriques et methodologiques," *Revue de Linguistique Théorique et Appliquée* (January 1985); G. Kubik, "African Graphic Systems: A Reassessment," *Mitteilungan der Anthropologischen Gesellscrhaft in Wien*, 114 and 115 (1984-1985); E. Jaritz, "Uber Bahmen auf Billardtischen-Oder: Eine Mathematische Untersuchung von Ideogrammen Angolanischer Herkunft," Mathematische-Statistiche Sektion, Research Centre A-8010, Graz, Austria.

84. Asante, *Kemet Afrocentricity and Knowledge* (Trenton, NJ: Africa World Press, 1990), 72-79.

4

African Socialism

The philosophy of negritude showed that for Africans to assert their values, practical problems had to be dealt with. The problems of colonization and its market economy had to be addressed. In other words, theory had to be supplemented by praxis, for without addressing the economic reality of most Africans, the quest for authenticity would be a luxury of the elite. The challenge before African intellectuals was now to engage liberal economics and political theory in order to find a mode of production and political theory that would enhance African values. Liberal political theory and economics had proven antithetical and destructive to African values and way of life.

A mode of production cannot be separated from the politics that defines its area of operation, its participants—who to include or exclude—and its values to be encouraged. A mode of production reveals how social institutions are structured, how people live and relate to each other, and how they think about nature or the material resources on which the economy depends. Liberal Laissez-faire economics maintains individual interest take priority over society and that there are laws or forces that govern the market. Adam Smith called these forces "the invisible hand."

> Every individual is continually exerting himself to find the most advantageous for whatever capital he can command. It is his own advantage, indeed, and not that of society, which he has in view. But the study of his own advantage naturally, or rather necessarily, leads him to prefer that employment which is most advantageous to the society. . . . In this case, as in many other cases, he is led by an invisible hand to promote an end which was no part of his intention. . . . I have never known much good done by those who affected to trade for the public good.[1]

Note here the heavy emphasis on individualism and its relation to capitalism. Equally stressed is the power of economic laws that should not to be interfered with; the unfettered market ought to make economic decisions. According to

Adam Smith, the market is the legitimate arbiter of equity and freedom, but a closer look at liberal economics reveals that in reality, the keys to understanding the market are power and competition, not market forces. Those with power manipulate and control the market. Power and competition also characterize the nature of relations within liberalism itself. Hobbes expressed the spirit of liberalism and its economics when he compared human life with a race: "But this race we must suppose to have no other goal, nor other garland, but being foremost, and in it." Concerning the specifications for the race he said:

> To consider them [competitors] behind is glory,
> To consider them before, is humility.
> To fall on the sudden, is disposition to weep.
> To see another fall, is disposition to laugh.
> Continually to be out-gone, is misery.
> Continually to out-go the next before, is felicity.
> And to forsake the course is to die.[2]

In *Leviathan*, Hobbes asserted that the first "general inclination of humankind" is "a perpetual and restless desire of power after power, that ceaseth only in death." This claim and the specifications above show that competition is a way of life in liberalism, and in this competition everyone is on her or his own. To what extent one succeeds depends on one's power. Individualism, therefore private ownership of the means of production, becomes a sacred institution. In a system with private ownership of the means of production, there is bound to be increasing concentration of power and wealth. Control over the decision-making processes of the economic system rests with those who own and control the means of production. Thus those with a large amount of accumulated wealth also have a large amount of economic power; inequality is built into the system. This means, economic well-being is denied those at the bottom, the powerless.

Given the basic presuppositions of liberal economics—power, competition, private ownership, and control of the means of production—African nationalists saw that this economic system could not foster African values, especially community and the dignity of persons. Nationalists feared that the "death" Hobbes spoke of could be of their people and possibly African civilization itself. To avoid this "death," nationalist leaders sought the mode of production that would allow African values to emerge and flourish. For them, such a system had to be communal. Such a mode already existed in traditional society; nationalists called it African socialism. Almost all first-generation nationalist leaders entertained socialist views in one form or another. The concept of African socialism was subscribed to by Léopold Senghor, Sekou Touré, Julius Nyerere, and Kwame Nkrumah, all of whom were the first presidents of their respective countries Senegal, Guinea, Tanzania, and Ghana. This chapter will consider whether African socialism succeeded in disengaging Africans from liberal economics and politics.

The term *African socialism* was employed with caution by African intellectuals. Some nationalists, Tom Mboya, for example, argued that some Africans used the term uncritically, thus falling into what he called Western "intellectual imperialism."

> We have Africans who call themselves socialists—"African socialists"—but if you scrutinize their thought process you discover that they are so blindly steeped into foreign thought mechanics that in their actions they adopt standards which do great violence to the concept of African brotherhood. These so called "socialists" peddle and parrot foreign slogans and allow themselves to be swept away by emotions which have nothing to do with the noble aspirations of our people.[3]

Mboya called for attempts to formulate "a new political philosophy—a philosophy of our own—that will explain, validate and help to cement our experience."[4] Mboya's definition of socialism focused on African values, "those proved codes of conduct in the African societies which have, over the ages, conferred dignity on our people and afforded them security regardless of their station in life. I refer to a universal charity which characterizes our societies and I refer to the African thought process and cosmological ideas which regard humankind, not as a social means but as an end and entity in the society."[5] Nyerere's definition of socialism emphasized the importance of care in society: "Socialism—like democracy—is an attitude of mind. In a socialist society it is the socialist attitude of mind, and not the rigid adherence to a standard political pattern, which is needed to ensure that the people care for each other's welfare."[6] Senghor distinguishes African socialism from the European type: "Our socialism is not that of Europe. It is neither atheistic communism nor, quite, the democratic socialism of the Second International. We have modestly called it the African Mode of Socialism."[7] Senghor maintained that African socialism was different because of the unique African experience of colonialism: "It is evident that African Socialism can no longer be that of Marx and Engels, which was designed in the nineteenth century according to European scientific methods and realities. Now it must take into consideration African realities. This is particularly necessary because Marx and Engels were not anti-colonial. Engels defended classical slavery and Marx supported British colonialism in India."[8]

In order to be faithful to the African experience and cultural values, Sekou Touré suggested that the term *communaucracy* be used in place of *socialism*. For him, *communaucracy* included also all the aspects of traditional life and values. "Africa is essentially 'communaucratic.' Collective life and solidarity give Africa a humanistic foundation which many peoples may envy. It is also because qualities that an African cannot imagine organizing his/her life outside that of his/her social group—family, village, or clan. The voice of African people is not individualistic."[9]

Sekou Touré underscored the fact that African socialism was original and that Africa was not trying to import an ideology from Europe.

> We use the expression "communaucratic" precisely in order to avoid all equivocation and all false analogies. . . . Our solidarity, better known under its aspect of social fraternity, the preeminence of group interests over personal interests, the sense of common responsibilities, the practice of a formal democracy which rules and governs our village life—all of which constitutes the basis of our society—that is what forms what we call "communaucratic realities."[10]

Nyerere gave further clarification concerning the nature of African socialism. Proponents of socialism in Europe, Lenin in particular, saw socialism as an antithesis to capitalism; they thought that a nation had to go through a form of capitalism before socialism could be established. Nyerere rejected this thesis, arguing that from his own experience in tribal socialism, he found contradiction between socialism and capitalism "quite intolerable. It gives capitalism a philosophical status which capitalism neither claims nor deserves. For it virtually says, 'Without capitalism, and the conflict which capitalism creates within society, there can be no socialism.' This glorification of capitalism by the doctrinaire European socialists, I repeat, I find intolerable."[11]

According to Nyerere, African socialism did not need to follow the path of its European counterpart. African socialism might "get the benefits of European society . . . and yet retain the African's own structure of society in which the individual is a member of a kind of fellowship."[12] Kenneth Kaunda, the first President of Zambia, expressed the same idea when he asked: "Is there any way that my people can have the blessings of technology without being eaten away by materialism and losing spiritual dimension of their lives?"[13] For the late Malawian economist Dunduza K. Chisiza, the path for Africa to follow was clear: a pragmatic form of socialism:

> It is both unnecessary and objectional to narrow the range of choice to two systems: capitalism and communism. As a matter of fact the chances of either . . . being adopted in its unadulterated form are slim. In Africa, the tendency is towards a pragmatic approach which discards the irrelevant and incorporates the best of both systems.[14]

Similarly, Mamaduo Dia, the former Prime Minister of Senegal, contended: "A synthesis will be possible between individualistic and social values, harmony between them being achieved in the complete human personality. This synthesis of a true socialism and a true humanism, which will rest on African reality and African values, while not rejecting the enriching contributions of other cultures, will be genuinely African, but will at the same time have universal importance."[15]

For Senghor, this pragmatic approach would be incomplete if African spiritual values were excluded: "A middle course . . . a democratic socialism, which goes so far as to integrate spiritual values, a socialism which ties in with the old ethical current of the French socialists."[16] Elsewhere says: "For us, socialism is merely the rational organization of human society, considered as a whole, according to the most scientific, modern and effective means. . . . More than the use of the most efficient techniques, it is the sense of community which is the return to Africanness."[17] Senghor summarizes African's understanding of socialism as follows: "Our socialism is nothing but the technical and spiritual organization of human society by intelligence and the heart."[18]

It is interesting to note that I. I. Potekhin, the orthodox Marxist, agreed with African nationalists on the claim that the existence of a specific tradition of life could lead to socialist means of production without capitalism running its full course. Potekhin highlighted some unique African experiences which set Africa on a different path to socialism.

> In discussing the possibility of noncapitalist development we consequently have in view mainly the countries of tropical Africa. The most typical feature of the social structure of the peoples in this part of Africa is the absence of clearly defined class divisions and still incomplete formation of antagonistic classes. There is no class of big landowners exploiting a dependent peasantry; some exceptions to this rule are Ethiopia, Buganda, and the northern regions of Nigeria and Cameroon. Neither does the national bourgeoisie exist as a class. There are semifeudal, patriarchal—feudal forms of exploitation, there are capitalist elements which exploit wage labor, but there is no class of feudal lords in opposition to a peasantry, there is still no class of bourgeoisie in opposition to a working class.[19]

Potekhin explained how this situation would have led to a socialist form of production.

> It is impossible to create a socialist system of social production without socialization, in one form or another, of the means of production. This fully corresponds to the interests of the working class, since it is the only class in contemporary society which is not connected to private ownership of the means of production. The African peasantry, too, is vitally interested in socialization of the means of production, since there is no other way for it to get rid of poverty. The peasant, however, owns some, although extremely limited means of production; he is attached to his small plot of land and this hinders him from realizing that socialization of the means of production by the setting up of cooperative farms is the only way forward to a happy life.[20]

THE DEVELOPMENT OF AFRICAN SOCIALISM

The rise in popularity of socialism in the African intellectual arena can be said to have evolved, in part, from the philosophy of negritude. The development of the notion of African socialism may be described as a "paradigm shift" in

Kuhn's sense. Kuhn has shown that in the field of history of natural science, changes in paradigm occur when the old paradigms are no longer able to explain a new phenomenon and the appearance of an anomaly in a scientific paradigm calls for a shift in that paradigm.[21]

This development in paradigm shift is clear in the work of Senghor. The new paradigm of socialism was for him revised negritude:

> Our revised negritude is humanistic. I repeat: it welcomes the complementary values of Europe and the white man, and indeed of all other races and continents. But it welcomes them in order to fertilize and reinvigorate its own values, which it then offers for the construction of a civilization which shall embrace all humankind. The neo-humanism of the twentieth century stands at the crossroads where the paths of all nations, races and continents meet, where the four winds of the spirit blow.[22]

For the most part, the concept of socialism rose as a continuation of the struggle against liberalism in its different manifestations: (1) liberal economics as it presented itself in colonial economy and (2) liberal thought. Senghor insists that it was the experience with liberal economics through colonial capitalism that made nationalists seek "a return to original sources," that is, African socialism.[23] Senghor rejected capitalism, saying, "It is because private capitalism finds it repugnant—or more precisely, finds it impossible—to transcend its material bounds, it is because of its transformation into colonialist imperialism that we were converted, after much hesitation to socialism."[24] African socialism emerged to fight against liberal forces which had destroyed African culture, robed Africans of self-esteem, and undermined their self-determination, all of which are important factors in achieving selfhood. By undermining these factors, liberalism was able to destroy African society. African socialism was an attempt to recover traditional values in order to create a new social order.

African socialism sought to address the problems of post-colonial Africa: dependence, poverty, and the value of community living. Albert Tévoédjré extolled the nobility of poverty, for in the poverty of traditional society people had what they needed and had respect for each other. He contrasted life in traditional society with the condition of people in modernity where they do not have basic things: their life is a constant struggle for survival. In this struggle for survival, people lose creativity and happiness; yet in the poverty of traditional society people relaxed and were happy. The present situation is what he preferred to call destitution for in destitution there can be no honor for people and thus no respect for life. Tévoédjré quoted from the Bible to support his thesis of nobility of poverty.[25]

The values of dignity of persons and community life arise from the African concept of the world. In the African world, the human is the central character. The importance of the human in African world makes the idea of community central in African society. Community in traditional culture exists to uphold the sanctity of life and maintain and sustain the value and respect of persons. Dia

Thiam explained the relation between individuals and community in African cosmology:

> It is often said that Africa is traditionally socialist. Sociologists and enthonologists inclined to African societies stress this dominant trait of African societies. The individual is not defined apart from the group, one is defined in and with group to which he belongs. The group and individual are not two distinct realities, but one and the same reality. R. P. Tempels and Professor Marcel Griaule, in particular, have written explaining this phenomenon which goes to the root of Negro-African philosophy. Negro-African socialism rests on a cosmology, an explanation of the universe according to which being is not divided, not a reducible reality, but constitutes elements of a whole in which it inserts itself and which gives its force and its life.[26]

The same views were expressed by Kwame Nkrumah:

> The traditional face of Africa includes an attitude towards humankind which can only be described, in its social manifestations, as being socialist. This arises from the fact that humankind is regarded in Africa as primarily a spiritual being, a being endowed originally with a certain inward dignity, integrity and value. This idea of the original value of humankind imposes duties of a socialist kind upon us. Herein lies the theoretical basis of African communalism. This theoretical basis expressed itself on the social level in terms of institutions such as the clan, underlining the initial equality of all and the responsibility of many for one. In this social situation, it was impossible for classes of marxian kind to arise.[27]

Pierre Kanoute agreed with both Thiam and Nkrumah that African society is predominately socialist. According to Kanoute, socialism in Africa was held in bondage by colonialism. He argued, "African socialism is a reality which was subjected, for a certain time, to the shock of colonialism: we must now rethink it in its new context. Frightened by the spectacle of Western individualism, we prefer to correct the abuses of our traditional socialism and to retain the community aspects of our civilization."[28] Nyerere agreed that the African was always a socialist, arguing that he himself lived in traditional community and that he "saw no struggle between his own interests and those of his community."[29] Like Kanoute, Nyerere wanted to reclaim African socialism: "We must . . . regain our former attitude of mind—our traditional African Socialism—and apply it to new societies we are building today."[30] The new African socialism sought to develop a new concept of the human, that is, the human as a social, political, and spiritual creature. Mamadou Dia explained the aim of African socialism:

> We aim at developing a new type of humankind, inspired by an awareness of the world and also by a sense of the spiritual values of the forces of life whose rhythm forms our aesthetic valuation. . . . This spiritual humanism will be in harmony with the Christian as well as the Moslem way of life, for we are in profound sense a

people of believers. . . . Our African socialism is not a scholastic theory, but a vital challenge and hence an ethic and an obligation.[31]

SENGHOR ON AFRICAN SOCIALISM

In formulating his socialism, Senghor draws from African cosmology and culture, and this is particularly clear in his understanding of persons and community. Concerning the basis of socialism Senghor says: "Negro-African society is collectivist, or more exactly, communal, because it is rather a communion of souls than an aggregate of individuals"; and he adds, "we already realized socialism before the coming of Europeans" and that "our duty is to renew it by helping it to regain spiritual dimensions."[32] In talking about African society, Senghor refers to it as a collectivist society, it brings together into a collectivity a number of individuals, who remain individuals in society. This collective and communitarian society makes the person feel that he or she can develop his or her originality only in and through society.[33] Thiam adds to Senghor's claims about the mind of traditional society, asserting that in the collective community, while each person had her or his own interest but the interest of each agreed with the interest of all. This led to a solidarity of members of a given village. Senghor contends that the productive efforts of a village appealed to this solidarity.[34]

Almost all of the advocates of African socialism were influenced by the writings of some non-Africans. Senghor was informed by dialectical materialism of Marx and Pierre Teilhard de Chardin. Senghor read Marx after the war in the deputies' library of the Palais Bourbon, admiring him as a true humanist who sought to enrich human life and its liberation from material necessity. Senghor quoted from *Das Capital*: "What from the very first distinguishes the most incompetent architect from the best of the bees, is the architect has built a cell in his head before he constructs it in wax. The labor process ends in the creation of something which, when the process began, already existed in an ideal form. . . . He realizes his own purpose." Senghor considered this the most profound and beautiful passage Marx ever wrote, for it depicts the human as purposive, acting with consciousness and liberty.[35] He took Marx's theoretical basis so seriously that he made the theories of Marx and Engels a starting for his own political theory for in spite of the limitations, inadequacies, and errors of their theories, the two revolutionized the political thought of the nineteenth century. The consequences of that revolution are still discernible in the twentieth.[36]

Senghor was especially impressed by Marx's concept of matter, which is at the heart of Marx's theory of knowledge.[37] Senghor saw Marx as one who integrated knowledge with practice, and this separated him from Hegel and materialism from idealism. Senghor observed that matter was central to Marx's thought not as the object of natural science but as the human social matter of nineteenth-century Western Europe. This was matter was composed of contradictions and was perpetually changing. It was matter animated by dialectical movement. "For dialectics, before it is method, is the very movement of 'material' realities," noted Senghor.[38] Senghor liked the idea of dialectical materialism, which he traced to Heraclitus, who the West believes was the first to affirm that matter is not static but always in motion or in the process of becoming. This mutability and instability of matter is due to principles of contradiction, reciprocal action, and change. Underlining these principles is the force of negation within matter, which destroys and changes matter itself thereby creating a new reality—a synthesis.

The concept of synthesis was developed by Hegel but it was Marx who gave it a materialist interpretation. Marx and Engels accused Hegel of "having deduced the laws of dialectics from the mind rather than from nature; of having maintained that the mind with its forms and categories created nature the real world," says Senghor. According to him, Marx, and Engels "it is from the history of nature and human society that the laws of dialectics are abstracted."[39]

Senghor liked Marx's dialectical materialism because its logic attempts to go "beyond the form, principles and categories of understanding and of common sense, thus allowing thought to enter into immediate rapport with the varies, changing content.[40] Put simply, dialectical materialism "catches" the three principles of mutability and instability: contradiction, reciprocal action and change. Marx's theory of knowledge, as Senghor interprets it, lies in the evolutionary, objective, contradictory character and originality of the object studied. Inasmuch as dialectical materialism made sense to Senghor, he cautioned against considering it as a panacea for Africa's ills. He maintained that the European dialectic remains abstract, for not only is it close to formal logic, but it also retains the categories and concepts, inductions and deductions of logic.[41] Formal logic with its principles of identity, non-contradiction, and exclusion, concentrates on objectivity and visual realism, thus producing an abstract theory of knowledge which remains so even when it is applied to reality. Marx's dialectical materialism stands in opposition to African theory of knowledge, which according to Senghor is based on confrontation and intuition.[42] Senghor rejected scientific materialism as deterministic and atheistic. Senghor saw Marx's rejection of Christianity as a reaction against the historical deviations of the religion, which violated the essence of religion. At the same time, the idea of alienation found in Marx's theory is of religious origin.[43]

While Senghor was impressed by Marx's humanism, he was a critic of doctrinaire Marxism on five points: (1) The "class struggle" is much more complex than Marx thought; in fact the working class is not a simple reality. (2) The peasants, whom Marx considered more or less impervious to revolutionary ferments and dedicated to "the stupidity of rural life" have, in non-Western countries, belied this judgment. (3) The theory of capitalist concentration of wealth has not been borne out by the facts. (4) Though periodic economic crises have not ceased, they are becoming rarer, and we cannot reasonably foresee a general cataclysm ending the capitalist system. (5) "Socialism" has not triumphed in the industrial nations of the Western world as Marx had predicated it would, but rather in the underdeveloped nations of Eastern Europe and Asia.[44]

In general, Senghor rejected the whole idea of calling Marx's theory of economics and socialism "scientific," as if this "science" had "the exact knowledge and formulation of economic facts in laws that permit one to foresee and organize a balanced economy."[45] Further, Senghor questioned the bases of the humanism of dialectical materialism. He argued that Marx's notion of humankind and his bases for moral value and judgment were distorted. For Marx, thought moves from "an equivocal conception of humankind" and of the universe; that is, humankind is treated as mere matter. In other words, his concept of *species being* or *species nature* does not take into consideration the other qualities of humankind, the spiritual dimension in particular. For Senghor, an ethic or idea of the human that is not informed by something beyond humankind, was faulty:

> In the name of whom or what, after all, does Marx dare affirm the dignity of humankind and humankind's right to appropriate the products of its labor? In the name of whom or what does he condemn night labor, child labor and African slave trade, unless it be in the name of a certain quality or transcendent something beyond humankind? Science notes facts and their relations; it explains, it does not demand. It cannot pass from factual to a value judgment.[46]

Here we see Senghor rejecting Marx's theory because of its mechanistic materialism, which leads into determinism and atheism. Moreover, Marx's theory of knowledge seems to deny that the activity of thought is to comprehend the object through the categories of understanding, in a subject and object reciprocal action.[47] Mechanistic materialism (determinism) and atheism are incompatible with African socialism. To solve the contradictions in Marx's theory, Senghor turned to the work of the Jesuit scientist, philosopher, and theologian Pierre Teilhard de Chardin. The work of Teilhard de Chardin had provided Senghor hope in reconciling not only Marx's theory, but also reaching a "*rendezvous de donner et recevoir*," a grand moment of give and take between African and European cultures. Senghor declared that the goal of the twentieth century was to create a rendezvous between national development and technical advances.[48] He further asserted that such a meeting had been envisioned by Marx, who said that the natural and social science would one day be incorporated into a single science.[49]

The concept of reconciliation Teilhard de Chardin discusses includes a harmonious relation between faith and science, spiritualism and materialism. Having been disappointed with Marx's materialistic determinism and atheism, Senghor found Teilhard de Chardin inspiring because the latter's theory allowed people to keep the positive contributions of socialism and justified their faith.[50]

He was also drawn to Chardin as a scientist who used the dialectical method. Like Marx, Teilhard de Chardin combined evolutionary theories in natural science with human science, studying the biological and psychological history of the humanity from the pre-life to the future, or what he called survival, studying the evolution of human life "from seemingly inanimate matter to the Omenga point (God), while crossing the critical thresholds of the biosphere (life) and noonsphere (thought)."[51] Teilhard de Chardin transcended the mind-matter dichotomy of Marx and Engels, maintaining that there is only a single reality in the universe which manifests itself as spirit-mind, in the same way there is space-time.[52]

In developing his ideas of socialism Senghor drew on Teilhard de Chardin's theory of matter and mind expressed by his law of complexity—consciousness.[53] According to this law, consciousness is always in the process of developing and rises to its fullest power in humankind's consciousness of itself. When people know who they are, they depict a consciousness of consciousness at its highest power. This law is based on mind-matter development. In the pre-life is scientific matter, characterized by change (complexity). Through critical changes within matter, a transformation to life and consciousness takes place. This movement from matter to consciousness takes place in stages: instinct, reflection, co-reflection, and ultra-reflection. The universe is divided into two spheres of influence: the biosphere for instinct, for reflection, the noonsphere for co-reflection, and ultra-reflection.

In de Chardin's materialism, matter and spirit belong together as network of forces of reflection. There are two forms of energy: (1) *tangible energy*, the external, material, and quantitative force linking the particles that make up matter; (2) *abstract* or *radical energy*, the internal, psychic, and qualitative force that organizes into a complex center to center relations of the various internal particles of matter. Energy is force, therefore radical energy is the creative force, the very substance of matter that which makes life. Tangible energy is secondary, it derives from interactions within the minor centers of consciousness. This means that physical-chemical laws, or determinism, apply only where there is no life, for where life exists the psyche increases in consciousness until it reaches freedom.

The law of complexity says the constitutive elements of consciousness are foresight, language, technique, and co-reflection. Foresight sets humankind apart from all other creatures as the only group of creatures with the capacity for planning. Foresight points to human responsibility and freedom in the world. Planning destiny of humankind is possible because humans have the ability to communicate with one another through speech, script and symbols. Technique allows humankind to implement its ideas and thereby realize its chosen ends. Co-reflection reveals the way people decide to live together as a group or community. Co-reflection discloses the economic, social, and political theories operative in a given community. The way people choose to live is reflected in the institutions and structures they create for themselves; this is to assert that social, political and economic theories and practices reveal people's ideas about life and community.

Senghor places de Chardin's categories alongside African values, especially the meaning of person and community. Senghor intends to use Teilhard de Chardin's categories to produce a universal understanding of a new humanity and society. The new person he has in mind is a totality of new consciousness, a person with a mission to the world that says people come first, for they constitute the measure of all planning and action:

> A nation that refuses to keep its rendez-vous with history, that does not believe that it bears a unique message—that nation is finished, ready to be placed in a museum. The Negro-African is not finished before he even gets started. Let him speak; above all let him act. Let him bring like a leaven, his message to the world in order to help build the civilization of the Universal.[54]

Here Senghor moves away from the negritude of his youth. The new person he now presents is not only produced by a cultural revolution—negritude—but is a synthesis of different traditional values and cultures. This is a universal person.

NYERERE'S *UJAMAA*

The development of socialist thought in Nyerere came as he struggled with the issues of colonial economy, the problems arising from the unequal distribution of worth and world resources due to the world market system. To put it simply, the problem of poverty. The concern that Nyerere had for his people in the post-independence era is also expressed by President Habib Bourguiba: "It is necessary to inculcate a sense of dignity in those of our Tunisian citizens who live in poverty, misery and hunger. It is clear that they are happy to be delivered from French domination. . . . It is equally necessary that they feel the need to improve their living conditions . . . and live honorably as advanced people do."[55] To live honorably for Nyerere, however, is to live as African communities lived prior to the destruction of their culture and thought by Western influence. For Nyerere, African socialism is a practical way to regain African values and the most appropriate means to deal with the problem of unequal distribution of wealth in modern Africa. Nyerere's socialism is a socio-economic and cultural critique of the liberal paradigm.

Like Senghor, Nyerere in his project places people at the center of his philosophical thinking.

> under socialism mankind is the purpose of all social activity. The service of humankind, the furtherance of his development, is in fact the purpose of society itself. . . . The word "man" to a socialist, means all people—all human beings . . .

> all human beings who are its purpose—are equal. . . . Socialism as a system is in fact the organization of humankind's inequalities to serve their equality. Their equality is socialist belief.[56]

Nyerere's socialism does not arise from a shift of paradigm from a capitalist paradigm to an Eastern form of socialism. Neither systems fits Africa because both create classes in society, and he maintains that social classes are alien to African society. European socialism was born out of what he calls a civil war between the landed and the landless masses: "Civil war no longer was looked upon as something evil, or something unfortunate, but as something good and necessary. As prayer is to Christianity or Islam, so civil war (which they call class war) is to the European version of socialism—a means is inseparable from the end. Each becomes the basis of a whole way of life. The European socialist cannot think of his socialism without its father—capitalism."[57] Nyerere insists that African socialism "did not start from the existence of conflicting 'classes' in society. Indeed, I doubt if the equivalent for the word 'class' exists in any indigenous African language."[58] The absence of class is due to the African concept of *Ujamaa* (familyhood). "'*Ujamaa*,' then, or 'familyhood,' describes our socialism. It is opposed to capitalism, which seeks to build a happy society on the basis of exploitation of man by man; and it is equally opposed to doctrinaire socialism which seeks to build its happy society on a philosophy of inevitable conflict between people by people."[59] Therefore, African socialism will have to contend with the problem of accumulation and poverty existing in both the capitalist West and the socialist East. "The world is still divided between the 'haves' and 'have nots.' This division is not between capitalists and socialists, or between capitalists and Communists; this is the division between the poor and the rich of the world. . . . The rich countries of the world today may be found on either side of the division between the capitalist and socialist countries."[60]

Nyerere rejects the mentality of accumulation for it is based on the idea of rewards or the Puritan spirit that argues that those who work hard reap their rewards.[61] He questions the whole concept of rewards: "There must be something wrong in a society when one man, however hard-working or clever he may be, can acquire as great a 'reward' as a thousand of his fellows can acquire between them." Nyerere argues that the concepts of reward and wealth imply exploitation by the powerful. He says that wealth and power go hand in hand. However, wealth itself is only bad when it is sought in order to dominate others. In his "Speech to the Second Pan-African Seminar, World Assembly of Youth," Nyerere explained the problem with accumulating wealth for personal power and prestige.

> The true purpose of wealth is to satisfy very simple needs: the need for food, the need for shelter, the need for education, and so on. . . . There is enough wealth in every state for every individual to satisfy these simple needs. But the moment individuals in any single state begin to use wealth not for the satisfaction of those

> needs, nor for the banishment of poverty, but for the purpose of acquiring power and prestige—then there is no longer enough. Then wealth tolerates poverty: then wealth is no longer to poverty what light is to darkness. For there is not enough wealth in any nation to satisfy the desires for power and prestige of every individual.[62]

Nyerere expresses his fear that some Africans seek wealth for the purpose of acquiring power:

> Unfortunately there are some of us who have already learned to covet wealth for that purpose (to dominate others)—and who would like to use the capitalist uses in its acquiring it. That is to say, some of us would like to use, or exploit, our brothers/sisters for the purpose of building up our own personal power and prestige. This is completely foreign to us, and it is incompatible with socialist society we want to build here.[63]

For Nyerere, accumulation in general, or "the very desire to accumulate," for whatever reason, is "antisocial" and "must be interpreted as a vote of 'no confidence' in the social system." He argues that if society organizes itself is such a way that it cares about its individuals, then provided one is willing to work, no one within that society should worry about what will happen to him or her if the person "does not hoard wealth today. This is exactly what traditional African society succeeded in doing."[64] Nyerere sees this as socialism—none accumulates yet none suffers. He argues that the presence of accumulation while others live in dire misery would be a contradiction in terms in a socialist society, for "there can be no such a thing as acquisitive socialism. Socialism is essentially distributive. Its concern is to see that those who sow reap a fair share of what they sow."[65]

Nyerere finds all these elements of socialism present in traditional African society. He therefore draws upon traditional society in his attempt to build a contemporary African socialist society. From traditional society he invokes the concept of *Ujamaa* to inform him in his project. (Familyhood refers to what the West calls extended family.) The concept of family is important to Nyerere because it is in the family that the concern and care for the other develop. Nyerere felt that the lack of care in modernity is due to the loss of the true meaning of family (community) and knowledge of the responsibilities that individuals have to the other members of the family. Therefore the "first step" Africans must take, "must be to re-educate ourselves; to regain our former attitude of mind. In our traditional African society we were individuals within a community. We took care of the community and the community took care of us. We neither needed or wished to exploit our fellow humankind."[66]

It is also within the family that dignity and respect of persons develop. People are respected for who they are—people and members of one's family! In traditional society old people, who are usually poor and weaker members of society, are respected because they embody traditional values and wisdom handed down through generations. Thus Nyerere states: "Just as the elder, in our former society, was respected for his age and his service to the community, so, in our modern society, this respect for age and service will be preserved."[67]

The family in the traditional African society was not only a socio-cultural and political unit, but also a production unit. Nyerere outlines three means of production that the family unit employed: land, tools and labor. With these, everyone worked. Nyerere uses the term "worker" in opposition to "employer" also opposed to "loiterer" or "idler." What he means is that each and every able-bodied person did something toward the well-being of the whole family. "One of the socialistic achievements of our society was the sense of security it gave to its members, and the universal hospitality on which they could rely. But it is too often forgotten, nowadays, that the basis of this great socialist achievements was this: that it was taken for granted that every member of society—barring only children and the infirm—contributed his/her fair share of effort toward the production of its wealth."[68] The family as a production unit depended on its land. In traditional society land was life itself, for it was the only means of livelihood.

> To us in Africa, land was recognized as belonging to the community. Each individual within our society had a right to the use of land, because otherwise he could not earn his living, and one cannot have the right to live without also having the right to means of maintaining life. But the African's right to land was simply the right to use it; he had no other right to, nor did it occur to her to try and claim one.
>
> The foreigner introduced a completely different concept—the concept of land as a marketable commodity. This idea is alien to our society.[69]

Nyerere in his project seeks to re-establish the network of social relations that provided security to individuals in traditional society. One's obligations to such network of social relations and security enjoyed, was through labor seen in the production of goods common to all members of society. Surplus goods were distributed among society assuring security and preventing accumulation for power and prestige. In other words, traditional society was a moral force, and as such, it structured its institutions in such a way as to prevent unequal distribution of wealth, thus domination of the wealthy few.

The objectives of *Ujamaa* are stated in Tanzania's Second Five Year Plan, referred to as the Arusha Declaration. The *Arusha Declaration* was Tanzania's blueprint for development and promotion of social, political, and economic equality, its objective being "to create a society based on cooperation and mutual respect and responsibility, in which all members have equal rights and equal opportunities, where there is no exploitation of one person by another, and where all have gradually increasing level of material welfare before individual lives in luxury."[70] The Declaration says that the guiding principle in process of creating such a society is the thought that "where capitalism put machines and technique in the first place, socialism puts people and people's political consciousness first."[71] Nyerere realizes that building such a society will require the involvement of all people and government institutions. Writing on the strategy for achieving African socialism in light of the concept of *Ujamaa*, Nyerere says: "United action from all government ministries and public organizations concerned with rural areas is of vital importance to the whole success of the new approach for the promotion of *Ujamaa* villages and the cooperative production units which we hope to be staged on the way to full *Ujamaa* villages. It is essential that all ministries put their services, and that of staff to the promotion of these policies to the maximum extent possible."[72]

As seen from above, Nyerere is very practical and systematic in his approach to African socialism. Unlike Senghor, Nyerere grounds his philosophy in a specific traditional socialist practice and thought—the concept of *Ujamaa*. *Ujamaa* identifies people as a socio-political unit as well as a unit of production. Nyerere seeks to move his people toward self-reliance and self-determination and to eliminate exploitation and excessive differentiation of wealth, income, and power in society through the concept of *Ujamaa*.[73] As an economic unit, the *Ujamaa* villages are to increase productivity in agriculture, a time honored labor in traditional society. Through *Ujamaa* he hopes to help his people to achieve dignity and selfhood—a new humanity. In sum, Nyerere's socialism is a prescription for ending liberal thought and practice.

KAUNDA'S HUMANISM

The theme that dominates the writings of the exponents of African socialism is that of a dignified humanity. Senghor addressed the theme of dignity in his early works on negritude; in his later life the quest for dignified human life appeared in his writings on socialism. Nyerere's socialism was a social, political, and economic approach to the African quest for dignified humanity. And thus Sekou Touré writes: "We have placed humankind at the end of everything."

Among the African thinkers, perhaps, Kenneth Kaunda has dwelt most on a conscious awareness of human dignity. Like Senghor, Kaunda admits being indebted to Teilhard de Chardin: "What he has discovered as a philosopher I can testify to as a politician."[74] In his discussion on "philosophical basis of nationalism," Kaunda commented on Teilhard de Chardin's understanding of humanity's

> growing capacity to situate itself . . . to 'situate oneself in space and time' is surely to discover one's identity, which was beaten out of shape by the impact of colonialism, and to 'become conscious of place and responsibility in relation to the universe' speaks of the dignity and stature of humankind. Humankind must measure itself not against the rest of the animal world, nor in terms of the little fragment of local history through which humankind has lived, but against the Universe itself.[75]

Kaunda's humanism develops from his understanding of nature and belief in humankind's ability to achieve goodness. He declares: "I believe that the Universe is basically good and that throughout it great forces are at work striving to bring about a greater unity of all living things. It is through cooperation with these forces that Humanity will achieve all it is capable."[76] Humankind is dependent on nature. Dependence on the rhythms of nature teaches humankind humility and how "to live harmoniously together because they know that only by acting together can they reap the benefits and try to overcome the hardships of Nature."[77] When people cease to see themselves as part of nature, when they are driven by the technological mind, they lose their capacity to appreciate and value each other as people. The technological mind objectifies nature, and others so that they are no longer considered a part of one's life but a thing. The technological mind objectifies people and reduces them to means to one's goal. To diminish the value of persons is to bring society, indeed the world itself, to an end. The respect for humankind is to take precedence over all else. Kaunda says that in "our task of fighting to preserve Human centered society . . . we must remember that it is people above ideology; humankind above institutions. We must continually refuse to slavishly tie humankind to anything. Society is there because of humankind. . . . In other words, whatever we take to do we have got to remember that it is Humankind that is the center of all human activity."[78] Again Kaunda says,

> No earthly idol, whether the state, the family or anything else, ought to take priority over respect for humankind; they are only worthy of respect in as far as they are images of the human spirit, enshrine its presence, aid its self-fulfillment, but where the cult of these idols seeks to usurp the place of the spirit, they should be put aside. They become dead husks, destined to decay. No injunctions of old creeds, religious, political, social, or cultural, are valid if they diminish persons. Science even, one of the chief idols of the modern world, must not be allowed to serve any lesser goal than greater humanizing of persons.[79]

Kaunda acknowledges that technology does indeed free humankind from hardships of nature, but his concern is that it leads to "materialism and losing the spiritual dimension of" human life.[80] According to Kaunda, the spiritual dimension of human life is very important for it makes humankind sacred. This sacred value of humankind should inform a way of life: "No mechanical, political or administrative unity of humankind is remotely possible until the sacred value of Man and Woman possesses not only your imaginations as a vision, but also your wills as a program of action and a way of life."[81]

Having made a critique of the liberal mind, Kaunda turns to traditional society in his quest for human dignity. According to Kaunda, the structure of African traditional society forms the basis for understanding humanism in modern Africa. "African humanism stems from the structure of traditional society and its effects upon African psychology," asserts Kaunda describing traditional society as "a mutual society. It was organized to satisfy the basic human needs of all its members, therefore individualism was discouraged."[82] Even human conduct was dictated by human need: "Human need was the supreme criterion of behavior."[83] It is in light of these attitudes of traditional society that he also speaks of traditional society as "an accepting community . . . an inclusive society," suggesting "web of relationships which involved some degree of mutual responsibility."[84]

The subject of human dignity is rooted in the attitudes of traditional society toward persons, therefore to realize human dignity in contemporary Africa means eliminating the colonial socio-economic and political structures. For Kaunda, humanism is the spirit of nationalism or Pan-African unity. By moving people to assert their dignity by fighting colonialism, humanism would allow peoples to see themselves as one people struggling together for a higher cause—to be fully human by realizing their personhood. Kaunda warns against false optimism about change of people's attitude at the dawn of independence, making it clear that the new humanity that people sought would not appear on the day of independence:

> It is still the same *old* people who constitute the new state. No blessed amnesia steals over them on the morning after Independence Day. They carry with them into the new society as part of their baggage the experience and heritage of their colonial past in spite of all their attempts to wipe the slate clean. Human nature is not, in the short run, changed by constitutional instruments. . . . Even the formal symbols of colonialism have been removed, its ghost-like presence persists.[85]

Humanism is a political principle and ethic as well as a cultural or socio-economic basis for transformation. Kaunda explains: "Humanism as a way of life is modelled on the mutual aid society," as exemplified by traditional society.[86] Kaunda acknowledges the power of liberal economics and what it has done to African society: "While there is plenty of good that Africa is justly proud of in its set-up of a mutual aid society . . . one has got to understand and appreciate that the powerful forces from the West which have been aggressively shattering in their individualistic, competitive and possessive approach, have had serious and grave consequences on the African society."[87] Although acknowledging the crisis of African values, Kaunda still believes that Africa can play a leading role in transforming the world. He believes that from the understanding of persons in traditional society, Africa can provide on the whole a rich meaning of being human.

> *Humankind has not yet understood its own importance. And yet we can say with justification and without any sense of pride that the African way of life with its many problems has less setbacks toward the achievement of an ideal society. We in Zambia intend to do everything in our power to keep our society human-centered. For it is in this that what might be described as African civilization is embodied and*

> *indeed if modern Africa has anything to contribute to this troubled world, it is in this direction that it should.*[88]

On the socio-economic front, "humanism is intended to arm the nation for the challenge of development and against the dangers of 'an invading money economy.'"[89] Traditional economics focused on basic human needs, security for all individual members of the community—that is, the distribution of wealth. In modern humanism, economics will pay attention to enhancing human dignity and happiness.[90] This will mean that the economic calculus will have to take into consideration the impact of development programs on the lives of the people.[91]

Finally, humanism is to take seriously the religious nature of the human. As indicated above, Kaunda understands the sacred value of the human that makes persons moral and religious creatures and sets them apart from all other creatures. Apart from drawing from traditional morality, Kaunda develops his understanding of humanism from the teachings of the Christian faith, especially from the work and life of Jesus Christ. For Kaunda, humanism can *only* be Christian humanism, since humanism is an attempt to follow the examples of the life of Jesus. A humanism that is not founded in religion fails to understand the principle of sacrificial love and life, claims Kaunda:

> Mankind must be the servant of a vision which is bigger than itself; that its path is illumined by God's revelation and that when a person shows love towards a fellow human being, the person is sharing the very life of God, who is Love. . . . Nor do I deny the reality of *sin*. The besetting sin of the humanist is Pride. The significance of Jesus Christ is surely that he spells death to our pride by showing us how far short of God's design for us as we are.[92]

NKRUMAH AND SCIENTIFIC SOCIALISM

Nkrumah understands African socialism as the way to fight Africa's economic problems. He considers the economic problem as the root cause for the loss of time-honored values of African peoples. Nkrumah focuses on values of dignity of persons and community, especially as these manifest themselves in economic life of traditional society, that is, egalitarianism as it informed the means of production. He maintains that the egalitarian and humanist traditional society was "ravaged by colonialism." To re-establish these values in modernity is the task of African socialism. With the economic problems in mind, Nkrumah's project of socialism centers on four issues: public ownership of the means of production, industrialization, education, and planning.[93] As the issues indicate, Nkrumah's socialism aligns more than others with Marxism. This is quite a contrast to Nyerere, who prefers traditional basis for socialism and speaks of "rejecting the capitalist attitude of mind which colonialism brought into Africa."[94] For Nkrumah, the task of African socialism is to bring people forward. Like

Bourguiba, he feels that African dignity will come when the question of poverty has been addressed. In "War on Poverty," Nkrumah expresses his understanding of African socialism.

> In this tremendous task of bringing our peoples forward out of poverty, the whole of our nation—civil servants, teachers, farmers, peasants—indeed, all able-bodied men and women, must stand together.
>
> How are we to achieve our goal within the shortest possible time?
>
> My assertion is that socialism is the only pattern that can within the shortest possible time bring good life to the people. For socialism assumes the public ownership of the means of production—the land and its resources—and the use of those means for production that will bring benefit to the people.[95]

Again Nkrumah says, "All talk of socialism, of economic and social reconstruction, is just empty words if we do not seriously address ourselves to the question of basic industrialization and agricultural revolution, just as much as we must concentrate on socialist education."[96]

Nkrumah argues that economy is the number one issue for African socialism. "Above all," he maintains, "our economic advancement must be the foundation upon which to erect an equitable and happy society."[97] To achieve this foundation Nkrumah says it will mean that "our planning must aim at a twofold purpose: to increase productivity, and to accumulate capital for the expansion of industrial development."[98] Like Nyerere, Nkrumah says that a new outlook is necessary for the new economic order to emerge—namely, a socialist attitude. "If this new economic and industrial policy is to succeed, there must be a change of outlook in those who are responsible for running our affairs. They must acquire a socialist perspective and a socialist drive keyed to the socialist needs and demands. They must not remain the servants of a limping bureaucracy."[99]

Nkrumah's ideas of socialism come from different sources but his starting point is his understanding of African traditional society, specifically the egalitarianism of traditional society, what he calls "communalism." This egalitarianism is seen in the attitude of traditional society toward land and the means of production; that land and the means of production belong to the community and not to the individual. Nkrumah sees the forces that created communalism in the traditional society also present in modern circumstances.

> In socialism the principles underlying communalism are given in modern circumstances. Thus, whereas communalism in an untechnical society can be laissez faire, in a technical society where sophisticated means of production are at hand, if the underlying principles of communalism are not given centralized and correlated expression, class cleavages will rise, which are connected with economic disparities, and thereby with political inequalities. Socialism, therefore, can be and is the defense of the principles of communalism in a modern setting.[100]

Nkrumah here agrees with Nyerere concerning the absence of social classes in traditional society. He says: "The African social system is communistic. In the African social system the foundation of a pauper class is unknown, nor is there antagonism of class against class."[101] However, Nkrumah fears that if the technological mind is left on its own the formation of such classes in technological society will be inevitable. On the other hand, if the technological mind is guided by principles of communalism, the benefits of modernity will enrich human life, ending poverty in Africa. Communalism within African socialism is the fight against the growth of inequalities between people (class) created by the "capitalist habit of colonialism" or the forces of neo-colonialism. In the manner of the other African socialists, Nkrumah rejects the classical Marxist view that a revolution has to take place before socialism is realized. "Revolution is an indispensable avenue to socialism, where the antecedent social-political structure is animated by principles which are a negation of those of socialism, as in capitalist structure (and therefore also in a colonialist structure, for a colonialist structure is essentially ancillary to capitalism). . . . But from the ancestral line of communalism, the passage to socialism lies in reform, because the underlying principles are the same."[102]

While Nkrumah here rejects the subject of class struggle, in his subsequent writings his thoughts changed. In a revision to *Consciencism*, Nkrumah speaks of the presence of social class in Africa and treats the struggle against neo-colonialism as class struggle on the international scale.

> Marx had argued that the development of capitalism would produce a crisis within each individual capitalist State because within each State the gap between the "haves" and the "have nots" would widen to a point where a conflict was inevitable and that it would be the capitalist who would be defeated. The basis of his argument is not invalidated by the fact that the conflict, which he had predicted as a national one, did not everywhere take place on a national scale but has been transferred instead to the world stage. World capitalism has postponed its crisis but only at the cost of transforming into an international crisis. The danger is now not civil war within individual States provoked by intolerable conditions within those states, but international war provoked by the misery of the majority of mankind who daily grow poorer and poorer.[103]

Nkrumah not only rejects his own old assumptions but also rejects the claims made by Senghor and Nyerere about traditional society.

> Today, the phrase "African socialism" seems to espouse the view that the traditional African society was a classless society imbued with the spirit of humanism and to express a nostalgia for that spirit. Such a conception of socialism makes of the communal African society. But an idyllic, African classless society (in which there were not rich and poor) enjoying a drugged serenity is certainly a facile simplification; there is not historical or even anthropological evidence for such a society. I am afraid the realities of African society were somewhat more sordid.[104]

This shift in positions can be accounted for Nkrumah's growing appreciation of dialectical materialism, which held that African societies shared the same laws of social evolution present in other societies. In his deeper struggle with the problem of poverty, Nkrumah employed dialectical materialist thought to argue that traditional (Akan) understanding of the world allows for a "minimal materialism." This claim is maintained by such eminent Ghanian thinkers as William Abraham. Indeed, there may be other reasons accounting for the shift in paradigm, political for one, but this is not clear either.

In an attempt to promote African socialism, Nkrumah sought to present to the whole of Africa a philosophical approach to the subject, thus the writing of *Consciencism*. This book might be described as Nkrumah's socialist manifesto. His burden in this book is to go beyond the traditional arguments for African socialism and to ground the concept of socialism in metaphysics, hence the term scientific socialism. In *Consciencism*, Nkrumah concerns himself with fundamental philosophical questions of existence, namely, "what there is" and "how 'what there is' may be explained." In exploring these questions he gives material examples of "what there is" and reduces it to some ultimate cosmic raw material.[105]

By following the materialist approach to the fundamental question of origin of life, Nkrumah does not seek to state that mind is the only reality, rather that it is the fundamental reality from which all others are derived. He introduces a process which he calls "categorical conversion" as the main factor in the derivation process. According to categorical conversion a given reality generates a reality of a higher category. It is through this process that matter generates mind. From here Nkrumah uses the language of the philosophy of dialectical materialism to advance the idea that minimum materialism is present in African socialism—a point he struggles to connect to the traditional understanding of the world. He presents his understanding of materialism as follows: "That matter can exist unperceived, that it has a continuance independent of mind, should really be axiomatic."[106] He further states:

> Materialism is a serious, objective, almost descriptive kind of metaphysics. As a minimum, it affirms the existence of matter independent of knowledge by mind. This minimal conception is obviously grossly inadequate. It is open to a materialist philosophy, but compulsory, to assert for its second thesis the primary reality of matter. Here matter would be whatever has mass and is perpetually active; and in its manifestations, matter would be coextensive with the universe.[107]

He engages in this complex philosophical thought mainly to explain the idea that a particular thought system influences a particular socio-economic and political system. This point, and indeed the aim of his total project in *Consciencism*, is made clear when he declares: "There are two real philosophical alternatives. These alternatives coincide with idealism and materialism. . . . Idealism favors oligarchy, materialism favors egalitarians."[108]

Nkrumah's project attempts to find an answer to the question of the origin of life. He finds his answer in a materialist metaphysic that asserts matter over mind, invoking dialectical materialism. In his autobiography, he makes it clear that he is "a non-denominational Christian and a Marxist socialist" and that he does not find any contradiction between the two.[109] Nkrumah defends his following dialectical materialist thought: "Dialectical materialism recognizes differences between mind and brain, between quality and quantity, between energy and mass. It however gives a special account of the nature of the differences. Both in metaphysics and in theory of knowledge, it does not allow the differences to become fundamental and irreducible."[110] The other reason he gives for following materialism arises from his uncritical appropriation of Marx on the role of religion in society. He argues that there is cause for "what is," which implies that there is something outside the world, which in turn implies for Nkrumah, "an acknowledgement that there is a conversion of a process which commences 'outside' the world into the world and its contents."[111] Then Nkrumah states: "But especially when this conversion is thought to be reversible, a definite contradiction is created in society, the contradiction between interests inside the world and interests outside the world. This kind of contradiction is made articulate in religion. . . . The contradiction takes effect when with the gaze steadfastly fixed upon things outside the world, the requirements of earthly life, which in fact conditions the existence of every human being, suffers neglect."[112]

This shows that Nkrumah followed a "pick and choose" method in developing the metaphysics he presents in *Consciencism*. For following his traditional Akan world, there is no way by which he could have come to the conclusion that religion creates a "contradiction" in life.

Sekou Touré and Léopold Senghor also have entertained Marxist thinking. But like Senghor, Touré, although a committed Marxist, rejects "scientific" dogmatism:

> Society is not made for principles, for a philosophy, for a doctrine, for a given science. On the contrary, science, philosophy and principles of action must be determined for the people and as a function of the realities of the people. Instead of applying society to science, we must apply science to society. This is why Marxism, which has served to mobilize the African peoples and particularly the working class and lead them toward success, has been shorn of those characteristics which do not correspond to the African reality.[113]

Nyerere considers it wrong to treat the ideas of "scientific socialism" as the norm for all forms of socialism. Nyerere calls for originality in socialist thought. He denounces the

> apparent tendency among certain socialists to try to establish a new religion—a religion of socialism itself. This is usually called "scientific socialism" and the works of Marx and Lenin are regarded as the holy writ in the light of which all

> other thoughts and actions of socialists have to be judged. . . . The task of socialists is to think out for themselves the best way of achieving desired ends under the conditions which exist now. . . . Africa's conditions are different from those of the Europe in which Marx and Lenin wrote and worked.[114]

Nyerere, not influenced by dialectical materialism, is politically astute when it comes to the role of socialism, because he does not address religion at a metaphysical level but at a political level. Nyerere is aware of the role and power of religion in traditional society, and is therefore ready to incorporate it in his socialism. He recalls that a "fundamental force in African traditional life was religion which provides a strict moral code for the community." He then declares, "This will be a permanent feature of African socialism."[115] He therefore takes religion and religious tolerance as fundamental to African socialism.

> This necessity for religious toleration arises out of the nature of socialism. For people's religious beliefs are important to them, and the purpose of socialism is humankind. Socialism does not seek to serve some abstract thing called "the people"; it seeks to maximize the benefit of society to all the individuals who are members of it. It is thus the essentially personal nature of religious beliefs which makes it necessary to leave religious questions alone as far as possible—which makes it necessary that socialism should be secular. And being secular involves trying to avoid upsetting deeply held religious beliefs however stupid they may appear to non-believers.[116]

The project of Nkrumah in *Consciencism* is not without difficulties. For example, in this project Nkrumah puts metaphysical discourse on a one-to-one correspondence with ideas of political discourse. For an explanation on his metaphysic in relation to the Akan world, one has to go to those who influenced him. William Abraham, for example, explains the meaning of "categorical conversion": "The distinction between spirit and matter, the most fundamental in Akan metaphysics, is reinforced by their distinction between quality and property. Whereas property might come to be founded on the quantitative, in Akan thinking no room was left for quality also being resolvable."[117]

The work of Abraham also sheds light on what Nkrumah was trying to do with his doctrine of *Consciencism*, to write a philosophical base for humanism in African socialism. Through materialism, he wanted to institute a complete ethic and a political doctrine on that metaphysic. In other words, Nkrumah sought to present a solid base for an egalitarian and humanist ethic. The influence of Kant is clear in the development of this ethic. For example, he writes that "the great moral principle of consciencism is to treat each human being as an end in itself and not as a simple means."[118] Compare this to what Kant says: "Act in a such a way that you treat humanity, whether in your own person or in the person of any other, never simply as a means, but always at the same time as an end."[119] The opening sentence of Chapter 4 of *Consciencism* also reflects the influence of Kant on Nkrumah: "Practice without theory is blind; theory without practice is empty." Kant states: "Concepts without intuitions are empty; intuitions without concepts are blind."

While Nkrumah gained some insight from Kant, he also drew from traditional culture, as Abraham shows: "The civilization operated an essentialist doctrine of person, according to which a person had an irreducible essence, which was constant and unchanging. This is a point on which one should expect similarity if there is a unity of African cultures. This similarity is in fact there."[120] According to Abraham, ethics was based on this essentialist pluralism of personality. Abraham states that the Akan employ a deductive system in their philosophical thought since they consider that as rational. To begin with, they understand "what is" as spirit. (Note that Nkrumah begins by asserting that "what is" is matter. If Abraham is correct, how then does Nkrumah arrive at the position that the Akan are materialistic in their metaphysics? Nkrumah is unclear.) Abraham says spirit exists in a hierarchy because the primary properties of spirits are qualities which are called moral.[121] Second relations between ideas take on body and flesh in their relations between things in nature. From this system of thought it follows that morality, politics, and medicine derive from metaphysics.[122] This relation explains why Nkrumah makes an easy correspondence between metaphysical and political discourses.

Speaking about the unity of African cultures, Nkrumah believed that his project of *Consciencism* would provide a solid base for a socialist ideology, which would unite Africa. This idea was also shared by the collective editorial of *The Sparks*, expressed by Julius Sago: *Consciencism* "will provide the rallying ideology for all sincere African patriots who feel that the socialist ideology should more closely reflect the African background."[123] According to Paulin Hountondji, *Consciencism* addresses two political issues: (1) a demand for a nationalist ideology which reaffirms the right of all people for self-determination which appeared in Nkrumah's earlier work[124] and (2) "the construction of socialism in a liberated Africa." Hountondji concludes, "The most interesting point, however, is the author's assertion that the three panels of the triptych (metaphysical, ethical and political) are closely linked and inseparable. *Consciencism* thus appears as a vast ideological structure in the fullest sense, a complete system of thought with multiple but independent aspects."[125]

In *Consciencism* the concept of African socialism is given a philosophical foundation. In addition, Nkrumah has explained what he perceives the tasks of African socialism. The first task of African socialism is to establish an egalitarian and humanistic society based on the African socialist past before it was "ravaged by colonialism." Such a society in modernity will need a sound economic base, founded on strong industrial production. To achieve this economic foundation, African socialism will seek and adapt from colonialism ways of industrial production and organization. This is the second task of African socialism. The problem is that colonial economy is capitalist, and as such it creates class inequalities and antagonism. To crush these classes, the third task of African socialism, "colonial mentality" will have to be erased by African socialism. The final task will be to defend the security of the people.

Nkrumah is not a theorist without practical knowledge. In *Consciencism*, he brings theory and practice together by making concrete and practical suggestions on the implementation of African socialism. Nkrumah describes the principles, strategy, and methods by which the "liberated territories" can make their transition to socialism.

CONCLUSION

The struggle for authenticity has prompted Africans to try different avenues in their attempt to recover their values. The attempts we have examined include the cultural revolution, which was the focus of Senghor's negritude and Nkrumah's "African personality." The concept of "African personality" was transformed into the concept of "communalism." An attempt to fully capture the dimensions of "communalism" and shift in the negritude paradigm has turned Africans to socialism. This is to say, in the crisis of meaning, amid the complexities of colonial and neo-colonial socio-economic and political history, or the forces of the liberal project, Africans have sought to retrieve their values by breaking with the liberal project and to establish their societies on the pattern of traditional community. Socialism is that pattern.

African socialism is a frame of reference for development in post-colonial Africa consisting of philosophical and ethical foundations for a new social order. It is pragmatic in its approach to the creation of a new social order. Africans realize that they cannot return to a socialism of pre-colonial Africa. In light of this fact, African socialism is informed by the values of traditional society while drawing upon technology and organization of modernity in order to combat poverty and promote the well-being of Africans. Africans are very concerned about the effects of technology, for they realize that it *can* and *has* destroyed values of traditional society and relationships between people. African socialism seeks to guard against the dehumanizing tendencies of technology by inculcating in people new attitudes of traditional African socialism. As Nyerere has stated, socialism is "an attitude of mind."

African socialism draws on traditional society so as to deal with the crisis of meaning in post-colonial Africa. In constructing a new social order, African socialism addresses three main issues: identity, economic development and formation of social classes. In dealing with the question of identity, African socialism is informed by three elements of traditional society: communal ownership of land (or what in modernity would be called a common ownership of the means of production), "egalitarian character of society (or a low degree of stratification) and the extensive network of social obligations that lead to considerable cooperation."[126] In short, the goal of African socialism is to give Africans a sense of identity by stressing the values of traditional society: community, egalitarianism, and cooperation.

African socialism addresses problems of economic development. The crisis of economic development in post colonial Africa has manifested itself in the dependence of African economies on the metropolitan centers of Europe and North America. To reduce dependence on the metropolitan centers, African socialism encourages economic development through industrialization and "international commodity agreements and other trade arrangements which help either to bring higher and more stable prices for primary products or to provide new outlets for ever increased production of these exports."[127] Furthermore, African socialism encourages the formation of regional common markets to reduce dependence on Europe and North America. The abandoned East African community was a direct result of the efforts of African socialism toward dependence. Regional economic organizations such as the South African Development Cooperation (SADEC) and the Economic Community of West Africa (ECOWA) encourage trade and other forms of cooperation between member states in order to reduce dependence on the metropolitan centers. African socialism makes it clear that African economic development will be largely in the public sector, challenging liberal economics and its emphasis on accumulation and individualism. In stressing the role of government in providing capital and guiding economic development, African governments have discouraged the formation of an entrepreneur class. The governments inhibit the development of this class by regarding it as self-interest. The African concept of wealth is that it should be for the welfare of all; therefore, to become an entrepreneur is to go against traditional ethical conduct to be against society itself.

Perhaps African socialism's most direct attack against individualism is through the formation of class through private ownership. Felix Houphouët-Boigny, the first president of Ivory Coast, revealed that one of the reasons for breaking with communism was because "the class struggle, which lies at the base of communism, has no meaning in classless society."[128] Senghor consistently maintained that there were no classes in African society, but he also expresses fear that classes may come. He notes that "analysis reveals a certain tendency, a 'real movement' toward the *formation of classes*." By this he refers to the gap in income between those employed in industry, trade and commerce, and the civil service, and the subsistence farmer. He adds, "the proletarian is not necessarily the one who claims the title."[129] Nyerere sees the elite moving toward privileged positions, and thus beginning the evolution of class formation.

> As nationalism becomes successful, the chances of the Europeans and the Asians maintaining a permanently privileged position in our countries will diminish. But the chances of the educated Africans to become a new privileged class will multiply. Yet this will not be so obvious while the Europeans and Asians are strikingly wealthier than the Africans. The would be African exploiter can masquerade as a

> great social reformer by concentrating the attack on European and Asian privilege. Before we know where we are, what is now essentially a dying-out privileged class will have been replaced by a permanent class of educated Africans.[130]

In the attempt to prevent formation of a permanent class, African socialism rejects "private ownership insofar as it heightens individual ambition and produces a desire for personal gain, destroying those characters in African society that are highly prized." African socialism argues that this "'alienation' is not only an essential feature of capitalist society but equally common in communist society."[131] Leo Apostel also states that it is the fear of alienation that has led Africans to reject both

> Western capitalism and European socialism . . . because both *could* reproduce a society in which the individual is alienated from others. Not the will of the majority but the will of the community should be realized; and even in a classless society African tradition is still afraid of solitude and closed individuality. The desire to avoid these evils, and realize the autonomy of the person, avoiding any fusion in the whole, is a reflection of the tension met in African art and expressed in African philosophy.[132]

The law of comparative advantage, known in its modern form as the Hecksher-Ohlin principle, states that a country gains more by producing and trading those commodities whose factor-intensity corresponds to that with which the country is well endowed. Unlike the Hecksher-Ohlin principle, African socialism takes seriously economic relations—the relations of people to work and wealth, and of person to person in the productive context. Because it is humanist, African socialism considers these relations of fundamental importance in the process of economic development "man above ideology," declared Kaunda; and Nyerere said, "under socialism man is the purpose of all social activity." Nkrumah explained why African socialism puts emphasis on people: "This arises from the fact that man is regarded in Africa as primarily a spiritual being, a being endowed originally with a certain inward dignity, integrity and value." In the process of economic development, African socialism focuses on the needs of people, "rather than the rights of property, and on cooperation rather than competition," observes Chandler Morse.[133] Because it is people-centered, African socialism attempts to provide the populace "with a sense of participation in an effort to modernize the economy for the common good."[134] Morse notes why Africans emphasize the significance of human relations in productive context.

> African elites, familiar with less savory features of industrialization in Europe and the United States, and themselves emerging from a traditional society structured more to maintain and solidify human relations than to manage the environment of productive increase, recognize the inherently divisive tendencies of competition as a regulator of economic activity and have sought ways to mitigate the conflicts of

> interest over distribution. Precisely because of its primary concern with this problem, and its potential ability to mobilize cooperative effort, socialism has a wide appeal in the sympathetic and favorable African environment.[135]

There is no single understanding of African socialism, but that does not mean that there is no sense of direction in the project. Nyerere says that the universality of the phenomenon of socialism and the various stages at which different people are "on the way to socialism" lends itself to different understandings.

> The universality of socialism, does not imply a single, worldwide uniformity of social institutions, social habits or social language. There is no reason why a dozen fully socialist societies should not have a dozen different methods of organizing themselves, a dozen different sets of customs relating to social intercourse, a dozen different styles of political address and description. It is by no means necessary to call people "comrade" in order to be socialist; it is not necessary to insist on a civil marriage ceremony in a socialist society; it is by no means certain that a centralized economy is an inherent part of socialist organization. It is my contention that socialist societies in different parts of the world will differ in many respects even when they are fully developed instead of being, as now, at different stages on the road to socialism.[136]

African elites see socialism as summing up their aspiration and views for a humanistic society, that is, an egalitarian society as exemplified by traditional society. In other words, African socialism is a critique of the liberal heritage and economics, including Hobbes's concept of power. In African socialism power is understood as participation of all and not a war of one against all. Hobbes states that the need for power and more power leads to competition but in African socialism power is taken as participation and cooperation, not competition, is the way of life. In focusing on the welfare of the whole community, individuality is not fused in the whole but affirmed by the community.

African socialism struggles with many other elements of liberalism: colonialism, neo-colonialism, dependence, the profit motive or market economy, and the dignity of persons. The struggle may be summarized as a quest for self-realization or authenticity. To be authentic is to be able to assert one's values and to reach selfhood. Selfhood does not appear until people have asserted themselves as subjects of history. African socialism seeks to recover African values, as well as African past, and transform these for modernity. The aim of African socialism is to produce a new "social order: an egalitarian, cooperative collectivistic, welfare state in which however, simultaneously the autonomy and dignity of humankind (the *muntu*) is maximized."[137]

African socialism differs from orthodox Marxism by its "mystical character," as Apostel has put it, to the understanding of persons in the African world. The religious nature of African humanism makes it easy for African socialism to accept Christianity although it has difficulties with the teachings of liberal

Christianity with its emphasis on the individual. African socialism takes the existential human condition seriously, but liberal Christianity minimizes it and instead emphasizes "other worldliness." It is due to this weakness of liberal Christianity that Nkrumah borrowed the language of dialectical materialism in order to speak of his "minimal materialism." It is the over-emphasis on "other worldliness" that led Nyerere to borrow the language of eighteenth-century European philosophers in his critique of liberal Christianity: "Unless we participate actively in the rebellion against those social structures and economic organizations which condemn people to poverty, humiliation and degradation, the church will degenerate into a set of superstitions accepted by the fearful."[138] Compare this quotation with the views of the Enlightenment: "the supposed revelation of God's purposes through the Holy Writ was a fraud, or at best an illusion born of ignorance, perpetuated, or at least maintained, by the priests in order to accentuate the fears of humankind, and so hold it in subjection."[139]

The concept of person in African thought and society is too strong to be compromised by any teaching that does not struggle against the present human condition; thus the break with liberal Christianity. When a particular teaching focuses on the existential human condition but ignores the sacred nature of persons, African socialism will have nothing to do with it—hence the separation with orthodox Marxism. It is clear from these views that the African struggle for authenticity, the quest for a new social order, is a struggle for a new vision of the world and meaning of life that seek to institutionalize the sacred nature of the human in a political and economic order to fully express the meaning of persons or personhood.

Did African socialism help Africans disengage from liberal economics and politics? There is no African country that is fully socialist in ways envisioned by the advocates of African socialism. Attempts are continually being made by various governments toward an economic system that integrates African values. We might say then that in its consciousness raising task, African socialism accomplished a very significant step toward Africa's liberation. But efforts to fully implement socialist ideas are often frustrated or dislodged by the world market economy, international money borrowers, and donor agencies, all of whom are informed by liberal theories of economics and politics. A case in point is Tanzania, which in spite of its political determination and practical programs has not been allowed to carry through its socialist agenda. Despite massive opposition and frustration, Tanzania has made some advances. African socialism is not merely rhetoric, but an unfinished agenda, a project, and a discourse on African values.

NOTES

1. Adam Smith, *An Inquiry into the Nature and Causes of the Wealth of Nations* (New York: The Modern Library, 1957), 421, 423.

2. Thomas Hobbes, *Body, Mind and Citizen*, ed. Richard S. Peters (New York: Collier, 1962), 224-25.

3. Tom Mboya, "African Socialism," *Transition*, no. 8 (March 1963).

4. *Ibid.*

5. *Ibid.*

6. Julius K. Nyerere, "Ujamaa: The Basis of African Socialism," in *Freedom and Unity* (London: Oxford University Press, 1967; Dar-es-Salaam, 1968); *Tanganyika Standard*, April 1962.

7. Léopold Sédar Senghor, *Discours d'Oxford.*

8. Léopold Sédar Senghor, *Afrique Nouvelle*, no. 800, 11.

9. Sekou Toufé, *L'Action du Parti Démocratique de Guinée et lutte pour l'émancipation africain* (Paris: Editions Présence Africaine, 1959), 108.

10. Sekou Touré, *Texts des Interviews Accordes aux Journalistes* (Conakry, 1959), 149, 151.

11. Nyerere, "Ujamaa," 170.

12. Julius Nyerere, "Africa's Place in the World," *Symposium on Africa* (Wellesley, MA:1960).

13. Kenneth Kaunda and Colin Morris, cited in Alyward Shorter, ed., *African Christian Spirituality* (Maryknoll, New York: Orbis Books, 1978), 136.

14. Dunduza K. Chisiza, *Africa: What Lies Ahead* (New York: African-American Institute, 1962), 28. William J. Fortz has cited other reasons that some West African countries have adopted a pragmatic approach. See his article, "The Radical Left in French-speaking Africa" in William H. Lewis, ed., *Emerging Africa* (Washington, D.C.: Public Affairs Press, 1963).

15. Mamadou Dia, in William H. Friedland and Carl G. Rosberg, eds., *African Socialism* (Stanford, CA: Stanford University Press, 1964).

16. Senghor, *On African Socialism*, trans. Mercer Cook (New York: American Society for African Culture, 1959), 45-46.

17. Senghor at the Dakar Colloquium on socialism, December 1962. *West Africa*, (December 29, 1962), 149.

18. *Ibid.*, 146.

19. I. I. Potekhin, "On African Socialism: A Soviet View," In Friedland and Rosberg, eds., *African Socialism*, 103.

20. *Ibid.*, 104.

21. Thomas S. Kuhn, *The Structures of Scientific Revolutions*, enlarged edition Chicago: University of Chicago Press, 1970).

22. Senghor, *Discours d'Oxford.*

23. Senghor, *On African Socialism*, 26.

24. Senghor, "Negritude and African Socialism," 15.

25. Albert Tévoédjré, *La Pauvreté: Richesses des peuples* (Paris: Editions Ouvriéres, 1978).

26. Dia Thiam, *La Politique extérieure des états africains* (Paris: Presses Universitaires de France, 1962), 33-34. Cited in L. V. Thomas, *Le Socialisme et l'Afrique: Essai sur le socialisme africain* (Paris: Le Livre Africain, 1966), 7-8.

27. Kwame Nkrumah, *Consciencism*, rev. ed. (London: Heinemann, 1964), 69.

28. Pierre Kanoute, "Le Socialisme africain: Expression de l'homannisme africain," *Afrique Nouvelle* (November 30-December 6, 1962).

29. Julius Nyerere, "Africa's Place in the World," 157.

30. Nyerere, *Freedom and Unity*, 170.

31. Mamadou Dia in *Socialist International Information* (London), vol. 11, no. 18 (May 6, 1961), 276-77.

32. Senghor, *On African Socialism*, 32.

33. Senghor, *Nation et Voie Africaine du Socialisme* (Paris: Présence Africaine, 1961), 123-124.

34. Mamadou Dia, *Contribution à l'étude du movement cooperatif en Afrique noire* (Paris: Présence Africaine, 1958), 11-12, 17; Mamadou Dia, *Reflexions sur l'economie de l'Afrique noire*, new ed. (Paris: Présence Africaine, 1960), 27.

35. Senghor, "Marxisme et humanisme," *La Revue Socialiste*, 19 (March 1948), 201-16.

36. Senghor, *On African Socialism*, 26-27.

37. *Ibid.*, 39.

38. *Ibid.*, 40.

39. *Ibid.*, 126.

40. *Ibid.*, 124.

41. *Ibid.*, 70.

42. *Ibid.*, 72.

43. *Ibid.*, 38.

44. *Ibid.*, 32.

45. *Ibid.*, 31.

46. *Ibid.*, 36.

47. *Ibid.*, 128.

48. Full argument in Léopold Sédar Senghor, "Pierre Teilhard de Chardin et la politique africaine," in *Cahiers Pierre Teilhard de Chardin*, no. 3 (Paris: Seuil, 1962), 15-65.

49. Senghor, *On African Socialism*, 134.

50. *Ibid.*, 45.

51. *Ibid.*, 135.

52. *Ibid.*, 183.

53. See Pierre Teilhard de Chardin, *Les Unités humaines naturelles*, vol. III of *Oeuvres* (Paris: Seuil, 1963).

54. Senghor, *On African Socialism*, 49-50.

55. Habib Bourguiba, "Neo-Destourian Socialism," address delivered June 24, 1961 (published by Tunisian government).

56. Julius K. Nyerere, *Freedom and Socialism* (London: Oxford University Press, 1968), 4.

57. Nyerere, *Freedom and Unity*, 170.

58. *Ibid.*

59. *Ibid.*

60. *Ibid.*

61. Max Weber expressed the relation between hard work and reward in *The Protestant Ethic and the Spirit of Capitalism*, trans. Talcott Parsons (New York: Charles Scribner's Sons, 1958).

62. For the full text of the speech see Paul E. Sigmund, Jr., ed. *The Ideologies of Developing Nations* (New York: Frederick A. Praeger, 1963), 205.

63. *Ibid.*, 162.

64. *Ibid.*, 164.

65. *Ibid.*, 163.

66. *Ibid.*, 242.

67. *Ibid.*

68. *Ibid.*, 164-65.

69. *Ibid.*, 170-71.

70. Richard Juma, "A Case Study of People's Participation in Development: The Tanzanian Experience," *People's Participation and People's Movements*, Commission on the Church's Participation in Development (World Council of Churches), Document no. 22 (May 1982).

71. *Ibid.*

72. Julius Nyerere quoted in *ibid.*

73. See the Arusha Declaration and also Nyerere's *Socialism and Rural Development.*

74. Kenneth Kaunda and Colin Morris, *A Humanist in Africa* (Nashville, TN: Abingdon Press, 1966), 20.

75. *Ibid.* Kaunda's understanding of humankind has been informed by Pierre Teilhard de Chardin, *L'Avenir de l'homme* (Paris: Seuil, 1959).

76. Kaunda and Morris, *A Humanist in Africa*, 19.

77. *Ibid.*

78. Kenneth Kaunda, speech at the National Council of the United National Independence Party in 1967, reproduced in Kaunda, *After Mulungushi* (Lusaka, Zambia, 1967), 12.

79. Kenneth Kaunda, Letter to My Children in *African Christian Spirituality*, Alyward Shorter, ed. (Maryknoll, NY: Orbis Books, 1980), 118.

80. *Ibid.*

81. *Ibid.*, 119.

82. *Ibid.*

83. *Ibid.*

84. *Ibid.*

85. Kaunda and Morris, *A Humanist in Africa*, 83.

86. Kaunda, *After Mulungushi*, 5.

87. *Ibid.*, 9.

88. *Ibid.*, 16. His emphasis.

89. *Ibid.*, 7.

90. *Ibid.*, 19.

91. *Ibid.*, 40-41.

92. Kaunda and Morris, *A Humanist in Africa*, 85-86.

93. Kwame Nkrumah, "The Basic Needs of African Socialism," *Pan-Africa* (April 19, 1963).

94. Nyerere, *Freedom and Unity.*

95. Nkrumah, "The Basic Needs," 13.

96. *Ibid.*

97. *Ibid.*

98. *Ibid.*, 14.

99. *Ibid.*

100. Kwame Nkrumah, *"The Old and the New: Law in Africa.* Address to the Ghana Law School." Accra: Ministry of Information and Broadcasting, January 4, 1962.

101. *Ibid.*

102. *Ibid.*, 74.

103. Kwame Nkrumah, *Neo-Colonialism: The Last Stage of Imperialism* (London: Heinemann, 1965), 255-56.

104. Kwame Nkrumah, *Two Myths* (New York: Panaf, 1970), 8.

105. Nkrumah, *Consciencism*, 7.

106. *Ibid.*, 19.

107. *Ibid.*, 20.

108. *Ibid.*, 75.

109. Kwame Nkrumah, *The Autobiography of Kwame Nkrumah* (New York: Nelson, 1957), 12.

110. *Ibid.*, 23.

111. Nkrumah, *Consciencism*, 11.

112. *Ibid.*, 12.

113. Sekou Touré, *Textes des interviews accordées aux representants de la press* (Conakry: 1959), 107.

114. Nyerere, *Freedom and Socialism*, 14-15.

115. Nyerere, *Ujamaa: Essays on of African Socialism* (London: Oxford University Press, 1968).

116. Nyerere, *Freedom and Socialism*, 14.

117. W. E. Abraham, *The Mind of Africa* (London: Weidenfeld and Nicolson, 1962), 107.

118. Nkrumah, *Consciencism*, 95.

119. Immanuel Kant, *The Moral Law*, trans. H. J. Paton. (London: Hutchison University Library, 1948), 91.

120. Abraham, *The Mind of Africa*, 113.

121. *Ibid.*, 50.

122. *Ibid.*, 47.

123. *The Spark*, March 26, 1964. Cited by Colin Legum, "Socialism in Ghana: A Political Interpretation" in Friedland and Rosberg, eds., *African Socialism*, 157.

124. Kwame Nkrumah, *I Speak of Freedom: Statement of African Ideology* (New York: Praeger, 1961).

125. Paulin J. Hountondji, *African Philosophy: Myth or Reality*, trans. Henri Evans and Jonathan Rée (Bloomington, IN: Indiana University Press, 1983), 153.

126. William Friedland in Friedland and Rosberg, *African Socialism*, 5.

127. *Ibid.*, 6-7.

128. Quoted by Alan Rake, "My Ivory Coast," *Africa Report*, no. 7 (April 1962), 4. Rake quotes from *L'Afrique Noire* (December 6, 1951).

129. Senghor, *On African Socialism*, 38.

130. Nyerere, speech at the awarding of an honorary degree at Makerere College, April 9, 1962. Cited by William Friedland in Friedland and Rosberg, *African Socialism*, 24.

131. Friedland, Friedland and Rosberg, *Ibid.*, 9.

132. Leo Apostel, *African Philosophy: Myth or Reality* (Gent, Belgium: Scientific Publishers, E. Story-Scientia, 1981), 380-81. His emphasis.

133. Chandler Morse, "The Economics of African Socialism," in Friedland and Rosberg, *African Socialism*, 42.

134. *Ibid.*, 43.

135. *Ibid.*

136. Nyerere, *Freedom and Socialism,* 3.

137. Apostel, *African Philosophy*, 386.

138. Nyerere, "Is Poverty the Real Problem," address to the Maryknoll Sisters General Chapter, New York, 1970, cited in Laurenti Magesa, "Return to the World," *African Ecclesiastical Review*, 16, no. 3 (1974), 279.

139. Carl Becker, *The Heavenly City of the Eighteenth-Century Philosophers* (New Haven, CT: Yale University Press, 1932), 51.

5

African Concepts of the World, Life, and Person

In this chapter attention will be on liberal cosmology as it affected African philosophers and theologians. We will enter this discussion by first exploring African concepts of the world, life, and person. In light of these fundamental concepts, the task of African intellectuals has been to explore their world and capture the meaning of life and persons. This task is important in two ways: (1) to stop, or at least slow down, the erosion of loss of meaning of life now present in African society, and (2) to integrate African values within the contemporary African socio-political situation. The crisis of meaning has a lot to say about the exploitation of people and resources, the loss of personhood and the relationship between people and nature. The task of retrieval of the notions of persons and life could lead to a new understanding of living together in the world, thus a reordering of society.

We have seen that the task of retrieval has been of a great concern among nationalists. They have demonstrated that the African way of life—socialist or communitarian—is grounded in the traditional African world. An outstanding work in this field is Kwame Nkrumah's *Consciencism*, which showed that socialism was in line with traditional African life. In addition, he wanted to emphasize that while the African world is spiritual, it also maintains a concept of minimal materialism. Nkrumah came up with the idea of minimal materialism, as a way of fighting against liberal Christianity which substitutes the material world with the hereafter. On the other hand, he wanted to distinguish African socialism from the European type by stating that African traditional society deals with the totality of persons. By making a break with liberal Christianity and drawing distance from European socialism, Nkrumah sought to point out that in African thought the concept of person is related to the meaning of life. This means that one cannot speak about life without talking about human life.

Nkrumah, Senghor, Nyerere, and Kaunda all emphasize that it is human life that gives creation meaning. Indeed, a world without persons is unthinkable to the African, for it is a world devoid of meaning—it is incomplete. By interacting with nature, both creation and people give themselves a new meaning of life and through this relationship people discover themselves within the totality of all creation. As nature opens itself up to humankind, it presents possibilities of experiencing life in its fullness. In the interaction with nature, people discover their being inseparably bonded to all life.

The African universe is one full of life—life transcending itself through fecundity. In its abundant creativity, life continues to cross frontiers and breaking forth into new dimensions, always re-creating itself, thereby presenting humankind with ever new possibilities. This self-transcending life is not just "nature life," that is, material; it is also sacred life. Nature, life, is sacred by origin in the African world, because it is given by God. By the fact of its divine origin the question of life becomes a spiritual issue. Since the cosmos is spiritual, then all considerations about human life have religio-moral implications as well as political ramifications. This means that the question of human life cannot be fully addressed until the religious and moral and political questions have been answered; life always has to be seen in its totality. The question of life is central in African thought because it is concerned with the ordering of social structures, behavioral patterns, relations, and possibilities within society and with nature. It is a question of the meaning of creation; therefore, life provides the basic framework of interpretation of the world. The question of life concerns developing structures which will allow or enhance possibilities for human life and the continuity of all creation.

The African world is concerned with fullness of life; it is in its fullness that life's meaning is realized. Fullness of life is realized when human potential and possibilities are allowed to reach their maximum in personhood. However, the question of human life cannot be understood apart from nature, to which it is bonded. Nature plays an important role in the process of human growth by providing all that is necessary, food, air, sunlight, and other things. This means that nature and persons are one, woven by creation into one texture or fabric of life.

It is this understanding of being inseparably bound to nature that makes it alien for an African to objectify nature as the other, as only something to be used or treated aesthetically. This is not to say that Africans do not enjoy aesthetics. However, a work of art is never abstracted or objectified but always rooted in the context of life from which it originated; there is no "claim to immediacy."[1] They do this to emphasize that art or any other work is significant only in the context of life. Art is a way of self-understanding in the world and discovering bondedness to other things in life. In sum, aesthetics (art) in African thought is a way of appreciating and expressing bondedness in life or unity of all creation. Just as the self cannot be objectified or used but is appreciated with love and care, so do Africans treat nature with respect and care, for without it no life would be possible. An example is seen in the way Africans think of the forest.

The forest provides the African with all basic needs—food, materials for building a home, medicine, and rain; it also provides a sanctuary for religious practices as well and a home for the fugitive; in addition, it serves as a cemetery and the abode of ancestral spirits. In short, the forest is everything for the African. It is this understanding of belonging to one texture of life which gives Africans the sense of respect and care for creation. This sense of respect for nature is also grounded in the African notion of sanctity of life. This sanctity does not mean that nature is to be worshiped but that it is to be treated with respect, which means allowing life or the rhythms of life to flow—the course of life should not be interrupted. Since people belong to this fabric of life, human life is to be respected. Respect for human life encourages nature's process of growth and maturity. Furthermore, this respect is a charge to the community to create possibilities for persons to realize personhood. Nature is alive in the African world; it interacts with people but is not worshipped.

The African concept of person is grounded in the concept of life, which is the basis for understanding all creation and is a central, all-embracing and overarching notion informing a manner of living in the world. This sense of being connected, bonded in one common life informs human relationships and defines behavioral patterns. The African concept of community also arises from this understanding of bondedness to natural life or the feeling of being in the network of life. From this it follows that the ethical imperative is not to treat the other or nature as a means, since the other is also part of the self. People belong to each other, being bonded in one common life. Therefore consciousness is not consciousness of self but always consciousness of the flow of life in the community and world.

The debate on the African concept of person emerged to correct the Western misunderstanding of African thought and society. To put this debate in perspective calls for an outline of Western intellectual history, especially concerning its attitude toward other races. This chapter makes a critical analysis of the major works in the area.

Western scholars have long written on the African world, its social and religious institutions and practices. This work has been done mainly by sociologists and anthropologists. Interest in the African world and values has grown since the work of Lucien Lévy-Bruhl on what he called the "primitive mentality" of non-Western societies. The work of Lévy-Bruhl was to show the disparity between the European mind and "primitive mentality" as manifested in their value systems. He took this task to refute once and for all the ideas and claims of Thomas Hobbes on the equality of all races. The ideas of Hobbes very much informed the British school of anthropologists, whose main representatives included Edward B. Tylor, Herbert Spencer, James Frazer, and L. H. Morgan.

According to Tylor, there is some connection between all races in how they think, especially about the future. The development of humankind through the ages shows similarities in how different races think.[2] This understanding comes from Hobbes's conclusion in his studies concerning the "state of nature." Hobbes maintained that all people are "by nature equal. Nature hath made men so equal in the faculties of the body, and mind." Hobbes further stated that in a natural condition people are "savages" for they are ruled by passion and as a result, "every man is enemy of every man."[3] Hobbes considered passion as human nature. This passion was the source of the spirit of "competition, diffidence" and "glory"—basic causes of savage behavior.[4] Since people in their natural state are "savages," they look for the possibility to move forward from the "ill condition" in which nature has placed them.

It was upon Hobbes's views concerning the state of nature that Tylor maintained the idea that all races are basically the same and all have a potential for change. Lévy-Bruhl contended that Tylor and company are wrong, for there are two forms of mental operations in the world. These forms produce two types of societies and cultures. He maintained that in order to determine what form of mental operation was present in a particular culture, the value systems of the given culture had to be examined. Lévy-Bruhl's argument for this approach was that mental operations are sociologically determined and culturally bound. With this theory, Lévy-Bruhl fulfilled the theory of Spencer on social or organic evolution which holds that moral improvement is the extension of the concept of biological adaptation, and social well-being is equated with survival of the fittest. Spencer saw a relation between biological adaptation and moral progress. He argued that socially valuable behavior, once established, constitutes moral prescription as habits, then it translates into anatomical changes that are transmitted by inheritance.[5]

Lévy-Bryhl's project centered on how the mind works. The dominance on consciousness in Lévy-Bruhl's work reveals that he was influenced by the French school of ethnographers. The school's main interest was on how "primitive" people construe their world. In its attempts to understand the "primitive mind," the school studied myths, proverbs, and sayings of these people, on the consciousness, imagination and linguistic analysis of "primitive people." We will see how this approach influenced the study of the African world and the consequent formulation of the African concept of person. The French school included Lévi-Strauss and Marcel Griaule of Ecole des études hautes but who is also identified with the French Africanists school at the Musée de l'Homme in Paris, and Paul Rivet, director of Musée. French anthropologists were influenced by Jean-Jacques Rousseau's understanding of the "state of nature." Rousseau described the state of nature "as one of innocence," harmony, fellow feeling, and empathy, a time of happiness.[6] In the state of nature people were not self-conscious; consciousness appeared when people started to settle down in family groupings, with the concurrent self-interest, vanity, and competition. In other words, society is responsible for producing self-preservation; thus, egotism awakens passion which people did not know in the state of nature. For Rousseau, the state of war is not a natural outcome of conditions in the state of nature.

Hobbes maintains the opposite and finds it a basis for the need to have a social contract. For Rousseau, the idea of having a social contract has no basis in nature but in the ideal of freedom and equality. In other words, voluntary agreement is the only basis for political authority and obligation. Rousseau argues that the state of nature was the "happiest and most durable epoch . . . the best for man. . . . He must have come out of it by some fatal accident."[7]

Taking a cue from Spencer, and with the influence from the French anthropologists, Lévy-Bruhl developed a method of studying non-Western cultures. It was through these studies that he came to the conclusion that non-Western civilizations had no principle of identity, idea of causality or concept of time which according to Lévy-Bruhl, are the principles of (Western) logic. Non-Western societies therefore were "pre-logic," backward, thus his notion of "primitive mentality." In this way he credited Western mind with rationalist philosophy and positive science, while magic and superstition characterized "primitive mentality." According to Lévy-Bruhl, a European does not have to use much effort to use abstractions and simple logical operations, because everything has been made easy by the language. On the other hand, the thought and language of a "primitive" person are exclusively concrete. He therefore concluded that European mentality was "conceptual," while that of "primitive" people was not.[8]

Here Lévy-Bruhl continued Hegel's project of crediting rationality to the Western mind alone and setting Europeans above other societies.[9] Hegel provided the philosophical foundations of ethnocentricism in anthropology. Hegel's philosophy and Lévy-Bruhl's anthropological work were to have a great bearing on colonial ideology. A stage had now been set for Western culture to claim to be the prototype for true development, a hierarchy of values and a reference point for true civilization. Lévy-Bruhl's work stimulated Europeans in general, and French anthropology in particular, to study the value systems and "primitive mentality" of non-Western cultures. Among the "pre-logical" people in Lévy-Bruhl's work were "Negroes."[10] It was at this time in the history of Western intellectual thought that Europeans studied African ethnic, social and political institutions and religious beliefs. Much literature appeared as a result of these studies.[11] This literature entrenched the negative attitudes of whites toward Africans, whether they went to Africa as colonialists, traders, or missionaries. The objectivity of these studies was not at all questioned in the West. The general understanding about Africans was clear: Africans could not think in abstract terms, had no system of thought, and were interested in magic and superstition. In addition, they were biologically and morally inferior, and unprogressive and uncivilized as a result of their biological inferiority. Once in a while, a missionary would write something positive about African moral life which would repudiate popular views about Africans. The following quotation is an example of such missionary writings.

> Those of us who have lived any length of time in the country and who have been in close contact with native life in all its phases must have often been struck with the high tone of native morality amid their social surroundings, and bear testimony to the fidelity of the native women to their husbands. . . . Native morality must be gauged by the conditioning thing in the native villages—we claim to speak from some experience of native life in these parts (about Blantyre and Domasi) and during the period of welnigh 20 years we have never seen an immodest action on the part of native women or heard an immodest word. Could we say the same of any district in either England, Scotland or Ireland?
>
> How can anyone describe native moral code as "low" among a people where the crime of adultery is classed in the same category as that of murder, and must be atoned for by the price of life, and where the criminal caught in the act may be killed on the spot—"he is only a hyena!" Where temptations of polygamy are so strong, it has always been a marvel to us to find things as they are. That native ideas regarding the crime are not those of the Christian moralist we will at once admit. How could they be so? But that the crime of unfaithfulness is anyway condoned by either native thought or ethics we absolutely deny.[12]

Such writings did not change the general attitude toward Africans. The reports of missionaries failed to convince Western scholars who argued that missionaries did not analyze the African value system in its totality—they dealt only with aspects of a people's culture. In short, these reports failed to grasp the ontology and epistemology of the African world. Without a systematic study of African ontology, it was impossible to understand African thought and its magic. Consequently, their reports failed to present the real dynamics of "primitive mentality." Thus, missionary writings were dismissed as unscholarly since they did not reflect African metaphysics.

The first work in "defense" of the African world was by a Belgian missionary to Zaire, Fr. Placid Tempels, who belonged to the French school of anthropologists influenced by Jean-Jacques Rousseau. His work, *Philosophie Bantoe*, was published in 1945. We will begin our exploration of the African notions of life and person by examining Tempels's work.

PLACID TEMPELS'S BANTU ONTOLOGY

Placid Tempels's main project was to refute Lévy-Bruhl's theories on "primitive mentality" and the traditional (anthropological) use of such terms as mana, animism, fetishism, totemism, magic and dynamism to conceptualize African thought, society, and religion. Tempels rejected these, terms for they implied lack of knowledge of cause and effect on the part of Africans, and therefore a lack of ability to grasp abstract thought. He argued that these terms revealed nothing about Bantu epistemology, and were in fact misleading. He further charged that the disciplines which used these terms "have so often had vague ideas of, approached near to, or even touched upon, the fundamental concept of *Bantu* ontology. Yet we find scarcely any systematic study of this ontology."[13] He went on to say:

> To declare on *a priori* grounds that primitive peoples have no ideas on the nature of beings, that they have no ontology and that they are completely lacking in logic, is simply to turn one's back on reality. Everyday we are able to note that primitive peoples are by no means just children afflicted with a bizarre imagination. It is as men that we have learned to know them in their homes. Folklore alone and superficial descriptions of strange customs cannot enable us to discover and understand primitive man. Ethnology, linguistics, psychoanalysis, jurisprudence, sociology and the study of religions are able to yield definitive results only after the philosophy and the ontology of a primitive people have been thoroughly studied and written up.[14]

Tempels had two objectives to accomplish in his project: to accord Africans with rationality and to stop the influence of materialist philosophy on African society. In the first task, Tempels claimed to have both internal and external "evidence" which would earn Bantu ontology respect: that it was rational (in Western terms). With this "evidence" he would prove that Africans had a system of thought based on a different ontology, but nonetheless a clearly defined system of thought. In the second task, he wanted to show that Western civilization was guided by materialistic and positivist philosophy which were alien to African thought and would only destroy African culture. He considered the imposition of such a concept of the world as the "crime" of Western culture. "It is a crime against education to impose on a human race a civilization devoid of philosophy, devoid of practical wisdom and spiritual aspirations. It would be an even more serious crime to deprive a people of its own patrimony, of an heritage which alone can ensure their full human dignity, of the only good which can serve as the starting point for cultural development."[15]

In his enterprise Tempels sought to define the African world. Having defined African system of thought, he would establish possible foundations for the development of African civilization which hitherto had been rejected or relegated to an inferior status as "primitive" or pre-scientific. Tempels's hope was to save Africans from being corrupted by ideas of a civilization that confused having with being.[16] A true civilization is founded on a true knowledge of a people's world, said Tempels: "Does it not mean, first of all, a capacity for having a meaningful conception of the world and life, for having convictions as regards its purpose and for letting oneself be impregnated and fired with enthusiasm for this purpose. . . . What meaning does a civilization have, which is devoid of wisdom and of vital enthusiasm? How can one imagine a civilization deprived of philosophy, of an ideal of an inspiration?"[17]

Tempels had still another objective with his project. This goal was perhaps the most important to Tempels since it concerned the meaning of *mission civilisatrice*: Tempels wanted to provide Europeans with the basic dynamics of an African mind. "A better understanding of the field of Bantu thought is equally necessary for all those who are called to live among natives. Therefore this first concerns colonials, but more especially those who are charged with the administration and justice of the Blacks, all those who want to civilize, educate, raise the Bantus. But if this concerns all colonials of good will, it is addressed more particularly to missionaries."[18]

Tempels claimed to have discovered how the African mind works, how the African discerned values. By analyzing and synthesizing African thought and language patterns, he had discovered the working of the African mind and was able to put in words what the African was only dimly conscious of. "Let us not expect the Black in the street (especially if he is young) to give us a systematic account of his ontological system. Nevertheless, this ontology exists; it penetrates and informs all the 'primitive's' thinking and dominates all behavior. Using the methods of analysis and synthesis of our own intellectual disciplines, we can and therefore must do the 'primitive' the service of looking for, classifying and systematizing the elements of his ontological system."[19] Tempels had come to understand the African world so well that he was ready to do Africans "service": do for them what they could not do for themselves. In short, Africans did not know how to present their world, their epistemology, since they were not able to use Western abstract categories.

> We do not claim that Bantus are capable of presenting us with a philosophical treatise complete with an adequate vocabulary. It is our own intellectual training that enables us to effect its systematic development. It is up to us to provide them with an accurate account of their conception of entities, in such a way that they will recognize themselves in our words and will agree, saying: "You have understood us, you know us now completely, you 'know' in the same way we 'know.'"[20]

In his dealings with Africans he had come to "discover" that they operated on a principle different from the European mind: "What has been called magic, animism, ancestor-worship, or dynamism—in short, all the customs of the Bantu—depend upon a single principle, knowledge of the Inmost Nature of beings, that is to say, upon their Ontological Principle. For it is not by means of philosophical term that we must express their knowledge of being, of the existence of things."[21] He further claimed that "the key to Bantu thought is the idea of vital force, of which the source is God." Tempels meant that Africans experienced the world as an interrelation of forces. Force is the most fundamental term in African thought. "I believe that we should most faithfully render Bantu thought in the European language by saying that the Bantu speak, act, live as if, for them, beings were forces. Force is not for them an adventitious accidental reality. Force is more than a necessary attribute of beings: Force is the nature of being, force is being, being is force."[22]

For Tempels then, the African world was based on this theory of forces. It was this theory, so Tempels claimed, that made Africans equate being with power. The theory of forces influenced the different ways in which westerners and Africans perceived the world. Western epistemology considered power as an attribute of being while for the African to be was power—power was essence of being. Tempels explained:

> For the Bantu power is not an accident: it is more than a necessary accident; it is the very essence of being. . . . Being is power, power is being.
>
> Our notion of being is "that which is," theirs is "the power that is." When we think in terms of the concept of "being" they use the concept of "force." Where we see concrete beings, they see concrete forces. When we say that "beings" are differentiated by their essence or nature, Bantu say that "forces" differ in their essence or nature.
>
> They hold that there is divine force, celestial or terrestrial forces, human forces animal forces or mineral forces.[23]

Tempels claimed that force is everything in African thought and society, that the force concept dictates all relationships between people, and between people and God, and that it is the foundation of African ethics, law, psychology, and wisdom. In sum, all action is directed toward increasing vital force. He therefore concluded: "The key principle of Bantu philosophy is that of vital force. The activating and final aim of all Bantu effort is only the intensification of vital force. To protect it or to increase vital force, that is the motive and the profound meaning in their practices. It is the ideal which animates the life of the 'muntu,' it is the only reality . . . the only thing for which he is ready to suffer and to sacrifice himself."[24] Tempels also says that in this universe of forces, humankind is central. He writes: "The Created Universe is centered on man. The present human generation living on earth is the center of all humanity, including the world of the dead."[25] People are interrelated to different forces in the cosmos. This idea of interrelatedness of forces captures how Bantus conceive the world. This is to say that Africans "cannot conceive a man as an individual existing by himself, unrelated to animate and inanimate forces surrounding him. It is not sufficient to say he is a social being; he feels himself a vital force in actual intimate and permanent rapport with other forces—a vital force both influenced by and influencing them."[26]

Having claimed an elevated system of thought for Africans, with its own "local color," as he put it, Tempels established a relation of identity between African spirituality and Christian theology as follows: "We arrive, therefore, at the unheard of conclusion, that Bantu paganism, the ancient wisdom of the Bantu, reaches out from the depths of its Bantu soul toward the very soul of Christian spirituality."[27]

The conclusions of Tempels analysis may be summarized as follows:

1. Tempels deals with the category of essence. He claims that in Bantu thought *l'être est force* (being equals force).[28] Therefore, to say something exists is to

imply that something exercises as a specific force. Therefore "existence of anything is in its being a force." In general, Tempels's work is full of Thomist ideas and analysis.

2. "Every force is specific." This implies that there is no Western dynamism and energetism in African thought. Furthermore, cosmic forces do not penetrate every existent. This means that the specificity of the forces is an indivisible individuality, or what Tempels calls radical individuality, which may come about as a result of a force combination.

3. From assertion 2 it follows that "different types of beings are characterized by different intensities and types of force." However, each force can be strengthened or weakened. Tempels interprets all Bantu action and practice as an attempt at strengthening vital force. His comment about Bantu knowledge affirms this: "All knowledge is to the Bantu knowledge of forces and takes into account the general laws of growth and influence."[29]

4. The forces are not static; there is always an interaction between the forces. In this interaction they can influence and act upon each other. This interaction of forces is based on a metaphysical of forces or immutable laws of an ontological system. It is in light of the interdependence of forces that Tempels introduces the Bantu idea of human dependence on the creator: "the creature is, by its very nature, permanently dependent on its creator for its existence."

5. The universe is a hierarchical order of forces arranged according to their strengths. God is at the apex as maximum of forces. The come spirits and divinities, founders of various clans, ancestors or the living dead of each tribe, and the living. The living are stratified "not only by law but in accordance with their being, with primogeniture and their organic degree of life, in other words with their vital power."[30] Animals, plants and minerals are at the bottom of the hierarchy. This hierarchical order allows beings of higher rank to influence those below them; however, beings of equal rank (force)—people for example—can weaken or strengthen each other. Tempels also claims that the theory of hierarchy of forces is the foundation of social order, the hierarchy of forces is actually the metaphysic bedrock upon which the Bantu social structure stands.

The theory of forces and essence is very important to Tempels, for it gives him the basis for formulating Bantu ontology from which arises Bantu wisdom (Chapter 3), Bantu psychology (Chapter 4) and Bantu ethics (Chapter 5). The vital force ontology becomes the foundation on which he develops the Bantu notion of *muntu*, or the Bantu concept of person. To begin with, he states that in Bantu philosophy, creation is centered on people, the living generation, "for the living, earthly human generation is the center of all humankind, including the world of the dead." Second, Tempels defines the Bantu concept of person, *muntu*, which is a force principle and as such can be weakened or strengthened. However, *muntu* is free to act in accordance with or opposition to the hierarchy of the universe. He concludes by saying that "the Bantus see in man the living force; the force of being who possesses life in its truest, most complete, most elevated form."

Apart from this freedom Tempels gives no other human qualities. Freedom is one of the two forms of transformations which Rousseau postulates. The first transformation is of human nature that comes when consciousness emerges in the state of nature. The second transformation lies in the possibility for the future or destiny, a possibility that stands on individual freedom when people, as individuals and equals, freely accept political obligation. To be precise, for Rousseau, freedom is the capacity to be self-governed or self-regulated: the ability to formulate rules and be governed by them as required by one's true interests. Tempels follows this idea of self-governance and self-regulation when he cites freedom as the essential and only quality Bantu attribute to *muntu*. By appropriating the concept of freedom, Tempels brings into the Bantu world a Western philosophical problem, namely, the age-old problem of freedom and destiny (determinism versus indeterminism). One of the twentieth-century Western theologians who has reflected on this problem is Paul Tillich. His work may help to put into perspective what Tempels was trying to achieve by attributing freedom only to people and not other forces or things. This is how Tillich re-opens the problem: "The human being is human because he has freedom, but he has freedom only in polar interdependence with destiny. . . . The human experiences the structure of the individual as the bearer of freedom within the larger structure to which individual structure belongs. Destiny points to this situation in which the human finds him or herself; facing the world to which, at the same time, he belongs."[31] Tillich then goes on to discuss determinism.

> The traditional discussion of determinism and indeterminism necessarily is inclusive because it moves on the level on which the polarity of freedom and destiny lies. Both conflicting parties presuppose that there is a *thing* among other things called "will," which may or may not have the quality of freedom. But by definition of a *thing* as a completely determined object lacks freedom. The *freedom* of a *thing* is a contradiction in terms. Therefore determinism is always right in this kind of discussion; but it is right because, in the last analysis, it expresses the tautology that a thing is a thing. Indeterminism protests against deterministic thesis, pointing to the fact that the moral and the cognitive consciousness presupposes the power of responsible decision. However, when it draws the consequences and attributes freedom to an object or function called "will," indeterminism falls into a contradiction in terms and inescapably succumbs to the deterministic tautology. Indeterministic freedom is the negation of deterministic necessity.[32]

Is this not revealing why Tempels claimed freedom the quality only people have? Tillich shows us why freedom is important to understanding of persons. He regards freedom and destiny as ontological polarities of being a person.

> Destiny is not a strange power which determines what shall happen to me. It is myself as given, formed by nature, history, and myself. My destiny is the basis of

> my freedom; my freedom participates in shaping my destiny.
>
> Only he who has freedom has destiny. Things have no destiny because they have no freedom. God has no destiny because he *is* freedom. . . . Man is man because he has freedom, but he has freedom only in polar interdependence with destiny.[33]

With the concept of freedom, Tempels fails to give foundation for the importance of *muntu* in creation. Even his discussion of radical individuality of forces fails to capture the importance of *muntu* in African thought.[34] Tempels treats *muntu* as a center of forces that exists in relation to other forces—*muntu* acts and is acted upon. For Tempels understanding *muntu* as an aggregate of forces explains for him, humankind's relation with the external world or creation. It is important to note here that *muntu* is not essence in Tempels's ontology, but is force. Tempels describes *muntu* in a purely Hegelian metaphysic of exteriority and interiority; that is to say, *muntu* is considered as having internal forces which respond to or have resonance with external forces.

The force ontology leads Tempels to understand Bantu ethics intensifying what he calls the "life force" of *muntu* or of one's group. In the force metaphysic, evil is the decrease of life force of *muntu*. Tempels gives three understandings of evil all of which are quasi Nietzschean: it can be committed (1) intentionally, better understood by Nietzsche's concept of "resentment," (2) as a result of provocation, and (3) unwillingly.

Tempels's vital force thesis has been rejected by some African scholars while others have modified and re-interpreted it. Among those who have rejected it are John Mbiti, Tshimalenga, Theophilus Okere, p'Bitek, Vincent Mulago, and Fabian Eboussi Boulaga. Mbiti simply says:

> The book is primarily Tempels's personal interpretations of the Baluba, and it is ambitious to call it "Bantu Philosophy" since it only deals with one people among whom he had worked for many years as missionary. It is open to a great deal of criticism, and the theory of "vital force" cannot be applied to other African peoples with whose life and ideas I am familiar. The main contribution of Tempels is more in terms of sympathy and change of attitude than perhaps in actual contents and theory of the book.[35]

Mbiti comments on Tempels's motive for writing: "His motive and that of the fellow colonialists whom he addresses, is 'to civilize, educate and raise the Bantu.'" Beyond this, Mbiti says nothing more.

Tshiamalenga agrees with Mbiti: "In effect, Tempels's method is simply one of sympathy (*einfuhlung*) and communion with Luba Shaba behavior, a method of rapid and superficial comparison, and premature generalization. If it is clear that sympathy can allow a hypothesis, that cannot mean that the latter is founded."[36] P'Bitek rejects Tempels's generalization of what he found to be Baluba: "Tempels invites us to accept this thought-system, not only as Bantu but as African. Can serious . . . scholars concerned with correct appraisal and analysis of African beliefs and philosophy afford this kind of generalization?"[37]

Mulago sympathizes with Tempels. Mulago's criticisms of Tempels are in an article in which he is trying to break from Tempels's influence—the vital force thesis. Unfortunately, Mulago does not succeed because of two problems: (1) his earlier interest in Tempels's analysis which keep reappearing throughout the text, and (2) he has not made a break with his Thomist/Aristotelian background. Mulago's mild criticism of Tempels appears in two footnotes in the article "Vital Participation." In the first footnote he states that Tempels's conclusion may be philosophically unsound but could be justified from a phenomenological viewpoint.[38] In another footnote Mulago rejects Tempels's assertion that being equals force: "For the Bantu there is no interaction of being with being, that is to say, of *force* with *force*."[39] Mulago contends that this assertion is wrong: "We do not agree that being and force are identical and interchangeable." He rejects this idea as foreign to Bantu thought.

Theophilus Okere argues that the whole force theory is alien to African thought. He charges that the force theory is the theory of magic revived at a higher level. He contends:

> In short, *La Philosophie Bantoue* is the theory of magic promoted to ontological status. What the author has called philosophy is hardly a *Weltanschauung*: no customs, rites, myths, or theologies are presented in a coordinated fashion or even described individually at length. *La Philosophie Bantoue* is *Bantu* only in as far as the author takes the scattered examples he invokes to prop his theory from the *Bantu* among whom he lived. The theory could well have been formulated on Oceania or Melanesia and the author freely generalises about *Bantu* or all primitives, that is, magical societies without discrimination.[40]

Okere further argues:

> The essence of Tempels's revolution is thus the systematic substitution of the word "force" wherever one formerly read "magic" or indeed wherever one formerly read "mana" in the theories of religion and magic formulated by the rationalist-evolutionist school of ethnology. The result reads like the application sometimes of Newton's Mechanics, sometimes of scholastic philosophy to Frazer's theory of magic. . . . It would seem here, too, "force" pervades everything, invades all departments of life. Knowledge is force, value is force, sickness is a loss of force. Primogeniture is force, hunting is trail of force. There is force all over. The term explains so many things that one has the right to suspect that perhaps it really explains nothing. When a word becomes so overworked, it is probable that it has lost all its force.[41]

Boulaga also has rejected the life force thesis, accusing Tempels of not defining force or giving concrete evidence for his construction.[42] Boulaga calls Tempels's project a "doubly interpreted misinterpretation." He further charges that the concept is ambiguous: if being equals force, then the universe must be completely static, for the possibility of change becomes nonexistent. He argues that the result of Tempels's force would be a complete amoralism, for force is the refusal of reason. Boulaga points out that in Bantu thought there are good and evil forces; therefore Tempels's notion of force defining its value is false.

Boulaga argues that an ontology based uniquely on force is inadequate and contradictory. He says that the contradictions in Tempels's work can ultimately be reduced to "an interplay of value and counter value . . . which characterizes the colonizer's judgments on the colonized. Bantuism is partly admirable and partly abominable. It is valuable when the colonized wish to forsake it for equality: then they are reminded that when they are losing their 'souls.' But Bantuism becomes a vile hotchpotch of degenerate magical practices when the colonizer wishes to affirm his pre-eminence and legitimize his power."[43] In general, Boulaga considers Tempels's project ideological, that is, as a representative of colonial force making its last ditch attempt to save the colonial system by preventing real political liberation by means of an ideological liberation. Boulaga's charge is supported by Tempels's own paternalistic views that (1) he is doing Africans a service by writing about their philosophy and (2) he knows Africans more than they know themselves.

Tempels has been accused of introducing an abstraction, a diversion from the concrete historical reality of the people of the Belgian Congo. In the first place, Tempels blinds people from the real issues of colonial economic domination. He does this by introducing ethnocentrism or what he claims to be the world of the Baluba or Bantu ontology. After he has pulled Bantu ontology from his hat, he quickly claims the white person belongs to the Bantu world. He then claims that Bantu ontology puts the white person in a higher position according to the hierarchy of forces. It is strange that a white person, a new phenomenon in the Bantu world, could be understood by Bantu categories, "incorporated into the world of forces, in the position that was his by right according to the rationale of Bantu ontological system . . . an elder a superior human force greater than the vital force of any black man."[44] It is in light of the idea of white superiority that Aimé Césaire makes a biting criticism of Tempels's Bantu ontology:

> Bantu thought being ontological, Bantus are interested only in ontological satisfaction. Decent wages? Good housing and food? I tell you these Bantus are pure spirits: "What they want above all is not an improvement in their material or economic situation, but recognition by the white man and respect for their human dignity, for their full human value." In short, one or two cheers for Bantu vital force, a wink for the Bantu immortal soul, and that's that. A bit too easy, perhaps?[45]

These charges have been rejected by the Cameroonian Johannes Fabian. In his defense of Tempels, Fabian has cited Tempels's commitment to social change by recounting his missionary life and his subsequent rejection by his superiors and formation of the *Jamaa* (brotherhood) movement, which aimed at bettering Bantu community life.[46] Fabian, however, agrees with Boulaga that Tempels's vital force lacks concrete evidence.

It appears to me that Tempels has failed to understand the central thought in the African world. The organizing power in the African world, or what he calls the key principle of Bantu ontology, cannot be described by the concept of vital force but by life. The concept of life is at the end of this chapter. Second, Tempels admits that *muntu* is at the center of Bantu thought. He writes: "The Bantus see in man *the* living force; the force of the being who possesses life in its truest, most complete, most elevated form." Inspite of this awareness, Tempels's theory of forces does not put *muntu* at the center of things until Tempels moves from ontology to psychology and describes how the Bantu construe the world, Tempels places *muntu* at the center only in the case of the theory of being.

One of Tempels's main reasons for writing Bantu ontology was the desire to show a closeness between Bantu and Christian worlds, but his concept of force failed to show that closeness at three points: on the concept of God as creator, on divine immutability, and on the meaning of the Incarnation.

1. God in Christianity is a creator. To make this claim is to put God before anything else. Following his Bantu ontology, Tempels identifies the divine mystery as a God-force. As a God-force, God's existence would have to begin, and this is what Tempels seems to claim when he says God is the originator, the divine being itself. That would imply that God is not "the one who was" of the Christian teaching. With this claim, Tempels has not only failed the Christian understanding of the divine mystery but also misrepresented African thought by equating the divine with force.

Africans maintain that the divine is the Eternal or Great Spirit. God is the active, creative spirit: the one who piles up rocks to make mountains, causes branches to grow, and gives rain to humankind.[47] This is the life-giving spirit, the one the Ashanti refer to as "the fathomless Spirit" (implying that the divine mystery is immeasurable or simply the immeasurable One), whom the Bakongo calls "the Marvel of Marvels" (the incomprehensible One) whom the Ngombe call *Endalandala* (the Unexplainable),[48] and the Massai call "*Ngai*" (the Unknown).[49] God is unknown because the divine mystery cannot be named. In African society to name is to describe personality or basic nature. Since divine personality and nature cannot be described or captured by human language and categories, then the Divinity is unknown. In African thought and language the Divinity is simply referred to as the Giver of life, meaning the Divinity is the beginning. This is more clearly expressed in my language, Chichewa. The Malawian attributes for the divine mystery include such terms as *Chisumphi* (spring or fountain of life), *Namalenga* (maker of life), and *Mulungu* (creator of life). The Divinity is the beginning; nothing was or will be beyond the Divinity. That is why the *Bashi* call the Divinity *Nyamuzinda* (the One who is at the end of everything). The idea that the Divinity is the limit, the beyond point after which nothing exists, is expressed by a traditional Mbuti hymn:

In the beginning was God,
Today is God,
Tomorrow will be God.
Who can make an image of God?
The one who has no body.
The one who is a word which comes out of your mouth.
That word! It is no more,
It is past, and still lives!
So is God.[50]

The hymn and all these "names" of God above illustrate that Tempels has misrepresented African ideas of the Divinity.

2. Tempels's second failure is related to the Christian teaching that God is self-sufficient. When the divine mystery is referred to as God-force, then the idea of self-sufficiency cannot be applied to God. Forces in Tempels's Bantu ontology are interrelated and interdependent. This means God, being a force, would depend on other forces. Therefore, the immutability of God would not be present.

3. Tempels's Bantu ontology, with its concept of vital force, undermines the centrality of the Incarnation. To bring the issue of the Incarnation into Tempels's theory of force is not to introduce a category outside the theory or to impose on Africans a foreign idea. This category is implicit in Tempels's theory, for he states that his principal objective is to provide a guide for those who would work in Africa—colonizers and Christian missionaries—to reach the African "soul." Missionaries could not proclaim the Gospel without reference to Jesus; the Incarnation is too central to the Christian faith. It is therefore necessary to discuss the Incarnation, although this is not a category present in Bantu thought, at least not in the way Christianity appropriates it.

The concept of vital force would imply that the Incarnation would not be possible or that if possible, the power of Jesus could be limited or changed by people. According to the theory of vital force, *muntu* is a center of forces or a force principle and as such acts and is acted upon. Furthermore, *muntu* can have his or her vital force increased or diminished based on the principle of the hierarchy of forces. Christ as *muntu* would be limited in His power therefore of no use to anybody for redemption.[51] Tempels used Rousseau's idea without developing it within the framework of human relations as Rousseau himself did.

KAGAME'S PHILOSOPHY OF BEING

Tempels's Bantu ontology was followed by other writings, the most important those of Alex Kagame, advanced Tempels's concept of vital force. Informed by the categories of Plato, Aristotle, and Kant, he developed a theory of semantic analysis that he applied to his native tongue, Banyarwanda. Kagame believed that by appropriating Kantian categories (which are informed by Aristotle) he would arrive at categories of African cultures and thus at a philosophy of his own people. In short, he wanted to follow up and verify Tempels thesis of vital force by exploring the world of his people. Kagame explains his aim as "to verify the validity of the theory of force advanced by this excellent missionary."[52]

The main source of his project was his language.[53] He studied its syntax, semantics, proverbs, and poems, and the socio-political institutions of the Kinyarwanda (Rwandese people). In his study of the categories of Banyarwanda he distinguished 11 categories, or word classes, which he correlated.[54] Kagame states that a word has four main parts: a prefix (a vowel), the determinative, the radical (which signifies the abstract), and the suffix. The classification of words begins with the determinative. In Banyarwanda, words with the determinative *-mu-* in their singular form and *-ba-* in their plural are in the category of people. In other words, *-mu-ba-* class is used only in reference to people. The determinatives *-ki-bi-* refer to inanimate objects. The class of determinatives *-ha-de* (determinatives of place), is used for locating things or people. The determinative *-ku-* signifies modalities of being. These four classes of determinatives stand for four types of being. All of them have the radical *-ntu-*, which in Kagame's analysis signify being.[55] The radical *-ntu-* is the all pervasive vital force of Tempels. However, Kagame, unlike Tempels, does not include the Divinity in his vital force theory. For Kagame the vital force thesis is concerned with humankind and the living and non-living things in creation for the enhancement of human life. He says that "God is not the end of humankind, God is not the purpose of human life. The end of the universe is humankind, and the end of humankind is its own eternity through procreation."[56] *Immana* (the source of all good and happiness—the Divinity) is absolutely transcendental. Kagame further claims that the conception of the Divinity among his people does not show any analogy between the existence of beings in the universe and the existence of the Divinity.

Kagame's four categories of words or categories represent four (Aristotelian) essences. Having given the type of essences, Kagame matches his categories with Aristotle's categories of substance.

Kagame	Aristotle
Umuntu—human being	substance
Ikuntu—non-human being	substance
Ushantu	time
Ukuntu	quantity, quality, relation, action, passion, position, possession

In Aristotle's analysis, people and things belong to the same category of substance. But we see above that Kagame has split Aristotle's substance into two in such a way that the two sides are no longer the same, although they belong to one category of substance. Kagame puts people in a primary status within Aristotle's substance because people have intelligence, which allows them to use other things in nature to enhance their lives. Kagame seeks to emphasize that *ibintu* (things) are defined only in relation to *abantu* (people). Kagame says he puts *abantu* in a primary status because they are a unique species.

> Some Europeans have taken great pleasure in the "naivete" of the Bantus, when asked "*Umuntu ni iki?*" ("What is man?"). Called upon to give the definition of the being endowed with intelligence, our Bantus, after much embarrassment, ended by answering: "*Umuntu, ni umuntu nyine*!" ("Man"), precisely, is which meant something like this: "By formulating the question, you have yourself given the answer, and it is impossible to explain further! You have stated the genus and the unique species! What would you answer if you were asked: 'What is the rational animal (i.e. man)?'"[57]

A question correctly stated gets a right answer. The "naivete" Kagame speaks about lies in the question itself, therefore, a proper answer should not be expected. The question presupposes a common understanding of the world between the person asking and the respondent, which in fact does not exist.

Kagame does not give a classification of essences but classifies types of existence. It is important to note how he analyzes the verb to be in Banyarwanda. He tells us that there is not a single term that denotes being. Instead radicals *-li-* and *-ba-* are used, and they have to be completed by an object to make sense. He points out that even then, these radicals are never used to denote to exist. He emphasizes that radicals *-ba-* and *-li-* are used only in reference to terrestrial beings. In short, Kagame asserts that among his people "existence is localized action, either continuous or discontinuous."[58]

Kagame struggles with the issues of essence and existence in order to emphasize the importance of two categories, namely, *muntu* and *kintu*. Kagame does not reach the same conclusions as Tempels that being equals force; he restates the formula by saying that being (if it is substance) equals *muntu* or *kintu*. What distinguishes the two substances is consciousness. Kagame puts it in this way: *muntu* characterized by consciousness has faculties which enables her or him to use other objects. On the other hand, *kintu* has properties which enables *muntu* to use it and act upon. Kagame says: "The independent form of matter is principle of activity and the simple substantial form is principle of substantiality. Thanks to these forms, a being that has intelligence can use properties of all beings who do not have intelligence."[59]

It seems that Kagame is unaware of his dependence on Cartesian epistemology. Consciousness and reason which distinguish people from inanimate objects in Cartesian epistemology, but Kagame argues that he takes this way to show the difference between being alive and existing.[60] Kagame says plants exist, that is to say, they do not have life; animals too do not have life, although they are "life."[61] To be alive, for Kagame, is to have the principle of *magora*, that is, intelligence. He argues that this principle is typically human.[62] However, people share a principle with the animal world, *ubuzima*, the unity of matter with the life principle. Kagame concludes that it is the union of *amagora* and *ubuzima* that characterize humankind.[63] Finally, Kagame asserts that the foundation of Kinyarwanda philosophy is the conception of *muntu*, the existent endowed with intelligence. According to Rwandan philosophy, all other living or non-living beings are placed at the service of humankind to strengthen human life force and procreative ability. "*Ibintu ni iby abantu: . . . personne ne vous dira que suivant notre philosophie traditionelle Dieu ait été considéré comme fin ultime des êtres*." (In our traditional philosophy is it not said that God is always considered the ultimate of beings?)[64]

KAGAME AND TEMPELS: A COMPARISON

There are several points at which Kagame agrees with the "excellent missionary." In the first place, both assert that African institutions and culture are based on a collective philosophy, consciously recognized by every African. Kagame puts it in these words: "Philosophical principles . . . are invariable: since the nature of beings must always remain what it is, their profoundest explanation is inevitably immutable."[65] Second, Kagame also agrees with Tempels on the "sources" of their philosophical enterprises. Kagame writes: "We shall have to resort to a kind of institutionalized record. . . . Even if the formal structure of these 'institutions' is not the expression of philosophical entity, it may be shown to be a direct consequence of a mode of formulating problems within the purview of philosophy."[66] However, among the "institutionalized records," Kagame used only linguistic analysis of the Banyarwanda.

Both Kagame and Tempels have followed Aristotelian-scholastic philosophy and categories, ecclesiastical scholasticism to be specific, thereby claiming that European concepts can be used to understand other cultures. In other words, European categories form the common denominator in understanding how other races construe the world. We also find this approach in the work of Vincent Mulago[67] and the other followers of Tempels. The result of using European categories (Aristotelian in this case) to understand the African world has been a philosophy that resembles the thought of a given African people—for example, the Baluba—but is in fact alien to those people and difficult to verify. It is difficult to verify because it is the philosophy of the particular writer and not of the people the author claims to represent. If people cannot see themselves in a given work, then that work does not represent them. We do not find it strange that a given people cannot identify themselves with a philosophy that bears their name for this "philosophy" is not intended for "home consumption," it is for people abroad from whom are received the "tools of the trade!"

Even with a very systematic and rigorous work such as that of Kagame, the African is lost in Aristotelian language and categories. An example of such categories is the celebrated *ntu* of Kagame, claimed "as representative of a philosophy which extends throughout all Africa. The majority of the ideas reflecting the African art of living are found in the *Ntu* philosophy."[68] The main argument in favor of the use of *ntu* is that it shows the unity of the African world, thereby enabling writers to reject the subject-object duality of Western thought. Mulago explains why some consider *ntu* as a fundamental category of African philosophy. "The dynamology of the *ntu* is around them; beings interact with one another through 'being' influences which establish the increase or diminution of the beings. This is true above all the *ntu* who are in contact through some of their belongings."[69]

Janhein Jahn also maintains the dynamism of *ntu*. He considers it to be "the universal force . . . which however, never occurs apart from its manifestations: *muntu*, *Kintu*, *Hantu* and *kuntu*. *Ntu* is the being itself, and cosmic universal force. . . . *Ntu* is that force which being and coalesce. . . . *Ntu* expresses, not the effect of these forces, but their being. But the forces act continually, and are constantly effective."[70] According to Jahn, this force *ntu* would be known only if the whole world came to a standstill. Jahn was never in Africa. He writes from what he has read about Africa from various sources. On the section on African philosophy he is informed by Tempels's force ontology and he also adopts Kagame's categories.

What is forgotten or not realized by Mulago, Jahn, and all who consider *ntu* a central category of African thought is that Kagame based his analysis on the structures of Aristotle. In other words, *ntu,* though African, is actually within the structures of Aristotle. If we take a basic structure of anything, we must also take the constitutive elements. This means that a philosophy informed or ordered by the *ntu* category must be understood within the Aristotelian structure. Such a philosophy cannot be properly called a Bantu philosophy; it is an Aristotelian philosophy couched in Bantu thought and language. Thus Mulago, Kagame, Tempels, and their followers remain caught in Lévy-Bruhl's theory and application of "primitive mentality." Put simply, Tempels's project was part of the European ethnophilosophy that started with Hegel and was continued by Lévy-Bruhl. In turn it produced an African ethnophilosophy whose first subscribers were Kagame and Mulago. Tempels and his followers set up the West and its categories as the norm for understanding all the races. The African world can only be understood by using African concepts. Anything short of that cannot give us a true understanding of the African world.[71]

Other themes that are found in these philosophers include Bantu concepts of the Divinity and person. Kagame rejects the idea that the Divinity is a substance as Tempels maintains, but he shares Tempels's view that the Divinity is the begetter of people rather than their natural parents. Kagame also agrees with Tempels that the Divinity is the author of personal destiny. Furthermore, Kagame and Tempels share the idea that in Bantu thought persons are understood as indivisible units. This is unlike the West, where the concept of person includes the understanding that a person is a compound of body and soul. To emphasize this difference, Kagame asserts that among his people, the Kinyarwanda, no word exists for soul as long as a person is still alive. One wonders whether he has not been misled by Western thought, Christianity in particular for even when a person is dead, he or she does not get a soul in Kinyarwanda. Spirit is human life that has been transformed to transcend death and it takes the personality of the particular individual from whom it has been released. Therefore spirits are addressed by name. A soul has no personality. In African prayers, spirits are invoked by their names—these are names of particular persons who died—because they have personalities.[72] It appears that the concept of soul is a foreign idea among a number of African peoples.

Mulago also fails us too at this point, for Like Kagame, he follows the Christian teaching and scholastic philosophy and speaks of soul. He quotes P. Colle's "The Bashi Notion of the Disincarnate Soul":

> We may affirm with the author quoted above that the Bashi, the Banyarwanda and the Barundi, are not spirituality philosophers, since they recognize in humans a spirit distinct from matter, a suprasensible spirit which is free, responsible, and immortal, but further, spiritualists of rigorous sort since they implicitly presuppose in living beings, in humans above all, the existence of matter and form. For at bottom the *muzimu* for them is none other than the form which animated what has now become a corpse.[73]

Does not Mulago, through Colle, here tell us that *muzimu* is what in scholastic language is known as "the substantial form of the body?" How different is Mulago's analysis from scholasticism? Does *muzimu* mean soul or spirit? Or is Mulago using soul and spirit interchangeably? In connection with the concept of person Tempels claims that it is the notion of freedom which distinguishes a person from other creatures. Kagame, on the other hand, argues that it is intelligence that sets *muntu* apart from *ibintu* (inanimate things). In this claim Kagame has recalled the Cartesian epistemology.

While Kagame's project has many similarities with the work of Tempels, there are some differences. Kagame rejects Tempels's main thesis that being and power are central categories of Bantu thought. Without mentioning Tempels by name, Kagame argues that it is wrong to claim that the difference between European and Bantu philosophies lies in their conception of being: that being is static in European thought while it is dynamic in Bantu philosophy. He says that when considering the ontologies of European and Bantu cultures the main issue is not motion (dynamic) or rest (static) of being. The subject matter is the same—being, but considered in two different ways.

While Kagame has rejected Tempels's thesis, he has also claimed Bantu and European thought use the same categories with only "a slight nuance" between them. The "slight nuance" is the idea that European thought understands being as static while in the Bantu world being is dynamic but the two remain complementary and inseparable in mode of thought. Kagame states:

In both systems, indeed, there are inevitably a static and a dynamic aspect at the same time.

1. Any structure, considered apart from its finality, must appear static.
2. If you then consider a structure as having an end, as being structurally oriented to action or being used for an end, that structure will present its dynamic aspect.

It therefore follows that if the philosophy of Bantu culture is called dynamic, it must be remembered it is in the first place static. If the philosophy of the European culture is described as static, it must not be forgotten that it is in the second place dynamic. Let me summarize these two correlative aspects in a double axiom:

1. Operational predisposition presupposes essence.
2. Essence is structured in terms of its finality.[74]

Here Kagame reduces African thought to a common ground with European philosophy, thereby making European categories a common denominator for understanding different worlds. Kagame admits inspired by Aristotle's work. Kagame wanted to do for his people what Aristotle did for the Greeks, namely, to ground the world of Kinyarwanda in their language just as Aristotle had grounded Greek metaphysics in structures of Greek language. But Kagame overlooks the fact that Aristotle's project had a broader aim: it was intended to transcend the contingencies given by language structure itself and then claim universality of ideas and categories. Aristotle hoped to transcend the contingencies by grounding Greek language in a universal and necessary order.

ON THE IDEA OF SOUL

A number of African philosophers claim to have the concept of soul in their societies. Bussia, Danquah, Gyekye, and Wiredu, for example, say that among the Akan, there is a tripartite concept of the person: *okra* (soul), *sunsum* (spirit) and *honom* (body). *Okra* is the divine spark in humans, which one receives from the father at conception. This is the principle of life and that part of the human concerned with destiny. *Sunsum* on the other hand, is personality and character. Gyekye says that *sunsum* may be understood as "part—the active part—of the *okra*."[75] *Okra* and *sunsum* form a constitutive unity which transcends death.

A tripartite division of the human is not present among the different ethnic groups of Malawi. Among the Achewa, Yao, Tumbuka, and other language groups, the human has *thupi* (body) and *mzimu* (spirit). *Mzimu* is the principle of life, the divine element in people, which is able to transcend death. The heart is considered the seat of feeling and consciousness, those elements that make up personality or the characteristics of *umunthu* (personhood). Accordingly, people speak of one having a good or bad heart, cold (calm) or hot (temper) heart. It is the heart which gives one individuality. More important, the heart houses *mzimu*, that lives after the heart stops in death. After death, *mzimu* embodies the personality of the heart as its identity. Thus people speak of the spirit of the deceased being incarnated in a newborn. Among Malawians there does seem to exist a term for soul; it is always translated *mzimu* (spirit).

The Malawian concept of person does not regard the brain as the seat of consciousness. Although thinking is understood as the function of the brain, learning or internalizing is the function of the heart. It is from this understanding that, to translate conscience, missionaries coined the term *chikumbumtima*. The term is a combination of the verb *kumbu* (dig), and the noun *mtima* (heart). Missionaries explained conscience as an act of digging within one's heart. Memory and feeling form conscience, so Malawians associate with functions of the heart.

The Malawian concept of person as composed of physico-material (with emotion and thinking attached to functions of the body) and spirit seems to be similar, in some ways, to the Yoruba. Segun Gbadegesin tells us that the Yoruba concept of person includes *Ara*, "the physico-material part of the human being," and *Okàn* (heart), "the physical organ for circulation of blood emotional and psychic reactions"; while *èmí* is the spirit from Olódùmarè, the supreme deity; and *orí* (head), the seat of the brain and bearer of destinies.[76] The Yoruba do not speak of the soul either.

Among the Ghanian philosophers mentioned above, there is a debate over the nature and role of *okra* and *sunsum*. Following the debate, one begins to wonders whether there is really an etymological or ontological difference in these terms, or if the differences do not lie in their lexical usage. It is important to note that African philosopher-theologians such as Kagame and Mulango, who have claimed the existence of soul among their people, have been greatly influenced by Aristotelian categories. This makes one ask: are these scholars not forcing Aristotelian (or Thomist) Christian categories into African thought? It appears that the terms soul and heaven have appeared only with Christianity. Boulaga reminds us that the concept of soul in Christianity goes hand in hand with its understanding of persons as individuals. "The expansion of the individual comes before all else. This is the absolute value. All other things shall pass—individuals alone shall abide, in immortal individuality, in their souls. The aim of faith is to save souls, to immortalize that individuality."[77] Here Boulaga contends that the doctrine of soul emphasizes the Western concept of individualism; soul is the abstract form of individualism.

THE AFRICAN CONCEPT OF LIFE

The theory of force is the thesis of Tempels's project. From this theory come the terms that are used indiscriminately and interchangeably such as force, vital force, life force, and being. Of these terms, force and vital force are dominant and controlling terms used almost like magic words. For Tempels these words mean everything in the Bantu world; they are connected with power and knowledge in Bantu thought and key to understanding the Bantu concept of person. Force, Tempels claims, has to do with the increase and decrease of life; it has to do with human happiness: "The supreme happiness, the only kind of good fortune, is for the Bantu the possession of the fullest vital potency. The worst adversity and, indeed, the only kind of misfortune is for him the diminution of this power. Every sickness, affliction or adversity, each injustice and every frustration is all regarded and described by the Bantu as a diminution of the vital force."[78] The decrease of life is what Bantus fear most, claims Tempels. By implication, Tempels alleges that the Bantu world is one of fear, a world in which the main preoccupation is the manipulation of forces to increase one's life force. Tempels promotes the idea of European anthropologists such as Lévy-Bruhl that the African world is one of magic and so is African religion.[79]

Tempels's theory of forces fails to grasp a basic framework of interpretation in the Bantu world: the theory reduces the Divinity, people, and everything else to force. Furthermore, it claims that the motivation for all human action is to increase one's vital force. In Bantu thought, the *raison d'être* for all creation is *life*. Nothing else informs action and orders human dwelling other than the concept of life. The concept of life provides the basic framework for both conceptualization and interpretation in the African world. Life orders the African world.

In traditional African thinking all life is knit together in a fabric of life. Life, not force, is the central and all-embracing concept in African thought. Any attempt to grasp the nature of the African world, must begin with it, other ideas derive from it and it governs every action. Life is the beginning and the end of all action, but life itself does not end. This is what the concept of the ancestors stand for. Life is the most important concern in the African world, constituting the most fundamental and authentic way of living in the world—it is the basis of community life.

"What is this life?" asks Mulago as he explains the notion of unity of life in the African world. He replies:

> It is a whole of life, individual inasmuch as it is received by each being which exists, communal or collective inasmuch as each being draws from a common source of life. . . . It is life as it has been derived from the source of "power," as it turns towards power, is seized by it and seizes it. This life is not destroyed by death, although death may subject it to a change of condition. It does not move in a straight

> line; it is better to compare it with a circumference of a circle. In other words, there is no break between life and death, but continuity between the two.[80]

By saying that life is the all-embracing concept of African thought, we are not suggesting here that it will do simply to replace Tempels's terms force and vital force with life for we would still be operating within the same framework of interpretation. To assert that life is the basic framework of living is to completely reject the Western Aristotelian view of the world. It is to say that Western categories are useless for understanding the African world; it is to call for a totally new orientation to the world, because force cannot be equal to life. Neither can we speak of "life force" but only of life. By speaking about life, we will be able to address problems preventing continuation of life. The theory of force has no basis or reason for asking political questions. The concept of life addresses political questions because human life is not lived in abstraction but in a real world where political decisions directly affect human life for good or ill. It is through this concept that spiritual questions are addressed, for the cosmos is spiritual. The concept of life deals with the world in its totality since it also confronts concrete historical realities. "This life is therefore neither purely bodily nor purely spiritual, but a life of the 'whole man.' It is the whole of life, the entire being, being in its totality. This totality of being includes all that belongs to it: inheritance, family or group capital etc. Indeed for the *muntu*, the human personality cannot be thought of without its belongings."[81]

The difference between vital force thesis and the concept of life is not just a matter of semantics, but their ways of comprehending the world. The force theory is about some abstract ideas, while the concept of life is concerned with the ultimate question and reason for all creation, the continuity of creation that is the self-transcendence of life in concrete historical situation. This question is not a discussion about metaphysical ideas, but about possibilities and hindrances, enhancing or preventing personhood and transcendence of life. Second, the language of the vital force theory is empty of meaning to Africans and cannot therefore mobilize them to transform themselves and the world. We cannot speak of being or essence in the African world for these terms mean nothing to Africans. In fact, they do not exist in African thought systems—only life does. The theory of force with its being speaks about abstractions, leaving untouched the real issues that concern living in the present, which gives meaning and purpose to human life.

Tempels seems to have a sense that life is the central and inclusive concept in African thought, as observed in the following words:

> Force, the potent life, vital energy are the object of prayers and invocations to God, to the spirits and to the dead, as well as of all that is usually called magic, sorcery or magical remedies. The Bantu will tell you that they go to a diviner to learn the worlds of life, so that he can teach them the way of making life stronger. In every Bantu language it is easy to recognize the words or phrase denoting a force, which

> is not used in an exclusively bodily sense, but in the sense of integrity of our whole being.[82]

Here Tempels let the real issue, life, slip through his hands, because he was busy forcing African world into European categories. In the Bantu world knowledge comes second to life; epistemology is a second level question. The most important question is life, how it is experienced, and how it is to be lived.

The African notion of person derives from the idea of what human life is in the totality of life as a whole. Human life is a fiber in the fabric of life, people and nature are one. Boulaga has defined this integrative symbol of person as "being-in-plenitude." The idea of "being-in-plenitude" emphasizes the unity or connectedness of persons to one another and to nature. Kwesi Dickson has described this relationship as "fellow-feeling with nature."[83] The idea maintains that people understand themselves only in a total framework of all life, that is, in nature or the world around them. Identity is derived from some other referent "outside" one's life, but it is derived in *LIFE*. This referent could be non-human—an animal or tree, for example. This referent gives one identity *via negativa*, that is, by showing what one is not. But full awareness of identity comes from the people themselves for it is what people do that gives them a sense of identity. As one engages in work, ritual practice, and symbols, one is defined by them and in them. Boulaga writes: "Thus people become who they are 'persons'—only by confirming to the 'conditionings' of their existence, only by inserting this existence into the framework proper to all life, only by liberating within themselves the necessary power to act contained within this life, and so taking up and accepting the law of all fecundity."[84]

Mulago, seeking to emphasize how life is lived in "plenitude," has termed human engagement in life "vital participation." His explanation of vital participation is reminiscent of the vital force theory, although Mulago realizes that life, not force, is central in African thought. But in Mulago's work life is subsumed under participation, which he makes the key concept in understanding the African way of life and world:

> The key to an understanding of Bantu customs and institutions would thus appear to be the fact of community, unity of life. The handing on of this life, the sharing in this one life, is the link which unites members of the community. *Everything is thus explained by participation in life.* The closer the point at which one is to the source, the higher one's status. The *Muntu's* primary concern is never to interrupt this vital circuit, to give it an ever wider and intenser "magnetic field," to remain united with the first sources and the first channels of life.[85]

The term participation describes a relational framework, however, the term has to be used with caution, for it has been used in Western philosophy from Plato to Lévy-Bruhl to mean different things. The history of the term in Western theology demands that we be critical of appropriating it for a theological interpretation of the African way of life.

The concept of participation appeared in Western theology in connection with the doctrine of *analogia entis*, and earned its theological significance in the work of Thomas Aquinas. Participation has a neo-Platonian ancestry, and it underlies Aristotelian vocabulary of analogy. Montagnes shows the connection between Plato and Aristotle through the idea of participation within the doctrine of analogy: "The doctrine of analogy is composed of the synthesis of two themes: one of Aristotelian origin, that of the unity of reference to a first; the other of Platonic origin, that of participation."[86] Geiger's definition of the doctrine is illuminating: "Analogy is the logic—more precisely, part of the logic—of participation."[87] Raeymaeker makes the point that in the work of Thomas Aquinas the doctrine has also to do with causality:

> It is through concrete participation and according to an individual mode that each particular being possess its *esse* and takes part in perfection of perfections. We must conclude from this that the principle of unity of the totality of the concrete and individual beings cannot itself be anything but real as well. Located at the point where the lines of participation converge, it is the real source from which particular beings, and upon which, by virtue of their participation, these beings never cease to be entirely dependent.[88]

This agrees with what Aquinas himself writes on the subject: "Whatever is said of both God and creatures is said in virtue of the order as that creatures have to God as to their source and cause, in which all the perfections of things pre-exist transcendently."[89] According to Aquinas, being is the ontological keystone of the theory of analogy.

This is where the term participation becomes problematic for a theological enterprise: the concept is grounded on the notion of being. The African world talks about life, not being. Furthermore, when *participation* is used to express bondedness, it brings to a Western mind a picture of individuals coming together to form collectivities. This is not the case in Africa; people are already within the texture of life—they do not have to come together. What is needed is communication within the texture of life. Participation not only fails to express the African idea of living in the fabric of life, but also defines persons in terms of agency. If people are understood in terms of what they can do, then the concept of person is reduced to a tool of production. By this mentality, if one faces a physical or a mental predicament that prevents one from doing something, one ceases to be a person. This is what I call the production or utilitarian mentality according to which one's "worth" is dependent on function, ability or capacity. This mindset entails serious ethical problems, especially in terms of care: Are people to be cared for because of what they can do for society or by the mere fact they are humans? Functionalism is not the way Africans understand by living in bondedness in life. To live in bondedness is to live in communication with others and nature.

This relatedness has not been well understood by some "Africanists," for example, John Taylor. Following Tempels's thesis of forces, Taylor has described the African notion of self as "scattered." Taylor claims that this notion of "complex scattered self" emerges from the idea of extension of one's power-force.

> The African self is not limited to "souls," even in considerable numbers. A man's shadow is an extension of his self; its intensity or faintness may disclose the condition of his power-force; through it others may harm or be blessed.[90] His name also is a most sensitive and powerful extension—one might almost call it a limb of the self, one which he must never put into the grip of an enemy. Possessions may also be regarded as imbued with the selfhood of their owner, particularly those, like a spear-shaft, sleeping mat, or shirt which are impregnated with perspiration or dirt from his body.[91]

Such wrong ideas about the African concept of self have led to a misrepresentation of the African notion of personhood. Understanding the self as dynamic, these "Africanists," and unfortunately some Africans too, have equated the African notion of personhood with existentialist philosophy. The confusion lies in the fact that existentialist philosophy has a dynamic view of persons. While there may be some dynamism in African notion of person, there is a difference between African and existentialist philosophies in their understanding of personhood. In African thought, community plays a crucial role in the process of identity and personhood, but that is not the case in existentialist philosophy, especially Sartrean existentialism, where, the individual alone defines the self one is to become.[92]

In the African world, identity comes as society inserts one in the activities of the total framework of life. Through work, rites and symbols, one belongs to the world or nature. One sees oneself as belonging to a larger framework of life—to nature as a creature, "not as that of a simple animal, a mere searcher after nourishment to digest and shelter for sleep, but as the issue of what the human being has already transcended: the cycle of seasons, the rhythms of life, and the being-together with the earth, sky and the dead."[93] Death is understood within the framework of life. Life comes from death and death from life, forming a continuum of life. Through death people "are born to that which they have been." "Dying people are part of the universal dynamics of presence; they are present to each and all, without distance implied in the space and time of the living. Now they are all to all. Death has meaning, and death with meaning is durable, lasting word—on going form, informing the life of the living. The death become spirits, and these spirits are the instructors and guardians of the living."[94]

The idea of connectedness, or "being-in-plenitude" is the foundation for the concept of community and justice, which are central in African thought. Tempels refers to it: "For the Bantus man never appears as an isolated individual, as an independent substance." The notion of community in African thought is different than in the West—an association of atomic individuals coming together for self-interested reasons—Menkiti demonstrates:

> Western writers have generally interpreted the "community" in such a way that it signifies nothing more than a mere collection of self-interested persons, each with his private set of preferences, but all of whom get together nonetheless because they realize, each to each, that in association they can accomplish things which they are not able to accomplish otherwise. In this primarily additive approach, whenever the term "community" or "society" is used, we are meant to think of the aggregated sum of individuals comprising it. And this is argued, not just as an ontological claim, but also a methodological recommendation to the various social or humanistic disciplines interested in the investigation of the phenomenon of individuals in groups; hence the term "Methodological Individualism" so much bandied around in the literature.[95]

The African idea of community refers to bondedness, the act of sharing and living in one common symbol—life—which enables people to live in communion and communication with each other and nature. Living in communication allows other's stories or life experiences to become one's own. Sharing of life experiences affirms people and prepares them for understanding each other. To understand is to be open to the life experience of others, to be influenced by the world of others, and this is fundamental in living together as a community. Bondedness to others and the cosmos makes one aware that there are selves other than ourself yet all are united by one creation, one life. This calls for a sense of justice or "just-ness, a correct insertion and reciprocity, in respect toward what is 'ourselves otherwise.'" Boulaga explains how the idea of justice is conceived and how it works in African society: "We must leave everything in place. There is time for each thing. We must repair every breach of harmony, every wound and lesion. We must demand reparation for ourselves because we are not merely ourselves, and for others because they are also ourselves, the what-and-who of our pre-existence and survival, the what or who of some manner of our 'presupposing' ourselves."[96] Justice is not only to others, but to oneself too. Absent are the Western terms will, reason, and capacity which often appear in Western legal language in the West. Compare the African notion of justice with what Rawls says about equal justice in Western society:

> Thus equal justice is owed to those who have the capacity to take part in and to act in accordance with the public understanding of the initial situation. One should observe that moral personality is here defined as a potential that is ordinarily realized in due course. It is in this potentiality which the claims of justice come into play.
>
> We see, then, that the capacity for moral personality is sufficient condition for being entitled to equal justice. . . . It should be noted that the sufficient condition for equal justice [is] the capacity for moral personality.[97]

In the African notion of justice not only is the legal notion absent, but also everyone is responsible for everybody else. It is within this framework of understanding that others are not considered strangers; they are selves other than ourself. In such a relationship, the issue is not to find the guilty party, for the most important point is that the order of life be reestablished by all and for all. Boulaga explains what is understood as disorder in African society.

> Every transgression, conscious or not, is disorder, and demands a restoration of order. Disorder is not only in the spirit wide-awake and fully aware; disorder is also in the body and its mutism. And because he or she is "total part," the individual is not the only one concerned. Failing, fault, is the intrusion of a strangeness that isolates human beings from one another, that dislocates them, makes them monads of them when their genuine being is being-oneself-together with others. Fault is evil. It is the failure that cuts off and isolates; it is the short coming, the want, the lack, which engulfs individuals in their own whirlwind of night. What is important is the reestablishment of community, the reestablishment of the circulation of life, so that life can go on transcending itself, go on bursting the barriers, or the intervals, the nothingness, go on being superabundant.[98]

The theory of force or a force ontology naturally leads to a world of magic, but a concept of life as the basic framework of interpretation and a way of living presents a world that demands respect for life and persons. This understanding of the world is based on notion that all life is sacred and must be allowed to flow. Founded on sanctity of life, this understanding encourages building of a community characterized by justice, or justness, for the circulation of life. Life is to be lived in solidarity, communication, and reciprocity among the living and the dead.

To encourage this solidarity and communication, communion meals are eaten at various ceremonies: marriage, rituals, and sacrifices. Stephen Okafor has termed these communion meals "commensality," which "in practice means the act of eating together or sharing a common meal." He calls commensality a sub-framework "of African cosmology . . . the one dealing with social organization; that is, social relationships." This is how it works: "In one sense it is a philosophical concept forming the basis of social relationships; in another, it is a traditional political ideology answering to the reasons for societal political actions. It negates both extreme individualism, considered as destructive to healthy community, and totalitarianism in all its forms requiring instead consensus as its life-line."[99] These meals are eaten by "those who are, or wish to be, on peaceful, friendly or brotherly terms," says Mulago. He adds, "Eating from the same dish or drinking from the same straw, means entering into interaction with someone else, letting his vital [life] influences be exchanged with one's own."[100] Okafor warns against being misled concerning what these meals are truly all about.

> We must avoid falling into the error of thinking that commensality is no more than a mere act of eating together. We are mislead if we think that a whole community

> is regarded as a commensal group on the ground that they can be said to dine together on the same table. . . . In commensality we are in fact dealing more with an ideology than with an act or acts. The notion expresses an understanding, a societal bond. It is a mechanism that expresses a negation to hostility, a force of social control symbolized in the act of sharing meals or the possibility of so doing. Thus while the actual eating on the same table may not be practicable the notion as a possibility is.[101]

These meals and other activities are intended to build a community of life emphasizes being together for life to continue to flow.

Okafor has made a good criticism of Tempels's force thesis. He contends that the theory fails to grasp the basic framework of interpretation in Bantu thought, namely, the concept of life. Okafor asserts that there is also a sub-framework in the African way of life—commensality. But he errs when he introduces the concept of phenomenon aura. "The notion is axiomatic to Africans," Okafor claims, "Now we hardly need to emphasize that traditional Africa holds it as axiomatic that every existent, be it animate or inanimate matter, emits a certain essence peculiar to it." Like a student of Lévy-Bruhl, Okafor claims that "the role of medicine men or sorcerers as traditional Africa understands it will be lost to us if we fail to make this conceptual axiom seriously."[102]

With the concept of phenomenon aura, Okafor asserts that the real framework of interpretation in the African world is the one described by Tempels, namely, the force ontology. But what is phenomenon aura but another term for forces? If the African way of living is understood through phenomenon aura, the work of traditional healers can be interpreted as manipulation of forces. The question that one struggles with is whether an understanding of a people's ontology can be based on antisocial behavior of some members of society, sorcerers, for example—the same magic theory upon which Lévy-Bruhl based his concept of "primitive mentality." The concept of phenomenon aura derails Okafor's earlier claims that life and commensality are central to the African way of life. This habit of defining African community with negative terms is also found among African theologians who dwell on the concept of witchcraft as if it alone explains African thought and world. This way of approaching the African world only serves to promote the ideas of Lévy-Bruhl, anthropologists, and "Africanists" who have completely failed to understand the African world.[103]

The two frameworks that Okafor has identified—life and commensality—inform the African way of life together. The concept of togetherness emphasizes that "life is the actuality of currently living," as Boulaga puts it.[104] To live this way is to live as a working, sexual, and political being.

> In these three modes of that human existence, the human being is a being of relationship, and is fulfilled only by visible reticulation with the other, by the institutionalization of this complexes of relationships with the other.
>
> The life that acknowledges these three mediations as constitutive—as uncircumventable dispositions by which the human being arrives at the fullness of his and her

call to personhood—is not profane, even though it must not be identified with the cultic life.[105]

To live in this complex of relationship leads to different ways of living, there may be problems, but people must be together if life has to continue. To be human is being-together with others and the cosmos. Boulaga expresses this idea beautifully: "Human being-together is the enigmatic form of the unity of human beings, which is asserted by fact that different manners of this being-together mutually limit each other, cause mutual problems, and have meaning only by their mutual relationship. Each taken by itself is contradictory, destructive."[106]

CONCLUSION

The African world and its understanding of bondedness could provide a corrective to ideas of exploitation of people and resources. The idea of being in a fabric of life has a rich meaning for persons and community. Persons are not individual entities, strangers to one another, but "nature" life seeking fullness in the "actuality of presently living," other selves seeking to discover themselves and creation through work, ritual, and symbolism. (Work is not production resulting from exerting effort but self-expression integral to personhood. As self-expression all work is equal. As work is necessary to realizing personhood, it is dehumanizing to rob someone of the opportunity to work.) Others are selves forming community, which creates possibilities for one to reach personhood. It is a community of justness, care, and fellowship. It is a community that seeks all life to flow, to transcend itself—a community of possibilities.

The concept of life emphasizes the historicity of persons. People live in a life process as historical persons whose lives find meaning and purpose as they communicate with one another and nature. Life experience is always constructed in communication with the life experience of others. Sharing life experience is only possible when people share a common symbol that informs them a way of life. Understanding between people takes place through what is common between them, in this case the symbol of life. Life allows them to live in communion and communication with each other and nature. Such a way of life enables the development of identity of each and everyone, while at the same time preserving the identity of all.

These views could offer African society an authentic way of living by emphasizing basic values of African society, namely, persons and community, justice and fellowship, and communion with each other and the dead. African societies could recapture the vision of life transcending itself. This is the vision and intention of the Divinity for human life and all creation, actualized for Christians in the person and life of Jesus. In other words, the mission of Jesus was to declare a divine plan for life: that life must transcend all barriers and reach its fullness. This mission is the meaning of the incarnation. The mission of Jesus is the foundation upon which the church stands. Since Jesus became human to reveal divine intention for life; and the Church is the embodiment of the life and ministry of Jesus, therefore the Church exists to declare the divine vision. The Church is to be a bearer of life or a place where life is experienced in its fullness it is to be a community of life. Mulago maintains that this vision of the church is what John the Apostle refers to when he writes:

> That which was from the beginning, which we have heard, which we have seen with our eyes, which we have looked upon and touched with our hands, concerning the world of life—the life made manifest, and we saw it, and testify to eat, and proclaim to you the eternal life which was with the Father and was made manifest to us—that which we have seen and heard we proclaim also to you, you that you may have fellowship with us; and our fellowship is with the Father and with his Son Jesus Christ.[107]

The Incarnation is central to the Christian faith because it brings into the world hope of life; life breaking all barriers. Jesus himself says, "I have come that they may have life, and have it abundantly."[108] The idea of life transcending barriers is what makes Christianity a celebration of life. This is the meaning of the Paschal mystery, says Boulaga.

> The content of the message [the Paschal mystery] is the everlasting victory of life over death in every one of our lives. Liturgy and daily existence alike actualize this drama in ongoing fashion. One enters the mystery with one's being, to receive there meaning of life, life in all its gratuity and superabundant measure, pressed down and overflowing. Even death puts no end to life. This is festive Christianity. It sings, it dances all the way to Passion. Death is not explained by fall or fault—death is explained by life. The Paschal mystery is joy, not because it solaces human beings languishing under weight of their guilt, but because it shows forth life in the midst of death. . . . It is not a matter of being saved so much as it is of taking part in life in its fullness. Faith becomes jubilation in the dead of the divine power. The redemption that is sought after is the redemption that bestows fullness of reality on all the conditions of human life.[109]

NOTES

1. In *Truth and Method*, Hans-Georg Gadamer critiques immediacy or the abstraction of aesthetic consciousness in the Western world (New York: Crossroads, 1982), 80-90.

2. Edward B. Tylor, *Primitive Culture*, 2 vols. (London: John Murray, 1871). Also see James Frazer, *The Golden Bough* (London: Macmillan, 1922); L. H. Morgan, *Ancient Society or Researches in the Lines of Human Progress and Savagery, Through Barbarism to Civilization* (New York: Holt, 1877).

3. Thomas Hobbes, *Leviathan*, ed. Michael Oakeshott (New York: Collier Macmillan Publishing, 1962), 98.

4. *Ibid.*, 99.

5. Herbert Spencer, *On Social Evolution*, ed. J. D. Y. Peel (Chicago University of chicago Press, 1972), Chapter 2.

6. See Jean-Jacques Rousseau, *Discours sur l'origine et les fondements de l'inégalité parmis les hommes* (London: Oxford University Press, 1922).

7. *Ibid.*, 151.

8. Lucien Lévy-Bruhl, *Les Fornictions mentales dans les sociétés inférieures* (Paris: Alcan, 1910).

9. See Georg Friedrich W. Hegel, *Lectures on the Philosophy of History*, trans. E. S. Haldane and Frances H. Simon (London: Routledge and Kegan Paul, 1955).

10. See Lucian Lévy-Bruhl, *Primitive Mentality* (New York: Macmillan, 1923); also his *How Natives Think* (New York: Allen and Unwin, Macmillan, 1926).

11. Among the popular works in this field are the following: Marcel Griaule, *Dieu d'eau* (Paris: Editions du Chéne, 1948); also by the same author, "L'Image du monde au Soudan," *Journal de la Société des Africanistes*, 19, Fasc. 2 (1949); Germaine Dieterlen, *Essai sur la religion bambara* (Paris: Presses Universitaires de France, 1951); E. E. Evans-Pritchard, *Witchcraft, Oracles and Magic among the Azande* (Oxford: Claredon Press, 1937); E. E. Evans-Prtichard, *Nuer Religion* (Oxford: Claredon Press, 1956); Margaret Joyce Field, *Religion and Medicine of the Ga People* (London: Oxford University Press, 1937); Daryll Forde, ed., *African Worlds: Studies in the Cosmological Ideas and Social Values of African Peoples* (London: Oxford University Press, 1954); Monica Wilson, *Rituals of Kinship among the Nyakusa* (London: Oxford University Press, 1966) and Merville Herskovits and Francis S. Herskovits, *An Outline of Dahomean Religious Belief*, memoire 41 (New York: American Anthropological Association, 1933).

12. Alexander Hetherwick, *Life and Work*, vol. 165 (December 1902), Malawi National Achieves (London: United Society for Christian Literature), 7, 8.

13. Placid Tempels, *Bantu Philosophy* (Paris: Présence Africaine, 1959), 59.

14. *Ibid.*, 16.

15. *Ibid.*, 113.

16. For a detailed discussion on the subject see Gabriel Marcel, *Etre et avoir* (Paris: Editions universitaires, 1935), 230.

17. Tempels, *Philosophie Bantoe*, 115.

18. *Ibid.*, 17.

19. *Ibid.*, 15.

20. *Ibid.*, 24.

21. *Ibid.*, 22.

22. *Ibid.*, 35.

23. *Ibid.*, 36.

24. *Ibid.*, 114.

25. *Ibid.*, 44.

26. *Ibid.*, 30.

27. *Ibid.*, 121.

28. *Ibid.*, 35. His emphasis.

29. *Ibid.*, 53.

30. *Ibid.*, 43.

31. Paul Tillich, *Systematic Theology*, vol. 1. (Chicago: University of Chicago Press, 1951), 182.

32. *Ibid.*, 183. My emphasis.

33. *Ibid.*, 185, 182. His emphasis.

34. Tempels, 62-67.

35. John Mbiti, *African Religions and Philosophy*, 2nd ed. (Portsmouth, NH: Heinemann, 1990), 10.

36. N. Tshiamalenga, "La philosophie dans la situation actuelle de l'Afrique," in *Combats pour un chtistianisme africain* (Kanshasa: Faculté de Théologie, 1981), 179.

37. O. p'Bitek, *Africa's Cultural Revolution* (Nairobi: Macmillan, 1973), 59.

38. Vincent Mulago, "Vital Participation: The Cohesive Principle of the Bantu Community," in Kwesi Dickson and Paul Ellingworth, eds., *Biblical Revelation and African Beliefs*, (Maryknoll, NY: Orbis Books, 1971), 137, n. 2.

39. *Ibid.*, 148.

40. Theophilus Okere, *African Philosophy: Historical Hermeneutical Investigation of the Conditions of its Possibility* (Lanham, MD: University Press of America, 1983), 5.

41. *Ibid.*, 5.

42. Fabian Eboussi Boulaga, *Le Bantu Problématique* (Paris: Présence Africaine, no. 66, 1968), 9.

43. *Ibid.*, 32.

44. *Ibid.*, 45.

45. Aimé Césaire, *Discours sur le colonialisme*, 4th ed. (Paris: Présence Africaine, 1962), 44.

46. Johannes Fabian, "Philosophie Bantoe: Placid Temples et son oeuvre, vus dans un perspective historique," *Études Africaines du Centre de Recherches et d'Information socio-politiques*, T. A. no. 108-9 (Bruxelles: C. R. I. S. P., 1970), 18ff.

47. Edwin W. Smith, ed. *African Ideas of God*, 2nd ed. (London: Edinburgh House Press, 1959), 127.

48. *Ibid.*, 167.

49. Sidney L. Hinde and Hildegarde Hinde, *The Last of the Massai* (London: Heinemann, 1961), 99.

50. T. Collen Young, *Contemporary Ancestors* (London: n. p). I have changed the beginnings of lines 5 and 6 from "He has no body," "He is a word" because the Mbuti, like all Africans, use a neutral gender for God and people.

51. I prefer to use the term *redemption* as opposed to *salvation* because the word *salvation* was used as an ideology by liberal Christianity in Africa. *Salvation* was used to produce an ahistorical Christianity concerned only with a salvation of souls. The present historical realities did not matter. What was important was to lay up treasure in heaven, where moths and ants would not destroy it. This was a Christianity of souls without bodies, a resurrection without the cross founded on an incarnation that never was. Boulaga distinguishes the two terms, redemption and salvation: "Redemption concerns the here below, time and history. Salvation tells of the invisible, of eternity, of the beyond. Salvation promises endless happiness after death, when there shall be no more tears, or needs or sin. The world of redemption is the one where every proposition calls for visible process, every idea has its material referent. *It is indeed the place of finitude, of death,*

the 'place under the sun.'" Fabian Eboussi Boulaga, *Christianity Without Fetishes*, trans. Robert Barr (NY: Orbis, 1984), 199.

52. Alex Kagame, *La Philosophie bantou-rwandaise de l'être*, memoire in 8 de l'Academie Royale des Sc. D'outre-mer (Arsom) Nouvelle Serie, Tome 7, 1 (Brussels: Editions du Marias, 1956), 8. This was a doctoral Dissertation.

53. *Ibid.*, 22.

54. *Ibid.* See his chapter entitled: "*A recherche des catégories Bantu rwandaises*," 95 ff.

55. *Ibid.*, 107.

56. Quoted by Leo Apostel, *African Philosophy: Myth or Reality?* (Gent, Belgium: Scientific Publishers, E. Story-Scientia, 1981), 83.

57. Kagame, *La Philosophie bantoe-rwandaise*, 118.

58. Apostel, *African Philosophy: Myth or Reality*, 74.

59. Kagame, *La Philosophie bantoe-rwandaise*, 282.

60. Ibid., 179.

61. *Ibid.*, 176.

62. *Ibid.*, 182.

63. *Ibid.*, 210.

64. *Ibid.*, 368.

65. *Ibid.*, 17.

66. *Ibid.*, 23.

67. I have in mind these works of Mulago: "Dialectique existentialle des bantou," *Recherches et Debats*, Centre Catholique Intellectuel Francais, no. 24 (1958), 146-71; *Un Visage africain du christianisme* (Paris: Présence Africaine, 1965). See especially Chapter 8, "Philosophical Outline" of "Dialectique existetialle des bantous et sacramentalisme," in *Aspects de la culture noire* (Paris: 1958).

68. *Meeting the African Religions* (Rome: Secretariat for Non-Christians, 1969), 29. For the content of *Ntu* see the summary of Kagame, *La Philosophie bantoe-rwandaise.*

69. Mulago, *Un Visage africain*, 154.

70. Janheinz Jahn, *Muntu: An Outline of the New African Culture* (New York: Grove Press, 1961), 99 ff.

71. The term ethnophilosophy was first used by Kwame Nkrumah as a topic of his master philosophy thesis. However, Paulin Hountondji used it to denote collective works about the African world, peoples, myths, folk roles and philosophy. Hountondji had in mind the works of anthropologists, ethnographers, sociologists, and philosophers including Placid Temples, Alex Kagame, Leopald Senghor, and John Mbiti in their attempts to "describe a world outlook or thought system of a particular African community or the whole Africa." Hountondji, "Le Mythe de la philosophie spontanee," *Cahiers Philosophiques Africains* (Lubumbashi), no. 1 (1972).

72. See Aylward Shorter, *Prayer in the Religious Traditions of Africa* (London: Oxford University Press, 1975), 75-77, for prayers from Tanzania, Malawi, and Siera Leone. See also John Mbiti, *The Prayers of African Religion* (London: SPCK, 1970). Mbiti has a detailed discussion on the personality of ancestral spirits in his classic *African Religions and Philosophy.*

73. Vincent Mulago, *Un Visage africain*, 150.

74. Kagame, *La philosophie bantoe-rwadaise*, 121-22.

75. Kwame Gyekye, *An Essay on African Philosophical Thought: The Akan Conceptual Scheme* (New York: Cambridge University Press, 1987), 98.

76. Segun Gbadegesin, *African Philosophy: Traditional Yoruba and Contemporary African Realities* (New York: Peter Lang, 1991), 29-41.

77. Boulaga, *Christianity Without Fetishes*, 61.

78. Tempels, *Philosophie Bantoe*, 34.

79. A full discussion on fear as a basis of African religion is found in E. E. Keller, *A Short History of Religions* (London: Gollancz, 1957), 9-37.

80. Vincent Mulago, "Vital Participation: The Cohesive Principle of the Bantu Community," in Dickson and Ellingworth, eds., *Biblical Revelation and African Beliefs*, 138.

81. *Ibid.*, 138-139.

82. Tempels, *Philosophie Bantoue*, 45.

83. Kwesi Dickson, *Theology in Africa* (Maryknoll, NY: Orbis, 1984), 48. The West does not maintain this idea of human bondedness to nature. However, the Judeo-Christian tradition maintains the idea of bondedness as illustrated by the creation accounts in Genesis. There is a difference in accent between the J and P accounts. In the J account human bondedness to nature comes first. Adam is made from clay and begins life as a companion of animals. In the P story of creation, humankind is created on the same day as the animals, yet as totally different creatures.

84. Boulaga, *Christianity Without Fetishes*, 80.

85. Mulago, "Vital Participation," in Dickson and Ellingworith, eds., *Biblical Revelation and African Beliefs*, 143. My emphasis.

86. Bernard Montagnes, *La Doctrine de l'analogie de l'être d'après St Thomas d'Aquin* (Louvain, Paris: Nauwelaerts, 1963), 23.

87. Louis-Betrand Geiger, *La Participation dans la philosophie de St. Thomas d'Aquin*, 2nd ed. (Paris: Vrin, 1942, 1953), 78.

88. L. de Raeymaeker, "L'Analogie de l'être dans le perspective d'une philosophie thomiste." See also Etienne, *The Christian Philosophy of St. Thomas Aquinas*, trans. L. K. Shook (New York: Random House, 1956), 105.

89. Thomas Aquinas, *Summa Theologia*, vol. 1. ed. Thomas Gilby (New York: Image Books, 1969), question 13, art. 5, 208.

90. Here Taylor quotes Acts 5:15 to support the idea of extension of power-force. The verse there says, "they even carried out the sick into the streets and laid them on beds and pallets, that as Peter came by at least his shadow might fall on some of them" (RSV). John V. Taylor, *The Primal Vision: Christian Presence amid African Religion* (London: SCM Press, 1977), 56.

91. Mulago, "Vital Participation," in Dickson and Ellingworh, eds. *Biblical Revelation and African Beliefs*, 56.

92. Jean Paul Sartre, *Essays in Existentialism*, Wade Baskin, ed. (Secaucus, NJ: The Citadel Press, 1965). See also Sartre, *Being and Nothingness: An Essay on the Phenomenological Ontology*, trans. Hazel E. Barnes (New York: The Philosophical Library, 1956).

93. Boulaga, *Christianity Without Fetishes*, 80.

94. *Ibid.*, 82.

95. Ifeanyi A. Menkiti, "Person and Community in African Traditional Thought," in Richard A. Wright, ed., *African Philosophy: An Introduction*, 3rd. ed. (Lanham, MD: University Press of America, 1984), 179.

96. Boulaga, *Christianity Without Fetishes*, 81.

97. John Rawls, *A Theory of Justice* (Cambridge, MA: Harvard University Press, 1971), 501-506.

98. Boulaga, *Christianity Without Fetishes*, 81.

99. Stephen O. Okafor, "Bantu Philosophy: Placid Tempels Revisited," *Journal of Religion in Africa*, 13, no. 2 (1982), 93.

100. Mulago, "Vital Participation," *Biblical Revelation and African Beliefs*, in Dickson and Ellingworth, eds., 155.

101. Okafor, "Bantu Philosophy," 94.

102. *Ibid.*

103. I have in mind Evans-Pritchard, *Witchcraft, Oracles and Magic Among the Azande*; P. Hughes, *Witchcraft* (London: Longman, 1952); J. Middleton and E. H. Winter, *Witchcraft and Sorcery in East Africa* (London: Routledge and Kegan Paul, 1963).

104. Boulaga, *Christianity Without Fetishes*, 187.

105. *Ibid.*, 181.

106. *Ibid.*, 188.

107. 1 John 1:1-3, (RSV).

108. John 10:10b (RSV).

109. Boulaga, *Christianity Without Fetishes*, 65.

6

Christianity and African Values

> A Christianity that presents itself as the best means of humanizing the human being can only face a crisis and lose its credibility with the arrival on the scene of real independence—when *Muntu* regain control over their destiny, and begin to seek the best possible means to ensure their development. In the best hypothesis, Christianity will continue to appear as a factor favorable to development. In the worst, it will appear as an obstacle and curb.[1]

Christianity is growing by leaps and bounds in Africa. According to the Center for World Evangelization in Nairobi, Christianity is growing faster than predicted in 1970. This is not a new phenomenon in Africa for statistics show that Christianity in Africa has grown at an average rate of 5 percent per annum since 1900. At the turn of the century there were an estimated 9 million Christians in Africa, about 7 percent of the total population of the continent. By 1960 there were about 86 million Christians, accounting for 30 percent of Africa's total population of 300 million. By 1980 the estimated number of Christians was at 200 million, about 45 percent of the population. Today, 67 percent of Africa is Christian, and it is now estimated that by the year 2000 Africa will have more Christians than Europe and North America combined. In general, the center of Christian will have shifted from the northern to the southern hemisphere.[2] John Mbiti has commented that "such a massive expansion within a short time is unprecedented in the history of Christianity."[3]

These figures reflect the work of over 650 Anglican, Orthodox, and Protestant bodies and well over 350 Roman Catholic dioceses. In addition, there are over 6,000 indigenous Christian movements, which scholars commonly call Independent Churches. As Christianity gains followers in the south, these organizations will have new challenges in their ministry and education.[4] The challenge is how to make the Christian faith credible, for although Christianity is growing, many people are becoming disenchanted with its mentality and practice as the continent faces growing socio-economic, political, and other problems. This chapter examines the attempts of African Christians to respond to the crisis of meaning occasioned by liberal Christianity, the impact of Western culture, the declining socio-economic situation, and mounting local and international political problems, all of which make the lot of many Africans miserable. This chapter focuses on issues raised by liberal Christianity and African attempts to recapture the essence of the Gospel to produce a meaningful Christianity that grapples with the problems of contemporary Africa while respecting African values and humanity.

The problem of credibility of Christianity in Africa arises from its apparent lack of interest in issues relating to the human condition in the world. Into the 1990s, many Church leaders did not want to say anything about politics. By refusing to identify with the struggle of the people, they have made Christianity an immobilizing force. Unwilling to be part of this world, Christianity puts emphasis on the otherworldly. Christianity has not only immobilized Africans but also led them to reject the values that inform their manner of living. People have rejected the traditional values that form a framework of interpretation and give meaning and a sense of direction in their lives. Historically, Christianity in Africa has always aligned itself with the forces that have destroyed African society. In most cases, it has denounced evil only when it was safe; otherwise it has supported the status quo and avoided confrontation. This is where the question of the credibility of Christianity arises. Christianity is a religion that preaches liberation of peoples, but in Africa it is concerned with self-perpetuation. During the struggle for independence Christianity endorsed political participation late, and this immediate identification of the faith with human emancipation and revolution was too sudden not to shock. The language smacked of opportunism. In the post-colonial society Christianity presents a lot of rhetoric concerning changing the human condition but fails to present a concrete plan of action.

> This new phraseology is totally lacking in verisimilitude in the context of neocolonial Christianity. We are showered with massive, lyrical assertions, but not favored with a theoretical presentation of the practice actually under way. The juxtaposition of these new goals and proclamations with the hoary data of tradition is lacking in any attempt to demonstrate the coherence and continuity of old and new—and surely lacking the courage to make any clarifying, liberating with the old.[5]

Christianity in Africa has always identified itself with the elite. Christianity as it first appeared was both colonialist and missionary, and as such, the "Christian message" included values of the liberal heritage. The result of this double heritage was a Christianity with elements of Western values—a bourgeois faith unfit for Africans. A few African theologians have analyzed African resistance to bourgeois Christianity and the initiatives to reinterpret what they consider the essence of the religion. This chapter will survey the analysis of four of those theologians, Fabian Eboussi Boulaga, Kwesi A. Dickson, Jean-Marc Ela, and

John Samuel Mbiti. This chapter will evaluate the works of these theologians as we seek to understand African resistance to Western values.

LIBERAL CHRISTIANITY

Boulaga's analysis of colonial-missionary or liberal Christianity demonstrates that there are contradictions within liberal Christianity. He focuses mainly on the contradictions within the liberal concept of faith: how it is related to community, love, and charity, or how it informs a way of life. Boulaga says that in liberal Christianity faith is related to violence, and violence is used whenever Christianity is resisted or challenged. He asserts that the concept of community in liberal Christianity is found in the formulas: "Men and women are sons and daughters of God, called to be such by faith and baptism, called to form a single 'body.' The middle-class Christian repeats these formulas but gives them a mystical meaning."[6] Boulaga derides middle-class understanding of community: "This unity, this communion are realized only in the invisible no-place where souls gather, whether here below or in the other world."[7] In these formulas, faith and baptism are shown as central teachings in missionary Christianity, which Boulaga prefers to call middle-class or bourgeois Christianity. But since baptism is a once-and-for-all ritual, faith becomes the principle teaching. Hence Boulaga writes:

> Faith is a community of beliefs in the same truths, a communion of adherence to the same values. Faith is a moral community of sentiments and minds. It is not that minds will be encountering one another by exchange and dialogue. Their oneness arises only from their orientation in the same direction, from the single object at which they aim. In faith, their unity is hidden in God.[8]

Boulaga charges that faith and community in missionary Christianity are not foundations of organic unity.

> *Conversions have not created a people, but crowds of people*, each appealing to the doctrine it has been brought and to the authority of those who have brought it. The bond among these believers is their subjection to the message and to the envoys. Their being-with is produced and maintained from without. There is no common, shared experience among them, nor could there be, since faith as a subjective, individual position with a particular, exterior, absolute content eludes each one of them. In this abstract objectivization, converts only elude themselves, along with the reality of their concrete world. Further, since the world of the converts' common experience is exiled in the utterly other universe of faith, they lose, when they adhere to new beliefs, the communication space that has subsisted among them, they lose the necessary material basis and condition of the relationships of human beings with one another. Deprived of the platform of realities that constitute it as a person and

> as a being-in-the-world, consciousness all in disarray "reflects" until it catapults into the empty heavens of credence and belief.[9]

Boulaga further argues that these converts give assent to enunciations that have no possible referent in experience. Subscribing to what is believed to be orthodoxy, the converts only remain strangers to themselves and one another. Boulaga calls the faith and practice of middle-class Christianity an ideology, because it does not point to an authentic life or create possibilities for an original way of being-with-world or being-in-the-world which leads to creating a community of the "sons and daughters of God." Boulaga says that an authentic way of living is informed by the knowledge of who God is—a parent who is metaphorically called Father:

> Calling God "Father" is not simple allusion to eternal subject, but an act that engages and involves the human beings performing it, and imposes on them certain rules of conduct: an original way of being—with-the-world, of being in society, of creating community. . . . It is a matter of the principle of illimitation (called God-who-is-Father, or God-who-is-Love).[10]

It is upon this understanding of community that Boulaga calls the faith and practice of middle-class Christianity an ideology which "serves to propagate the ideal image of oneself." He interprets the relationship between ideology and religion in middle-class Christianity as follows:

> Ideology is the sharing of the sacred, but nothing so sacred as material goods. In ideology, the offer of what is declared to be the most precious thing can go hand in hand with the refusal of what is most elementary. In a class society, founded on individualism and profit, religion is transformed into a superstructure. Its transcendence places it at zero degrees longitude and latitude, from whence it can arrange to fit all situations, and accompany either pole of a contradiction without modifying it, indeed by serving it as a metaphor or camouflage if need be. It is no longer a matter of astonishment that, in the presence of positions other than dogmatic—in the presence of this tautological on Christianity's irreducibility and identity, just as of its pretension to superiority and universality—Christian thought and practice should be diluted and fragmented into contradictory opinions and actions. Faith like the Hegelian Being, will be the poorest of concepts, while being asserted to be the first and the "All" to the point where, in a given Christian assembly, one may see persons united more on the bases of profane ideologies than on that of their common belief.[11]

According to Boulaga, missionary Christianity is a superstructure, an ideological framework for Western values.

While as religion functions as an ideology in missionary Christianity, it has a different role in African traditional society. Boulaga says that up to the time middle-class Christianity entered traditional society, religion "was a metaphor of life—the acknowledgment, in the acts of living, of the movement and power by which life's self-transcendence never abates. In accepting one's determinations and conditionings, one's radication in nature, and everything by which one was mediated—the earth, sex, strength—the African human being moved into a position with Life, with God."[12] Religion informed a manner of living. To live as well as to die, was to engage in interpretation of the nature of things and the world. In African thought, the nature of life was understood within the framework of religion. Boulaga further states that it was in being alive and dying, in particularly "in a manner of being a sexual creature . . . that wove the tissue of the religion of existence. . . . It was being born, living, and dying in the most empirical manner that ever could be, that furnished the framework, the matter and the experience of God's sacrality and sovereign immanence."[13]

Boulaga defines the middle-class Christian as "a creature free of all natural ties, one who has broken with the tribe—the great family—and is before all else an individual, a closed subjectivity, finished and perfect in itself, maintaining no purely extrinsic relationships with society. . . . The first and last reality is individual. . . . The expansion of the individual comes before all else. . . . This is the absolute value."[14] The strategy for inculcating this value in an African mind demanded that the convert first be disoriented through an "uprooting and alienating praxis."[15] Inherent in this praxis was the negation of temporality and historicity, thus creating what I call de-enspaced minds. These are minds without sense of space and time or what Boulaga calls familiar vectors in life. "There are familiar vectors in life—directions one is to go, calculated to provide one with a locus of presence to oneself as a corporeal being. Extirpation is a mode of disorientation via suppression of one's point of reference. It is disorientation by disjunction."[16] De-enspacement was the first necessary break with the thought and values of traditional society. Missionary Christianity claimed that it was necessary to break with one's traditional values in order to be saved, since there was nothing in these values to communicate true revelation. What will it benefit one to hold on to traditional values, one's culture or history and lose eternity? Voluntarism thus becomes the key to salvation. "The first breach demanded, and transformed into a precondition of adherence to the faith, is a renunciation of the texture of relationships with the dead and the living that makes the traditional human being a person, a being-oneself-with-the-others."[17] This praxis also presupposes the superiority of revelation, culture, and history, as Mbiti says:

> Evangelism has been carried out under a false cultural superiority and the Church in Africa has developed in the context of a false inferiority. . . . Missionary culture told Africa in effect that "unless you were (culturally) circumcised, you cannot inherit the Kingdom of God." So unless they mutilated a large portion of their culture foreskins, unless they become culturally Westernized, and then Lutheranized, Methodistized, Anglicanized, Roman Catholicized, Presbyterianized, Africans could not inherit one centimeter of the Christian faith. We were told that if we wanted Christianity (and this we had been persuaded passionately to want) we had to pay

> the price: we had to lay down our cultures, despise them as the missionaries did, condemn them as the missionaries did, and run away from them since missionaries had declared them to be dangerously demonic. . . . A legion of sins suddenly mushroomed around and from African cultures. Almost everything in African culture was tabooed in the course of evangelism.[18]

The life of these people who were torn by their roots was difficult. Boulaga discusses some of the problems related with the transition that new converts faced.

> By taking the individual in isolation, by separating the individual from what constitutes him or her a part of reality, one creates insurmountable problems of passage, together with obsessional hypertrophy of human being. These transitional problems come down to questions like these: How does what is not individual come to be added to him or her? How, and how far, can foreign elements come together in unity? What sort of unity do they form? What is the common element, intermediary of passage from one to the other? And what is the precise nature and quality of this element?[19]

The praxis of middle-class evangelism consisted in suppression of a person's sense of situation. When a person loses the sense of being located in particular place and time, the self is rid of any obligation to the demands of a given situation. In this manner of life faith can only mean estrangement.

> Faith is consciousness torn out of the worldly realities that it had taken upon itself and by which it was being mediated, so that it has become a stranger to its own self. Delivered up to a totally different world, it fixes the object of belief only as "other" to this subject—as an outsider vis-à-vis its new world, its beyond, its abstraction, its reversal. The absolute appears with the traits of a Strangeness, with recognizable references. As a result it cannot be coined arbitrary, predetermined material, inaccessible to examination and verification. Now faith becomes an authoritarian orthodoxy.[20]

Again Boulaga says: "Faith is psychologized, just as sin is psychologized. Bourgeois Christians no longer recognize the originating, constitutive relationships of human existence: they no longer see that these are given and are anterior to every act of the individual, that they are the conditions which make possible the rise of the latter as concrete reality, as culturalized nature, historicized and socialized from the start."[21]

Boulaga contends that the term *faith* is completely misconstrued in middle-class Christianity as ascribing to orthodoxy and having nothing to do with the concrete historical reality but with "revealed" truth. This misinterpretation of faith separates believing from loving. "*The dissociation of faith and love is the reason for the discomfiture of the Christianizing enterprise today*," emphasizes Boulaga.[22] Through dissociation faith degenerates "into rites to be observed and the canonization of middle-class morality." He further describes the middle-class notion of faith in these words: "Faith as certitude of salvation in and by Jesus Christ alone, faith as assent to revealed event and doctrine *qua* revealed becomes the be-all and end-all. Faith absorbs charity. Charity becomes interior to faith, becomes one of its attributes. It becomes benevolence and beneficence that adorn the holy or pious life of God-fearing Christians—the faithful. Faith is required in order to be able to love with the love of charity."[23]

Boulaga defines true faith this way:

> A profession of faith is not a recitation of articles of belief. Faith is but the process by which human beings are constituted as beings of word, responsible, spontaneous, and gratuitous subjects who cannot be the "means of" anything, as they are in the likeness of God. Faith is the effectuation of this creative autonomy of the human gift, as real sharing in the Spirit who works in the force of illimitation that creates universe.[24]

Middle-class Christianity not only misunderstands faith but also reverses the order of relationship between faith and charity. Faith is made absolute and concretized; consequently, faith ceases to be "a moment in a process—the process of creative love—it succumbs to bigoted particularism bound to singular events, places, things, and persons. . . . Cut off from its soul, faith begins to draw its value from orthodoxy, from mystery, from miracle, from a system of wonders, from human corruption and the arbitrary divine will."[25] Such a notion of faith leads to a misunderstanding of what love and charity mean. Charity will be equated with faith and will take the place of love. Hence Boulaga's biting remark: "Where human love is wanting, charity alone abides. Where slavery and racism reign, there is charity." This understanding of faith makes it possible to condemn others while at the same time bearing them "a radical love—the love of charity—because one is seeking their salvation by faith."[26] This kind of charity is lethal. It is not surprising then that such charity does not establish solidarity between the missionary and the evangelized in a community of a shared lot. Boulaga maintains that it is not possible to have a true community with this understanding of charity and love.

> It is not a power that creates persons, that is, it is not a force for rendering persons autonomous beings existing for and by themselves. When all is said and done, it is offensive, and it will be rejected as the very caricature of love, as love's opposite. Membership in the established Churches will be experienced and felt as an institutionalized denial of oneself and a source of continual humiliation. The independent and dissident Churches are the expression of the contemptuous rejection of this association, this caricature of *philadelphia* which calls forth such sarcasm and "ridicule by the infidel." (See how they love one another!)[27]

How could the work of a few people, missionaries and colonialists, have such a devastating influence on African life? Boulaga says the answer is found in the phrase "trial by might," the use of violence to achieve a desired end. "Violence by nature is instrumental," says Hannah Arendt "like all means, it always stands in need of guidance and justification through the end it pursues."[28] The end, for missionaries, was submission of Africans to the "saving power of Christ." The problem for Africans was that this power identified itself with the power of subjugation by missionaries. Missionaries and colonialists both wanted to have power over Africans, use of violence was only a logical means. "Power and violence, though distinct phenomena, usually appear together. Whenever they are combined, power . . . is primary and predominant factor," writes Arendt.[29] It is beside the point to argue that missionaries were only few in number to have created such a destruction of society. "Violence, we must remember, does not depend on numbers or opinions, but on implements, and the implements of violence . . . like all other tools, increase and multiply human strength."[30]

Boulaga says the violence of bourgeois Christianity was based on its theology, expressed by the language of derision. This language establishes inferiority of the other's culture and values and the inanity of the other's beliefs:

> trial by might establishes the inanity of the gods by their helplessness to express their ire in the face of sacrilege. The God of the Christians, on the contrary is a strong God, with vigorous passions. He experiences anger. He feels jealousy. He speaks. He reacts to prayer, crime, and defiance. To be sure, he is slow to anger and prompt to forgive, but one must repent, and acknowledge him in truth—acknowledge him as he reveals himself.[31]

It is truth that the world must know at any cost. "Anyone who opposes Christianity or seems to be about to turn it to derision can and should be destroyed. . . . Truth coincides with might. Truth as the right and duty to impose itself by force."[32] These are the presuppositions of middle-class Christian practice, says Boulaga who calls this supernatural terrorism.[33] Supernatural terrorism creates "submission to those who have power constraint and whose ethnic religion is Christianity. . . . Thus trial by might is trial by failure, misfortune, or humiliation of another. You can see it on face of Africans, the curse of God."[34]

Boulaga has not defined what he means by violence but we take him to mean dehumanization, or rejection of personhood of the other by any means. In missionary Christianity this is accomplished by negating people's values through the use of language of derision and appealing to theology to disorient Africans through an uprooting praxis. It is in view of this fact that Boulaga says "the decline or ebb of imperialism . . . is the refutation in practice of trial by might. One of the reasons for the loss of credibility of African Christianity is its dangerous alliance with might and force."[35]

AFRICAN RESISTANCE TO LIBERAL CHRISTIANITY

Values of missionary Christianity are too alien to African way of life and sense of the sacred not to be resisted. Missionary Christianity is resisted by individuals and by communities. Given the negative experience that Africans have with middle-class Christianity one would think that African resistance would take the form of total rejection of the religion. On the contrary, African resistance is not a rejection of Christianity but an attempt to recapture the teachings of Christ presented to them in a distorted manner. Africans neither seek to break with Christianity altogether nor part with traditional values and practices so as to embrace the new religion.

> The "necessary break" theory is refuted by practice, by a *probo ambulando*. Instead what must be broken with is evil symbolized by sorcery. There is no need to break with one's solicitude for the dead or any other ancestral traditions. The message of Christ is not in competition with them. On the contrary, this message has come to fulfill the dream of a life in all its fullness, a life destined to triumph even in the collapse of the framework of a way of life that had been consecrated from time immemorial.[36]

Before Boulaga wrote these words, John Mbiti had already commented that one of the main factors accounting for the rapid growth of Christianity in Africa was the religiosity of traditional society itself. Mbiti actually considered the spirituality of African traditional religion as *preparatio evangelica.*

> It is in this religiosity that the preaching of the Gospel makes sense; it is this preparedness that has undergirded the spreading of the Gospel like wildfire among African societies which had hitherto followed and practiced traditional religion. Consequently people are finding that the biblical faith is not harmful to their religious sensibilities. . . . African religion has equipped people to listen to the Gospel, to discover meaningful passages in the Bible, and to avoid unhealthy religious conflict.[37]

Mbiti considers it natural that "theology in Africa must inevitably grow within this religious setting. For this reason some African theologians consider traditional religions as one of the sources of theological reflection (besides the Bible, Christian heritage, etc.)."[38]

Africans are resisting ideological Christianity that aligns itself with the powerful and does not seek to be part of the struggle for an authentic life of dignity and respect for persons. To live such a life is to experience personhood. The resistance movement seeks to reinterpret Christianity within African reality so that people can realize what it means to be fully human. Nowhere is this resistance movement more active and visible than in the Independent Churches. The term *Independent Church* was coined by Bengt Sundkler, a Lutheran missionary among the *Amazulu* in Southern Africa. He used the term to describe Churches started by Africans, not by Western missionaries, and without Western influence.

The term has earned much usage among scholars. I, too, used the term in an earlier work.[39] In that article I described these Churches and their work in this way:

> It cannot be overemphasized that most Independent Churches aim at making the Church really African in the African context. Indeed, Independent Churches are workshops for reinterpreting the Gospel into African thought forms and culture. Independent Churches try to peel off the Western dress in which Christianity has come to us, thereby remaining with the "essence" of the Christian message and clothe it in African dress. The act of de-Westernization, if I may be allowed to use that term, should be the task of every African Church. For time has come when our Churches can no longer keep the Western marks of a Church as the marks of a Church in Africa. Independent Churches are not just a mini-phenomena but a real power pressing on for a radical change in the African Churches.[40]

De-Westernization is key to understanding indigenous Churches. Boulaga says

> The whole phenomenon is a response to a certain situation in the sense that it is both reflection of this situation and a protest against it. The dissidence is determined in respect to missionary, middle-class Christianity. The dissidents interiorize certain aspects of Christianity and are content with mimicking other aspects, either as they are or by setting them on their heads; and finally, they react to still other aspects, or even to the whole ensemble, via an "initiating breach" consisting of resumption and transposition, on the level of faith, of the real, social, political, and economic conditionings of the African man and woman today.[41]

Indigenous Churches are concerned with keeping faith and identity. There is a lot about Christ's message that finds affinity with basic traditional values. In his proclamation, Jesus used cultural symbols, traditional ideas, and values to express an authentic way of living in the world. This is the agenda of African Churches resisting missionary Christianity. These Churches are often accused of being unorthodox. They reject the charge and argue that orthodoxy is an ideology missionary Christianity uses to hoodwink the African. Indigenous Christianity says its goal is to make Christianity relevant: "The exegesis of the sects is neither philological nor historical—critical. It is not situated in a hermeneutical tradition that is forever resuming and elaborating the meaning of an already event. It is a creative interpretation or, better, a prophetic actualization, a fulfillment: what the Scriptures tell, what Jesus did, is being reactualized here and now."[42]

These Churches cannot be understood unless one comprehends the spirituality that leads and sustains them. People can only be sustained by a spirituality that springs from their own tradition and culture. It is African culture that is fueling and sustaining the struggle of these Churches. What is this spirituality?

"Describing it negatively, we might say that African spirituality is a logic that organizes attitudes of resistance to alienation or estrangement," says Boulaga.[43] We must first locate this "logic that organizes" a way of living in the world. A manner of living in the world is informed by the concept of life. It is through the concept of person that the concept of life is fully comprehended. It can therefore said that the "organizing logic" of African spirituality is found in the concepts of life and person. Negative experience with Christianity has not changed the basic foundations upon which this spirituality rests. Africans have been able to maintain this spirituality because it springs from their own culture and not from alien sources, thus the strong appeal to culture in African Churches. Concerning African spirituality, Boulaga says

> In spite of the onslaught of Christianity, African spirituality abides, as human beings' conscientizations of their position in the world through the cycles of tasks and seasons and ages of life and social roles, through the bond among the generations, through healing and festival. It abides as the permanent, regulatory metaphor of structures and basic activities of existence, by which are accomplished the genesis of human beings, the conditions of their being, and their access to their humanity until death comes and is accepted as necessary to the truth of life, and as a source of solidarity, communication, and reciprocity among the living. African spirituality is a spirituality in which the afterlife is in the hands of others. My survival is other people's problem, not mine. The important thing is to exist really, without ever seeming to have discharged one's obligations toward others, living or dead. True life is never absent.[44]

Notwithstanding their shortcomings to redirect Christianity, Independent Churches have been powerful forces in both Christianity and politics. Most members of these Churches are of low-income, making the Churches sensitive to issues of justice and a voice of the poor. These Churches have been pressure groups and leaders of liberation forces in Southern and Eastern Africa. Indigenous Churches in South Africa were in many ways a precursor to black theology of liberation. Malawi's struggle for independence was started by the preaching of John Chilebwe and his Providence Industrial Mission. From 1900 to 1915, when he was shot dead in a violent uprising, Chilebwe challenged the colonial administration on human dignity and justice.[45] The down-to-earth message and consciousness to human suffering of these Churches present a challenge to missionary preaching and theology.

THEOLOGY AND AFRICAN CULTURE

The undertaking of the African Churches has slowly gained attention within the once missionary Churches, sometimes called mainline or historical. With the interest in these Churches has appeared a growing scholarship in indigenization.

Although indigenization started in Churches of African origin it has now become a universal phenomenon. Many Christians are now appropriating elements of their culture to make Christianity meaningful to them as Africans. Among the leading advocates of indigenous theology is John Mbiti who argues that indigenous theology is central to proclamation and human development. He contends that imported theology fails to speak to Africans:

> This theology is largely ignorant of, and often embarrassingly impotent in the face of, human questions in the Churches of Africa, Latin America, parts of Asia and the Islands. Thus the Church has become kergmatically universal, but is still theologically provincial, in spite of the great giants of theology. This is a serious dilemma, and if we do not resolve it, it will destroy our foundations as the Church in the world.[46]

To go beyond the present theological method is an immediate task for African theologians, says Mbiti. The universality of the Church can only be affirmed by the presence of indigenous theologies. Mbiti urges theologians to go beyond Western theological methodology and to affirm the universality of the Church by asserting their particularity. "Theology should strain its neck to see beyond the horizons of our traditional structures, beyond the comforts of our ready-made methodologies of theologizing; it should be with the Church where it is, rubbing shoulders with human beings whose condition, outlook, concerns and world views are not those with which we are familiar."[47]

Mbiti believes that the solutions to the problems Africans are facing, such as ethical problems arising from development, Church and state relation, and competing ideologies, must be informed by Christ's message and African values. This way of doing theology will force African theologians to break with traditional methodologies and it may also open the discipline to all Christians. The discipline has hitherto been a business of the privileged, middle-class Christians. It is not surprising that it fails to speak to the conditions of most Africans. Theology, according to Mbiti, is a reflection of all Christians—call it a people's theology.

> Theology need not . . . be the monopoly of the comfortable, the secure, the highly educated, the rich; it can come also from the songs and hymns of peasants as they till the ground; from the impromptu prayers of Christian parents as they nurse their sick child; from the unorganized sermons of the village catechist; from the charismatic leadership of an illiterate founder of an Independent Church; from the old man who is steeped in traditional religious life, who has been converted, together with his several wives and many children, to the Christian faith, and who is trying to make sense of it. Indeed, there is a great deal of spontaneous theologizing going on in the Church in Africa. It is informal, quiet, unwritten, unpolished theology, but nevertheless theology in its own way, and a theology which must be allowed a place in the Church universal.[48]

Burgess Carr, the former secretary-general of the All Africa Conference of Churches, agrees with Mbiti about the nature of African theology. However, Carr says that Christian presence in Africa forces theologians

> to search for the distinctive interpretation of the Gospel in theological terms deriving out of and utilizing African traditional values and beliefs which constitute a vital aspect of the African reality, inform and shape our world view, and endow our existence with meaning and worth. This is what we call *African theology*. Essentially it involves liberating the Gospel from its Western wrappings in order that the truths which Jesus of Nazareth reveals about God may encounter the spiritual, cultural and intellectual worlds of the African personality: the contours and contents of his mind, his cosmology and eschatology, his institutions and values, his history, politics, philosophy and ideology.[49]

The task of producing an indigenous theology arises from a particular understanding about culture and revelation. Missionary Christianity maintains that revelation and culture are one and the same, but Africans argue that they are different. It is therefore possible to separate culture from the basic teachings of the Gospel. The argument is that Christianity has something which transcends culture and yet allows to be mediated by it. This notion seeks to affirm that divine revelation is known and experienced through a particular cultural matrix. This transcendent characteristic of Christianity is what inspires African theologians in the task of indigenization. Kwesi Dickson illustrates how the transcendent characteristic of Christianity informs the African project.

> The basic assumption underlying the concept of indigenization is that there is a distinction between the "core of the Gospel" and Christianity, the later subsuming the former but including cultural elements which came with the Gospel through missionaries. In other words, around the Gospel had been woven cultural vestments which the missionaries considered to be a piece with the Gospel message. The argument, then, is that the Western cultural elements should give way to elements of African culture, thereby placing the Gospel message in a relevant setting.[50]

According to Dickson the term core is used by African theologians to express "the thought of the permanent as against the incidental . . . the salvation of God in Christ."[51] African theologians who have appropriated the concept of core understand the task of indigenous theology to be "a process of 'translation' whereby all that would need to be done in order to give the Church's theology authenticity in the context of Africa would be to examine the various Christian doctrines, as traditionally defined and stated in the West, and reexpress them in ways which would make them acceptable in light of the context of African cultural traditions."[52] From this, studies on the various doctrines of Christianity appeared, from which, it was believed, would emerge "a more culturally acceptable statement of Christian belief." Dickson contends that this approach is limiting, "for the rethinking of Christian belief would then be done along the lines of areas of thought defined in the Western context. . . . An uncritical resort to this procedure could very well stifle greater originality and result in confused thinking."[53] Dickson thinks the project of translation, or adaptation, as some call it, cannot produce a genuine African theology because "the quest for an African theology assumes that there is much more to be done than is implied by indigenization, which by its very nature does not encourage original thinking and analysis; African theology is meant to involve a sustained articulation of faith which would bear the marks of an original African experience."[54]

When Mbiti calls for an indigenous theology, he does not suggest adaptation. He is for a more serious interaction between African culture and the Gospel. It is upon the same understanding that Dickson rejects indigenization. Dickson, like Mbiti, believes that it is through culture that African theology will be able to address itself fully to Africans and their context. He sees the unity between African sense of the sacred, or spirituality, to be a force that would adequately address the problems Africans are facing.

> In adopting the cultural emphasis we wish to be understood to be giving recognition to the need for Christian theology to address itself to the *totality* of the African existence. Theology *judges*, but that can only be part of its task, for it also *affirms*, and what it affirms ranges from African humanity to the Christ; and there is much in the religion-cultural reality which could facilitate the actualization of the twin roles of judgment and affirmation.[55]

Dickson argues that the ambivalence or rejection of culture in a theological task arises from a wrong understanding of culture. He is specifically addressing advocates of black theology in South Africa and other African theologians in general who have argued that cultural theology is irrelevant because traditional African culture has no tools to deal with the modern social, economic, and political problems. Dickson defends appropriating culture for theology, arguing that

> there has been a cultural dislocation, the result of contact with the European world, and this dislocation has not perhaps been recognized for what it is—certainly not by the Church in Africa which continues to function in blissful ignorance, by and large, of the serious cultural handicap under which it labors. While the feeling that African culture cannot be relevant in the present situation may arise from a misunderstanding about, or even ignorance of, what the cultural reality is, there is also the possibility that the thought of giving recognition to this reality is a source of uneasiness arising from the feeling—unarticulated, and perhaps unrecognized—that in the order of things African culture is inferior to Western culture, aspects of which are to be encountered in the urban areas in Africa, in the educational institutions, in governmental systems and in the Church.[56]

Like Boulaga, Dickson believes that African spirituality has much to offer contemporary Africa. African humanity will appear only when Christianity has fully embraced the totality of African life.

> Theology will make a greater impact when it addresses itself to the situation in such a way as to underline the *fullness* of a people's humanity. The emphasis on culture . . . arises from the conviction that the realization of the African's full humanity would come from not only the winning of the socio-economic and political freedom, but also—and more importantly—the winning of the cultural battle, for it is the latter which defines, more fundamentally, the humanity of a people.[57]

Dickson states that the Church will have no business whatsoever to speak for the people if it does not take culture seriously. He maintains that the middle-class mentality prevailing in the African Church is a direct result of the cultural dislocation. A dislocated Church cannot speak for the people. "The Church can only claim the right to speak in the name of society when it is fully identified with it. A religio-cultural awareness should help shake the Church out of its middle-class fastness and reinforce Christian conviction regarding the just society. A rekindling of the awareness of meaning of life as enshrined in African religio-cultural values should underpin the quest for selfhood."[58] At stake in the question of culture and theology is the issue of life and selfhood, the affirmation of these as organizing logic for a manner of living in the world. For Dickson, these basic concepts of the African world are very important for understanding the Christian message in Africa. Life and selfhood do not stand in opposition to Christ's message; if anything, they enhance the relevance of the message to the African reality.

> Selfhood means *conscious existence*, an expression which aptly characterizes the goal of Christian preaching. Christ calls us to *live*, which implies having a personality, and all that it involves. The Church in Africa needs to live, so also do the people in whose name it speaks. Should the phrase "a new life" or "a new creature" be preferred as a description of what Christ seeks to make of use, we would say that if by this were understood the abrogation of selfhood, then this would be a contradiction in terms, for to make the recipient realize his full potential as one whom God in his wisdom and goodness has created. Looked at this way, the cultural emphasis becomes unavoidable.[59]

Cultural Retrieval

Discussion on African theology centers on the role of culture in informing a relevant theology. Mbiti, Dickson, and Bolaji Idowu, are some of the names associated with this project. Mbiti explained cultural retrieval in "Christianity and African Culture."[60] This article is a "classic" among African theologians.[61] While some criticisms have been made of the article, no other work has outdated its views expressed. Many African theologians have drawn from, or are guided by it. The thesis statement of Mbiti's article is: "African culture needs to be studied, analyzed and utilized in the evolution of relevant spirituality and worship of the Church." But Mbiti's article fails to fulfill its thesis. For example, where he discusses "African Culture and Church Life," Mbiti has remained very general.[62] In the conclusion, he presents fifteen areas of discussion, again they are given no depth treatment.[63] In spite of these limitations, it is a great article.

Mbiti begins the article by stating the importance of culture: "An African proverb says that 'the crown of a man is in his hands.' Culture is a person's crown. Therefore the question of culture and the Christian Faith is very important as exemplified by the fact that since the time of our Lord and the early Church, it has continued to come upon every generation of Christians in new demanding ways."[64] Mbiti reminds readers that Africans are not the only people to have invoked culture. He cites three world Christian conferences that have made statements on the importance of culture.[65] A question asked at one of the conferences is worth repeating here. The Bangkok Conference on Salvation today states, "Culture shapes the human voice that answers the voice of Christ" then asks, "How can we responsibly answer the voice of Christ instead of copying foreign models of conversion . . . imposed not truly accepted?" The World Council of Churches Faith Assembly in Nairobi answers: "We have found that He (Christ) is not alien to any culture."[66]

Mbiti understands culture "to mean pattern of life in response to people's environment. This pattern is expressed in physical forms (such as agriculture, the arts, technology, etc.) in interhuman relations (such as institutions, laws, customs, etc.), and in the form of reflection on the total reality of life (such as language, philosophy, religion, spiritual values, world view, the riddle of life-birth-death etc.)."[67] This is to say culture is considered a subframework of organization and interpretation of life. Mbiti argues that culture is the proper medium for understanding the Gospel, for through culture divine mysteries are experienced. In fact, Mbiti says, culture is central to understanding the Incarnation. His point is that it is in and through culture that God saves the world. His interpretation of John 3: 16 serves as a clue to his understanding of the interaction between culture and religion. Mbiti understands the verse to be about God's love "invading people in their culture. The incarnation of our Lord was God's act of intercepting human cosmic history. The Gospel was revealed to the world, in the context and language of culture, and not in an empty vacuum."[68] God continues to enter specific cultures and is mediated in and through them. This is to say revelation was not completed with God entering Jewish culture. Revelation continues every time the Gospel meets a culture. In light of this understanding Mbiti writes: "God gave us the Gospel. Humans give us culture. When the Gospel and culture meet, and if the Christian Faith is generated, then Christianity is the result."[69] For Mbiti the Gospel does not equal Christianity. Rather, his formula for Christianity can be stated as: Gospel+Culture+Faith=Christianity. In light of this formula he argues that "there is no divine form of Christianity which is 100 per cent suitable for all peoples and at all times. Every form of Christianity has impurities—because of human sinfulness. Therefore every cultural setting has a right to evolve its own form or expression of Christianity. No single form of Christianity should dominate another."[70] Mbiti writes:

> Conversion to the Gospel takes place within a cultural framework. . . . It is within culture that we have to wrestle with the demands of the Gospel, and it is within our culture that we have to propagate the Gospel of our Lord. The Gospel does not throw out culture: to the contrary, it comes into our culture, it settles there, it brings its impact on our total life within that culture. It is within our culture that God loves us and calls us to repentance; it is also within our culture that God wants us to love, worship and obey Him. God does not want us to be aliens to our culture—but only alien to sin. Our culture is the medium of receiving, diffusing, tuning in and relaying the Gospel. Without culture we would not hear the Gospel, we would not believe the Gospel, and we would not inherit the promises of the Gospel.[71]

Having argued for the centrality of culture in the propagation of the Gospel, Mbiti speaks against cultural domination, arguing that the Gospel is not a property of one culture; it belongs to all cultures in which Christ is proclaimed. "The Gospel is a stranger in every culture—a stranger who settles down, when it is so accepted in Faith, and yet a stranger who continues to wander on from culture to culture, from generation to generation, calling all people to a newness of life in Christ."[72] He then reintroduces the concept:

> Each culture must count it a privilege to have the Gospel as guest. African culture must extend its hospitality to the Gospel as an honored guest that, hopefully may stay for many centuries and millennia as the case may be. Some cultures of the world have rejected the Gospel while others have restricted its effectiveness. . . . So let African culture treat the Gospel with respect, gentleness, with all due hospitality—for it is a divine message coming into frail cultural vessels.[73]

The metaphor of guest does not imply that the Gospel is temporary, rather that it should be welcomed with openness and allowed to interact with African culture, the host. Mbiti is aware that culture can also be a stumbling block to the advance of the Gospel. In Africa culture has not yet been allowed to freely interact with the Gospel. On the contrary, it has been Western culture which has been a stumbling block to the Gospel in Africa. Cultural imperialism has prevented the growth of an authentic African Christianity and theology. That is why Mbiti writes that cultural imperialism must end to allow room for African culture to interact with the Gospel to produce a genuine African Christianity and theology. This interaction will ensure a viable Christianity in Africa: "Cultural imperialism must terminate first, in order to allow the indigenous culture to relate more effectively to the Gospel, on its own terms and without pressure from outside. . . . The only lasting form of Christianity in this continent, is that which results from a serious encounter of the Gospel with indigenous African culture when the people voluntarily accept by faith the Gospel of Jesus Christ."[74] He further contends:

> Until we can cultivate a genuine Christianity which is truly **MADE IN AFRICA**, we will be building on a shallow foundation and living on borrowed time. Let it be said once and for all, as loudly as technology can make it, that **IMPORTED CHRISTIANITY WILL NEVER, NEVER QUENCH THE SPIRITUAL THIRST OF AFRICAN PEOPLES**. The wisdom of our fathers speaks clearly about this, in a proverb: "That which comes from charity is never sufficient to fill the granary. . . ." Africa does not require imported Christianity, because too much of it will only castrate us spiritually or turn us into spiritual cripples who can only move on a broken and imported crutches.[75]

For Christianity to be viable in Africa, it has to become a mobilizing power. It has to enter into the daily lives of the people. For Christianity to get to a point where it will be a controlling force in the lives of the people, much will depend on how far Africans are allowed to inherit the Gospel. People can be recipients of promise when the Gospel pervades their culture; when it enters the African world and runs through all the channels of communication in their society; when Christianity identifies itself with African spirituality and becomes a framework of interpretation in the African world. Then Africans will become what Mbiti calls "depositaries of the Gospel," and he challenges Africans that "unless we can adequately become the depositaries of the Gospel, unless it can stretch out its roots in our cultural setting, we as the people of this continent, shall be found unfaithful in the sight of God, and the day would come when He would take away the Gospel."[76]

The challenge of African Christians and theologians is to be faithful to God amid all the problems facing Africans today. Mbiti, however, does not think God has left Africans without tools to meet their challenge. "The only tools needed to evolve a viable form of Christianity are: the Gospel, Faith and Culture. Thank God, we have these three fundamental tools in plenty in our continent. With them we are obliged to feel the spiritual granaries of our peoples."[77]

ASSESSMENT

Boulaga and Dickson both agree that the project of indigenous churches has not fully succeeded since they have not redirected African Christianity from the Western (middle-class) mentality to a full appreciation and appropriation of African values and spirituality in a creative manner resulting in a new Christianity. However, it is important to understand these Churches on the basis of what they are: they constitute both protest and reflection at the same time. Mbiti has shown these two elements in his description of these Churches.

> They are primarily a protest movement—against foreign domination in Church life, against foreign structures and leadership in the Church, against the imposition of foreign traditions on their lives as African Christians. They also want to create communities in which their members feel at home, in which there is warmth of fellowship, in which individual gifts and talents are fully utilized, and in which the individual feels that he or she matters very much. The independent Churches are trying to utilize much of African cultural and religious background which has not been so readily accepted in the missionary Churches. In many ways, in spite of dangers of straying away from some central Christian practices, these Independent Churches are affirming that they want to be both Christian and African. In commitment they are making a major contribution to the future of Christianity in Africa. At the same time, they are reaching beyond their local image toward the universal dimension of Christianity.[78]

Boulaga concurs with Mbiti that these Churches constitute protest and reflection at the same time. Boulaga considers these Churches a rejection of false love "caricature of *philadelphia*" and missionary Christianity "which calls forth such sarcasm and ridicule by the infidel." These Churches seek communities of brothers and sisters seeking love, health, and liberation. Boulaga insists that these Churches have reinvented the evangelical project in their reaction to missionary Christianity. The evangelical project "comprises of liberation in one's condition of life, healing of body and spirit, and the permanent celebration in one's life of the Paschal mystery as it aims at the community of brothers and sisters as a total and effective transposition of tribal solidarity into the modern world."[79] This evangelical zeal does not last in the newfound Churches their failure is because the evangelical ideas that originally animated the Churches are not "energetically thought and willed for themselves." The movement becomes side tracked, stagnate or regress. When these Churches do survive they quickly adopt the norm of Western or missionary Churches, copying the rituals, hierarchies, and teachings of the missionary Churches and thereby reproducing their values. Finally, a movement that started as a protest becomes part of the problem it protested.

Nevertheless, these Churches point in the right direction. The problem lies in their praxis. The task then is to put everything they have lifted up into perspective and find the right practice. The traits found in indigenous Churches reveal the nature of the African project: "These traits form an ideal model, type, which affords us a better view of what the force of this dissidence consists in, of what is at work here, even if its full expression and clear formulation is lacking in the actual Churches."[80] Boulaga calls missionary Churches syncretist. Syncretism must be taken into account when missionary Christianity is examined.

According to Boulaga, syncretism appears where people "have assimilated the notion that Christianity is hereditary." He defines it as

> that quality of religious phenomenon by which they have not yet become adequately conscious of their historicity, and so remain the prisoner of a substantialist conception of their own reality and that of others, to the point of seeking a solution for problems arising from acculturation, domination, and the collision of cultures of unequal strength, in some kind of mixture, in symbiosis, in grafting on, in adaptation, or in synthesis. . . . Syncretism is the formless, the amorphous, that which is compatible with whatever one pleases because it has no organizing structure of its own, no concern for internal consistency. Syncretism is an emulsion of trifles and vacuities.[81]

Syncretism also looks backward rather than forward. Its movement advocates glorifying the past, and never taking the future seriously. It is at this point that Boulaga says indigenous Churches are as misguided as missionary Churches in thinking that a return to the past alone could guide African Christianity into the future. "Syncretism fails correctly to take up and assume the past. It undertakes a return to the sources, a return to the tribal heritage and Judeo-Christian origins simultaneously—and the 'find' of course, is nothing but old treasure, where one can dig out a few 'new' ready-to-wear truths for all circumstances."[82] Boulaga says "these facile quests for the founts neglect the *distance* that separates us from times gone by." When a Christian movement does this, it finds itself engaged in the task of preservation and the Gospel then is reduced to "basic evidence" invoked to legitimize the status quo. In this type of Christianity revelation is a deposit of truth. This is what has made missionary Christianity "an ideology of conservation, camouflaging a helplessness in the place of profound change. Christianity becomes a veil for a cowardly, fogbound mentality."[83]

Several phenomena account for the shortcomings of indigenous Churches and the task of adaptation in the missionary Churches. The first is the failure of indigenous Churches to carry through the evangelistic project that originally sets them in motion. The second is that they stagnate as a result of copying the values of missionary Churches, which are steeped in syncretism. The Churches are syncretist because they do not treat revelation as a continuous process of recreation and renewal. Boulaga calls the approach of indigenous Churches the same imaginary praxis used by the missionary Churches, a "praxis operating with a network of symbols that fail to correspond to the infrastructure of real relationships among persons, whether it be in the production and distribution of goods or in the acquisition and distribution of knowledge and power."[84] Like magic, this imaginary praxis

> identifies the relationship between signifier and signified with that between cause and effect. By seizing control of signs and manipulating them, one believes has seized control of the realities they symbolize. In attacking superstructures, one thinks to

> have grasped the infrastructure as well. Religion and culture have been taken to be the secret power of the West. They have been the symbol of the totality of its social and historical being, the precise instances of its absolute legitimation and validation. Thus they appear as the reality-of-its-reality, its quintessence. Appropriate its symbolic universe and you have grasped the whole—science, technology, everything. To make these one's own it suffices to mimic their possessors—their manner of worshiping, of drinking, of eating, of making love.[85]

Such a praxis fails to grapple with historical reality, although it may point out some issues connected with the celebration of life and community. The problem, however, is that here the issues are raised in a such a manner that they seem to be a simple parenthesis in life's daily round, a kind of escape that fails to fill one with courage and a taste—communion falls prey to the imaginary. "One's personhood drowns in the collective emotion, and one escapes the daily prison of censure, injustice and humiliation." When all is said and done, "the need for numbness becomes desperate. Celebration is on its way to becoming an opiate, delivering and consoling human beings in a realm of the imagination."[86]

The efforts of indigenous Churches do, however, provide an authentic Christianity in Africa. The goal of these Churches was expressed by the Conference of Third World theologians held in Ghana in December 1977. In its communique, this conference of mostly African theologians said, "The God of history speaks to people in particular ways. . . . The beliefs and practices of the traditional religions in Africa can enrich Christian theology and spirituality." Africans are eliciting traditional spirituality to enrich Christianity. Traditional spirituality is informed by the meaning of creation which is understood as the bonding of all life, and all life is sacred. People are the epitome of creation, therefore of life. The concept of person then becomes central, informing all action and ordering institutional behavior and conduct as well as structuring the institutions themselves. To close the discussion on indigenous Churches on a positive note, Jean-Marc Ela says that these Churches "strive to develop a symbolism of faith that will take African tradition into account. The African syncretisms are the expression of an oppression rejected. In their protest of the particularity of European Christianity and of its protest of the system of Western domination, they oblige us to rediscover the elements of liberation in Christianity where its pretension to universality is concerned."[87]

Although Christianity had negative influences on African traditional life, Africans are reconstructing the Christian message and enriching it with indigenous spirituality. In their assessment of the African project, some African theologians have argued that it is not enough to address the problem of liberalism from the Christian perspective alone; the whole of society has to be dealt with as a totality. Christianity, politics, economics and other aspects of life must be treated together.

Jean-Marc Ela has evaluated the various dimensions of the African project: negritude, authenticity, adaptation, and indigenous Churches. Ela begins his assessment by evaluating the role of the sacraments, the eucharist in particular, in elite (missionary) Christianity. The eucharist is intended to liberate people, but Ela sees it as a sign of subjugation. Unless present eucharistic practices are critically examined, attempts to reconstruct faith and life in African society will be partial.

> This dependence is no less obvious when we examine the elements of the eucharistic rite itself. Notwithstanding verbal declarations in favor of a liturgical pluralism, a single rite is actually imposed on the ensemble of the Christian communities of black Africa: the Roman rite, whose substance must be respected integrally and faithfully. The rite we follow has not been of our choosing; it bears the mark of a culture not ours; it has not developed in function of our personality or the genius of our people. And so the Eucharist in the daily life of the Church has become the locus of our daily alienation.[88]

For Ela, the eucharist represents the bourgeois mentality of domination. The way the rite is conducted, even the elements themselves, bread and wine, are foreign to the African. The eucharist, then, instead of symbolizing freedom in Christ, stands for dependence experienced in all sectors of African life. At every partaking of the eucharist, the African confirms subjugation and dependence in all sectors of her or his daily life.

> It is paradoxical that, in celebrating Jesus' resurrection, the Church, in its current eucharistic practice, reveals our alienation at the hands of a world that imposes its products on us not only generally, but in the very liturgy that actualizes our redemption. . . . Imported bread and wine are not only nutritive elements that enter into the composition of a European's menu; they are cultural elements with a meaning for a people and connections with its history. We must admit, then, that through the eucharistic matter the Church is imposing Western culture and its symbolic structure on us.[89]

Ela says the eucharist loses its meaning when it fails to take into account African way of life, language, work, or symbols. The eucharist becomes a symbol of domination when it overlooks the realities of a given people. When the symbolism of the rite escapes people, so does its meaning, for what it claims to stand for is not delivered. Thus "the eucharist reveals the domination at the heart of the faith as lived in Africa, within a Christianity that refuses to become incarnate in our peoples."[90] Ela also writes, "In Africa, current eucharistic practice sheds light on an identity crisis of the de facto dependency. The ambiguity of this practice appears when one discovers that redemption is accomplished as part and parcel of a socioeconomic and cultural system that penalizes the food and drink of the earth if they happen to be from the wrong part of the earth."[91]

Ela's discussion on the eucharistic practice in Africa introduces the reader to the quest of indigenous Churches and society, a quest for liberation and dignity of persons. Some argue that it is wrong to begin deconstructing dependency by first considering the sacraments. To this argument Ela replies:

> The locus of our current questions is a situation of dependency and an insecure future. We are not dealing here with a historical context that might be considered peripheral to the Christian faith as lived in African milieu. In order to enter into the mentality of the many human beings around us, we must ourselves be defined in function of the project of liberation. Neither Christian reflection nor the celebration of the mysteries of worship can remain external to this project. Indeed, the understanding of faith, along with the liturgy and evangelical praxis, must be organized from a point of departure in the actual problem of the African peoples today. The faith cannot be lived atemporally: it must be inscribed in a historical context and expressed in a praxis, for it must manifest, in comprehensible signs, the Christian message of liberation in Christ Jesus.[92]

Ela turns to African attempts at liberation and reconstruction. Like Boulaga, Ela finds that African intellectuals are not dealing with the real issues confronting people. He finds their enterprise self-interested and their claims to cultural authenticity a mockery of the African past. Like Boulaga, he finds it of no help to invoke the past in trying to deal with the problems facing Africa today. The task of the African Church today: "In a sense the Church has its *raison d'être* only in the hopes of those who search and struggle for life. . . . How can we rethink the Church at the grassroots, from within a commitment to deprived, plundered peoples? How are the tasks of the Church to be situated within African revolution? If the experience of millions of Africans demands daring transformations, what can the role of the Church be in this process of change?"[93] He also asks: "If the Church is to be defined only in its conscious solidarity with the poor and oppressed, can the Church be itself in today's Africa without rediscovering itself among the little people who cry for justice and liberty?"[94]

This understanding of the Church leads Ela to reject indigenization as regressive. He also strongly condemns the undertaking of the African elite in philosophy and politics in particular, for negritude and authenticity have led to abuse of culture: "The clergy continue to exhaust their resources in the rhetoric of indigenization, and African leaders promote a return to the sources in Black Africa. Does not the quest for authenticity require a rereading of the Gospel and the search for language of faith in African society?"[95] Ela condemns negritude as not an African project but a resurrection of the Western stereotypes of the African as seen in the works of European philosophers and ethnologists. Negritude, like all attempts by the African elite to transform society, fails because it does not address the lot of the majority of the African people. Ela rejects the projects of the elite as ideologies of the petit bourgeois.

> Blackness emerges as a movement of the petit bourgeois, a movement for intellectuals straddling the fence between European culture and African tradition. Now the traumatic condition of elite groups in a state of breach with the real African world is laid bare. As the romanticism wears off, Blackness is seen to be ideology masquerading as a restoration and recognition of black culture but really a vehicle of the African's alienation. . . . Blackness . . . identifies itself as a cunning ideology of the ruling class, the objective ally of imperialistic international capital, dissimulating the defense of its hegemony and the pursuit of its interests.[96]

Ela seeks to underscore the fact that most Africans still live in traditional society and although they experience some shock as the result of the impact of a collision between their tradition and Western culture, they by far have retained a lot of cultural values and practices. "In the colonized world, it is not the masses who suffer from loss of their past; it is the intellectuals who suffer, snatched from their ancestral universe by colonial alienation. . . . The problem for African peasants is not a return to the sources. African peasants have never lost their living culture."[97] He condemns the idea of returning to the past, arguing that

> The return to the past is a vast entertainment project, whose purpose is to distract the exploited masses from the struggle of the present. It is manipulation of the past. It renounces a critical approach to tradition. African identity is not a heritage handed down. It is the deed of historical subjects, who transform themselves as they transform the world in which they live. We must have men and women who strive for new beginnings. Africa will have a different face, a different picture of itself, thanks to their courage and initiative.[98]

Ela does not intend to reject traditional culture, rather to make it the object of "radical revolution which will enable Africans to discover its creative thrust" for the language of faith. What he rejects is uncritical appropriation of culture which intends to legitimize the status quo. When culture is appropriated uncritically it becomes an ideology. "Accordingly, Christianity's incarnation in an African milieu cannot be by way of a facile, casual adaptation of the quaint and the traditional in its expressions of faith. Hence, without a doubt, the present danger of a certain literature concerned with indigenization, whose content its proponents refrain from defining. . . . The problem of acculturation of Christianity must be integrated into the lines of a deliberately liberative strategy of evangelization."[99]

CONCLUSION

All attempts to deal with the crisis of meaning present in both the Church and society began with recognizing the need to recapture Christianity and ground its spirituality in African culture. To transform society African Christianity must rediscover its evangelical zeal. Although Christianity has credibility problems,

Africans have not abandoned it. There are two reasons that account for this: (1) African religiosity and (2) that most Africans practice a Christianity that is infused with indigenous spirituality and traditional values. African spirituality has played a significant part in organizing the way of life of those converted to Christianity. Spirituality is the dynamic power in shaping societal values.

It is from this background that Africans approach the crisis of meaning. Since the crisis has appeared with the presence of missionary Christianity, the first task in recapturing basic human values is to create structures of resistance to Western values. African resistance to bourgeois Christianity is at two levels: (1) African resistance accounts for the formation of indigenous Churches appearing everywhere south of the Sahara, where two-thirds of African Christians are found; (2) African resistance has inspired African theologians to undertake a quest for an indigenous theology. In pursuing this quest, these theologians have advocated appropriating culture, using terms such as *adaptation*, *inculturation*, and *indigenization*. The main reason for appropriating culture is to enable the Christian faith to interact with traditional spirituality to make Christianity authentic and to help in shaping societal values. Christian spirituality alone is powerful, but it has been corrupted by liberalism so that it promotes only middle-class values. Unless Christianity fully enters the African world, it will remain an alien faith.

Culture is the hermeneutical key in a theological process. This approach is based on the view that the Gospel is mediated through culture or that divine revelation is manifested in the ideas and language of a given people. Indigenization has some limitations it must overcome if it is to produce an authentic faith. The first problem is defining its area of operation. At present, it is carried out within missionary Churches and follows the same theological method as missionary Christianity. By sharing the same locus and method, indigenization fails to develop its distinctiveness. The task seems to be a window dressing; preoccupied with outside appearance and not content. This explains why there are no fundamental changes taking place in indigenization. Although the project has noble aims, it is caught in itself. Because of this, indigenization fails to create possibilities for an authentic African Christianity to emerge. Such a Christianity will not appear as long as indigenization is caught in itself because it cannot produce an empowering praxis. This is a praxis which comes as a result of critically examining social reality in its totality. In Africa, this praxis will empower the people and guide them in their struggle for a full humanity.

As cultural retrieval has failed to transcend these limitations it has fallen into abuse. This is what Jean-Marc Ela is referring to when he says that African intellectuals and politicians invoke culture to advance their own ends. His pessimism about the ability of cultural retrieval to address the problems facing the powerless is based on this negative or ideological appropriation of traditional culture. Invoking culture as a means to create possibilities for an authentic faith is a second order of business, says Ela. The first task for Church leaders, nationalists, and intellectuals is to address problems facing most Africans: powerlessness and marginalization—the dependence syndrome into which the whole of Africa is deeply steeped. The task of the Church is to produce a faith that will empower people to deal with this situation.

> This faith must embark upon a self-examination in depth where spoilation of the masses is perpetuated in African society. Or, to put it another way: Christian faith is here put to the test in a determinate historical context. Here the poverty of the majority of Africans is due to a lack of power, lack of the ability and opportunity to speak, the outgrowth of an unfair position in the interplay of socioeconomic factors. The situation of poor populations cannot be analyzed solely in fiscal terms. It is first and foremost a situation of marginality and dependency.[100]

Ela's understanding of the African reality is correct. Unfortunately he leaves his readers with no concrete suggestions for transformation of faith and society, except saying that the Church has a task to rekindle hope among the "little people" and practicing a faith that will liberate "the human person."

> One thing is clear: We can no longer understand and live our faith apart from a context of the liberation of the oppressed. It is here that we must reinterpret the whole of the revealed message, here that we must rethink the Church and its mission, here that we must redefine the lifestyle of our evangelical communities in society. Our manner of reading the Bible is jostled on every side by a society in ferment of question and quest. We must be ready to listen to the people with whom we live and take our position, as women and men of faith and hope, in the becoming of a society that must be led to liberation.[101]

Indigenization could provide Africans ways and means to address the marginality of the people. However, this can only be possible if the indigenization deals with the subject of self-authentication of the people, Dickson says, because this is what people are struggling for. Through cultural retrieval, theology would discover "wisdom in African thought as would make for stability and self-authentication in today's world; in other words, the achievement of *selfhood* which has been delayed by . . . socio-economic and political problems . . . would be immensely facilitated by an appreciation and appropriation of some of African religio-cultural values. Selfhood is a concept which is essential to this study of Christian theology."[102]

Three issues arise in the African reaction to Christianity: indigenization, the quest for indigenous theology that Mbiti calls for; the question of marginality, which follows from a situation of dependence as Ela explains and the subject of selfhood which up to now has not been realized in both the African Church and society. The African agenda is a quest for indigenous theology, liberation from dependence and selfhood. There is one common theme running through the works of African Christian theologians: the African condition is generalized domination seeking liberation. Here liberation means setting free of people and the Christian faith in Africa. Christian faith in Africa needs to be set free so that it can be a creative power in reconstructing society. Boulaga describes the African situation as follows:

> The context is one of domination. The reality denoted by the word "domination" is reducible to a lack of groups and collectivities, and at times individuals as well, of a minimum of the power of to build and grow as societies and persons—the power to ensure their own mental coherence and to have taken hold of the production and reproduction of the material and symbolic conditions of existence. If domination is capability of disposing of the human substance of others, then the question of power becomes inseparable from that of freedom of faith. A "faith" refusing to face this question would be the reflection of a situation of dependence, an alienated credence that would play its powerlessness by investing it in imaginary, "spiritual" power and freedom. The faith of human beings, once they become the agent of their destiny again, can only be in the *form* of rediscovered, rectified power and self-determination. The structuring that will render its content perceptible, enunciable, and hence real for us, will be that of a power of actual, historical self-determination.[103]

African Christians are seeking a faith that will lead them out of the situation of dependence; an authentic faith that will be able to address abuse of power and help people achieve self-determination. An authentic faith will create right relationships in the Church and society.

> The end pursued by the resumption of the founding deeds of African Churches is not to reproduce (not even by indigenizing it) a Christianity whose acculturation is that of other times and places and erected into a way of life. The reality seems to call for the transformation of the human condition as such, the transformation of the system of relationships currently prevailing among human beings, among Africans, and between Africans and the others. The horizon here is one of the risky hope of a metamorphosis that will be the anticipation of "salvation"—its symbolizing or better, its effectuation in our world and our time.[104]

The challenge before Christians in Africa is to transform their faith and society. Transforming the faith would change the concept of power from domination to a means of enabling others to achieve self-determination. With the emphasis on empowering people there would be a restructuring of relationships in Church and society. Power understood as letting others be, would promote dignity and respect of persons. A new concept of power would provide a paradigm and praxis for transformation. Praxis is not something that is given beforehand; it is realized in the process of the struggle for self-determination. Genuine practice for liberation arises out of lived experience, so a model for transformation of faith would be defined by a praxis ensuing from the struggle. Signification, meaning, or sense of ideas and things are gifts of the lived moment of self-determination for people who struggle together to see themselves into being; people joined together to conquer banality of evil and unhappiness, a society ready to work with Christ to liberate people from servitude and to create new life. Boulaga is right in asserting that power and self-determination can be the "sacraments of salvation."

> Power and self-determination, then, inasmuch as they restore life to the dead and liberty to slaves, will be able to be the sacraments of salvation, at once the effect and the condition of salvation, its "demonstration" and its production. Power and self-determination in the service of creation of life—"letting others be" in their consistency and for themselves—will constitute the radical rectification in question. Miracle is power become service, and thereby multiplying life, bursting the vicious circle of violence and the will to power that institutionalizes murder and feeds on the "flesh" of others and abjection. . . . In this context, the task before us is to develop significations from within the very interior of the movement by which societies and persons structure themselves and come to be.[105]

Self-determination is arriving at a creative autonomy, and for this autonomy to become a reality the African Church will have to be "converted to liberty, in its teaching, activity and its relationships. . . . It should be able to initiate an ecclesial practice that would reverse, within itself and for itself, the general tendencies and manners of acting."[106] This would be a process of self-healing that would enable the Church to promote healing in larger society. The process of self healing takes into account the third suggestion for action given by Boulaga: that the Churches need to communicate. "Such a communication will imply autonomy, and must be sought for itself, without the constraint of material and intellectual dependence or dogmatic blackmail."[107] This, then, would be one way to establish independence from the Western Churches.

African Christians and their theologians have done a good job in identifying the problems facing African Christianity. The task to recapture the Gospel has been undertaken; however, the suggestions presented by African theologians to transform Christian faith and society need a much broader and integrated approach. The theological task must be entered upon by taking culture seriously. By appropriating culture as a way to establish an authentic faith (Mbiti), theologians will fully address the issues of selfhood (Dickson), power (Boulaga), marginality, and dependence (Ela).

These theologians have appealed to culture to locate the symbols of ultimate values in African thought and life. The dominant symbol is community, and with it, is the concept of persons. The symbol of community and the quest for dignity of person were first appropriated by indigenous Christianity. It is important to appropriate symbols because people live their symbols. These symbols have within them moral claims which bear the people's values. When symbols fail to function, to deliver the promise, people become demoralized consequently, corrupted. If critically examined, symbols can show what people are struggling for or what they consider ultimate reality and values. At the same time, symbols can furnish a critique of society. Therefore, the transformation of society constitutes a hermeneutics of symbols. This is an interpretation of symbols which reveals the nature of structures within a society mediating (or failing to mediate) people's values. The symbols can then be related positively to the scripture, the sacred oral and written traditions referring to ultimate meaning and reality. In the present work the symbols are life, persons, and community. These form metaphoric structures which challenge missionary Christianity and liberal values, while at the same time elevating respect for persons and affirming personhood, self-authentication or self-determination.

NOTES

1. Fabian Eboussi Boulaga, *Christianity Without Fetishes: An African Critique and Recapture of Christianity*, trans. Robert R. Barr (Maryknoll, NY: Orbis Books, 1984), 48.
2. David Barrett, ed., *World Christian Encyclopedia* (London: Oxford University Press, 1982).
3. John Mbiti, "The Encounter of Christian Faith and African Religion," *Christian Century* (August 27-September 3, 1980): 818.
4. John Mbiti spoke about this challenge in his convocation address to the Senate of Serampore, at the United Theological College, Bangalore, India, on February 5, 1983. "As Christianity Tilts to the South," *The Indian Journal of Theology*, 33, nos. 1, 2, 3 (January-September, 1984).
5. Boulaga, *Christianity Without Fetishes*, 48.
6. *Ibid.*, 59.
7. *Ibid.*
8. *Ibid.*
9. *Ibid.*, 66. His emphasis.
10. *Ibid.*, 111.
11. *Ibid.*, 60.
12. *Ibid.*, 27.
13. *Ibid.*, 27.
14. *Ibid.*, 61.
15. *Ibid.*, 19-28.
16. *Ibid.*, 24.
17. *Ibid.*, 61.
18. John Mbiti, "African Indigenous Culture in Relation to Evangelism and Church Development," in Robert Pierce Beaver, ed., *The Gospel and Frontier Peoples* (South Pasadena, CA: William Carey Library, 1973), 81, 82.
19. Boulaga, *Christianity Without Fetishes*, 62.
20. *Ibid.*, 26.
21. *Ibid.*, 62.
22. *Ibid.*, 67. His emphasis.
23. *Ibid.*, 67.
24. *Ibid.*, 110.

25. *Ibid.*, 67.
26. *Ibid.*
27. *Ibid.*, 69.
28. Hannah Arendt, *On Violence* (New York: Harcourt Brace Jovanovich, 1970), 51.
29. *Ibid.*, 52.
30. *Ibid.*, 53.
31. Boulaga, *Christianity Without Fetishes*, 45.
32. *Ibid.*, 44.
33. *Ibid.*, 46.
34. *Ibid.*, 44, 46.
35. *Ibid.*, 44.
36. *Ibid.*, 64.
37. John Mbiti, "The Encounter," 819.
38. *Ibid.*
39. Harvey J. Sindima, "A General Survey of Independent Churches in Malawi 1900 to 1976," *All Africa Council of Churches Bulletin* (1977).
40. *Ibid.*
41. Boulaga, *Christianity Without Fetishes*, 63.
42. *Ibid.*, 64-65.
43. *Ibid.*, 77.
44. *Ibid.*, 82-83.
45. For full details of the mission and the uprising see George Shepperson and Thom Price, *The Independent African* (Edinburgh: Edinburgh University Press, 1958).
46. John Mbiti, "Theological Impotence and the Universality of the Church," *Lutheran World*, no. 3 (1974): 253.
47. *Ibid.*, 253.
48. *Ibid.*, 257-58.
49. Burgess Carr, "The Relation of Union to Mission," in Gerald H. Anderson and Thomas F. Stransky, eds., *Mission Trends, Number 3* (New York, Paulist Press, 1979), 162.
50. Kwesi Dickson, *Theology in Africa* (Maryknoll, NY: Orbis, 1984), 116.
51. *Ibid.*, 118.
52. *Ibid.*, 119
53. *Ibid.*, 119, 120.
54. *Ibid.*, 120. I have discussed the limitations of adaptation theology in my *Drums of Redemption: An Introduction to African Christianity* (Westport, CT: Greenwood, 1994), 160-61.
55. *Ibid.*, 136. His emphasis.
56. *Ibid.*, 138.
57. *Ibid.*, 139. His emphasis.
58. *Ibid.*, 139.
59. *Ibid.*, 139-40. His emphasis.
60. John Mbiti, "Christianity and African Culture," *Evangelical Review of Theology* (World Evangelical Fellowship, Theological Commission), 3, no. 2 (October 1979), 183-197. All references shall be made to *Evangelical Review of Theology.*

61. Classic denotes that which has withstood the test of time. This does not imply that the text has eternal truth, rather that something rooted in its own historical time continues to invite people in different times and ages to reinterpret it. Culture and tradition are best examples of classics.

62. *Ibid.*, 189-91.

63. *Ibid.*, 37-38.

64. *Ibid.*, 183.

65. The Conference of Salvation Today, Bangkok, Thailand, 1973; Congress on World Evangelization, Lausanne, 1974; The World Council of Churches Faith Assembly, Nairobi, 1975. To this list may be added the 1978 Williwbank Consultation on the Gospel and Culture.

66. See Preparatory Document for the Colloquium as "Confessing Christ in Different Cultures" in John Mbiti, ed., *Confessing Christ in Different Cultures: Report of a Colloquium held at the Ecumenical Institute, Bossey 2-7 July 1977* (Geneva, Switzerland: Ecumenical Institute, 1977).

67. Mbiti, "Christianity and African Culture," 183-84.

68. *Ibid.*, 184.

69. *Ibid.*, 184.

70. *Ibid.*, 186.

71. *Ibid.*, 185.

72. *Ibid.*

73. *Ibid.*, 186.

74. *Ibid.*, 187.

75. *Ibid.*, 187-88. His emphasis.

76. *Ibid.*, 189.

77. *Ibid.*, 188.

78. John S. Mbiti, "Learning from Africa," *Cross Currents*, 28, no. 4 (Winter 1978-79), 392.

79. Boulaga, *Christianity Without Fetishes*, 69.

80. *Ibid.*, 69.

81. *Ibid.*, 71.

82. *Ibid.*, 72.

83. *Ibid.*, 73.

84. *Ibid.*, 73.

85. *Ibid.*, 74.

86. *Ibid.*, 75.

87. Jean-Marc Ela, *African Cry*, trans. Robert R. Barr (Maryknoll, NY: Orbis Books, 1986), 50.

88. *Ibid.*, 3-4.

89. *Ibid.*, 5.

90. *Ibid.*, 5.

91. *Ibid.*, 6.

92. *Ibid.*, 86-87.

93. *Ibid.*, 55-56.

94. *Ibid.*, 76.

95. *Ibid.*, 122.

96. *Ibid.*, 123, 125.
97. *Ibid.*, 126, 130.
98. *Ibid.*, 129.
99. *Ibid.*, 129, 130.
100. *Ibid.*, 136-37.
101. *Ibid.*, 94.
102. Dickson, *Theology in Africa*, 85. His emphasis.
103. Boulaga, *Christianity Without Fetishes*, 221.
104. *Ibid.*, 218.
105. *Ibid.*, 221-22.
106. *Ibid.*, 223, 224.
107. *Ibid.*, 225.

7

Community of Life: A Framework for Transformation

The African quest is for the meaning of being human. However, to be fully human is not something that one can achieve by one's own initiative. Traditional African wisdom is emphatic that people realize their humanity in the company of others; the union between person and society is indivisible. Social relations and structures promote or limit fullness of life, and accordingly, the meaning of being human concerns community and relations. Therefore, the term *person* implies society and exists only via the instituting action of the latter. From this it follows that the African struggle is for a community that will provide possibilities for Africans to realize their full potential. This chapter presents a framework of a community where fullness of life will be the organizing logic of all relations, the very foundation of community living.

Relations and similarly the meaning of living together as a people in Africa today are distorted. The elite have distorted these relations by corrupting the understanding of basic values or the symbols of these values. Symbols represent structures of wholeness of people and nature.[1] As structures, symbols are lived through networks of relations, institutions, and activities of daily living. Symbols regulate present activities as well as invoke the past in which they stand and the future to which people are bound. Stated differently, symbols invoke memories of the past while challenging people to the future, or that symbols have the ability to present the interplay of past, present and future. This ability invokes people's creativity and it is a creativity which mediates a future even as it presents a present. Without creative symbolizations people do not know how to live in the present and consequently have no future. It is for this reason that symbols and values become the foundations upon which the community rests. The point is that communities organize themselves around particular symbols or values. Some symbols further life while others destroy it. In a way, symbols form the organizing logic and power which give people a sense of direction. When these organizing symbols become corrupted or eroded, people experience loss of meaning of their work and of a sense of direction. Life becomes meaningless and this is reflected in the way people treat each other. Since there exists no common understanding of values, every person tries to fulfill her or his own goals and aspirations. Consequently, relations become corrupt since one treats others as means toward desired goals. Society no longer cares how people are treated or whether they lead a truly human life. When symbols and values no longer have organizing power, the result is a crisis of people's identity and rupture of society.

Relations are distorted at a fundamental level in African society evidenced by the fact that symbols, having been emptied of their meaning and values, no longer perform their work. Boulaga and Ela have shown that life, the central symbol in African tradition, has been eroded by bourgeois Christianity and the bureaucratic elite. Other symbols include the concepts of person and community. In traditional society everything was directed toward personhood and building of community. The concept of personhood no longer informs people how to treat each other. The understanding of community among the elite, is based on political association. In single party-states, the party organizes these associations. Community is a political unit, but only if politics is understood as the art of living together. However, this life together should not be based on self-interested ends. Communities are not constituted, but develop as relations between people grow. They are networks of relationships of care and concern; associations are self-interested.

Ela laments that relations among people have become so self-centered that even the symbols that are supposed to have redemptive power do nothing to change the African crisis. If anything, these symbols lead people to their own destruction. This is the lament of Ela in regards to the role of the eucharistic elements in the African church. The elements are distorting the meaning of life together in the world since they no longer provide the transformative power that changes people and relations. Instead, the symbols of life are mediating subjugation and death. In both church and society symbols have been emptied of their meaning and people no longer know how to live, how to make sense of their situation. The result is a crisis of thought, meaning, and identity.

For this change to take place, there will have to be a radical transformation, making the symbols stand on their heads—a total critique. The transformation will then have to be a change of relations at a fundamental level. This is the level at which interpretation of basic values takes place. Since basic values or symbols have been distorted, the task of transformation of relations and society will involve a reinterpretation of basic values and symbols. This is to say that reconstruction of African society will be done as a hermeneutics of symbols of basic values. This hermeneutic will serve as a foundation for building basic values in society.

A hermeneutics of symbols will reveal how life has been corrupted in contemporary Africa as a result of distorting basic values. The task will allow us to appropriate anew basic symbols, values and structures. The reappropriation of these will give us a new framework of relations. This framework will not be imposed on the people's struggle but will arise from their own understanding of values and symbols. As such, the framework will be able to include people's dreams and aspirations. For a true transformation to take place, the paradigm for change must emerge from within the people themselves because a paradigm imposed from outside can never include people's hopes and fears. The hermeneutics of symbols is emphasized to avoid prescriptions from without which will not bear the fear and aspirations of the people. At present, Africans fear the meaninglessness of life. Human life has lost value and thus people have lost respect and dignity. People are crying for liberation; their hope is for a new and transformed society in which men and women will have respect, dignity, and self-authentication, and self-determination will be the order of the day.

The distortion of symbols in Africa has occurred in both the church and society. Symbols have also been corrupted at a theological level. Distortion of symbols at this level obliterates people's correct understanding of the Divinity. Such a distortion degrades people because it negates their true humanity. This is very serious in Africa where people understand themselves and their values in light of their relation to Divinity as the source of all life. It is to this effect that Boulaga writes: "Human beings who suffer the loss of their perception of 'values' lose as well a perception of the God who constitutes the basis of these values, or rather, who prescribes them. The converse is equally true: the one who, explicitly or implicitly, denies the true nature of God falls prey to passions and vices."[2]

In light of this theological crisis, the task of reconstruction in Africa will require a theological reinterpretation of symbols. In other circumstances, the task of transformation would require a decoding of secular and sacred symbols, but in Africa this distinction does not exist. Life as a symbol stands for human life, human bondedness to nature, and the Divinity. As was shown in chapters 3 and 4, the symbol of person refers to the special role that humankind has in creation. Chapter 4 demonstrated that the concept of community plays an important role in informing personal and collective identity, and is a symbol for security.

The African quest is for fullness of life. To speak of fullness is to imply that there is a level of life that is realized when people take control of their own future as they appropriate their past. In living in the present, they share and enjoy the material and spiritual benefits available and take responsibility in the shaping of their future. To participate in creating one's destiny or that of one's people is being the subject of history. Subjecthood is fulfilled humanity, or personhood at its fullness. Boulaga puts it in this way: "Personhood is perfectly itself when it is the presence both of what is no more and of what is not yet, when it fulfills the former and proclaims the latter all at once. Personhood arrives at self-realization in accordance with the ancient figures. Better, it actualizes and renews these. It is a process of activation of the past and invocation of the future."[3] This understanding of personhood demands that the task of the reconstruction of society include a hermeneutics of the symbol of personhood. This also means that the notion of personhood be appropriated for a theological framework of transformation.

A HERMENEUTICS OF SYMBOLS

The burden of the present work is to provide a paradigm for transformation via a hermeneutics of symbols. Although Africa is too vast to make generalizations, there are certain fundamental values that Africans share, such as the concepts of life, person, and community. Among the Achewa of Malawi, *moyo* (life) and *umunthu* (personhood) are foundational concepts of self-understanding and identity.

Moyo is an all-encompassing and overarching symbol of living. It forms the basic framework of interpretation in Malawian society, because it speaks of what creation is for and what it is intended to achieve. Creation is intended to be the home of life and to serve life as life breaks frontiers and reaches super-abundance. The first meaning of *moyo*, then, has to do with the cosmos. *Moyo* refers to cosmos since it inhabits life; creation is therefore understood as life. Life begins and ends, biologically, yet life continues to transcend itself in different ways. *Moyo* as the foundation of all creation has no end. It is both material and yet spiritual; humankind participates on both levels of *moyo*. It was from this understanding that the universe shares life with people that the notion of bondedness was developed in Chapter 5. The idea underlying the concept of bondedness is rooted in the symbol of *moyo*.

At the anthropological level, *moyo* refers to biological existence. Here, *moyo* means the act of living connected with activities of biological existence. Fundamental to biological existence of all creatures is blood; consequently, blood is considered the sign of *moyo* as biological existence and is itself called *moyo*. Breath, a vital sign of biological existence, is also called *moyo*. People speak of *moyo* as breath when talking about someone taking a last breath in death. The Achewa will say, life went out of the person. *Moyo* has other meanings in connection with human life. *Moyo* refers to physical well-being or simply health. In everyday speech, *moyo* also refers to health and well-being, as well as the estate of an individual or community. In light of these interpretations, the term is used as word of salutation, wishing good health, well-being, and peace.

It must be emphasized that life is not defined by activity: motion (vibration), heat, mutation or nutrition. Among the Achewa these conditions are not the only indicators of life, for their opposites could also indicate the presence of life. Take, for example, the question of heat as indicator of life. Achewa wisdom says there are other forms of life that are not destroyed by heat. This means that heat only tells us about *some* forms of life and this is true of motion and mutation. Of course some forms of life manifest themselves through these conditions, but these are not the only ways we can tell the presence of life. The Achewa hold that life manifests itself in opposites: heat (fire) and cold (water), mind (thought) and word (action), good and evil, male and female, day and night, and so forth. In addition, they believe that forms of life are always in pairs. When life is not thought of in light of its opposite—say, heat without cold, or activity without state, it leads to very narrow and erroneous views about the nature of creation; take, for example, the idea that a stone has no life. Achewa thought maintains that a stone is full of life in the core of the particles that make up the stone, but we are unable to see or feel it. Achewa wisdom says that given the limitations of human intelligence and senses, humans are unable to either know or understand all forms of life. There are many forms of life beyond human comprehension or sensory perception. Just because we are not able to experience other forms of life through our senses, it does not mean there is no life in them. African wisdom insists that the cosmos is full of infinite varieties of *moyo* unknown to humans, and that these varieties of *moyo* are indestructible, and only change forms and patterns.

Apart from biological and cosmological meanings, *moyo* means other things, such as right relations between people, sharing, openness, and spiritual well-being. All these are non-material things but nonetheless necessary to support biological life. To exclude the socio-religious dimension of *moyo* would be to neglect the fact that *moyo* is constitutive in the meaning of persons. Central to the meaning of persons is respect, that attitude and act of affirming someone as human. This notion emerges from the understanding that people have something sacred in them, *moyo*. External things are immaterial when it comes to respect of persons. Rather than wealth or status, it is only *moyo* in a person that demands respect at all times and everywhere.

To respect someone is to affirm a person which is more than acknowledging the other's presence but a willingness to enter into that person's world, to share *moyo* and to open up one's world to others for dialogue. To dialogue is to make the experience of others one's own, thereby making understanding possible. Unless people understand each other or have a sense of the "said," they cannot truly communicate. By experience we are referring to the possibility or condition for understanding. To speak of a particular experience, the African experience, for instance, is to refer to a historical condition that allows for understanding of what it means to be an African. This historical condition also opens up future possibilities for understanding. For Africans, the historical condition provides possibility for self-understanding, while for non-Africans this condition serves as a hermeneutical key for the possibility for understanding African life in a given period. Experience is not a completed event, but a possibility for disclosure of the nature of things. Experience is a process that continues to unfold and has a potential to transform those participating in it. This transformation is what we call understanding. Communities are built on shared experience or *moyo* gained through communication.

To speak about experience is to imply the possibility for understanding and communication, which transforms those involved. African traditional society realizes the potential for harmonious living that comes with shared experience. To encourage understanding between people, traditional wisdom in Malawi teaches that it is dehumanizing for people to rush into business when they meet. The first few minutes after meeting are taken up with sharing with each other the experience of *moyo*. To share *moyo* is more than a salutation; it is getting to know what informs the other's world at a given time or day. To share one's *moyo* is to tell others about one's experience. It is the sharing of *moyo* which enables real communication or historization of people and events to take place.

Moyo as the historization of people, is the art of learning to live together by accepting and affirming one another as persons and establishing genuine communication. In traditional society, one begins to learn about this art of living together as a community, in a ritual process. Through ritual one learns about self-respect and about dignity of persons. The key to both is the art of sharing *moyo*. Through ritual one is not only grafted, as it were, or affirmed as a person and member of a particular group but also taught the fine art of being open, essential for character building. Being open is also the foundation for true communication through which *moyo* can continue to flow. The continuity of the life of a community depends on how open the channels of communication are. Distorted relations are a direct result of not being open to each other or living together as people informed by the symbol of *moyo*.

It has been shown in earlier chapters that according to African thought all life has its origin in the Divinity. Furthermore, it was mentioned that Africans maintain that the Divinity as the giver of all life is *Life* itself. This relation between human life and the Divinity allows people to discern divine intention for human life and the cosmos. From a religious perspective, *moyo* refers to that part of human life that has the capacity for self-transcendence and the ability to seek and respond to spiritual things or to communicate with the Divinity. This is the part of human life that can respond to divine presence or to the source of life itself—Divinity.

In the post-colonial period, *moyo* as a symbol of the act of living has been distorted. By distortion we imply that the symbol has become misleading because its original meaning has been twisted and changed to mean other things other than what it actually shows. There may be some truth in a distorted symbol, but the truth is so clouded that it is impossible to draw out the original meaning. By truth it is implied the condition of the state of things or how things are in themselves. This is the uncovering of people's temporality and of the language that mediates them. Language mediates the world because it shows people how the world is. Distorted symbols fail to show or mediate the world for people to see how things really are. The distortion of *moyo* as the symbol of interpretation of the world and human life, is clearly seen in its usage by the bureaucratic elite. To them, the term means "enjoying oneself" or "feeling good," betraying a utilitarian view of life. The understanding of *moyo* here is material only. In this respect, *moyo* has come to mean having power needed to acquire status symbols; material things that "spell success." Here power does not refer to freedom and the creative urge that enable others to live an authentic life. Creative freedom is power known as love; it is life. *Moyo* as power in the elite sense denotes capacity or force. Power understood as capacity or force knows no limit, it is therefore destructive. Here we see how some Malawians have bought into Hobbes's view that one must have power over others to protect oneself against others and to maximize self-interest relative to desired ends. This notion of power often leads to greed, and with greed there can never be enough resources to go around. People fight for the scarce resources and use underhanded means to acquire them. Thus corruption, the handmaid of injustice, sets in. Real power is not over others or toward self-interested ends, but the concern to enhance life together. The corruption of the meaning of *moyo* by the bureaucratic elite is the result of their disorientation in African values and assimilation of Western ones. With this mentality they fail to realize the potential of the concept of *moyo* for nation building.

We have seen that *moyo* is an all pervasive symbol of interpretation. But this symbol can remain simply an abstract idea if not grounded in reality. In order to ground the symbol of *moyo* one has to address the question of fullness. For the Achewa, fullness is in realizing *umunthu* (personhood), that state of experiencing all that is good and worth human life—a historization of *moyo*. In other words, *umunthu* stands for basic values of human life, that which gives human life meaning. By articulating basic human values, the term distinguishes people from the cosmos or nature and other creatures with whom people share a common life. *Umunthu* is rooted in the Achewa understanding of the meaning of person (*munthu)* as a member of humankind or a particular community (*anthu*). *Umunthu* does not refer to person or people; it refers to quality and fullness of human life. We can therefore say that *umunthu* is concerned with the actuality of living in time and space. It is about being a historical and temporal creature. Since fullness is sought in concrete historical conditions, *umunthu* is about authentic living, accordingly, *umunthu* is against all that relativizes human life or prevents its fullness. To underscore: *umunthu* is about subjecthood of persons. As in the case of *moyo*, *umunthu* is about the meaning of relations in a given community. Relations are determinative because they provide and limit possibilities for self-discovery and actualization of *moyo*.

Umunthu involves moral development and character building. In all relations, morality and character play important roles in determining how people treat each other. Through the symbol of *umunthu* we meet people as moral characters, therefore, they can be agents of change when recognized as persons. To be recognized as a person is to have self-respect, or to realize self-determination. In order to respect others, there is a need for character development or training in basic values of a particular society. Character development deals with how one conducts self and behaves toward others. This is a discovery of basic values and a realization of one's duties and responsibilities. When the Achewa say, "*uyu ndi munthu*" (this is a person), they imply that the person knows her or his duties and responsibilities, and is truthful and generous. *Umunthu* includes the virtues needed to have a strong moral society: truthfulness, generosity, self-respect and respect for others, integrity, duty, and responsibility.

Generosity is a very important virtue in African society because it is the foundation upon which rests the notion of sharing, a key idea in the concept of community. Sharing is one way of expressing bondedness and selflessness. Generosity as a virtue promotes unselfishness which allows people to stand together in want or plenty. Readiness to share is a complete surrender of individualism in favor of a communal life. This is a lesson a child learns as soon as he or she becomes conscious of him- or herself as a person. A request must express a readiness to share with others. A child puts the request like this: "*ndipemphe nao*" (Please, give to me *also*). Implicit in this phrase is the assumption that the child is not the sole recipient. Children learn that individualism is unacceptable behavior.

To be generous is a moral obligation in Africa; generosity is considered a virtue par excellence. While it is expected of everyone, people do not go around asking that they be given something. Against development of such a practice, the wisdom of the ancestors says: "*npatse, npatse nkulanda, mwana wa mfulu adziwa yekha*" (To demand a gift is to rob someone, for a generous person needs no asking). This saying seeks to make it clear that traditional society is against creating situations of dependence resulting from a habitual practice of asking for gifts and hand-outs. In traditional society everyone has to work. Idlers and beggars have appeared with the new economic order—capitalism. As stated in Chapter 4, in traditional society those who were too weak to work, the sick, the aged, or the handicapped, were taken care of by society through its practice of sharing.

Generosity as a moral obligation assures security, mutuality, and a means for social communication. It is about production and distribution of goods in society, as a complete circulation of available resources and benefits. This circulation gives everyone a chance or possibility for self-realization. Everyone controls the desire or temptation to accumulate for self-centered reasons; it is in sharing of the products realized through one's labor that one's life becomes meaningful and at the same time useful to the community. Such a person can therefore expect to enjoy the fruits of others' labor. In traditional society production for its own sake is an alien idea; neither does it make sense to enjoy the fruits of one's labor all by oneself. While sharing presupposes production, it is not a mere function of production, but rather the opposite: production emerges from the fact of sharing. Everyone works to share the fruits of labor with others. Every uncorrupted African works not for him or herself but to assist parents, family, friends, and others. This is a moral obligation that underscores the traditional wisdom that no one is self-made, therefore no one should live for him- or herself. In a society where everyone is responsible for the other, failure to give aid when help is needed is a rejection of responsibility and virtues. This moral obligation seems to be universal in Africa. Bukasa Mpansu comments about this obligation as people of Zaire think about it:

> The moral obligation to give is synonymous with living itself and its opposite is, clearly, in the refusal to give. Those who refuse to give are not merely socially ostracized and placed beyond protection; they are also real enemies of society for they expose it to the danger of death. If refusal to give is refusal to identify with others (since giving implies relations with others) then by the same token it is a kind of killing, since living is essentially "being with" others.[4]

Among the Achewa, and Malawians in general, anyone who does not help others is not *munthu*, for the individual does not know the meaning of living together as a people. One may accumulate wealth and gain status, but people will not say, "*Uyu ndi munthu*" (This is a person). Anyone who does not share lacks the value of *umunthu*, the meaning of *moyo*, or living in the world as a bonded creature. One may have physical qualities of *munthu*, but inside the individual is like an animal. The human face that such a person has is only a mask. Sharing begins when *moyo* is announced as a salutation. When people exchange *moyo* as a greeting, they begin an authentic way of living in the world—sharing. To live in bondedness is to know that sharing is the "organizing logic" that holds creation together. "The principle of sharing begins to operate when on the first encounter of the day people wish each other health and peace. To 'salute' or greet someone is, etymologically, to wish them well! Sharing food and drink, especially with an unexpected visitor, is a practical expression of the principle. Everywhere what is sought is satisfaction of everyone's needs rather than satiety for the individual."[5]

The development of these essentials qualities is the task of the individual as well as the community. Society teaches one how to be truthful, generous, develop self-respect and perform one's duties and responsibilities. These virtues are included in the package of basic values that society teaches, but the development of these virtues is the responsibility of anyone willing to be fully *munthu* by being virtuous.

Umunthu is fullness or wholeness of *moyo*, that is, society's "yes" to the self-transcendence of *moyo*. *Moyo* more than seeks its maximum level, for it always seeks to transcend the limits imposed from within or without by people. When society says "yes" to *moyo*, it joins hands with *moyo* to say "no" to all that negates experience of fullness of *moyo* in peoples' concrete historical conditions. Saying "yes" to *moyo* is to affirm people. Society says "yes" to *moyo* by providing a morality and creating space for people to realize or actualize themselves. Herein lies the need for society to order itself in such a way that its structures will be conducive to a morality that will allow the people self-determination. This is an absolute necessity for every society if it is to be viable as a unit.

The way society is ordered can create, demean, or completely negate people possibilities of *umunthu*. This is to limit *moyo* or cut short the future of the community. Fullness of *moyo* as symbolized in *umunthu* cannot be achieved with structures that erode the meaning or value of *moyo* by creating inhuman conditions, such as the lack of food, health, justice, political participation, and education. The absence of basic needs denies people space to be people and to discover their potential and plan their future accordingly. What is the future of a society where its children die of hunger, malnutrition or basic lack of health care services? How can a society be viable when most of its minds are wasted because many parents cannot afford tuition and fees in an educational system that favors those already well-off? Practical experience rejects the idea that an elevated economic system, one in which the economic cycle is not complete, will benefit all. For a society to say "no" to *moyo* is to commit suicide.

Wherever people are denied their *umunthu* there develops a social and political system that seeks to effectively patronize them. Social relations are elevated with a handful at the top. In an elevated economic system, the people at the top are the benefactors. These are the ones who believe they know what the people need better than the people themselves. This happens at local and international levels. The economic centers of the world think they know what the periphery countries need. Such moral arrogance arises out of the lack of cognitive respect, or respect for persons. This disrespect presupposes that some people, by virtue of their status, wealth, or influence, are the "brains" of the poor. To patronize is to diminish human worth by crippling and stifling the creative energies of a people, which produces dependence. Dependence is denying people possibilities for realizing their *umunthu*, their subjecthood.

The term *umunthu* has to do with moral-political character of *munthu* or *anthu* in a particular community. As a term symbolizing moral-political character, *umunthu* focuses on how people live as subjects of history or how they order themselves and their institutions for all to truly actualize their potential and realize their future. *Umunthu* is the historization of persons in the continuum of *moyo*. To discover how people live as a political community, to see whether there is a process of historization in a given community, *umunthu* demands critical examination of the moral fiber of a society. An inquiry into the moral character of a society is undertaken to examine how people's moral values guide or fail to affect relations and communication between them. Moral inquiry reveals how people affirm each other as persons or deny each other possibilities to be fully human. Moral inquiry is political ethics examining all structures and relations. In the inquiry, attention is given to issues of power, justice, freedom, and political economy, the last of which deals with the questions: Who gets what, and at the expense of whom?

Marriage illustrates how seriously the Achewa consider the question of *umunthu* in terms of moral-political character. Among the Achewa, marriage is between two families or villages, not just two persons interested in each other. Marriage is not arranged but mediated by representatives of the two parties, usually the uncles or some elderly person. When a young man tells his uncle that he is attracted to a young woman in another village, before his uncle goes to the woman's family to present a proposal for marriage, an inquiry is made into the moral character of the family and the village. The uncle or the man's family may ask: "Are those people real (*anthu*)?" In other words, do they affirm each other as persons? The interest is in whether the young man's *umunthu* will be realized, given the moral character of the woman's family and village. The decision to propose will depend on the result of the secret moral inquiry undertaken by the uncle or any other appointed person. Frequent quarrels, lack of respect for persons, injustices by the chief or the village head, and so forth may stop the whole matter, for these constitute a lack of understanding of *umunthu*. These cases affect moral values, relations, and communication in any given family or village. The secret inquiry reveals that the people in that village are not *anthu*, since they deny each other possibilities to be fully human or qualities of *umunthu*. *Umunthu* points to issues of communication, power, and justice, or human relations.

Moyo and *umunthu* form the symbolic framework for understanding the cosmos, nature, and above all meaning and authentic manner of living in the present. The function of these values, which have withstood the test of time, is to inform persons and society how *moyo* can reach its fullness. The values seek to ensure that humanity and the world are not cut short. The values have been passed down from one generation to the other, prescribed by ancestors and sanctioned by the giver and sustainer of life, the Divinity. Surely, the Divinity is always pleased with anything that enhances human life or allows people to live together in peace while making it possible for creation to have a future. Therefore, *moyo* and *umunthu* are "sacred" values of ultimate meaning. For in far as they order the political realm, they awaken consciousness of divine intention for human life and creation as a whole. The terms provide possibilities for reconstruction of society just as they have a potential for transformation of faith and religious structures.

THE SYMBOL OF LIFE

What kind of social structures would derive from *moyo* and *umunthu* if they were to be appropriated as a framework for transformation? First, let us recall some basic facts and what has led us to these symbols. We did not choose these symbols; they emerged and presented themselves to us as we sought to understand the struggle of the people. We arrived at them after going through Africa's biography. The purpose for studying Africa's biography was to learn the state of affairs and the factors informing the situation. We learned from the exercise that people are going through an identity crisis and it was argued that the crisis was caused by liberalism as it manifested itself in colonialism and the Christian evangelization of Africa. We have shown various attempts toward retrieval of traditional values through which it was believed people could rediscover their identity. These endeavors had limited success and it was demonstrated that the failure was partly because those engaged in the task had not broken away with the liberal tradition which had eroded symbols of basic values. On the other hand it was because the symbols and spirituality ordering societies and the lives of the people had not been considered when proposing paradigms for change. People live their symbols grounded in their spirituality or understanding of their world. It was because of these reasons that we went in search of the symbols informing a manner of living in the world. For the Achewa, we located basic values in the symbols now under investigation.

We are invoking these symbols to reorder society and since these are symbols of basic values and meaning among the Achewa, and many other African peoples, we believe they will be able to inform an authentic life. We must remember though, that authentic life cannot be given, it can only be developed. Authenticity is a project of self-discovery made possible by right relations in a given community and its structures. This is a way of living proper to people. Africans will discover and develop an authentic life as they engage in the task of establishing structures which will allow traditional values to form a social moral fiber. What we are saying here is that a paradigm for transformation of society about to be attempted, is only a sketch for the project of authenticity. As a sketch, there will be some loose ends; the full blown picture is never part of praxis. The "whole" has to be realized through experience. The sketch is seeing in part. The details of the "whole" or what it means to be fully human, awaits those who are in the struggle. We therefore argue that authenticity is cultural interpretation of basic symbols as understood and experienced by the people. An authentic life is lived interpretation of basic symbols and as an interpretation, it is a creative task.

In decoding the Achewa symbols of basic values it was stated that *moyo* and *umunthu* are primary symbols, and that *moyo* pervades all creation and regulates it. We asserted that *moyo* was the foundation upon which everything rests, and it was shown that the characteristic of this symbol was self-transcendence; even death cannot stop *moyo* from seeking its fullness. Traditional thought maintains that ancestors live beyond death, and that death is part of the self-transcendent character of *moyo*. The point is that *moyo*, as foundation, is before creation and it is always ahead of creation through its self-transcendent nature. *Moyo* never ends, it is eternal. Nothing is eternal but Divinity. It is because of this understanding of *moyo* that Achewa thought calls Divinity, *Moyo*.

Referring on Achewa anthropology we said the activity of being alive as a person is signified by *moyo*. (This also goes for the activities of all creatures.) Considering what has been restated here concerning *moyo*, we now define this pervading symbol as that *which is*, the foundation of creation, even as creation itself is mediated and held together by it. *Moyo* is the *all* in *all* value and meaning of creation. We therefore say *moyo* is the overarching symbol of all creation. Society is mediated by *moyo*, but also *moyo* mediates society. By saying society mediates *moyo* it is implied that the *raison d'être* of society is to provide possibility of *moyo*. This being the reason for having society, it is incumbent upon its members to make this possibility a reality by creating conditions that will not limit *moyo* as it seeks to transcend itself.

Achewa creation myths rank people above everything else although *munthu* is part and parcel of and shares the same destiny with creation.[6] Various traditions in Malawi maintain that all things evolve around *munthu*. In the order of creation only *munthu* is next to the Divinity, in life and death. This proximity gives people a special relation with the Divinity, which makes *munthu* the center of and the highest value possible in all creation. Not only does all creation evolve around *munthu*, but all value is based on *munthu*. If something is of the highest value, or if it has meaning at all, it has to do with *munthu*. Malawian thought maintains that *munthu* must be the embodiment of *moyo*.

Malawian thought maintains that *moyo* in *munthu* are of the highest value. This value is by the order of creation or of the divine origin. The Divinity-given value of *moyo* of *munthu* is what the Achewa call *umunthu*, a state or condition of fullness of *moyo*. This condition has to be a present reality. In this respect, then, *umunthu* is the quality and condition of *moyo* in a historical process, hence all action is to be directed toward the fullness of *munthu*. This explains why *umunthu* also refers to character and moral behavior. There are many Chichewa wise sayings pertaining to development of character and moral behavior, since it is through these that one really becomes *munthu*.[7] Real *munthu* is the one whose behavior, moral life, and relations with others are toward respect of persons. To respect someone is to acknowledge that person as the highest value possible. The one who respects the dignity of others does not treat them as if they were nothing; real *munthu* is the one who lets "others be" or live as persons. We therefore take *munthu* as the organizing concept of our framework for transformation.

It is not possible to live as a person or experience fullness of *moyo* without society's willingness to maintain the highest value possible—*munthu*. Society's readiness to maintain and protect *munthu* can be seen in its moral fiber as it regulates relations and structures. Since *munthu* cannot be understood apart from society, then the primary task in restructuring society should focus on the meaning of *munthu*. In our model for transformation we place community as one of the constitutive concepts essential for mediating *moyo*. For society to be able to mediate *moyo*, its moral fiber must be grounded in the people's values as expressed by their virtues. In Malawi the virtues include generosity, or sharing, and mutuality. These form an internal mechanism for assurance of continuation of community and the self-transcendence of *moyo* of its members. Only social structures and a morality dedicated to the continuation of *moyo* can assure a community of its own viability.

A community in which *moyo* is considered the highest value and people are treated with respect and dignity is a community of life. On other hand, a situation in which people are denied fullness of *moyo*, a context of domination, for example, is a community of death. This is a community where mutuality does not exist because everyone lives for self. Such a situation arises when justice is not maintained and power falls into abuse, or both justice and power are corrupted and distorted. In the liberal tradition justice means distribution, or giving each person his or her due in an equitable manner, as Aristotle writes: "Since the equal is the median, the just, too, will be a median. . . . 'To each according to his deserts.' . . . In distributions the just share must be given on the basis of what one deserves."[8] For Aristotle, equal distribution is among equals and for what they do. In Malawian thought, justice means right relations and what constitutes "right" is *moyo* or that which promotes *moyo*. Right relations are about *moyo* and *umunthu*. The primary goal of traditional legal system is to establish right relations between people. Right relations promote mutuality while at the same time controlling acquisitiveness and abuse of power arising from seeking self-centered ends. Understanding justice as right relations, power emerges as the common stock of a people in the service of *moyo* and *umunthu*.[9] People are both the base and mediators of power. This means that domination is expropriation of the common stock. Injustice is expropriation of the shared. The concept of right relations deals with rectifying power and self-determination.

The concept of justice as right relations concerns social structures. It is impossible for mutuality to exist in an elevated social structure or situation of dependence. The concept of right relations, then, concerns ordering social structures in such a way that *moyo* will flow and people will be affirmed. The concept of right relations means a critique of the situation of dependence that makes it impossible to realize *umunthu*. The value of *moyo* is reduced in dependence. People are not treated as the highest value possible but as tools for production for the elite. People labor and the bureaucratic elite and the entrepreneur get well off by reaping the benefits thereof. This is the expropriation of the common stock. Situations of dependence are complex. In order to rectify relations of dependence, the whole situation has to be fully examined. The complex nature of the situation demands a scientific approach. Scientific approaches have a tendency to become absorbed in themselves, therefore the given scientific approach must be informed by *moyo* and *umunthu*. This can be done by situating these basic symbols in the framework as the hermeneutical or organizing concepts. This task will reveal where power is abused and justice corrupted.

For Malawi, it will be very important to include the hermeneutic of symbols of *moyo* and *umunthu* in its development program. To situate these symbols in a total framework of transformation process is an imperative for all Africans especially at this time, when the leaders of the second republic and their bureaucratic elite are self-critical of their work in the past and are committed to a development program that will effect change in the living standard of the general populations. The symbols will reveal where power has been abused and justice corrupted in the past. On the other hand, having *moyo* and *umunthu* as organizing symbols in a development process will help the elite to create checks and balances within the system, and these will prevent corruption of power and justice in this second phase of Malawi's development process.

The last point to consider in a model for transformation is the relationship between people and nature. The African attitude toward nature is based on the understanding that all creation is knit in one fabric or texture, namely, *moyo*. Nature plays a role toward self-realization of persons and the whole cosmos. Nature provides needs necessary for human life: food, materials for shelter, and change of seasons are some of the basic human needs. Nature meets human needs through its cycles or seasons and other internal mechanisms for maintaining an ecological balance necessary for its own viability. Since human life depends on the generosity of nature, the Achewa consider nature as *moyo*. This connectedness means that people and nature share the same destiny, just as they live and belong to the same origin, that is, the Divinity, the giver of *moyo*, who is *Moyo*. From this follows the understanding that both people and nature are sacred since they have a divine origin. Respect and care of nature is grounded on this sense of oneness.

Oneness means that people have a moral responsibility toward nature since they share in *moyo*. Bondedness means being in the network of life. The responsibility that accompanies being located in this network is allowing *moyo* to transcend itself. Nature has rhythms and patterns through which *moyo* flows. It is human responsibility not to interpret the flow of *moyo* by changing or reversing these rhythms and patterns. The question of responsibility is about behavior and relations. In this case, it is human behavior toward the gifts nature provides, or how people relate themselves to nature. The future of people depends on how they relate themselves to nature or whether they exercise their responsibility.

Africa knows too well what happens when people no longer feel they are part of nature or take for granted that nature will continue to support human life no matter what they do to it. When people do not take care of nature they interrupt the patterns and rhythms responsible for maintaining an ecological balance. The result is that the ecological balance may be changed permanently with a very devastating impact on all life. Greed is perhaps the main reason for tampering with nature's flow—greed is the opposite of responsibility. The way people use natural resources reveals how much they care about nature. Unless people cultivate a sense of bondedness to nature they cannot care about nature. If nature is objectified as the other, then the beginning of the end begins, for the destiny of nature is the destiny of all people. Any model of transformation that does not take into account the value of nature is not worth a chance because such a model cannot mediate *moyo*.

The problem Africa has inherited from its colonial past is greed. The need for Africa's resources abroad has not only made Africans poorer, but has changed the ecological pattern of nature in Africa. Let us look at a few examples. The demand for ivory abroad is the reason for the large decrease of elephants in Africa. It is an established scientific fact that elephants play a very important role in ecological balance. While elephants may uproot some trees they contribute a lot to the welfare of others animals. Elephants are the only animals endowed with an extra sense to locate where water is in the ground and dig for it. With their tusks, elephants make a hole in the ground to get water from a depth as far as three feet. Elephants drink about 65 gallons of water at a given time. They like to play and bathe in mud which serves as moisturizer for their usually dry skin. Because of this great need for water and mud they dig up a large area, large enough for their massive bodies. In the process, they make a small pool from which other animals find water they need. This explains why many animals are found in areas where elephants are in large numbers. Kill elephants for their tusks to satisfy aesthetic beauty abroad, and many animals will die of thirst at home. The ecological balance elephants made is destroyed.

Ecological balance is also destroyed when people want to take more from nature at one time than nature's internal mechanism allows for the balance of the system. Science has the ability to promote *moyo* when rightly applied, but its potential to destroy the ecological system is great. Advised by marine biologists, an effort was made in the 1960s to increase tonnage of fish caught in Africa's largest lake (Victoria?). They recommended introduction of Nile perch, a river fish, into the lake. This is a giant perch, some of which grow to be six feet. The perch took to the lake with vengeance; they destroyed scores of all native fish. Once again, the ecological balance was changed with a negative result for the people who depend on the lake for their livelihood and protein. The desired increased tonnage is still in the future.

Attempts for high productivity may be good, but the price has always to be considered. Even when something is said to be scientifically true, the price must first be figured out to see if it is worth a try and who is going to pay the price. Usually, it is those already struggling to make ends meet, the poor, who pay the price for national gambles. Science has much to answer for in Africa in this respect. In the name of high productivity Africans were encouraged to use fertilizers. Most of these fertilizers were not tested for the particular soils in which they were being used. Consequently, soils were burnt by the fertilizers and were therefore unable to produce as much as had been hoped.

In Malawi, the staple diet for most of the population is made from corn flour. In an attempt to increase production of corn, agriculture experts recommended introduction of a hybrid corn, *Malawi Hybrid* commonly known by its scientific formula numbers MH 12, 15, 32 and now 41. This corn grows two to three long cobs with big ears on one stock, and it grows faster than the traditional corn. Its big ears, however, are softer and therefore absorbs water much quicker than the traditional corn. Because of its softness and quick absorption of water, weavers quickly develop inside the ear and rot sets in very fast. To preserve it for sometime, even for a few months insecticides have to be used. For reasons best known to agriculture "experts" in the country or because of economic considerations, the insecticide commonly used by local farmers is dichlorodiphenyltrichloroethane (D.D.T.). How safe is D.D.T. for human consumption?

This breed of corn is unsuitable for the tropics because of the high rainfall these areas get. The corn begins to rot even before it is harvested. For Malawi, the problem is compounded by the fact that rain water permeating through the walls of traditional granaries of bamboo or twigs with a grass thatched roof, gets to the corn. A roof on top of the granary prevents the corn from direct exposure to rain but does very little to keep it from getting rotten. Thus a family that worked very hard for months, may find it has less food to carry it through to the next harvest because all its corn is rotten. Worse still, the family will have no money, yet it has to pay back a loan from the local farmers' club from which it got the MH 41 seed. So much for high productivity!

These are a few instances where nature has been limited in its ability to support the self-transcendence of *moyo*. The result has been human suffering, which need not be. Until people learn to be responsible in their relations with nature and realize that nature is part of them and vice versa, unnecessary human suffering will abound. People need to learn to take care of nature. There are few encouraging examples of care for nature in Malawi. The reforestation of the country, which begins every year in December with the tree planting day, December 21, is a good sign of care for nature. The project is participated in by all Malawians. The Ministry of Forestry through its nurseries throughout the country sells the seedlings at a price cheap enough for most people to afford. Game parks are another sign of hope, especially when attention is given to animals that may soon be endangered species, such as elephants now under special protection in the game parks.

In an attempt to preserve nature, Malawi in 1982 became the first country in the world to create an underwater national park designed to protect fish. According to ichthyologists, Lake Malawi has nearly a thousand species of fish, many of which exist nowhere else in the world. But what will happen to this park if Malawi follows the U. N. proposal to introduce fresh water sardines into the lake? According to U. N. marine biologists, these sardines could produce as much as 100,000 tons of protein. At what price will that be in terms of the ecological balance of the lake? What will be the future of over 18,000 Malawians whose livelihood depends on the lake?

The examples given above give a clue of what will happen when moral responsibility is replaced by greed. Nature will not continue to support human life, or *moyo* will not be mediated by nature when human responsibility is neglected. The result of this neglect is the suffering of many. It is therefore necessary to make sure that preservation of nature is part and parcel of the process of transformation. This means that a country must think twice before it commits itself to some novel scientific ideas. This may include considering the impact of technology on nature. The kind of technology chosen must be of such type that will promote the community of *moyo*. For Africans, *moyo* is everything and it is the will of the Divinity that *moyo* should be allowed to continue.

Let us review the issues for consideration in transformation of society. The starting point is that people seek life in its fullness; therefore, transformation should begin with the question of *moyo*, the foundation of everything there is. Then the focus should move to *umunthu*, the ultimate value and organizing logic for meaning. Consideration of how people live together follows the subject of *umunthu*. The issue of community is about the self-transcendence of *moyo*. This is to maintain that community creates possibilities for realization of *umunthu*. Basic values are mediated by social structures. To ensure that social structures will permit fullness of *moyo* or consider *umunthu* a priority, it is necessary to critically examine social structures and moral life. Here it is important to analyze concepts of justice (right relations) and power operative in society. Human sciences may be invoked here to locate where power is abused. The last issue to be considered in the transformation of society is the people's relation to nature. Human destiny is tied with that of nature. Therefore the care of nature should be treated as one of the basic considerations for transformation. All the points proposed for transformation—*moyo*, *umunthu*, community, justice, power and nature—are not to be taken as isolated parts of a whole; they are inseparable, thus they have to be treated as a unit. This idea is explained by the concept of bondedness. This term also expresses a very profound idea that the Divinity creates and holds all things together.

Figure 1 represents the ideas about transformation. *Moyo* appears on all sides because it is the foundation and purpose of creation. All concepts in the sketch stand on *moyo*, but all the concepts in the paradigm are under the umbrella of *moyo*. As an umbrella, an overarching symbol, *moyo* is an organizing concept of value and meaning.

In community are included generosity, or sharing, and mutuality. These are necessary for a harmonious living. Nature includes care for everything in creation. Care does not mean worshipping nature but being mindful that the destiny of creation includes that of all people. Here may be raised the question of proper technology. The term *proper* defines the ability of a particular technology to promote or enhance *moyo* and *umunthu*.

Figure 1
The Community Of Life

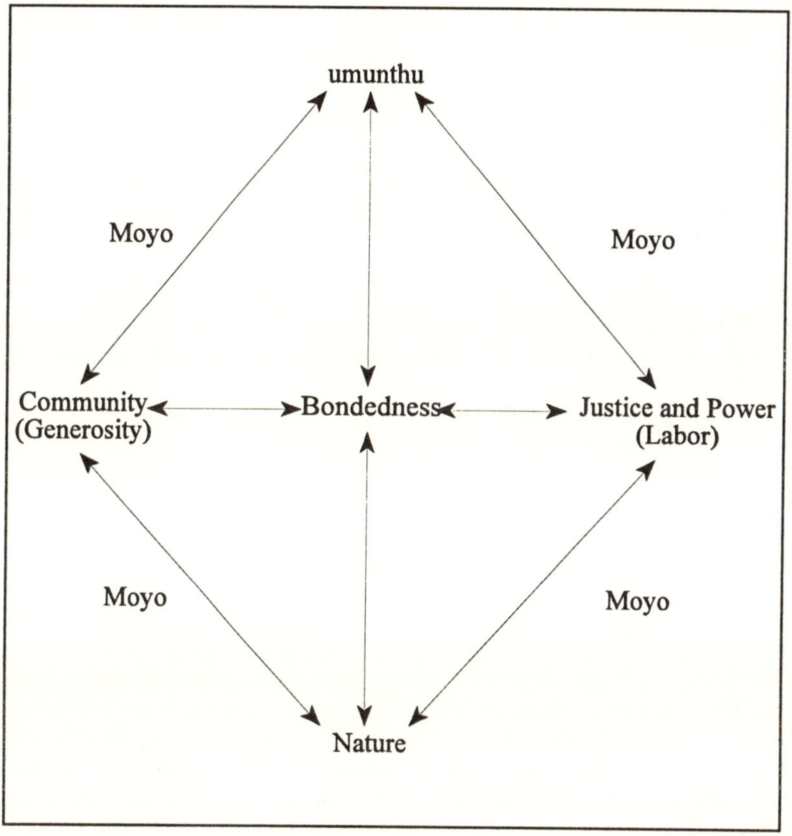

In considering power and justice, we have also included labor. Fullness of human life demands an opportunity for labor. A community that is dedicated to fullness of life (*umunthu*) cannot afford to have people sitting idle or dependent if they are physically and mentally fit. The concept of power and justice also deals with the question of freedom. The term *freedom* here refers to the moral and spiritual well-being of persons which allows them to be creative in community or to let others be. Here the focus is not on rights or civil liberties, but on moral and spiritual obligation which let others be. A society based on civil liberties stifles peoples creativity on how to live in a community because people feel little or no obligation at all toward the people in their community or to the community itself. Moreover, the language of rights from Locke on puts emphasis on self and not community.

We have bondedness at the center as the concept that makes people aware of their relatedness to one another, nature, and *moyo*. Bondedness gives people consciousness of their being part of others and sharing a common destiny with nature.

NOTES

1. My understanding of symbols in this book has been informed by the following works, among others: Gibson Winter, *Liberating Creation: Foundations of Religious Ethics* (New York: Crossroads, 1981); Paul Tillich, *Dynamics of Faith* (New York: Harper and Row, 1957), 41-57; Philip Wheelwright, *The Burning Fountain: A Study in the Language of Symbolism* (Gloucester, MA: Peter Smith, 1982), Chapter 1.

2. Fabian Eboussi Boulaga, *Christianity Without Fetishes: An African Critique and Recapture of Christianity*, trans. Robert Barr (Maryknoll, NY: Orbis Books, 1984), 19.

3. *Ibid.*, 132.

4. Bukasa Tulu Kia Mpansu, "The African Tradition of Sharing," *The Ecumenical Review*, 38, no. 4 (October 1986), 387.

5. *Ibid.*, 388.

6. J. M. Schoffeleers and A. A. Roscoe, *Land of Fire: Oral Literature from Malawi* (Limbe, Malawi: Popular Publications, 1985), Chapter 1.

7. See Stevenson Kumakanga, *Nzeru Za Kale*, 6th ed. (Blantyre, Malawi: Dzuka, 1975).

8. Aristotle, *Nicomachean Ethics*, trans. Martin Ostwald (Indianapolis: Bobbs-Merrill, 1962), book 5, section 3, 118. By giving this quotation I do not indent to imply that Aristotle belongs to the liberal tradition; rather that his understanding of justice prepared the stage for liberal interpretation of justice. For modern development and interpretation of the theory see John Rawls, *A Theory of Justice* (Cambridge, MA: Harvard University Press, 1971). Robert Mangabeira Unger shows how the theory of distributive justice fits into the total picture of liberal political theory in his *Knowledge and Politics* (New York: Free Press, 1975).

9. In traditional society property is owned by the community. A herd of cattle or stock, for example, is owned by all, although one may have bought the original cows and bulls.

8

Christianity and Social Change

CHRISTIANITY'S OBLIGATION

The African world is holistic; there is no dichotomy between the sacred and the secular. Concerning African religiosity, Mbiti has said: "Africans are notoriously religious. . . . Religion permeates into all the departments of life so fully that it is not easy or possible always to isolate it." Boulaga agrees: "Religion is the metaphor of life concerned with living life's self-transcendence, nature, earth, sex, anything that moves the African in the position of life." According to African ways of life one cannot talk about society without mentioning the role of religion.

The influence of the sacred in other spheres of life demands that a paradigm for transformation place religion at the center. The present undertaking is informed by the African way of life and sense of the sacred. The concepts guiding the study, *moyo*, *umunthu*, and community, have a sacred dimension to them. The paradigm for transformation suggested in Chapter 7 is complete as it stands; the concepts in the paradigm do not need to be complemented. However, the presence of Christianity in Africa forces one to examine these concepts in light of the Christian message. The task is necessitated by the fact that many Africans profess Christianity. To profess a particular religion is to make a decision to organize one's life along the lines prompted by that faith.

Perhaps the most compelling reason for discussing Christianity in a paradigm for transformation in Africa is the fact that the liberal heritage entered traditional society through Christianity. Christianity is not the only religion with a large following in Africa; Islam is also popular but it did not have as much negative influence on traditional values as Christianity. This is not to exonerate Islam, for there are evils that it perpetuated in Africa, the slave trade for one. But Islam was Africanized to the degree that it did not find African values incompatible with the life of faith. On the other hand, through preaching and education,

Christianity undermined the traditional value system. As traditional values crumbled, the hermeneutic ability of the people became deeply affected. Christianity weakened or impaired the ability of Africans to interpret and reconstruct their systems of representations, values, and norms, which gave meaning to their lives. Many Africans who have not attended primary school education still find their values greatly affected by Christianity. The values that were taken for granted in traditional society have become obsolete in areas where Christianity is dominant. When people lose their sense of values and norms, the symbolic function itself becomes blocked, because there is no possibility for the theological work required to analyze past traditions and gain a new understanding. People understand the present in light of their interpretation of past experiences. Since in the African world there is no dichotomy between the sacred and the secular, interpretation of the past is always a theological interpretation.

Because Christianity had devastating influence on African societies, it has a moral obligation to play a role in the people's attempt to recover their identity by retrieving symbols of value and meaning in their lives. Symbols have a theological function in the sense that they express the dimension of ultimate value and meaning. They are not picked arbitrarily—they are "born" out of people's experience, and as such, they embody a collective consciousness. They remind people of who they are, where they came from, and what they should be about. As a product of collective consciousness, symbols have the ability to disclose anything that denies people their values or identity, just as they are able to point people to the future. Traditional symbols of value and meaning may enrich Christianity in Africa and help African Christians understand their vocation in history while they await divine final intervention in history. The people's concepts of basic values would help churches in their task of biblical and theological interpretation. The process would enable missionary churches to discover themselves. It is only after the churches have discovered their own identity that they will truly be churches of the people and therefore be relevant and effective in their preaching, education, and other ministries.

African churches are drawing many people, in Malawi at an average of 16 percent growth per year. What is then implied by being "effective in their preaching, education and other ministries" when the churches are growing at this rate? The concern is for a responsible total ministry that leaves no department of people's life unserved. This means addressing the people's needs and aspirations, and answering questions concerning faith and practice in a context of the people's social reality. African churches are just beginning to show interest in the suffering of the people, after having focused on saving the souls without concern for bodies. In the Bible, people are a totality, with bodies and souls, therefore, to be faithful to the biblical message, churches will have to address issues about the people's socio-political reality. The churches must be able to address ethical questions raised by politics or the economy. The fact that churches say nothing to questions of faith raised in the context of national development is indicative of their apolitical nature due to biblical and theological misinterpretation of divine intent. This lack of interest in the human condition as seen in historical reality was a product of a cognitive theology whuch claimed the "Word of God" to be eternal, therefore politically neutral. This "Word of God" transcends all cultural, political, or economic boundaries, it is universal and all are one. Cognitive theology is in missionary churches. It is an ideology, a fetish under whose spell many of our people have preached universal love of God, that has no particularity. Cognitive theology glosses over, at best commits charity to poverty, ill health, all manner of suffering and contradictions in the world. It is an abstract revelation.

Cognitive theology faces a crisis when people begin to take their historical reality seriously, when the non-persons and marginalized begin to discover or demand meaning of faith in light of their condition. Historical theology (not to be confused with the study on development of doctrine), on the other hand, says that divine intention, or the meaning of the incarnation, is for people to experience *umunthu* and *moyo* in social, political, and economic dimensions of society. "Immanuel" (God with us), is divine revelation unfolding in historical reality: "Immanuel" is born to a young struggling couple who cannot afford a big sacrifice on his naming ceremony, save for two turtle doves, the offering of the poor (Luke 2:22-23). This is how Immanuel, divine revelation, enters human history.

Christianity emerged from a situation similar in some ways to the African condition today: from a situation of invincible military and political powers, cultural domination, and exploitation of resources and people by the elite. There were also internal problems: Christianity called into question religion, power, and even the law. Religious practices, traditions, and laws that were intended to mediate and enhance *moyo* and *umunthu* had become distorted to the extent that they were a burden to the poor and the powerless. Christianity emerged as a form of conscientization with respect to the people's history and divine knowledge. It was conscientization in respect to people's locality and temporality. This means that Christianity in its origin focused on the particular, the here and now. This is why it raised hope and expectation to the powerless. The call of Jesus, "Come to me all you that are heavy laden and I will give you rest," must be understood against this religio-political and socio-economic background. The religious and political infrastructure was such that the poor or powerless had no recourse.

The cleansing of the temple must also be seen as Jesus' attempt to stop religious, political, and economic corruption. Contrary to popular images, Jesus did not attack a clergy that become insensitive to the suffering of the people; he attacked the whole national infrastructure. The temple was the center of power, for it drew together people from all parts of the country, among them buyers, sellers, bankers, tax collectors, and priests (and it must be remembered that priests practiced law). The temple then was the seat of economic and political authority, but also a place of prayer, religious regulations, and religious authority. Money was generated, circulated in all sorts of transactions in the temple, the most important being the sale of sacrificial sheep, oxen, and pigeons. Money was made safe in the temple bank. Funds from the temple bank went to all parts of the country to serve self-interested goals of political figures.[1] The temple was the center of secular and religious activity. Jesus was angered by the prominence of economic activity in the temple. The objects of sacrifice that were sold in the temple came from farmers, the poor and powerless, far away from the capital, Jerusalem. These activities led Jesus to suspend business by turning over counters and chasing everybody out. It was a brief stoppage for soon business returned to normal. However, it was a symbolic gesture of divine disapproval of economic and political institutions. Operating under divine names and symbols these institutions exploited the powerless and the poor.

Although in some ways religious and political institutions were separate, each sought the help of the other when it was to its advantage. Anyone who dared question the authorities in either system paid the ultimate price—death by execution. The trial and sentencing of Jesus showed how vulnerable and defenseless the poor were before the political and religious powers. The fear of these powers was so strong that it created indifference and cowardice among the poor and powerless themselves. So the one who challenged the system suffered alone, deserted by friends and scorned by foes. But this challenge brought Christianity into being.

Christianity today has the same task: to challenge the forces that be and to participate in structures that seek to mediate life. Churches must be concerned with the suffering of the people and be involved in social change. In some areas in Africa, the Church may be the only hope the people have. This may put the Church on a collision course with the state, but the Church has no other way but to obey God. The Church may also not find wide support; there may be indifference in countries where people have been numbed by the activities of the ruling elite and the state. Dentation without trial, political killings, and intimidation do succeed in frightening and numbing the people. Still, the Church must call on national leaders to create conditions for fullness of *moyo*, for people to realize their *umunthu*.

In Christian-dominated areas it may be easier to work with the marginalized because there Church members also belong to the political elite. Raising the consciousness of such members will go a long way toward justice. Churches are obliged to participate in the process of building social structures that will foster the values and aspirations of the people. However, the churches need to develop a praxis informed by both the Christian message and traditional values. An authentic practice will emerge only after developing a biblical hermeneutics for a people in a changing socio-economic and political reality. Such a hermeneutics could also be informed by indigenous spirituality and its quest for fullness of *moyo*. Such a hermeneutics would empower the people as they seek a community in which they will realize themselves as daughters and sons of the Divinity. A biblical and theological interpretation which takes into account the people's values, in this case *moyo*, can properly be called a *hermeneutics of life*.

A BIBLICAL HERMENEUTICS OF *MOYO*: TOWARD AN AFRICAN CHRISTOLOGY

The hermeneutics of life has two sources: the biblical message and indigenous spirituality. The hermeneutics seeks to discern scriptural (biblical) understanding concerning the quality of human life, how it is to be lived and protected. A hermeneutics of life maintains that a fulfilled person is divine image. Scripture is that which mediates (divine) life, hence African oral sacred stories become scripture when they mediate life. Scriptures have meaning only after they become living substance of persons.

The hermeneutics of life draws from the prophetic writings but also from the gospels. The prophets strongly condemn socio-political systems that say "no" to life. They emphasize that the prerequisite to good relationships with God is doing away with injustice in society (Amos 2:6-16; 8:4-8; Isaiah 58:1-9). The gospels play a very important role in informing the hermeneutics, since it is there that God, through Jesus, shows how to live a full human life acceptable to God. Similarly, Malawian spirituality informs the hermeneutics with the basic values of *moyo*, *umunthu*, and other values that constitute fullness of life. By lifting out the prophets and the gospels, the hermeneutics does not presuppose that these parts of the Bible are unproblematic as texts. The hermeneutical epistemology, the "truth," of these texts is bound by history, culture, or socio-economic factors. The hermeneutician struggles with all these factors to decode how the texts mediate or fail *moyo*. Simply, the interest of the hermeneutician centers on how the text becomes living substance "scripture" of persons rather than dogma.

A hermeneutics of life will lead churches to a new interpretation of the Bible and reconsider their own ministries, their preaching and works, and the effect of their ministries in reaching all the departments of people's lives. By reforming from within, the churches will be better prepared for transformation of the larger society. Transformation from within will lead churches to confess mistakes and sins of past, and to conversion. Their conversion will be demonstrated in willingness to identify with the lot of the people. In addition, a hermeneutics of life will aid Christians in their understanding of the Bible. Some key passages of the Bible, such as the Prologue of John, will be better understood by reading them through the hermeneutics of life, which will produce a new theological interpretation centered on the question of life and the churches' moral and divine responsibility toward life.

Reading the gospels through the hermeneutics of life will lead to a new understanding of who Jesus is. The quest to know Jesus can be a basis of a confession of faith in Jesus as well as genuine Christian praxis, a historical theology. In our context the issue is who Jesus is for Malawians in their historical situation. There does not exist a universal knowledge of Jesus. Faith is a people's response to an encounter with a deity in all dimensions of their life and particular historical circumstance. Therefore, the knowledge of Jesus is always particular since it is a people's way of confessing what God has done through Jesus in a concrete historical situation. Faith is a particular response to the *kerygma.* To talk about faith as a response to *kerygma* is to declare that the disciples of Jesus proclaimed Jesus by means of christology as the one in whom God acted.

How would African churches develop a knowledge of Jesus which would be a particular confession, that is, a response that would reflect people's experience of divine mercies in Jesus? For Malawians the best way to understand Jesus will be to begin with the knowledge of God in traditional thought. We have stated elsewhere that in Malawi, the Divinity is the source of all life. No one can give out something unless he or she has it. According to Malawian thought, the one who can give life to all creation must be full of life. The Divinity is *Moyo.* The Bible asserts Jesus is the Son of God, or as the Nicene Creed states, Jesus is the very God of the very God. Since Divinity in Malawian thought is *MOYO,* therefore Jesus is the very life of the very life. Therefore, to understand Jesus through the hermeneutics of life, is to see divine life, an authentic life, in human form and to know the meaning of this life for humanity in history.

From this it follows that christology for Malawians will begin by considering *moyo.* Jesus is *moyo* expressing itself in the process of nature and history. This *moyo* reaches fullest articulation in the meaning of the person of Jesus. In other words, through historization of divine *moyo* in Jesus, all creation and humanity get *moyo.* Therefore, Jesus becomes the prototype, the real *munthu.* The one of whom Malawians can say "*uyu ndiye munthu*" (this is a person) is the one with a character and moral life of *umunthu.* We recall that the qualities of *umunthu* includes integrity, truthfulness, and generosity (sharing). The one who has realized *umunthu* respects others as the highest value possible. This is the person who lets others be. Jesus is the fullness of *umunthu* as the Divinity would have us realize it. In his *umunthu,* Jesus shares with humanity his *moyo* which is also divine *moyo.* In Jesus then, people share in the divine *moyo.* To claim that Jesus is divine *moyo,* is to assert that he is a fulfilled person, the visible image of the invisible Creator of *moyo, Namalenga,* and is himself *Namalenga.* Here Malawian understanding of Jesus agrees with the New Testament assertion about the nature of Jesus: Jesus is pre-existent; he was before anything was created, and that all things were created through Him, as the apostle Paul writes:

> He is the image of the invisible God, the first born of all creation; for in him were all things created, in heaven and on earth, visible and invisible, whether thrones or dominions or principalities or authorities—all things were created through him and for him. He was before all things, and in him all things, hold together. . . . For in him all the fullness of God was pleased to dwell, and through him to reconcile to himself all things, whether on earth or in heaven, making peace by the blood of his cross.[2]

Taking a cue from the hermeneutics of life, we argue that the Malawian understanding of *MOYO* as pre-existent opens the way for reading the Prologue of John as a basis for a Malawian understanding of Jesus. The prologue will reveal the meaning of *logos* for Malawians. Our reading of the Prologue will be in the form of translation.

Translation is a task of deconstruction and reconstruction, a creation of meaning arising from the conflict and tension or interaction between the world of a text and the world of the reader.[3] The tension between the text and the reader frees the spirit of the text which was bound or frozen by the script, to create a world of its own that makes demands on the reader. Translation is the setting free of a text, a bringing to life of what the hermeneutics tradition calls the "event" or the "said." It is resurrecting the spirit of a text that it may speak to a given situation in a voice clear enough for everyone to understand. To understand is not just to hear and listen; it is living the "event." Translation, then, is the creation of space as the text intended to create in the original setting. To understand a text is to live in the space and "spirit" of the text. The task of translation is to create a language that will mediate the space or world of the text. This mediation opens a whole new world to the reader. By responding to the demands of the spirit of the text, the reader is transformed or is offered a possibility to see things in a new light, to live in a new world. The fusion of the horizons of the reader and the text opens new possibilities for understanding.[4] True understanding transforms as one heeds to the claims of the spirit of a text. Since understanding is made possible by language, it is important that a translation struggles with language to make understanding possible.

The pre-existent Jesus is God and because God is *moyo*, Jesus is also *moyo*. By inference, the *logos* in John 1:1, 3, 14 is *moyo*. A Malawian reading of the prologue with *moyo* instead of *logos* in the text would make sense. At the present time, the Chichewa version of the Bible and the latest version of the New Testament both have *logos* translated as *WORD*.[5] The term *WORD* has negative connotations in Chichewa for it is associated with that which can cause or invoke harm. Of course the Divinity does not cause harm, but it is identifying Divinity with negative power. Indeed, a herbalist utters a "word" to invoke healing powers. In everyday speech, however, "word" mostly means to wish someone bad.

Translating *logos* as *moyo* would restore the original meaning of the text. John 1:1-18 is a religious poem, or a powerfully contrived psalm (hymn) to the eternal Divinity. A close reading of the New Testament indicates that singing of songs, hymns, and poems constituted an integral part of the liturgy within mission churches. Singing was not only an expression of the flow of new life but also a proclamation. This explains why hymn singing composed the liturgy of the daily Eucharist *Christo quasi Deo* (to Christ as to a God), to borrow from Pliny's famous *Letter X 96* to Trajan. Singing was praise and jubilation. In his letter to the Colossians, Paul encourages singing of praises: "Let the word of Christ dwell in you richly, teach and admonish one another in all wisdom, and sing psalms and spiritual hymns with thankfulness in your hearts of God" (Colossians 3:16). Praise took different themes: In the Book of Revelation, for example, praise is to the Eternal King, while Romans 11:33-35 extols God's inscrutable ways. In the Prologue, the theme is thanksgiving for deliverance. In the *Magnificat,* or Mary's Hymn of Praise (Luke 1:47-55), God is praised for raising the human condition at the Consummation. The same praise is also found in the *Benedictus* (Luke 1:68-79).

Logos is the Christian hymn about God's pre-existence and compassion. The prologue is the *kerygma* in a hymn. The climatic parallelism found in the text gives further evidence that the prologue is one of the early Christian hymns. There are three types of parallelism commonly used in poetry: synonymous, antithetic, and synthetic.[6] In synonymous the second line repeats the contents of the first line. In antithetic, the second line is the opposite of the first. In synthetic, the second line adds a new idea to the first. In John we find the synthetic form of parallelism, combined with another form parallelism, step or climatic parallelism, which has every line take up a word of the preceding line to a higher level. Climatic parallelism is clearly seen in John 1:4.

In him was *life*,
and the *life* was the *light* of all people
And the *light* shines in *darkness*,
and the *darkness* has not comprehended it.

The same form of parallelism is found in John 1:14b, 16.[7]

This parallelism indicates that the first line was sung by a precentor while the congregation followed or responded by singing the second line. The climatic parallelism of the text draws interest of an African reader for antiphonal singing is characteristic of African music. If all the climatic parallelism of the prologue were emphasized as it has been above, many Africans would identify with the text and perhaps it would be used more often in preaching than it is at present.

As can be observed from verses 14 through 18, the prologue is a confession of a believing community as well as a hymn of praise. In this respect, the prologue is like the other christological hymns in the New Testament; 1 Peter

1:20, 1 Peter 3:8-22, 1 Timothy 3:16, Hebrews 1:1-4, Colossians 1:15-20 and Philippians 2:16. In dealing with the prologue, as with the other New Testament hymns to the eternal *logos*, we are dealing with the question of the living God in human life. The writer of the fourth Gospel, (and these hymns in general), does not belittle the earthly life of Jesus. It is essential to the message of the apostle John that Jesus lived a real human life. It is for this reason that John uses the strong biblical metaphor *dwelt* in verse 14. The metaphor refers to God's presence, *Skenco*, as found in the Old Testament. For John to have used the term *dwelt* was a profound abasement of God; that God took on human body. This was an unacceptable idea in the time of John. It was very bold of him to claim that God became human in Jesus. What John sought to express with the term *dwelt* was to relate the life of Jesus to the life and total work of God. I believe the basic theme for John is life and that he wrote to tell the story of life. It is based on the centrality of the concept of life in the fourth Gospel that I translate the *logos* as *moyo*. This would allow the message of the *kerygma* to be clearly proclaimed and the confession of the believing community in verses 14-18 to be appreciated. Were the focus of this reading to be on *moyo*, John would be the most widely read of the Gospels, replacing Matthew.[8]

The pronoun used to refer to God might present a problem of transition from one sentence to the other, however, from the African perspective the pronoun is not an issue because African translations use a neutral gender for God. We thus translate the first verses and verse 14 of the prologue from a Malawian point of view:

Chichewa

1 Pachiyambi, zinthu zonse zisanakhale, panali *moyo*, ndipo *moyo* unali kwa Mulungu, *moyowo* ndi Mulungu. 2 *Moyo* unali ndi Mulungu kuchokera pachiyambi; 3 zonse zinalengedwa kupyolera mwa *moyo*, ndipo popanda *moyo* palibe chikanalengedwa. 4 Mwa Mulungu munali *moyo* ndipo *moyowo* unali kuunika kwa anthu.

14 Ndipo *moyowo* unafika mdziko lapansi mwa *munthu* amene anali ndi makhalidwe a uMulungu komanso a *umunthu* weni-weni; ndipo mu ulemerero ndi m'makhalidwe akewo tinaona kuti *munthuyo* anali mwana wa Mulungu.

English

1 Before all things were created, there was *life*, and *life* was with God, *life* is God. 2 *Life* was with God at the beginning; 3 all things were made through *life*, and without *life* nothing in the whole creation could have been created at all. 4 In God was *life* and *life* was the light of people.

14 And *life* came into the world through a *person* who had divine character and *fullness of human* qualities; and those qualities reflected a glory which us showed that the *person* was the son of God.

The English text here is almost a literal translation of the Chichewa text. In verse 14, the term *grace*, which appears in the NRSV, has been translated as *divine character*, to emphasize the deity of Jesus. The term used to translate "grace" in the Chichewa Bible is theologically very misleading. The word used by the *Revised Union Nyanja Version* to translate grace means "to be lucky" or "have a love charm" (*chisomo*). Jesus was not lucky; *grace* was part of his divine nature. In order to avoid creating the impression that Jesus was lucky or had some magical powers, the translators of the New Testament in modern Chichewa decided to use *kind hearted* (*wokoma mtima*) for *grace* (*chisomo*). While *kind hearted* is an improvement on the earlier translation, it does not emphasize the deity of Jesus.

What is the significance of *moyo* in history? The answer to this important question is found in the titles people give Jesus. Let us then examine those titles from an African perspective. Mbiti has already done an exploratory study on the titles of Jesus in light of the African understanding of the world. Mbiti says some of the major titles of Jesus have no relevance to traditional African concepts, and consequently have no appeal to Africans. Those titles include Messiah, Christ, Son of David, Son of Man. On the other hand, the following titles find some affinity in some African traditional concepts: Son of God, the Servant of God, and possibly Savior and Redeemer.[9]

African knowledge of who Jesus is based on two fundamental points: His humanity and His proximity to God. Hence, the titles Servant or Son of God. The concepts of savior and redeemer emphasize his humanity by indicating his proximity to people: he is savior and redeemer to people and not God. We can therefore say the titles of Jesus arise from the understanding that he is a special kind of *munthu*—one whose *umunthu*, relation to God and people, qualifies Him as a bridge. He is able to take this role because His proximity to God allows Him to know what God wants while His being human enables Him to understand human need for fullness of life. To know the fullness of human life is to realize *umunthu*. The qualities of *umunthu* include truthfulness, integrity and generosity. In Jesus these qualities reach their fullness and because of that he is the prototype.

Maintaining the notion that Jesus was *munthu* and had realized the qualities of *umunthu* to the fullest opens many possibilities for understanding him within Malawian culture. To begin with, his proximity to the Divinity and to people would earn him the title of *nkhoswe* (advocate, guardian, or counselor). In Malawian society an advocate plays a very important role in establishing relations or reconciling estranged parties. Only the person with fullness of the qualities of *umunthu* can be *nkhoswe*. In a society where right relations are fundamental, to be named an advocate is a public affirmation of fullness of qualities of *umunthu*. The role of *nkhoswe* is to mediate and in the person of Jesus we see a perfect mediator.

The concept that Jesus was *munthu* whose qualities of *umunthu* qualified him to become *nkhoswe* opens possibilities for a better understanding of key passages about Jesus. Being *nkhoswe*, Jesus is raised to a higher status as a mediator between people. Therefore, he is a special kind of *nkhoswe* and being associated with him brings one into a special kind of relationship with God. This understanding of Jesus would occur to Malawians reading the fifth chapter of Paul's second letter to the Corinthians:

> 16 From now on, therefore, we regard no one from a human point of view; even though we once regarded Jesus Christ from a human point of view, we regard him thus no longer. 17 Therefore, if anyone is in Christ, he is a new creation; the old has passed away, behold, the new has come. 18 All this is from God, who through Christ reconciled us to himself and gave us the ministry of reconciliation; 19 that is, in Christ God was reconciling the world to himself, not counting our trespasses against them, and entrusting to us the message of reconciliation.

Taking Jesus as pre-existent *moyo*, reconciliation could be understood as *moyo* seeking self-transcendence. This self-transcendence takes place in concrete historical conditions by Jesus' identification with people. This implies that the call of the Church to reconciliation is a call for identification with the people in their historical situation. It is a call to self-transcendence of *moyo* in concrete situations of human life. This further means the Church has to address historical situations that prevent *moyo* from reaching fullness. The Church errs in its christology when it calls for reconciliation without identifying with the people or addressing the issues causing estrangement between people and thus separation from God. Reconciliation with God without healing between people is a mockery of Christ's role as *nkhoswe*, thereby missing the Church's teaching on christology. Reconciliation means just relations, or justice. In seeking reconciliation, the Church will have to address questions of justice.

According to Malawian heritage, mediators usually emerge as prophets. They are selfless people and always willing to suffer for others. The maximum level of *umunthu* is willingness to mediate and suffer for others. Suffering for or with others, comes under the virtue par excellence in Malawi. This is true sharing —generosity at its best. The idea of suffering and mediating for others could explain why the *kenosis* passage in Philippians (2:1-11) is one of the favorite texts among many Malawian preachers. The passage is chosen mostly when preaching about Jesus as redeemer.[10] Mbiti has commented about the appeal of the title of redeemer in the context of African religious heritage.

> Jesus as the Redeemer opens way and possibility for men to be reconciled and to become akin to God. Because, in the African image of man, Jesus is seen as a perfect, complete man; and because he is seen as the Son of God, he is entitled to mediate between God and men. Many of our peoples know the need of mediators between God and men, and some provide them in persons of priests, spirits, or the

> departed. That we as men can become akin to God, touches upon a key concept in African traditional life.[11]

Malawians understand Jesus as the perfect redeemer who lays down his life for others. The oral sacred stories from southern part of Malawi have a story of Mbona. He was a man believed to have been born without a father. He was despised as a son of an illicit union, but his mother knew that she had conceived him without a man. The man grew up to be a savior of his people. He died for them. Commenting on this story Schoffeleers writes:

> The story of Mbona is widely known and has become a sacred oral text. His mother's only son, his parthenogenic birth marked him out from the beginning, and his whole career comes down to us, coincidentally or not, as bearing close parallels to that of Christ. In its present version the story is tightly woven in that it offers almost a complete diagram of Mbona's birth, rise, and fall. The need for a martyr to spill his blood for the sake of founding a nation's religious tradition is strong among *Bantu* people and here Mbona plays this role for the *Chewa*.[12]

Our short discussion on some aspects of a Malawian understanding of Jesus shows that the task will be informed by three concepts. The first is the symbol of *moyo*, and the attention must be on *moyo* as the foundation and beginning of all creation. The second is *moyo* incarnated in *munthu*, Jesus. The focus must be on the *umunthu* of Jesus and his relation to the eternal *Moyo* or God. He is *munthu* who shows Christians how to live as people made in the image of God. He is *munthu* like all humans, therefore he knows human suffering and yearning for fullness. A Malawian understanding of Jesus, then, must struggle with the meaning of being human in concrete historical situation. Jesus must be the model of the meaning of *umunthu*. To this end, a Malawian understanding of Jesus will not be interested in abstract formulations but practical relevance of the life and teachings of Jesus. Malawian churches must concern themselves with how to promote *umunthu* by overcoming all that limits it in the churches (the churches' preaching and ministries), socio-economic and political context. In doing this the churches will fulfill Jesus' own mission given in John 10:10b, "I came that they may have life and have it abundantly."

Umunthu must be the foundation of a Malawian approach to ethics. In his *umunthu* Jesus lays down the model of a perfect *munthu*: *umunthu* is the highest moral value in traditional society. People strive for fullness of the highest moral value. Jesus makes the ideal of moral values in Malawi a reality. Jesus challenges people to find creative ways to realize the ideal. As exemplified by his life, the task involves putting right relations with others and God. The challenge is for a praxis for a moral life in the concrete historical situation.

Jesus furnishes the process for arriving at a praxis for moral life in a concrete historical situation. As *munthu* he exemplifies how to live a perfect moral life in relation to others and the Creator. To know how to act is to discern divine intention in a given situation. In *umunthu* of Jesus we see a process by which one discerns divine intention for a particular situation. Divine intention is not otherworldly, but speaks of what is good in the world. In his own ministry Jesus continually defined "good" in light of divine intention and always did so in historical perspective. As we see him deal with the question of marriage (Mark 10: 2-9); he begins by developing a historical perspective on divorce and reveals original divine intention about marriage. From the way Jesus handles this case and others, we learn that moral theology, ethics, is the task of reflecting on a concrete moral value and the process that lead to its formulation in light of divine intention. If this process of moral theology or ethical inquiry were followed in Malawi, it would advance the task of the recovery of identity. Based on both prejudice and ignorance, missionary Christianity wiped away all traditional values without attempting to know their historical background or whether they were in line with divine intention for Malawians.

The third concept of a Malawian understanding of Jesus must center on Malawian understanding of the relationship. A way of life in traditional society focuses on creation of healthy relationships. Jesus is what he is, *moyo*, by virtue of his relationship to the eternal *Moyo*, the Divinity. He points to this relationship in many ways, for example, in John 6:33: "For the bread of God is that which comes down from heaven, and gives life to the world." It is his concrete relationship to the Divinity that makes him the Son of God. On the other hand, it is the relationship of Jesus to us which makes him our mediator.

The concept of relations is about reconciliation. According to Jesus, reconciliation has to do with right relations or justice. Reconciliation is justice, whether it involves relations between people or between the Divinity and people. In the divine-human relationship, it is the Divinity who effects justice by deciding not to count trespasses against people (2 Cor. 5:19b). The Divinity re-creates the situation with people as divinely intended at the beginning, not by overlooking sin, but by dealing with it in the *umunthu* of Jesus. Justice here then means re-creation or transformation of relations. The concept of relations underscores the need for transformation of relations in Church and society.

In the preceding paragraphs we have discussed some of the ramifications of *moyo* and *umunthu* theology. There are more implications or considerations for the agenda of African churches but here we want to look at one—liturgy, the aesthetic expression in worship. Liturgy has a great deal to do with *moyo* and *umunthu*. Liturgy is a way by which people constitute and express themselves as a community of faith. It is a manner of relating self to others and the divine, a self-presentation through word, deed, and art (symbols). As a ritual, it is a celebration linking people to the past, and to the instituting event—divine miracles. It is an expression of divine experience rooted in a particular manner of living and dying. Liturgy in missionary churches, however, is not a self-presentation or expression, for it is imported from the West where it was packaged with complete formula for world-wide consumption. Anything other than this prepackaged liturgy cannot be true expression of faith, missionaries warned. In truth, this liturgy cannot be true expression of faith elsewhere, even when it is tampered with by traditional tunes and drums, for it is rooted in alien theology. It stifles creativity, that essential element of *umunthu*, it dehumanizes. A complete overhaul of liturgy is needed to express people's manners of living and dying. It is therefore necessary to rethink how to historicize worship, rites of baptism, burial, marriage, and remembrance. In most parishes people have two marriage and burial ceremonies: the official, in a prepackaged liturgy, and a secret one, that satisfies them because it expresses indigenous spirituality. Indigenous churches are aware of this problem, and it is for this reason that they try holistic liturgies that express the people's cry to God and indigenous spirituality, presented in the people's idiomatic and style. This is what *umunthu* is all about: the freedom to express oneself in one's own manner of life. This is what liturgy should be about.

CONCLUSION

The African condition is marked by economic and political suffering. Dependence reigns supreme. Traditional values have lost their meaning and no substitute seems to work. The bureaucratic elite show little or no concern about the people's loss of values and economic and political dependence. For a long time the Church was ambivalent about getting involved. Yet political and economic suffering is the everyday reality of many. The situation challenges African scholars and Church leaders. Some African scholars have already written about the crisis and made economic and political suggestions toward transformation. However, most of those suggestions have not been grounded in African thought and symbols. A people's vision is found in their thought and is mediated by their symbolizations. A work that is not grounded in people's thought and symbols risks remaining an abstract quest that people fail to find identity with. It is almost impossible to mobilize a people for transformation if the plan of action is not in the thought and symbols they can readily identify with. An empowering framework moves from intellectual speculation to concrete situation by being grounded in the people's thought and symbols. Here I have attempted to go beyond intellectual speculation by providing a plan of action in the thought and symbols of the Malawians.

In this book an attempt has been made to present a framework for reconstruction of society. Reconstruction is a human attempt to make human life worthwhile; it is about people and their future. The project is about how people can take hold of their destiny by restructuring relations within their society and reordering their means of production as their symbols inform them. At stake in contemporary Africa is human life and when human life is at stake, the future of all creation hangs in balance. Life is given to be lived to its fullest; when the possibilities for fullness of life or the self-transcendence of *moyo* are short-circuited, the task of transformation is urgent. The task requires examining and interpreting the symbols that bear the dreams and visions of the people. The decoding of symbols of the people is the hermeneutic of symbols, and it is this hermeneutic which informs an authentic praxis, in that the praxis rises out of the struggle itself. Genuine transformation begins from within. The hermeneutic of symbols has informed the framework for transformation proposed in this book. The symbols in the Malawian struggle, *moyo* and *umunthu*, are so foundational that they enabled a framework for a transformation that would involve both Church and society. Genuine transformation does not leave religious institutions untouched since these institutions represent the ultimate meaning in the world.

The presence of Christianity in Malawi makes it necessary to let traditional symbols of *moyo* and *umunthu* interact with this religion. Such a task would give rise to a reinterpretation of fundamental theological concepts. This is a much needed task for the development of a genuine Christian life and practice that would prepare Malawians to face the challenge of modernity. The influence of modernity continues to erode traditional values, causing an identity crisis in both the Church and society in the post-independence era. The 1990s and beyond will be the time of national reconstruction in many African countries. Should the interest of African countries lie in building national infrastructure only, the nations will be doomed. A nation without a strong moral fiber cannot be viable, for it is given to corruption.

As indicated above, Christianity played a major role in creating and developing the crisis of values prevailing in society. This current crisis situation calls the churches to repentance. Apart from confessing past mistakes, Malawian Christians would like the churches to move away from their reluctance to become involved in the struggle of the people. The churches have maintained their apolitical and thus ahistorical position by arguing that they have no business with "temporal" issues. Some Christians wonder whether the spiritual can be disregarded by the political and vice versa. This prompts a theological question concerning the meaning of faith and Church: What does it mean to believe and to be a Church? To exist as a Church is to live as an ensemble of those who confess Jesus Christ as redeemer and to live by faith inspired by Jesus. This means that the Church, through its preaching and ministries, guides people in how to implement the faith they have in Jesus. Faith can only be implemented in the present—faith will not be needed after the *parousia*. It is therefore wrong for the Church to preach faith as a premium for salvation. To implement faith is to respond to divine invitation to fashion one's life in the divine image (*umunthu*) and to transform others and the world. The task of transformation is to remove every obstacle that prevents people from fully actualizing *moyo* and realizing their *umunthu*.

To implement faith is to proclaim the Gospel. Faith discloses the human relationship to God in history. It would be misrepresenting Jesus and his ministry for the Church to live as of the other world. Vincent Cosmao reminds us that the gospel has to do with the present even as it speaks of the future. Asserting that the Gospel is a divine force for the transformation of the world, he writes:

> The worse fate to befall the gospel message, in terms of the inner dynamics of its history, would be to have it seen as a message from another world that leaves this world as it stands. So viewed, the gospel message would dissociate its earnest followers from the collect effort of humankind to make the earth habitable for all.
>
> The gospel is the word of God, of course. As such, its first and last aim is to bring our relationship to God as the most important structure of human existence. This evident certitude is so basic a part of the gospel universe that it automatically serves as the chief reference point in elucidating the radical nature of our relationship to others: to love our neighbor is identified with the love of God. To ground our relationship on this relationship to God is not, however, to live out the history of some other world. It is to unveil the first and last structure of this world, where human beings fashion themselves into humanity as best they can.[13]

Transformation is about restructuring relations in society as well as putting right human relations with God. The apostle John says it is hypocrisy to claim right relations with God, or to love God, whom no one has ever seen, while hating those made in the divine image and likeness (1 John 1:11; 4:7-12). Transformation of society is about a reordering of relations and value systems so that all people can live a truly human life. It is only when people have realized their *umunthu*, or live as God had intended human life to be, that the destiny of the whole creation, all *moyo*, is assured. It is only when *moyo* and *umunthu* will inform all action and control all relations that true transformation in the whole of Africa will take place. In Africa there are no ultimate values, no symbols so foundational, nothing so empowering as *moyo* and *umunthu*. In these two symbols lies the present and future of society and the churches in Malawi, Africa, and perhaps the whole world. *Moyo* and *umunthu* are terms rich with meaning, symbolizing all that is significant in human life and the world. *Moyo* and *umunthu* are the keys to true transformation in Africa.

NOTES

1. Neill Q. Hamilton, "Temple Cleansing and Temple Bank," *Journal of Biblical Literature* (December 1964): 365.
2. Colossians 1:15-17, 19-20. See also the prologue of Hebrews 1, especially verses 1-3.
3. I have in mind here the work of Paul Ricoeur, *Interpretation Theory: Discourse and Surplus of Meaning* (Fort Worth, TX: Christian University Press, 1974); and Hans-Georg Gadamer, *Truth and Method* (New York: Crossroads, 1982).
4. Gadamer, *Ibid.*, 273f, 337f.

5. The Malawian version of the Bible, the *Revised Union Nyanja version with References*, was originally translated directly from the Greek, while the latest New Testament version is based on contemporary English versions, namely, *Today's English Version* (TEV), the *New English Bible* (NEB), and the *Revised Standard Version* (RSV).

6. Charles F. Burney, *The Poetry of Our Lord: An Examination of the Formal Elements of Hebrew Poetry in the Discourses of Jesus Christ* (Oxford: Claredon Press, 1925).

7. For a detailed discussion on the climatic parallelism in the Prologue of John, see a short work by Joachim Jeremias, *Der Prolog des Johannasevangeliums Johannes 1:1-18* (Stuttgart: Calwer Verlag, 1967).

8. A short scientific study of sermon texts in African Christian movements has shown which gospels are most used by African preachers. According to the study, Matthew is the most popular of the four gospels, then John, Luke, and Mark. The work also reveals the passages and themes that dominate preaching in these movements, but those are of little interest to us at this time. See W. Harold Turner, *Profile Through Preaching* (London: Edinburgh House Press, 1965).

9. John S. Mbiti, "Some African Concepts of Christology," in George F. Vicedom, ed., *Christ and the Younger Churches* (London: SPCK, 1972), 58.

10. Personal scientific study.

11. Mbiti, "Some African Concepts of Christology," in Vicedom, *Younger Churches*, 61.

12. J. M. Schoffeleers and A. A. Roscoe, *Land of Fire* (Limbe, Malawi: Popular Publications). See also J. M. Schoffeleers, "Mbona Cult in Malawi," in I. N. Kimambo and T. O. RAnger, eds., *The Historical Study of African Religion* (London: Heinemann, 1972). The sacred story of Mbona forms the theme of a play by Steve Chimombo, *The Rainmaker* (Limbe, Malawi: Popular Publications, 1978).

13. Vincent Cosmao, *Changing the World: An Agenda for the Churches*, trans. John Drury, (Màryknoll, NY: Orbis Books, 1984), 59.

Bibliography

Abanda Ndengue, Jean Marie. *De la négritude au négrisme*. Yaoundé: CLE, 1970.

Abble, A., et al. *Des Prêtres noirs s'interrogent*. Paris: Cerf, 1975.

Abraham, I. *Land Commission Report* 1946. Zomba: Government Printer, 1947.

Abraham, W. E. *The Mind of Africa*. London: Weidenfeld and Nicolson, 1962.

Achebe, Chinua. *No Longer at Ease*. London: Heinemann, 1963.

________. *Things Fall Apart*. London: Heinemann, 1958.

Adotevi, Stanislas Spero K. *Negritude et négrologues*. Collection 10/18. Paris: Union Générale, 1972.

Ajayi, J. F. A., and M. Crowder, eds. *History of West Africa*. Vol. 2. London: Longman, 1974.

Ake, Claude. "The Congruence of Political Economics and Idiologies in Africa." In *Political Economy of Contemporary Africa,* 2nd ed. Peter C. W. Gutkind and Immanuel Wallersteing eds. Beverly Hills, CA: Sage, 1985.

Akpan, M. B. "Ethiopia and Liberia." In *General History of Africa*. Vol. 7. A. Adu Boahen, ed. London: Heinemann, 1985.

Amin, Samir. "Modes of Production and Social Formations." *UFAHAMU*, 4, no. 3 (1974), 57-85.

Anderson, Efraim, *Churches at Grassroots*. London: Lutterworth Press, 1968.

Anderson, Gerald H., and Thomas F. Stransky, eds. *Mission Trends Number 3*. New York: Paulist Press, 1979.

Annual Reports, British Central Africa Protectorate 1912-13. Cmd. 7050. London: His Majesty's Stationery Office.

Anyanawu, K.C. "The African World-view and Theory of Knowledge." *African Philosophy: An Introduction to the Main Trends in Contemporary Africa*. Edited by Ruch and Anyanwu, Rome: Officium Libris Catholici, 1984.

Apostel, Leo. *African Philosophy: Myth or Reality*. Gent, Belgium: Scientific Publishers, E. Story-Scientia, 1981.

Appiah-Kubi, Kofi. "Why African Theology?" *AACC Bulletin,* no. 7 (1974).

Appiah-Kubi, Kofi, and Sergio Torres, eds. *African Theology en Route*. Maryknoll, New York: Orbis Books, 1979.

Aquinas, Thomas. *Summa Theologia*. Vol. 1. Edited by Thomas Gilby. New York: Image

Books, 1969.
Arendt, Hanna. *On Violence.* New York: Harcourt Brace Jovanovich, 1970.
Aristotle. *Nicomachean Ethics.* Translated and introduction by Martin Ostwald. Indianapolis: Bobbs-Merrill, 1962.
________. *The Basic Works of Aristotle.* Edited by Richard Mckeon. New York: Random House, 1941
Arrow, K. *Social Choice and Individual Values.* New York: Wiley, 1963.
Asante, Molefi Kete. *The Afrocentric Idea.* Philadelphia: Temple University Press, 1987.
________. *Afrocentricity: The Theory of Social Theory.* Rev. ed. Trenton, NJ: Africa World Press, 1988.
________. *Kemet, Afrocentricity and Knowledge.* Trenton, NJ: Africa World Press, 1990.
Asante, Molefi Kete, and Karium Welsh-Asante, eds. *African Culture: The Rhythms of Unity.* Westport, CT: Greenwood Press, 1985.
Aschcraft. "Locke's State of Nature: Historical Fact or Moral Fiction?" *American Political Science Review*, 42 (1968).
Ayandele, E.A. *African Exploration and Human Development.* Edinburgh: Center for African Studies, University of Edinburgh, 1972.
Ba, Ahmadou Hampeté. "La Notion de Person en Afrique Noir." Centre National (1973).
Bâ, Sylvia. *The Concept of Negritude in the Poetry of Leopold Senghor.* Princeton, NJ: Princeton University Press, 1973.
Bacon, Francis. *Novum Organum.* Trans. R. Ellis and James Spedding. London: Routledge and Sons, n.d.
Baeta, C. G. "Missionary and Humanitarian Interests, 1940 to 1960." In *White Settlers in Tropical Africa.* Edited by L. H. Gann and Peter Duigan. Baltimore, MD: Penguin, 1962.
Baeta, C. G., ed. *Christianity in Tropical Africa: Studies and Discussions Presented at the International African Seminar: University of Ghana, April 1975.* London: Oxford University Press, 1968.
Ballie, Donald M. *God Was in Christ: An Essay on Incarnation and Atonement.* New York: Scribner's Sons, 1948.
Barber, W. G. "The Movement into World Economy." In *Economic Transition in Africa.* Edited by M. J. Herskovits and M. Harvitz. Evanston, IL: Northwestern University Press, 1964.
Barrett, David B. *African Initiatives in Religion.* Nairobi: East African Publishing House, 1971.
________. *Schism and Renewal in Africa.* Nairobi: Oxford University Press, 1968.
Barrett, David B. ed. *World Christian Encyclopedia.* London: Oxford University Press, 1982.
Baum, Gregory. *Religion and Alienation: A Theological Reading of Sociology.* New York: Paulist Press, 1975.
Beaver, Robert Pierce, ed. *The Gospel and Frontier Peoples: A Report of a Consultation, December 1972.* South Pasadena, CA: William Carey Library, 1973.
Becker, Carl. *The Heavenly City of the Eighteenth-Century Philosophers.* New Haven, CT: Yale University Press, 1966.
Beker, Donald. *Politics of Race: Comparative Studies.* Westmead and Lexington, MA: D. C. Heath, 1975.

Bentham, Jeremy. *An Introduction to the Principles of Morals and Legislation*. Edited by J. H. Burns and H. L. A. Hart. London: Athlone, 1971.

Berdyaev, N. *Freedom and Spirit*. Bles: T. P. Verso, 1935.

Bernstein, Richard J. *Praxis and Action: Contemporary Philosophies of Human Activity*. Philadelphia: University of Pennsylvania Press, 1971.

Boahen, A. A. *Britain, the Sahara, and Western Sudan*. Oxford: Clarendon Press, 1964.

Boni, Nazi. *Crépuscule des temps anciens*. Paris: Présence Africaine, 1962.

Booth, N. S. "African Religions and Philosophy," *International Quarterly*, 11, no. 2 (1971).

________. "Time and Change in Traditional African Thought," *Religion in Africa*, 7, no. 2 (1975).

Bornkamm, Guther. *Jesus of Nazareth*. New York: Harper and Row, 1960.

Bourguiba, Habib. "Neo-Destourian Socialism." Address delivered June 24, 1961. Published by the Tunisian government.

Brett, E. A. *Colonialism and Underdevelopment in East Africa: The Politics of Economic Change 1919-39*. New York: Nok, 1973.

Burke, Fred. *Africa's Quest for Order*. Englewood Cliffs, NJ: Prentice-Hall, 1964.

Burney, Charles F. *The Poetry of Our Lord: An Examination of the Formal Elements of Hebrew Poetry in the Discourses of Jesus Christ*. Oxford: Claredon Press, 1925.

Bussia, K. A. *Africa in Search of Democracy*. London: Oxford University Press, 1957.

Carr, Burgess. "The Relation of Union to Mission," *Mission Trends Number 3*, Gerald Anderson and Thomas F. Stransky, eds. New York: Paulist Press, 1979.

Cassirer, Ernest. *The Philosophy of the Enlightenment*. Princeton, NJ: Princeton University Press, 1979.

Césaire, Aimé. *Discours sur le colonialisme*. 4th edition. Paris: Présence Africaine, 1962.

________. "Négrerie-jeunesse noir et assimilation." *L'Etudiant Noir* (March 1935).

________. "La Négritude en question." *Jeune Afrique*, no. 532, (March 16, 1971), 65.

________. *Return to My Native Land = Cahier d'un retour au pays natal*. Edited and translated by Emile Synder. Paris: Présence Africaine, 1971.

Chimombo, Steve. *The Rain Maker*. Limbe, Malawi: Popular Publications, 1978.

Chisiza, Duduza K. *Africa: What Lies Ahead*. New York: African-American Institute, 1962.

Christian Science Monitor, April 4, 1957.

Colonial Reports, British Central Africa Protectorate 1904-5. Cmd. 2684 London: His Majesty's Stationery Office.

Commission on Theological Concerns of the Christian Conference of Asia, ed. *Minjung Theology: People as Subjects of History*. Preface by James Cone. Maryknoll, NY: Orbis Books, 1958.

Cosmao, Vincent. *Changing the World: An Agenda for the Churches*. Translated by John Drury. Maryknoll, NY: Orbis Books, 1984.

Cullmann, Oscar. *Die Christologie des Neuen Testaments*. Tubingen: J. C. B. Mohr, 1957.

Curtin, Phillip. *African Slave Trade: A Census*. Madison, WI: University of Wisconsin Press, 1969.

Curtin, P., S. Feierman, L. Thompson, and J. Vansina. *African History*. London: Longman, 1978.

Dadie, Bernad. "The Contribution of Religion to the Expression of the African Personality," *Africa in Search of Democracy*. Edited by K. A. Bussia. London: Oxford University Press, 1957.

Dallmayr, Fred R. *Twilight of Subjectivity: Contributions to a Post-Individualist Theory of Politics*. Amherst, MA: University Press of Massachusetts, 1981.

Dammann, Ernst. "A Tentative Philological Typology of Some African High Deities," *Journal of Religion In Africa*, 2 (1969).

Dampier-Whethan, William Cecil. *A History of Science and Its Relation with Philosophy and Religion*. New York: Cambridge University Press, 1929.

Davidson, Basel. *The African Past: Chronicles from Antiquity to Modern Times*. New York: Grosset and Dunlap, 1967.

________. *Black Mother*. London: Victor Gollancz, 1961.

________. *The Lost Cities of Africa*, Revised edition. Boston: Little, Brown, 1987.

Delafose, Maurice. "Les Civilisations Negro-Africaines." In *Da Postima, Filosofia Africana*. A. Pavian, ed. Milano: Estere Capucini, 1967.

de Sardan, Olivier J. P. "Personnalité et structures sociales à propos Songhay," *Colloque international sur le notion de personne en Afrique noir (Paris: 11-17 octobre 1971)*. Paris: Editions du Centre National de la Recherche Scientifique, 1973.

Descartes, René. *Discourse on Method and Meditations*. New York: Liberal Arts Press, 1960.

Dia, Mamadou. *Contribution à l'étude du movement cooperatif en Afrique noire*. Paris: Présence Africaine, 1958.

________. *Réflexions sur l'economie de l'Afrique noire*. New ed. Paris: Présence Africaine, 1960.

________. "Speech at the National Assembly in Dakar, April 4, 1961," *Socialist International Information*, XI, 18 (1961). Reprinted in *African Socialism*. Edited by William H. Friedland and Carl G. Rosberg. Stanford, CA: Stanford University Press, 1964.

Dickson, Kwesi A. "African Theology—Whence, Methodology and Content," *Journal of Religious Thought*, 33 (Fall-Winter, 1975).

________. "Consultation on African Theologians, 5-16 January 1966—A Review," *Bulletin of the All Africa Conference of Churches* (April 1966).

________. "Continuity and Discontinuity Between the Old Testament and African Life and Thought." In *African Theology En Route*. K. Appiah-Kubi and S. Torres, eds. Maryknoll, NY: Orbis Books, 1979.

________. *Theology in Africa*. Maryknoll, NY: Orbis Books, 1984.

________. "Towards a Theologia Africana." In *New Testament for Africa and The World*. Edited by M. E. Glasswell and E. W. Fasholé-Luka. London: SPCK, 1974.

Dickson, Kwesi A. and Paul Ellingworth, eds. *Biblical Revelation and African Beliefs*. Maryknoll, NY: Orbis Books, 1971.

Dieterlen, Germaine. *Essai sur la religion bambara*. Paris: Presses Universitaires de France, 1951.

Diop, Aloune. "Editorial." *Présence Africaine* (October-November 1947).

Diop, Cheikh Anta. *The African Origin of Civilization: Myth or Reality*. Mercer Cook, ed. and trans. Westport, CT: Lawrence Hill, 1974.

________. *Black Africa: The Economic and Cultural Basis for a Federated State*. Westport, CT: Lawrence Hill, 1978.

________. *The Cultural Unity of Black Africa.* Chicago: Third World Press, 1978.

________. *Nations nègres et culture.* Paris: Présence Africaine, 1954.

________. *Parenté génétique de l'égyptien pharaonique et des langues négro-Africaines.* Dakar: IFAN–Les Nouvelles Editions Africaines, 1977.

________. *Precolonial Africa.* Harold Salemson, trans. Brooklyn, NY: Lawrence Hill, 1987.

Diop, Maghemout. "L'independence totale," *Présence Africaine* (1959).

Dodd, C. H. *Founder of Christianity.* New York: Macmillan, 1970.

Dogbé, Yves-Emmanuel. *Négritude, culture et civilisation: Essai sur la finalité des faits sociaux.* Paris: Éditions Akpagnon, 1980.

Donders, Joseph G. *Non-Bourgeois Theology: An African Experience of Jesus.* Maryknoll, NY: Orbis Books, 1985.

Dorsemaine, Michèle, Alfred Fierro and Josette Masson, eds. *Léopold Sédar Senghor.* Paris: Bibliothèque Nationale, 1978.

Du Bois, W. E. B. *The Souls of Black Folk.* Greenwich, CT: Fawcett, 1961.

Durkheim, Emile. *The Rules of Sociological Method.* Translated by Sarah A. Solovay and John H. Mueller; edited by George E. G. Gatlin. New York: The Free Press, 1964.

Eboussi Boulaga, Fabian. *Le Bantu Problématique.* Paris: Présence Africaine, no. 66, 1968.

________. *Christianity Without Fetishes: An African Critique and Recapture of Christianity.* Translated by Robert R. Barr; foreword by Simon E. Smith. Maryknoll, NY: Orbis. 1984.

Ela, Jean-Marc. *African Cry.* Translated by Robert R. Barr. Maryknoll, NY: Orbis Books, 1986.

________. *From Charity to Liberation.* Ontario: Canadian Catholic Organization for Development and Peace, 1984.

________. "L'Eglise, le mode noir et le concile." In *Personnalité africaine et catholicisme.* Paris: Présence Africaine, 1963.

Essertier, D. *Les Formes inferieures de l'explication.* Paris: F. Alcan, 1927.

Etienne, Gilson. *The Christian Philosophy of St. Thomas Aquinas.* Translated by L. K. Shook. New York: Random House, 1956.

Evans-Pritchard, E. E. *Theories of Primitive Religion.* Oxford: Claredon Press, 1965.

________. *Nuer Religion.* Oxford: Claredon Press, 1956.

________. *Witchcraft, Oracles and Magic among the Azande.* Oxford: Claredon Press, 1937.

Ewing, A. C. *A Short Commentary of Kant's Critique of Pure Reason.* Chicago: Chicago University Press, 1938.

Fabian, Johannes. "Philosophie Bantoe: Placid Tempels et son oeuvre, vus dans perspective historique." *Études Africaines du Centre de Recherches et d'Information socio-politiques.* T. A. no. 108-9. Bruxelles: C. R. I. S. P., 1970.

Fanon, Franz. *Black Skin, White Masks.* Translated by Charles Lam Markmann. New York: Grove Press, 1967.

________. *The Wretched Earth.* Preface by Jean-Paul Awrtre; translated by Constance Farrington. New York: Harmondsworth, 1968.

Fasholé-Luke, E. W. "The Quest for African Theologies," *Scottish Journal of Theology,* no. 29, 1972. Also in G. H. Anderson and T. F. Stransky, eds. *Mission Trends, Number 3: Third World Theologies*. New York: Paulist Press, 1976.

________. "Footpaths and Signposts to African Christian Theologies," *Bulletin of African Theology*, no. 3 (January-June 1981).

Ferkiss, Victor C. *Africa's Search for Identity*. Cleveland, OH: World Publishing Co., 1966.

Fetter, Bruce, ed. *Colonial Rule in Africa: Readings from Primary Sources*. Madison, WI: University of Wisconsin Press, 1979.

Field, Margaret Joyce. *Religion and Medicine of the Ga People*. London: Oxford University Press, 1937.

Fitzgerald, A. V. K. "The New International Division of Labor and Relative Autonomy of the State: Notes for a Reappraisal of Classical Dependency." *Bulletin of Latin America*, 1, no. 1 (October 1981).

Forde, Daryll, ed. *African Worlds: Studies in the Cosmological Ideas and Social Values of African Peoples*. London: Oxford University Press, 1954.

Fortz, William J. "The Radical Left in French-speaking Africa." In *Emerging Africa*. Edited by William H. Lewis. Washington, D. C.: Public Affairs Press, 1963.

Frazer, James. *The Golden Bough*. London: Macmillan, 1922.

Freire, Paulo. *Pedagogy of the Oppressed*. New York: Seabury Press, 1972.

Friedland, William H. and Carl G. Rosberg, eds. *African Socialism*. Stanford, CA: Stanford University Press, 1964.

Fuller, Reginald H. *The Foundations of New Testament Christology*. Glasgow: William Collins Sons, 1979.

Fynn, J. "Ghana-Asante," In *West African Resistance*. Edited by M. Crowder. London: Heineman, 1971.

Gadamer, Hans-Georg. *Hegel's Dialectic: Five Hermeneutical Studies*. Translated by P. Christopher Smith. New Haven, CT: Yale University Press, 1976.

________. *Philosophical Hermeneutics*. Translated and edited by David E. Linge. Berkeley, CA: University of California Press, 1976.

________. *Truth and Method*. New York: Crossroads, 1982.

Gann, L. H., and P. Duigan. *White Settlers in Tropical Africa*. Baltimore, MD: Penguin, 1962.

Garbutt, H. E. "Native Customs in Nyasaland," *Man*, 12, no. 20 (1912).

Garrot, Daniel. *Léopold Sédar Senghor critique littérature*. Dakar: Les Nouvelles Editions Africaines, 1978.

Garvey, Marcus. *Philosophy and Opinions of Marcus Garvey*. 2 vols. Ed. Amy Jacques-Garvey. New York: Atheneum, 1971.

Gbadegesin, Segun. *African Philosophy: Traditional Yoruba Philosophy and Contemporary African Realities*. New York: Peter Lang, 1991.

Geertz, Cliford. *Interpretation of Cultures*. New York: Basic Books, 1973.

Geiger, Louis-Betrand. *La Participation dans la philosophie de St. Thomas d'Aquin*. 2nd ed. Paris: Vrin, 1953.

Gerth, H. H. and C. W. Mills, trans. and eds. *From Max Weber: Essays In Sociology*. London: Routledge and Kegan Paul, 1948.

George, James. *Stolen Legacy*. San Francisco: Richardson, 1976.

Gogbé, Yves-Emmanuel. *Negritude, culture et civilisation: essai sur la finalité des faits sociaux*. Paris: Éditions Akpagnon, 1980.

Gollmer, C. A. "On African Symbolic Messages," *Journal of the Anthropological Institute*, 14 (1985).

Gray, Chris. *Conceptions of History: Cheikh Anta Diop and Theophile Obenga*. London: Karnak House, 1989.

Griaule, Marcel. *Dieu d'eau*. Paris: Editions du Chéne, 1948.

________. "L'Image du monde du Soudan." *Journal de la Société des Africanistes*, 19, Fasc. 2 (1949).

Grierson, Denham. *Transforming A People of God*. Melbourne: The Joint Board of Christian Education of Australia and New Zealand, 1984.

Gusdoff, Georges. *Mythe et metaphysique*. Paris: Flammarion, 1953.

Gyeke, Kwame. *An Essay on African Philosophical Thought: The Akan Conceptual Scheme*. New York: Cambridge University Press, 1987.

Hamilton, Neill Q. "Temple Cleansing and Temple Bank." In *Journal of Biblical Literature* (December 1964).

Hardie, W. F. R. *Aristotle's Ethical Theory*. Oxford: Claredon Press, 1968.

Harrington, Michael. *Politics at God's Funeral: The Spiritual Crisis of Western Civilization*. New York: Holt, Rinehart and Winston, 1983.

Harris, Joseph E. *Africans and Their History*. New York: New American Library, 1972.

Hauser, M. *Essai sur la poétique de la négritude*. Lille: Université de Lille III, 1982.

Hazoumé, Paul. "L'Âme du Dahoméen révélée par sa religion," *Présence Africaine*, nos. 14-15 (1957).

________. *Le Pact du sang au Dahomey*. Paris: Travaux et Mémoires de l'Institut d'Ethnologie, 1937.

________. "L'Humanisme occidental et l'humanisme Africain." *Présence Africaine*, nos. 14-15 (1957).

Hegel, Georg Friedrich W. *Lectures on the Philosophy of History*. Translated by E. S. Haldane and Frances H. Simon. London: Routledge and Kegan Paul, 1955.

________. *Philosophy of History*. Translated by J. Sibree. New York: Dover, 1956.

________. *Phenomenology of Spirit*. Translated by A. V. Miller. London: Oxford University Press, 1977.

Herskovits, Mervile and Francis S. Herskovits. *An Outline of Dahomean Religious Belief.* Memoire 41. New York: American Anthropological Association, 1933.

Hetherwick, Alexander. *Life and Work*. Vol. 165 (December 1902). Malawi National Archives. London: United Society for Christian Literature.

Higgot, Richard A. *Political Development Theory: The Contemporary Debate*. New York: St. Martin's Press, 1983.

Hinde, Sidney L., and Hildegrade Hinde. *The Last of the Masai*. London: Heinemann, 1901.

Hobbes, Thomas. *Leviathan: Or the Matter, Forme and Power of a Commonwealth Ecclesiastical and Civil*. Selected and introduction by Richard S. Peters; edited by Michael Oakeshott. London: Collier Macmillan, 1962.

________. *Body, Mind and Citizen*. Edited by Richard S. Peters. New York: Collier, 1962.

Horkheimer, Max. *Critique of Instrumental Reason*. Translated by Matthew O'Connell, et al. New York: Continuum, 1974.

________. "Traditional and Critical Theory." In *Critical Theory: Selected Essays*. Edited and translated by Matthew J. O'Connell et al. New York: Herder and Herder, 1972.

Horkheimer, Max, and Theodore Adorno. *Dialectic of Enlightenment*. Translated by John Cumming. New York: Continuum, 1972.

Hountondji, Paulin J. *African Philosophy: Myth or Reality*. Translated by Henri Evans and Jonathan Rée; Introduction by Abiola Irele. Bloomington, IN: Indiana University Press, 1983.

________. "Le Mythe de la philosophie spontanée." *Cahiers Philosophiques Africains* (Lubambashi), no. 1 (1972).

________. "Histoire d'une myth." *Présence Africaine* (1974).

Houston, Jean. "Prometheus Rebound: An Inquiry into Technological Growth and Psychological Change." In *Alternatives to Growth*, vol. 1. Edited by Dennis Meadows. Cambridge University Press, 1977.

Hughes, Langston. "The Twenties: Harlem and its Negritude." *Africa Forum*, 1, no. 4 (Spring 1966).

Hughes, P. *Witchcraft*. London: Longman, 1952.

Hume, David. "Dialogues Concerning Natural Religion." In *The Empiricists*. New York: Anchor Books, 1974.

________. *On Human Nature and Understanding*. Edited and introduction by Anthony Flew. New York: Macmillan, 1962.

Hutchinson, Roger, and Gibson Winter. "Towards a Method in Political Ethics." In *Perspectives on Political Ethics: An Ecumenical Enquiry*. Edited by Kosan Srisang. Washington, D.C.: Georgetown University Press, 1983.

Idowu, Bolaji. African Traditional Religion—A Definition. Maryknoll, New York: Orbis Books, 1975.

________. *Biblical Revelation and African Beliefs*. Ed. Kwesi Dickson and Paul Ellingworth. Maryknoll, NY: Orbis, 1969.

________. *Towards An Indigenous Church*. London: Oxford University Press, 1965.

Irele, Abiola. "Contemporary Thought in French Speaking Africans." In *Africa and the West: Legacies of Empire*. Edited by Isaac James Mowoe and Richard Bjornson. Westport, CT: Greenwood, 1986.

________. *Selected Poems of Léopold Sédar Senghor*. London, New York: Cambridge University Press, 1977.

Isaacman, A. *Anti-Colonial Activity in the Zambesi Valley, 1850-1921*. Berkeley: University of California Press, 1976.

Jackson, John G. *Introduction to African Civilization*. Secaucus, NJ: The Citadel Press, 1970.

Jahn, Janheinz. *Muntu: An Outline of the New African Culture*. New York: Grove Press, 1961.

Jalee, Pierre. *The Pillage of the Third World*. New York: Monthly Review Press, 1968.

Jaritz, E. "Uber Bahmen auf Billardtischen-Oder: Eine Mathematische Untersuchung von Ideogrammen Anglolanischer Herkunft." Mathematisch-Statistiche Sektion, Research Centre A+8010, Granz, Austria.

Jeremias, Joachim. *The Central Message of The New Testament*. New York: Charles

Scribner's Sons, 1965.

________. *Das Evangelium nach Johannes: Eine Urchristliche Erflarung fur die Gegenwart.* Themniz und Leipzig: Verlag Max Muller, 1931.

________. *Der Prolog des Johannasevangeliums Johannes 1:1-18.* Stuttgart: Calwer Verlag, 1967.

Johnston, Leonard. *The Word and the Flesh: John 1-13.* London: Darton, Longman and Todd, 1969.

Jones, Thomas Jesse. *Four Essentials of Education.* New York: C. Scribner's Sons, 1926.

________, ed. *African Education 1920-1921.* New York: Phelps-Stokes Fund, 1922.

________, ed. *Education in Africa 1923-1924.* New York: Phelps-Stoke Fund, 1925.

Juma, Richard. "A Case Study of People's Participation in Development: The Tanzanian Experience." In *People's Participation and People's Movements.* Commission on the Church's Participation in Development. World Council of Churches Document no. 22 (May 1982).

Jung, L. Shannon. "Spatiality, Relativism, and Authority." In *Journal of the American Academy of Religion,* 2, no. 50 (1982).

Kagame, Alexis. *La Divine pastorale.* 2 vols. Brussels: Editions du Marais, 1952-55.

________. *La Philosophie bantoe-rwandaise de l'être.* Memoire in 8 de l'Academie Royale des Sc. D'outre-mer (Arsom) Nouvelle Serie, Tome 12, 1, Brussels: Editions Lumen Vitae, 1956.

________. "La Poésie guerriére." *Présence Africaine,* no. 11, 1957.

________. *La Philosophie bantoe comparé.* Paris. Présence Africaine, 1976.

Kane, Cheikh Hamidou. *Ambiguous Adventure.* Edited by Katherine Woods. New York: Walker, 1963.

Kanoute, Pierre. "Le Socialisme africain: Expression de l'homannisme africain." *Afrique Nouvelle* (November 30-December 6, 1962).

Kant, Immanuel. *Beantwortung der Frage: Was ist Aufklarung? (1784).* Frankfurt: Neuer Frankfurter Verlag, 1905.

________. *Critique of Judgment.* Translated by James Creed Meredith. Oxford: Claredon Press, 1952.

________. *Critique of Pure Reason.* Translated by Norman Kemp Smith. New York: St. Martin's Press, 1965.

________. *Foundations of the Metaphysics of Morals.* Translated and introduction by Lewis White Beck. Indianapolis: Bobbs-Merrill, 1959.

________. *The Moral Law.* Translated by H. J. Paton. London: Hutchison University Library, 1948.

________. *Prolegomena to Any Future Metaphysics Which Will Be Able to Come Forth as Science (1783).* Translated by Mahaffy-Carus. New York: Library of Arts, H. W. Sams, 1950.

Karenga, Maulana, and Jacob H. Carruthers, eds. *Kemet and the African Worldview: Research, Rescue and Restoration.* Los Angeles: University of Sankore Press, 1986.

Kaufmann, Walter, trans. *Hegel: Texts and Commentary.* New York: Doubleday, 1966.

Kaunda, Kenneth and Colin Morris. *After Mulungushi.* Lusaka, Zambia: 1967.

________. *A Humanist in Africa.* Nashville, TN: Abingdon Press, 1966.

________. "Letter to My Children." In *African Christian Spirituality*. Edited by A. Shorter. Maryknoll, NY: Orbis Books, 1980.

Kauta, Stephen. "Traditional Religion Among the Tumbuka and Other Tribes in Malawi." *Ministry Theological Review*, 9, no. 1 (January 1969).

Kayoya, Michael. *My Father's Footprints*. Translated by Aylward Shorter and Marie-Agnes Baldwin. Nairobi: East African Publishing House, 1973.

Keller, E. E. *A Short History of Religions*. London: Gollancz, 1933.

Kenyata, Jomo. *Facing Mount Kenya: The Tribal Life of the Gikuyu*. London: Oxford University Press, 1938.

Kesteloot, Lilyan. *Intellectual Origins of the African Revolution*. Translated by Alexander Mboukou. Washington, D.C.: Black Orpheus Press, 1972.

Kibanda, M. "L'Écriture dans la civilisation Kongo: Problèmes théoriques et methodologiques." *Revue de Linguistique Théorique et Appliqué* (January 1985).

Kimambo, I. N. and T. O. Ranger, eds. *The Historical Study of African Religions*. London: Heinemann, 1972.

Kramer, W. Christos. *Kyrios, gottensshon: Studien zur pualischen und vorpaulinische Christologie*. Zürich: Zwingli Verlag, 1962.

Kubik, G. "African Graphic Sytems: A Reassessment," *Mitteilungan der anthropologischen Gesellschaft in Wien*. 114 and 115 (1984-85).

Kuczynoki, R. R. "Population Movements." In *Black Mother*. Edited by Base Davidson. London: Victor Gollancz, 1961.

Kuhn, Thomas S. *The Structures of Scientific Revolutions*. Enlarged edition. Chicago: University of Chicago Press, 1970.

Kumakanga, Stevenson. *Nzeru Za Kale*. 6th ed. Blantyre, Malawi: Dzuka Publishing Co., 1975.

L'Afrique Noir, December 6, 1951.

Lane, Dermot R. *Foundations for a Social Theology: Praxis, Process and Salvation*. New York: Paulist Press, 1984.

Lévy-Bruhl, Lucien. *Les Fornictions mentales dans les sociétés inférieures*. Paris: Alcan, 1910.

________. *How Natives Think*. New York: Allen and Unwin, Macmillan, 1926.

________. *Primitive Mentality*. New York: Macmillan, 1923.

Lienhardt, Godfrey. *Divinity and Experience: Religion of the Dinka*. New York: Oxford University Press, 1987.

Lewis, W. E. "World Production, Prices and Trader, 1870-93." *Manchester School of Economics and Social Studies* (1952).

Life and Work. No. 165 (December 1902). Malawi National Archives, London: United Society for Christian Literature.

Linden, Ian. *Catholic Peasants and Chewa Resistance in Malawi*. London: Heinemann, 1974.

Livingstone, David. *Narrative of an Expedition to the Zambezi and its Tributaries*. London: John Murray, 1865.

Locke, John. *An Essay Concerning Human Understanding*. Book 1. 1690. Oxford: Claredon Press, 1894.

________. *Two Treatises on Government*. 2nd ed. Edited by P. Laslett. London: Cambridge University Press, 1967.

Lukacs, Georg. *History and Class Consciousness*. London: Merlin, 1979.

Lukes, Steven. *Individualism*. New York: Harper and Row, 1973.

Ly, Abdoulaye. *Les Masses africaines et l'actuelle condition humaine*. Paris: Présence Africaine, 1957.

Macdonald, J. "East Central African Customs" *Journal of the Royal Anthropological Institute*, 22 (1882).

MacIntyre, Alasdair. *After Virtue: A Study in Moral Theory*. Notre Dame, IN: University of Notre Dame Press, 1981.

Mackintosh, Hugh R. *The Person of Christ*. London: SCM Press, 1918.

Magesa, Laurenti. "Return to the World." *African Ecclesiastical Review,* 16, no. 3 (1974).

Malula, John. "Speech to the Congolese Elite and to Missionaries." *Revue du Cleqé Africain*, no. 5 (1960).

Manix, Daniel P. and Malcolm Cowley. *Black Cargoes*. New York: Viking Press, 1962.

Marcel, Gabriel. *Etre et avoir*. Paris: Editions universitaires, 1935.

Markovits, Irving. *Leopold Senghor and the Changing Social Function of Negritude as an Ideology: 1931-1966*. African Studies Association, n. d.

Masamba, ma Mpolo, Reginald Stober, and Everlyn V. Appiah. *An African Call For Life: A Contribution to the World Council of Churches Sixth Assembly Theme, "Jesus Christ the Life of The World*." Geneva: World Council of Churches and Contributors, 1983.

Mazrui, Ali A. *The African Condition*. London: Cambridge University Press, 1980.

Mbiti, John. "African Indigenous culture in Relation to Evangelism and Church Development," *The Gospel and Frontier Peoples: A Report of a Consultation December 1972*. Edited by R. Pierce Beaver. Pasedena, CA: William Care Library, 1973.

________. *African Prayers*. Maryknoll, NY: Orbis Books, 1975.

________. *African Religions and Philosophy*. 2nd ed. Portsmouth, NH: Heinemann, 1990.

________. "African Theology." *All Africa Lutheran Consultation on Theology in African Context* (October 5-14, 1978).

________. "African Theology." *Worldview* (August, 1973).

________. "As Christianity Tilts to the South." *The Indian Journal of Theology*, 33, nos. 1, 2, 3 (January-September 1984).

________. "The Biblical Basis for the Present Trends in African Theology." In *African Theology En Route*. Edited by Kofi Appiah-Kubi and Sergio Torres. Maryknoll, NY: Orbis Books, 1979.

________. "Cattle Are Born With Ears, Their Horns Will Grow Later: Towards an Appreciation of African Oral Theology." *Africa Journal of Theology*, no. 5 (1978).

________. "Christianisme et religions indegnes au Kenya." *Présence Africaine*, nos. 27-28 (1959).

________. "Christianity and African Culture." *The Journal of Theology for Southern Africa* (September, 1971). Also in *Evangelical Review of Theology* (World Theological Fellowship, Evangelical Commission), 3, no. 2 (October 1979).

________. *Concepts of God in Africa*. London: SPCK, 1970.

________. "The Encounter of Christian Faith and African Religion." *Christian Century* (August 27-September 3, 1980).

________. "The Future of Christianity." *Cross Currents*, 28, no. 4 (Winter 1978-79).

________. "Learning From Africa." *Cross Currents*, 28, no. 4 (Winter 1978-79).

________. *New Testament Eschatology in an African Background.* London: Oxford University Press, 1971.

________. *The Prayers of African Religion.* London: SPCK, 1970.

________. "Some Aspects of Christology," *Christ and the Younger Churches.* Edited by C. F. Vicedom. London: SPCK, 1972.

________. "Some Currents on African Theology." *Expository Times*, vol. 88, (1975-76).

________. "Theological Impotence and the Universality of the Church." *Lutheran World*, no. 3 (1974).

________, ed. *Confessing Christ in Different Cultures: Report of a Colloquium at the Ecumenical Institute, Bossey 2-7 July 1977.* Geneva, Switzerland: Ecumenical Institute, 1977.

Mboya, Tom. "African Socialism." *Transition*, no. 8 (March 1963).

McCraken, John. "The Nineteenth Century in Malawi." In *Aspects of Central African History.* Edited by Teremce O. Ranger. Evanston, IL: Northwestern University Press, 1968.

Meeting the African Religion. Rome: Secretariat for Non-Christians, 1969.

Menkiti, Ifeanyi A. "Person and Community in African Traditional Thought." In *African Philosophy: An Introduction.* 3rd ed. Edited by Richard A. Wright. Lanham, MD: University Press of America, 1984.

Metcalfe, M. "Some Nyasaland Folklore Tales." *Nyasaland Journal*, 7, no. 2 (1954).

Mezu, S. Okechukwu. *The Poetry of L. S. Senghor.* Rutherford, NJ: Fairleigh Dickinson University Press, 1973.

Middleton, J., and E. H. Winter. *Witchcraft and Sorcery in East Africa.* London: Routledge and Kegan Paul, 1963.

Milcent, Ernest, and Monique Sortdet. *Léopold Sédar Senghor et la naissance de l'Afrique moderne.* Paris: Seghers, 1969.

Milimo, J. T. ed. *Bantu Wisdom.* NECZAM, 1976.

Miller, John. *The Disappearance of God.* London: Cambridge University Press, 1963.

Mkandawire, J. A. K. "Reality and Symbolic Exchange in African Religion." *Journal of Social Science* (Malawi), 5 (1976).

Mohiddin, A. "Towards Relevant Culture and Politics in Africa." *Africa Development*, 2, no. 4 (October-December 1977).

Montagnes, Bernard. *La Doctrine de l'analogie de l'être d'après St Thomas d'Aquin.* Louvain, Paris: Nauwelaerts, 1963.

Morgan, L. H. *Ancient Society or Researches in the Lines of Human Progress and Savagery, Through Barbarism to Civilization.* New York: Holt, 1877.

Mowoe, Isaac James and Richard Bjornson, eds. *Africans and the West: Legacies of the Empire.* Westport, CT: Greenwood Press, 1986.

Mpansu, Buakasa Tulu Kia. "The African Tradition of Sharing." *The Ecumenical Review*, 38, no. 4 (October 1986).

Mphahlele, Ezechiel. *The African Image.* London: Faber and Faber, 1974.

________. "The Fabric of African Culture." *Foreign Affairs* (July 1964).

________. *The Living Dead and Other Stories.* Ibadan: Ministry of Education and Black Orpheus, 1961.

Mulago, Victor. "Dialectique existentielle des bantou." *Recherches et Debates.* Centre

Catholique Intellectuel Français, no. 24 (1958), 146-71.

________. "Dialectique existentielle des bantous et sacramentalisme." In *Aspects de la Culture Noire* (Paris: 1958).

________. *Un Visage africain du christianisme*. Paris: Présence Africaine, 1960.

________. "Vital Participation: The Cohesive Principle of the Bantu community," *Biblical Revelation and African Beliefs*. Edited by Kwesi Dickson and Paul Ellingworth. New York: Orbis Books, 1971.

Mumford, Lewis. *The Myth of the Machine, Part Two: The Pentagon of Power*. New York: Harcourt Brace Jovanovich, 1970.

Murphy, Jefferson E. *History of African Civilization*. New York: Delta, 1972.

Muzorewa, Henry. *African Theology: Its Origin and Development*. Maryknoll, NY: Orbis Books, 1985.

Myers, Max A. "Ideology and Legitimation as Necessary Concepts for Christian Ethics. "*Journal of the American Academy of Religion*, 59, no. 2 (June 1981).

Nabudere, D. Wadada. *Essays on the Theory and Practice of Imperialism*. London: Onyx Press, 1979.

Nardal, Paulette. "Eveil de la conscience de race." *La Revue du Monde Noir*, no. 6 (April 1932).

Ndabaningi, Sithole. *African Nationalism*. London: Oxford University Press, 1957.

Newman, John Henry. *The Scope and Nature of University Education*. London: Oxford University Press, 1915.

Ngal, Mbawil a Mpaang. *Aimé Césaire: Un homme à la recherche d'une partie*. Dakar: Les Nouvelles Editions Africaines, 1975.

Nkrumah, Kwame. *Africa Must Unite*. London: Heinemann, 1963.

________. *The Autobiography of Kwame Nkrumah*. New York: Nelson, 1957.

________. "The Basic Needs of African Socialism." *Pan Africa* (April 19, 1963).

________. *Class Struggle in Africa*. London: Panaf Books, 1970.

________. *Consciencism: Philosophy and Ideology of Decolonization and Development with Particular Reference to the African Revolution*. Rev. ed. London: Heinemann, 1964.

________. *Neo-Colonialism: The Last Stage of Imperialism*. London: Heinemann, 1965.

________. "*The Old and the New: Law in Africa*. Address to the Ghana Law School." Accra: Ministry of Information and Broadcasting, January 4, 1962.

________. *I Speak of Freedom: Statement of African Ideology*. New York: Praeger, 1961.

________. *Towards Colonial Freedom*. London: Heinemann, 1962.

________. *Two Myths*. New York: Panaf, 1970.

Nothomb, Dominique. *Un Humanisme Africain: Valeurs et Pierres d'attente*. Preface by Alex Kagame. Bruxelles: Editions Lumen Vitae, 1965.

Nthara, Simeon Yosia. *Headman's Enterprise*. Translated by Cullen Young. London: Lutterworth Press, 1949.

________. *Man of Africa* (1934). London: USCL 1943.

Nyamiti, Charles. "African Theology: Its Nature Problems and Methods." Gaba pastoral papers, no. 19, 1971.

________. "The Scope of African Theology." Gaba pastoral papers, no. 30, 1973.

Nyerere, Julius K. "Africa's Place in the World." *Symposium on Africa* (Wellesley, MA, 1960).

________. *Freedom and Socialism*. London: Oxford University Press, 1968.

________. *Freedom and Unity*. London: Oxford University Press, 1967.

________. *Man and Development*. London: Oxford University Press, 1974.

________. "Ujama: The Basis of African Socialism." *Tanganyika Standard*, April 1962.

________. *Ujama: Essays on African Socialism*. London: Oxford University Press, 1968.

Obenga, Theophile. *L'Afrique dans l'antiquité*. Paris: Présence Africaine, 1973.

Ojuka, A. "African Thought and the Concept of Essence." *Thought and Practice*, 1, no. 1 (1974).

Okafor, Stephen O. "Bantu Philosophy: Placid Tempels Revisited." *Journal of Religion in Africa*, 13, no. 2 (1982).

Okere, Theophilus. *African Philosophy: A Historico-Hermeneutical Investigation of the Conditions of Its Possibility*. Lanham, MD: University Press of America, 1983.

Oldham, J. H. "Aims of African Education." *International Review of Mission*, 14 (1924).

Olela, Henry. *From Ancient Africa to Ancient Greece: An Introduction to the History of Philosophy*. Atlanta, GA: Select, 1981.

Oliver, Roland and J. D. Fage. *A Short History of Africa*. 5th ed. New York: Penguin, 1978.

Oppenheim, Felix E. *Political Concepts: A Reconstruction*. Chicago: University of Chicago Press, 1981.

Parrinder, E. G. "Philosophy and Cosmology." In *Religion in Africa*. London: Pall Mall, 1970.

Parsons, Talcott. *The Social System*. London: Routledge and Kegan Paul, 1951.

Pateman, Carole. *The Problem of Political Obligation: A Critique of Liberal Theory*. Berkeley: University of California Press, 1985.

Pavian, A. *Da Postioma, Filosofia Africana*. Milano: Estere Capucini, 1967.

P'Bitek, O. *Africa's Cultural Revolution*. Nairobi: Macmillan, 1973.

Pegis, Anton C., ed. *Introduction to Saint Thomas Aquinas: The Summa Theologica*. New York: Random House, 1948.

Perier, A. G. "La Poésie ethnique." *La Revue du Monde Noir*, no. 6 (April 1932).

Phiri, Kings. "Chewa History in Central Malawi and Use of Oral Tradition 1600-1920." Ph.D. dissertation. Michigan University, 1975.

Potekhin, I. I. "On African Socialism: A Soviet View," *African Socialism*. Edited by William H. Friendland and Carl G. Rosberg. Stanford: Stanford University Press, 1964.

Preamble to the constitution of Central Africa Federation. n.d.

Rabinow, Paul, and William M. Sullivan, eds. *Interpretive Social Science: A Reader*. Berkeley: University of California Press, 1979.

Radin, Paul, ed. *African Folktales*. New York: Schocken Books, 1983.

Raeymaeker, L. de. "L'Analogie de l'être dans le perspective d'une philosophie thomiste." In Paul Ricoeur, *The Rule of Metaphor: Multi-disciplinary Studies of the Creation of Meaning*. Translated by Robert Czeny with Katheleen Mclaughlin and John Costello. Toronto: University of Toronto Press, 1977.

Rake, Alan. "My Ivory Coast." *Africa Report*, 7 (April 1962).

Ranger, Terence O., ed. *Aspects of Central African History*. Evanston, IL: Northwestern University Press, 1968.

Rawls, John. *A Theory of Justice*. Cambridge, MA: Harvard University Press, 1971.

Ricoeur, Paul. *The Conflict of Interpretation: Essays in Hermeneutics*. Evanston: Northwestern University Press, 1974.

________. *Interpretation Theory: Discourse and Surplus of Meaning*. Fort Worth, Texas: Christian University Press, 1974.

________. *The Rule of Metaphor: Multi-Disciplinary Studies of the Creation of Meaning of Language*. Translated by Robert Czeny with Kathleen McLaughlin and John Costello. Toronto: University of Toronto Press, 1977.

Robinson, John T. A. *The Human Face of God*. Philadelphia: Westminster Press, 1973.

Rodney, Walter. *How Europe Underdeveloped Africa*. Washington, D.C.: Howard University Press, 1981.

Rousseau, Jean-Jacques. *Discours sur l'origine et des foundements de l'inégalité parmis les hommes*. London: Oxford University Press, 1922.

________. *The First and Second Discourses*. Edited by R. D. Masters. New York: St. Martin's Press, 1965.

Roy, P. K. "The Principles of Ontological Balance and Social-Ethical Ideal in (Nigerian) Traditional Thought," *Philosophical Society*. Act 9.

Ruch, E. A., and K. C. Anyanwu. *African Philosophy: An Introduction to the Main Philosophical Trends in Contemporary Africa*. Rome: Officium Libris Catholici, 1984.

Salemohamed, G. "African Philosophy." *Philosophy*, 58 (1983).

Santos, J. dos. *Ethiopian Oriental*. Lisbon: Estudios de Ciéncias Politicas e Sociales, 1881. Also in Axelson, *Portuguese in South East Africa 1600-1700*. Johannesburg: Witwatersrand University Press, 1964.

Sartre, Jean Paul. *Being and Nothingness: An Essay on the Phenomenological Ontology*. Translated by Hazel E. Barnes. New York: The Philosophical Library, 1956.

________. *Black Orpheus*. Paris: Présence Africaine, 1967.

________. *Essays in Existentialism*. Edited by Wade Baskin. Secaucas, NJ: The Citadel Press, 1965.

Scanlon, D. G. ed. *Traditions of African Education*. New York: Columbia University Press, 1964.

Schmidt, Paul Wilhelm. *Die Religionen der Urvolker Afrikas*. Munster: Aschendorffsche Verlaghandlung, 1933.

________. *Der Ursprung der Gottesidee: Ein Historisch-kritische und Positive Studie*. 5 volumes. Munster: Aschendorffsche, 1926.

Schoffeleers, J. M. "Myths and Legend of Creation." *Vision of Malawi*, (December 1972).

________. "Mbona Cult in Malawi," *The Historical Study of African Religions*. Edited by I. N. Kimambo and T. O. Ranger. London and Nairobi: Heinemann, 1972.

Schoffeleers, J. M., ed. *Guardians of the Land*. Ngwelo, Zimbabwe: Mambo Press, 1978.

Schoffeleers, J. M., and A. A. Roscoe. *Land of Fire: Oral Literature from Malawi*. Limbe, Malawi: Popular Publications, 1985.

Schreiter, Robert J. *Constructing Local Theologies*. Maryknoll, NY: Orbis, 1985.

Schultz, Alfred. *On Phenomenology and Social Relations*. Edited by Helmut R. Wagner. Chicago: University of Chicago Press, 1970.

Schumpeter, Joseph. *Business Cycles*. New York: McGraw-Hill, 1939.

Segundo, Juan Luis. *Jesus of Nazareth Yesterday and Today*. Vol. 1, *Faith and Ideologies*. Translated by John Drury. Maryknoll, NY: Orbis Books, 1984.

Senghor, Léopold Sédar. *Discours d'overture du colloque sur Littérature africaine d'expression française*, March 26, 1963.

________. *Discours prononcé à l'Université d'Oxford*. October 1964.

________. "L'Esprit de la civilisation ou les lois de la culture négro-africaine," *Présence Africaine*, nos. 8, 9, 10 (June-November 1956).

________. *The Foundations of "Africanité" or "Négritude" and "Arabité."* Paris: Présence Africaine, 1971.

________. "L'humanisme et nous: Réne Maran." *L'Etudiant Noir* (1934).

________. "Le Problem Cultural en OAF," reprinted in *Liberté I, Négritude et humanisme*. Paris: Seuil, 1964.

________. *Liberté III: négritude et civilisation de l'universal*. Paris: Seuil, 1977.

________. *Liberté IV: Socialisme et planification*. Paris: Seuil, 1983.

________. "Marxisme et humanisme." In *La Revue Socialiste*, 19 (March 1948), 201-16.

________. *Nation et Voie Africaine du Socialisme*. Paris: Présence Africaine, 1961.

________. "Negritude and African Socialism." In *African Affairs*. Edited by Kenneth Kirkwood. Number Two: St. Anthony's Papers, no. 15. London: Chatto and Windus, 1963.

________. "Negritude: A Humanism of the Twetieth Century." In *The African Reader: Independent Africa*. Edited by W. Cartey and M. Kilson. New York: Random House, 1970.

________. *On African Socialism*. Translated by Mercer Cook. New York: American Society for African Culture, 1959.

________. *Pierre Teilhard de Chardin et la politique africaine*. Paris: Seuil, 1962.

________. *La poésie de l'action: Conversations de l'action avec Mohamed Aziza*. Paris: Éditions Stock, 1980.

________. "Pourquoi une idéologie négro-africaine?" *Présence Africaine*, no. 82 (1972).

________. *Pour une relecture africaine de Marx et d'Engels*. Dakar, Abidjan: Nouvelles Editions Africaines, 1976.

________, ed. *Anthologie de la nouvelle poésie négre et malgache de langue française*. Paris: Presses Universitaires de France, 1948.

Sewell, Elizabeth. *The Human Metaphor*. Notre Dame, IN: University of Notre Dame Press, 1964.

Shepperson, George, and Thom Price. *The Independent African*. Edinburgh: Edinburgh University Press, 1958.

Shorter, Aylward. *African Culture and Christian Church*. London: Geoffery Chapman, 1973.

________. *Prayer in the Religious Traditions of Africa*. London: Oxford University Press, 1975.

Shorter, Aylward, ed. *African Christian Spirituality*. Maryknoll, NY: Orbis Books, 1978.

Sigmund, Paul E., Jr., ed. with introduction. *The Ideologies of Developing Nations*. New York: Praeger, 1963.

Sindima, Harvey. "Bondedness, *Moyo* and *Umunthu* as the Elements of Achewa

Spirituality: Organizing Logic and Principle of Life." *Ultimate Reality and Meaning: Interdisciplinary Studies in the Philosophy of Understanding*, 14, no. 1 (March 1991).

________. "Community of Life." *The Ecumenical Review*, 41, no. 4 (October 1989).

________. *Drums of Redemption: An Introduction to African Christianity*. Wesport, CT: Greenwood Press, 1994.

________. "A General Survey of Independent Churches in Malawi, 1900-1976." *All Africa Council Churches Bulletin* (1977).

________. *The Legacy of Scottish Missionaries in Malawi*. Lewiston, NY: Edwin Mellen Press, 1992.

________. "Liberalism and African Culture." *Journal of Black Studies*, 21, no. 2 (December 1990).

________. "The Origin and Development of African Philosophy." *Africa Theological Journal*, 8, no. 3 (1989).

Smith, Adam. *An Inquiry into the Nature and Causes of the Wealth of Nations.* (1774). 5th. ed. Dublin: William Porter for G. Burnet, L. White, etc., 1793; New York: The Modern Library, 1937.

Smith, Edwin W. *The Christian Mission in Africa.* (Report of the International Missionary Conference at Le Zoute, Belgium, September 14 to 21, 1926). London: The International Missionary Council, Edinburgh House, 1926.

________, ed. *African Ideas of God.* 2nd ed. London: Edinburgh House Press, 1959.

Sobrino, John. *Christology at the Crossroads*. Translated by John Drury. Maryknoll, NY: Orbis, 1978.

Spencer, Herbert. *On Social Revolution*. Edited by J. D. Y. Peel. Chicago: University of Chicago Press, 1972.

Spleth, Janice. *Léopold Sédar Senghor*. Boston: Twayne Publisher, 1985.

Sraff, Piero. *Production of Commodities by Means of Commodities*. London: Cambridge University Press, 1972.

Srisang, Kosan, ed. *Perspectives on Political Ethics: An Ecumenical Inquiry*. Geneva: W. C. C. Publications; Washington, D.C.: Georgetown University Press, 1983.

Stenger, J. "The Congo Free State and the Belgian Congo Before 1914." In *Colonization in Africa 1870-1960*. Vol. 1. Edited by L. H. Gann, and P. Duigan. London: Cambridge University Press, 1969.

Strauss, Leo. *Natural Right and History*. Chicago: University of Chicago Press, 1953.

Taylor, John V. *The Primal Vision: Christian Presence Amid African Religion*. 5th impression. London: SCM Press, 1977.

Taylor, V. *The Names of Jesus*. London: Macmillan, 1953.

Teilhard, de Chardin Pierre. *Building the Earth*. Translated by Noel Lindsay. Wilkes-Bare, PA: Dimension Books, 1965.

________. *L'Avenir de l'homme*. Paris: Seuil, 1959.

________. *Les Unités humaines naturelles* vol. III of *Oeuvres*. Paris: Seuil, 1963.

Tévoédjré, Albert. *La Pauvreté: Richesses des peuples*. Preface by Helder Camara. Paris: Editions Ouvriéres, 1978.

Tempels, Placid. *Bantoue-Filosofie*. Antwerp, 1946.

________. *Bantu Philosophy*. Paris: Présence Africaine, 1959.

The Spark, March 26, 1964.

Thiam, Dia. *La Politique extérieure des états africains*. Paris: Presses Universitaires de France, 1962.

Thomas, L. V. *Le Socialisme et l'Afrique: Essai sur le socialisme africain*. Paris: Le Livre Africain, 1966.

Thompson, John B. *Critical Hermeneutics: A Study in the Thought of Paul Ricoeur and Jurgen Harbermas*. London: Cambridge University Press, 1981.

Tillich, Paul. Dynamics of Faith. New York: Harper and Row, 1957.

________. *Systematic Theology*, vol. 1. Chicago: University of Chicago Press, 1951.

Touré, Mamadou. "Responsabilité de l'économiste africain." *Présence Africaine*, nos. 27-28 (1959).

Touré, Sekou. *L'Action du Parti Démocratique de Guinée et lutte pour l'émancipation africaine*. Paris: Editions Présence Africaine, 1959.

________. *Textes des interviews accordées aux representants de la press*. Conakry: 1959.

Towa, Marcien. *Léopold Senghor: négritude ou servitude?* Yaoundé: Editions CLE, 1971.

Tshiamalenga, N. "La philosophie dans la situation actuelle de l'Afrique." In *Combats pour un christianisme africain*. Kanshasa: Faculté de Théologie, 1981.

Turner, Harold W. *Profile Through Preaching*. London: Edinburgh House Press, 1965.

________. "Typology of African Religious Movements." *Journal of Religion in Africa*, no. 1 (1967).

Turner, P. "The Wisdom of the Fathers and the Gospel of Christ: Some Notes of Christian Adaptation in Africa." *Journal of Religion in Africa*, 4, no. 1 (1971).

Tylden, G. "The Gun Trade in Central and Southern Africa," *Northern Rhodesia Journal*, 11, no. 1 (1953).

Tylor, Edward B. *Primitive Culture*. 2 vols. London: John Murray, 1871.

Unger, Robert Mangabeira. *Knowledge and Politics*. New York: The Free Press, 1975.

Vail, Leroy H. "Religion, Language and The Tribal Myth: The Tumbuka and Chewa of Malawi." Conference on the History of Central African Religious Systems, 30 August-8 September, 1972. Lusaka.

Vaillant, Janet G. *Black, French, and African: A Life of Léopold Sédar Senghor*. Cambridge, MA: Harvard University Press, 1990.

Vicedom, Georg F., ed. *Christ and the Younger Churches: Theological Contributions from Asia, Africa and Latin America*. London: SPCK, 1972.

Volney, C. F. *Oeuvres*. 2nd edition. Paris: s. n., 1836.

Voltaire, André. *Ouevres II*. Paris: Presses Universitaires de France, 1948.

wa Ilunga, Bakole. *Paths to Liberation: A Third World Spirituality*. Translated by Matthew O'Connell. Maryknoll, NY: Orbis Books, 1984.

Wallerstein, Immanuel. *The Modern World-system*. New York: The Academic Press, 1974.

________. *The Capitalist World-Economy*. London: Cambridge University Press, 1979.

________. "Three Stages of African Involvement in the World Economy." In *Political Economy of Contemporary African,* 2nd ed., Peter C. W. Gutkind and Immanuel Wallerstein, eds. Beverly Hills, CA: Sage, 1985.

Washington, Booker T. *Up From Slavery*. New York: Doubleday, 1963.

Wauthier, Claude. *The Literature and Thought of Modern Africa*. 2nd ed. London: Heinemann, 1978.

Weber, Max. *The Protestant Ethic and the Spirit of Capitalism*. Translated by Talcott Parsons. New York: Charles Scribner's Sons, 1958.

________. "On Church, Sect and Mysticism." In *Sociological Analysis*. Translated by J. Gittleman. 34 (1973).

West, Cornell. *Prophesy Deliverance: An Afro-American Revolutionary Christianity*. Philadelphia: Westminster Press, 1982.

Wheelwright, E. L. *Radical Political Economy: Collected Essays*. Sydney: Australia and New Zealand Book Co., 1974.

Wheelwright, Philip. *The Burning Fountain: A Study in the Language of Symbolism*. Gloucester, MA: Peter Smith, 1982.

Wilks, I. G. *Asante in the Nineteenth Century*. London: Cambridge University Press, 1975.

Williams, Eric. *Capitalism and Slavery*. Chapel Hill: University of North Carolina Press, 1944.

Wilson, Bryan. *Magic and the Millennium*. London: Heinemann, 1973.

________. *Religious Sects*. New York: McGraw-Hill, 1970.

Wilson, Godfrey. "An African Morality." *Africa*, 9, no. 1 (1936).

Wilson, Godfrey and Monica. *The Analysis of Social Change: Based on Observations in Central Africa*. London: Cambridge University Press, 1968.

Wilson, J. P. *Religion and Transformation of Society*. London: Cambridge University Press, 1971.

Wilson, Monica. *Rituals of Kinship among the Nyakusa*. London: Oxford University Press, 1956.

Winter, Gibson. *Elements for a Social Ethic: The Role of Social Science in Public Policy*. New York: Macmillan, 1971.

________. *Liberating Creation: Foundations of Religious Foundations*. New York: Crossroads, 1981.

Wiredu, Kwesi. *Philosophy and African Culture*. London: Cambridge University Press, 1980.

Wolff, Richard. *The Economics of Colonialism: Britain and Kenya 1870-93*. New Haven, CT: Yale University Press, 1974.

Wright, Richard A., ed. *African Philosophy: An Introduction*. 3rd ed. Lanham, MD: University Press of America, 1984.

Young, T. Cullen. *African Ways and Wisdom*. London: Lutterworth Press, 1937.

________. *Contemporary Ancestors*. London: n. p., n. d.

Zahan, Dominique. *The Religion, Spirituality, and Thought of Traditional Africa*. Translated by Kate Ezara and Lawrence M. Martin. Chicago: University of Chicago Press, 1979.

Zuesse, Evan M. *Ritual Cosmos: The Sanctification of Life in African Religions*. Athens, OH: Ohio University Press, 1979.

Index

About the Author

HARVEY J. SINDIMA is currently Assistant Professor of Philosophy and Religion at Colgate University in Hamilton, New York. He is the author of *The Legacy of Scottish Missionaries in Malawi* (1992), and *Drums of Redemption: An Introduction to African Christianity* (Greenwood, 1994).

ISBN 0-313-29479-8

EAN

90000>

9 780313 294792

HARDCOVER BAR CODE